In 1801, when he was ten years old, he made himself useful to his mother by inventing a washing machine (there were nine children in the family). Apprenticed to a New York coachmaker at fifteen, he contrived an apparatus which, by using the tides off Brandy Moody Point to compress air, *should* have been able to drive the Fulton ferry back and forth across the East River. Robert Fulton came to see it, but reserved comment. At twenty he purchased the rights to a cloth-shearing machine, improved it, and went into business for himself. On the strength of this he married, and—because he found inspiration in everything—signaled the arrival of his first child by inventing a self-rocking cradle.

The end of the war in 1815 brought back overwhelming competition from the British, so he left the textile business to run a green-grocery on New York's Stuyvesant Street. Because he distrusted banks and never borrowed, he had money during the depression of 1821 when others didn't, and with it he bought a factory that was soon to produce most of the glue used in America and to make him a fortune.

PETER COOPER

PETER COOPER
CITIZEN OF NEW YORK
BY EDWARD C. MACK

DUELL, SLOAN AND PEARCE · New York

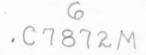

Contents

PREFATORY NOTE   ix

INTRODUCTION   xi

Part I THE LADDER OF SUCCESS (*1791-1828*)

   1. Hudson Valley Dutch and English   3

   2. A Rolling Stone   20

   3. Coachmaker's Apprentice   34

   4. A Taste of Independence   43

   5. Grocer and Inventor   56

   6. A Small Private Business   69

Part II A MAN OF AFFAIRS AND DREAMS
        (*1828-1859*)

   7. The Tom Thumb   99

   8. The Education of Peter Cooper   122

   9. Citizen of New York   138

 10. A Man's Castle   164

 11. Entrepreneur   183

 12. New Jersey Ironmaster   200

 13. Wiring Oceans and Continents   218

 14. The Opening of Cooper Union   243

Part III THE YOUNG ARE NEVER OLD
        (*1859-1883*)

 15. The Civil War   277

 16. Father Cooper   290

NOV 5 – 1949

CONTENTS

17. *Canals and Elevated Railroads*   308

18. *Cooper and His Union*   324

19. *Bearding the Tiger*   344

20. *Peter Cooper for President*   357

BIBLIOGRAPHIC NOTE   385

NOTES   388

INDEX   423

List of Illustrations
(beginning opposite page 208)

New York in 1808
Peter Cooper's 28th Street home
New York in 1817
Peter and his family
Lincoln at Cooper Union
Red Cloud speaks at the 'Institute'
Abram S. Hewitt as a young man
Hewitt in later years
'Let Papa Cooper Show His Hand'
Mathew Brady's photograph of Cooper
The Burling Slip office
Posthumous portrait of Peter Cooper
The endless-cable patent
Cooper and William Cullen Bryant
'Men of Progress'
Peter in extreme old age
'Three Monuments'
Puck's tribute to Peter Cooper
Cooper Union in the 1870's

For **D.M.** *and* **C.M.**

Prefatory Note

Fate has been unusually capricious in denying to Peter Cooper adequate biographical recognition during the sixty-five years since his death. Named (with Robert E. Lee) number eighteen on the original Hall of Fame list and called by Nicholas Murray Butler the Franklin of the nineteenth century, he has obviously deserved a full-dress biography. The director and trustees of Cooper Union, long aware of this need, asked me several years ago if I would undertake the task.

To recover at this long distance the record of Peter Cooper's life has not been easy. In my efforts to do so I have been offered every help and courtesy by the director of Cooper Union, Dr. Edwin S. Burdell, and by the librarians of that institution, Dr. Harold Lancour, Dr. David K. Berninghausen, Mr. Frederick A. Meigs, and Mr. Harold C. Whitford. Mr. Thomas P. Martin, keeper of manuscripts of the Library of Congress, gave me access not only to the Cooper-Hewitt papers but to many other collections in the library. The staffs of the American Historical Society Library, the Columbia University Library, the New York Public Library, the Queens Borough Public Library, and the New York City Hall of Records have all been extremely helpful. Mr. Edward Ringwood Hewitt and Mr. Norvin Green have aided me with advice and material. Garrett Mattingly, Millard Meiss, and John C. Thirlwall have read the book in manuscript and offered me the sort of invaluable criticism that only friends unsparing of their time can be counted on to give. For my wife, Ruth P. Mack, I have no words of thanks that are appropriate.

——E.C.M.

Introduction

A few minutes after Peter Cooper's eyes closed for the last time in the early morning hours of April 4, 1883, his brisk and efficient son-in-law, Abram S. Hewitt, began making preparations for the dignified private funeral appropriate to one of Cooper's wealth and respectability. By nine o'clock, when the editions of the morning papers bearing the tidings reached the streets, a private funeral was already manifestly impossible. The whole city had garbed itself in mourning. When the surprised stranger asked the reason, every hack driver was ready with his answer: "Peter Cooper, the best man in New York, is dead." Though Hewitt refused to permit the body to lie in state at City Hall, as the Common Council of the city desired, New York would not be denied its rights, and the casket remained open for six hours in front of the pulpit of All Souls' Church at 20th Street and Fourth Avenue. In those six hours, twelve thousand New Yorkers—draymen, shopgirls, millionaires—filed silently past the face so many of them had loved. Thousands more lined Broadway when the coffin was borne down its length in the late afternoon of the dreary April day. The *Herald* said that no funeral in the memory of anyone living—not Astor's or Clay's or Webster's—could compare with Cooper's, and the general sentiment from every editorial pen and from every pulpit the following Sunday was that New York had lost its most beloved and possibly its greatest citizen.

When Tom Hughes, author of *Tom Brown's Schooldays*, sat down to write the story of Cooper's life, this tribute both deeply impressed and baffled him. What had suddenly transformed a seemingly ordinary businessman and kindly old gentleman, a familiar and occasionally even laughable figure, into the hero of a city without heroes? He was neither statesman nor soldier nor prophet. Hughes could not believe, indeed, that he quite represented the 'typical hero whom our English speaking race desires just now to honour,' though when that hero appeared he would 'have much in common, both in aim and spirit, with the old philanthropist of New York.'[1]

Today, that long procession marching between closed shops and mourning crowds to the sound of tolling bells seems just as impressive as it did to Hughes, dreaming of it among the Welsh hills sixty-five years ago; nor has the mystery surrounding it entirely dissipated. Yet we are in a better position than was Tom Hughes, handicapped by his English background, his preconceptions about the heroic,[2] and his closeness to the scene, to understand what happened. Peter Cooper's apotheosis was the result of a fortuitous conjunction of an individual and a moment in history. A man who would have been loved and admired in any age, Peter Cooper received the almost unprecedented tribute that he did because, contrary to Tom Hughes's view, he seemed to the America of 1883 to represent precisely what it most desired, to be just the hero for whom it had been yearning. To the thousands who streamed in never-ending line past his coffin through a long gray day, Peter Cooper was both father-figure and reflection of their aspirations.

In the preceding eighteen years America had transformed herself from a predominantly agricultural country of small farmers and small manufacturers into the great industrial nation of today. The process had been going on before the Civil

War, but the cessation of hostilities immensely accelerated it. The 1870's saw at long last the complete unleashing of the amazing energies of a nation bent on exploiting the resources of a still half-occupied continent. The American people, previously inhibited by lack of capital, by puritan morality, by humanitarianism, rushed to partake of the feast prepared for them by previous generations. In a few years the 'robber barons' had carved out gigantic empires in steel and oil and railroads, and their deeds were being sung as the fulfillment of the American dream by a bewitched people.

By 1880, however, the inevitable public reaction was on its way. Even the more dim-witted could see that only a few were sharing in the great barbecue and that corruption, unprecedented in American annals, had swept through the legislative halls of the land. Many, infatuated by success, still glorified the rugged, the strong, the powerful, but they demanded that industrial leadership be accompanied by a show of morality and civic responsibility. Divines and educators—Bishop Lawrence of Massachusetts and Presidents James McCosh of Princeton, Noah Porter of Yale, and Mark Hopkins of Williams—developed the gospel of wealth, which was to be stated in its most cogent form by Andrew Carnegie six years after Peter Cooper's death: the great industrialists were the natural leaders of the people and the saviors of the nation, but they fulfilled their duty only when they acquired their wealth honestly and treated it as a trust. The true hero was a moneygetter who felt the responsibility of his position.

What better example of such a man could be found than Peter Cooper? Hughes, a dozen or more years before he undertook Cooper's life, had viewed him as one of the people who were justifying America's ruthless individualism. While rich Englishmen bought titles and castles, wrote Hughes on returning from his first trip to America in 1870, the Coopers and Cornells were establishing philanthropies in their names. Cooper had not only founded a great institution, but had been watching over it personally and lovingly, and devoting his life to its maintenance. Moreover, Cooper fitted the new pattern in its other basic essentials. He had begun with practically nothing and had worked his way upward by the force of his personality and by methods that were scrupulously honest. Endless variations on these themes were played by orators, ministers, and newspapers at his death. The only people who were not at the funeral, wrote one Jewish journal, reflecting popular feeling, were those who had attended Vanderbilt's ball the previous night and 'are probably not yet quite over their spree,' and the crowd who went to Philadelphia to witness the launching of Jay Gould's pleasure yacht *Atalanta,* whose absence would 'purify the moral atmosphere at the Cooper funeral.' [3] T. DeWitt Talmadge said that not violence but only an 'allopathic dose of Peter Cooperism' would cure the labor problem; in an age of dynamite 'who ever looked for a keg of dynamite in the cellar of Peter Cooper's house?'; in a time of public excitement 'no sentinel has ever stood at that man's door, and there has not been a time in the last forty years that the plainest man in New York and Brooklyn could not ring his doorbell and go in and shake hands with Peter Cooper.' [4] What made Cooper's death a public event, wrote the influential Godkin in the *Nation,* was the fact that Peter Cooper could take every dollar he owned up to God with him. Until we started honoring Peter Coopers instead of those who have merely 'contrived to outlive' their rascalities, and 'in trying times, successfully escaped the proper legal consequences of their misdeeds,' there was little hope for America. [5]

It was not solely, however, or even primarily as symbol of the virtues of the new industrialist that Peter Cooper appealed to the masses of Americans. By 1883 there were millions of farmers and artisans and workers who, disillusioned by nearly two decades of land thefts, Washington scandals, and callous profiteering, would not have worshiped the new industrialist had he come robed in the garb of an angel. They yearned for past days of independence and equality, and for a man with the simplicity, the great humanitarian heart, and the democratic impulses of an older America. To such people, too, Peter Cooper seemed a perfect symbol of their desires. As a great many of them knew from newspaper and magazine articles and from his own lips, Peter Cooper had been born in the presidency of George Washington and had spent most of his adult life in pre-Civil-War America. Only by a great stretch of the imagination could a man who was seventy when the Civil War broke out, and who, unlike the redoubtable Commodore Vanderbilt, had ceased to take an active interest in business before any of the new generation of capitalists were even heard of, be equated with a Carnegie or a Rockefeller. He grew up in a small town in an era of small towns, and made his money as a small independent manufacturer in the days when textile mills stood beside rushing streams, and iron bloomeries and blast furnaces were found near charcoal supplies. In his thinking and behavior, too, he belonged for the most part to pre-Civil-War America. Craftsman, untutored inventor, individualist businessman, and Jacksonian Democrat, he had little in common with either the great bankers and merchants of his own day or the industrialists of a later day. And after the Civil War he dedicated his remaining years to a vigorous fight in the name of democracy against the basic principles of the very capitalists who praised him so highly. No wonder the disinherited of the 'eighties no less than the rich and successful claimed him as their own. Even when they knew nothing about his economic theories—theories which the upper classes ignored as the harmless fancies of an old man—they instinctively recognized Peter Cooper as their friend. A man of the people, he was striving by deed and word, they dimly sensed, to save the old American dream of Jefferson and Jackson from the corrosion of the new industrialism. In Peter Cooper a simpler America called to the America of the 'seventies and 'eighties across the chasm of civil war.

Very seldom is it possible for one man thus to symbolize the aspirations of two worlds at a single moment of history. And Peter Cooper was not, of course, either a perfect symbol or an ideal hero. His weaknesses and inconsistencies were at least as apparent as those of far greater figures like Lincoln and Jefferson. But the remarkable thing is how eminently fitted he was for the dual role that was assigned him at his death and that lifted him for a brief moment to such heights of adulation. Bred amid the harsh conditions of an earlier day, he had been toughened for the struggles of the new but not hardened by his experiences. He brought from the past for the enlightenment and benefit of the present a tender social conscience perfectly blended with oldfashioned probity and simple austerity and dignity. Behind the director of great corporations was always the craftsman who worked with his hands; behind the entrepreneur of the new industrialism was the common man and the democrat. Acquisitive, inventive, and self-reliant, he was also a lover of his fellowmen, who aided them not only because it was right to do so but because he truly wished them well. His long, full, richly various life spanned the whole development of America from the framing of the Constitution to the heyday of capitalism. And in his own person he embodied for nearly a century his country's peculiar talents, aspirations, and virtues.

PART ONE

The Ladder of Success

(1791-1828)

Chapter 1

HUDSON VALLEY DUTCH
AND ENGLISH

IN THE year 1713 there was living in the little town of Albany, still governed by its first mayor, Peter Schuyler, a tailor by the name of Obadiah Cooper. Albany, which a half-century before had been a tiny cluster of houses surrounding Fort Orange and which had achieved its independence of the Van Rensselaers only a generation previously, was now a fast-growing community of many hundreds of English and Dutch settlers. Obadiah Cooper was one of its solidest if not most aristocratic citizens, and his name appears frequently in church and land records of the period. A short time before 1713 he had enhanced his prestige by marrying a Huguenot heiress, Cornelia Gardenier, whom he had met while living at Kinderhook, and by whom he had a progeny of seven sons and five daughters. Spreading far and wide over the Hudson Valley, these dozen children were themselves to produce numerous offspring, among whom was the father of Peter Cooper.

Where this Obadiah Cooper came from is a mystery. According to family tradition he was English and his father was one of three brothers who came to America in 1662. One brother, according to the story, settled on the east end of Long Island, one in New Jersey, and the third, the father of Obadiah the tailor, in Fishkill. (Obadiah, born about 1685, was supposed to have been the fourth male child of white parents in Dutchess County.) Someone, indeed, has discovered that a Thomas Cooper, one of the twenty-four grantees of William Penn, had three sons who came to America and who were probably the aforementioned brothers. A tradition shared by several branches of an extensive family cannot be lightly discarded, but there is not a scrap of evidence to support the tradition and much to cast doubt on it. If the Cooper family was English, it seems very curious that the entries in the family Bible were written in Dutch until well into the eighteenth century, and equally strange that Obadiah's children should have Dutch, not English names: Annatje (Hannah), Maria (Mary). Cooper—in English a maker of barrels—is the same as the Dutch name Kiuper, or Kuper, or Cuyper, and it is not surprising that one genealogist has turned up a fine Dutch ancestor, Claes Janson Cuyper, alias Claes Jansen, who had the good sense to marry the daughter of Cornelius Van Voorst, director of the Hoboken Trading Station, around 1620. At least two of Peter Cooper's relations were elders of the Dutch Church at Fishkill village, and one was a deacon. The Coopers were certainly either Dutch or had adjusted to and been completely accepted by the Dutch community. As a matter of fact, Coopers of all generations married Englanders and Hollanders and Huguenots with a fine disregard for ancestry, suggesting how completely national lines were being broken down among the farmers and artisans of the Hudson Valley.

It also seems highly unlikely that a Cooper settled in Fishkill as early as 1662. The wilderness of Dutchess County had no white inhabitants before the 1680's, when Nicholas Emigh fled there from the feudal jurisdiction of the Van Rensselaers, and only in 1688 did a second settler arrive. The 1714 census of Dutchess and Putnam Counties lists 445 inhabitants, among whom there is no Cooper mentioned, so that if Obadiah's father came there in the interval—and there is no record that he did —he was now dead, and his offspring, if he had any except Obadiah, were departed. The one solid fact that remains is the existence of Obadiah the tailor in the Albany directory of 1713.[1]

The history of Obadiah's wife's family is less obscure. Cornelia's grandfather, Jacob Janse Gardenier, was one of the many well-to-do Huguenots who early settled in New York State. A carpenter by trade, he came from Holland in 1637 and settled at Beverwyck, later Albany. In 1666, under the alias of Jacob Janse or Jansen Flodder, he bought with Captain John Baker a large tract of land from the Indians at Kinderhook, and secured a patent for it from Governor Nicolls. The deed of conveyance for this land, which included twelve miles of river frontage and ran back for thirty miles into the wilderness, is in the approved English legal form, though whether the Indian chief, Wathwaett, who put his mark to the document knew what he was signing is another matter. It stipulated that he, 'Wath-waett, for and in consideration of one blanket, one axe, three horses, two bars of lead, three handfuls of powder, one knife, one kettle . . . covenanted, bargained and sold unto Captain John Baker and Jacob Jansen Flodder, their heirs and assigns for ever, all that bushland and Kill, with the Face Fall running north and south, lying and being upon the north side of Enneke's and at Kinder Hook, on the west side of the Great Kill.'[2] Though the English patent for this land passed into the Cooper family on the marriage of Cornelia Gardenier to Obadiah Cooper, it did not make any of them rich. During the Revolutionary War a small colony of squatters settled on the land, and, according to Peter Cooper, the Coopers were unable to oust them, despite the best efforts of Aaron Burr, their attorney. Burr, Peter's father told him, 'would not take any pay for what he had done' because he thought the Coopers had been 'shamelessly cheated out of their property.'[3]

Cooper's ancestors were not, then, to be great landowners to rival the Van Cortlandts and the Van Rensselaers; nor were they to have the capital to invest in shipping and to lend money to farmers and manufacturers and thus grow rich. Peter's grandfather's heirs—seven in number—realized a total of six hundred pounds on their joint inheritance. But the Coopers were also not among that impoverished lower class of itinerant artisans and laborers and servants which swelled the population in the eighteenth century and led to so many conflicts over voting privileges and debts. This should particularly be kept in mind when we hear Cooper tell countless audiences of Cooper Union students and workingmen how he, too, was a workingman and had risen from nothing to affluence by hard work. Peter himself was well aware in his less sentimental moments that he did not start entirely from scratch, and was displeased when a writer in *Frank Leslie's Popular Monthly* alluded to his parents as poor and obscure and to himself as self-made.[4] From the days of Obadiah Cooper for three-quarters of a century, until Peter's birth, the Coopers were master artisans and well-to-do farmers, part of that great middle stratum of society that was later to lead an independent America to industrial greatness.[5]

The master artisan's was a good life but a hard one. And it bred distinct patterns of behavior, patterns that were to form the groundwork of Peter Cooper's long life. Forced to work hard on slender capital, the artisan put a premium on thrift, skill, carefulness about business detail, and work. There was little time for leisure or indulgence, and family life was close and strict. Parents were honored, the rod was used unsparingly, and a stern moral code condemned unrestraint. Though materialism and rationalism had undermined an older Calvinism, the Methodist revival led by the great evangelist, George Whitefield, brought back a Godfearing religion to the Hudson Valley in the middle of the eighteenth century. Yet expansive tendencies predominated over repressive. Owning his own shop and his own tools, the artisan was self-sufficient and independent; if he owned land, he held a substantial position in the community; and in a developing economy he had high hopes of improving his condition. All this made him ambitious, energetic, proud, and incorrigibly optimistic. Throughout the century he fought the great landed patroons, into whose ranks he had no chance of being admitted, over the privileges of voting, of controlling taxation, of electing justices, of having a militia. An individualist, he assumed his right to the property that he owned and that he might acquire. It was easy for him to imagine that personal success would crown honest effort, that failure was due to defects of character, and that his self-interest served society, since he saw around him conditions far better for the average man than could be found in Europe. He was sure that through self-education and effort he could conquer the world.

Obadiah Cooper's children and grandchildren followed the familiar pattern. Hardworking, honest, religious men and women, they supported themselves comfortably but left no fortunes, and what they had they divided equally among their numerous offspring, scorning the aristocratic system of primogeniture. Their family motto was *Perseverance conquers all things,* and most of them followed its dictum. While their father was alive his children remained around him, but after his death in 1742 most of them struck out down the river on their own. Obadiah, Peter's grandfather, the fourth son, stayed in Albany until the death of his first wife, Maria Fonda, a descendant of one Jellis Fonda, who settled in the Albany region as early as 1651. Maria died in the fifth year of their married life, in 1748, as did their two-year-old son Pieter. Obadiah, then aged twenty-eight, with his daughter Cornelia followed two of his older brothers into the region of Dutchess County broadly called Fishkill. Here he quickly established himself as a farmer and merchant, and made an advantageous second marriage in 1749 to a girl named Hester (or Esther) Bos (or Terboss). (Henry and Rosekrance Terboss were said to have been the first settlers in Fishkill village, and the family boasted a judge of the Court of Common Pleas in 1761, one Jacobus.) This twenty-two-year-old Dutch girl presented Obadiah with five children in five years, the last of whom, born in 1755, was Peter Cooper's father, John Cooper. So, whether or not the Coopers were Dutch, Peter Cooper had at least one Dutch grandparent.[6]

Though as late as the Revolution Fishkill had not more than fifty houses in a two-mile radius, it was the largest town in the county, having an academy, two churches, a schoolhouse, a hotel, a printing press, and in 1789 one of the seven post offices in the state. Obadiah lived there or near there all his life, and, as the scanty records show, was a respected and well-to-do member of the community. He is on the tax rolls from 1753 to 1775, listed as a merchant; on October 10, 1761, he is recorded as residing in Rombonts Precinct, which included Fishkill and other towns, and as buying six and three-quarter acres and eight roods of land from Robert Brett; on September 13, 1763, he bought a meadow of Matthew DuBois, Jr.; and in the last year of his life, the first year of the Revolutionary War, he served at the age of fifty-six in the second regiment of the Dutchess County militia. The old Cooper family Bible was his book, and in it, beginning in 1746, he carefully recorded in Dutch the births and deaths and marriages of his children and relations. He was very consciously the head of a growing and prosperous family.

It is hard to say what sort of man he was. Since he and his wife both died before Peter Cooper's birth—the grandfather fifteen and his wife two years before—the grandson had no personal memories to record, though he was once in his grandfather's home in Fishkill and was told how a large black snake nearly swallowed the foot of one of his young nephews or nieces. But it is rather remarkable that Peter, always avid for stories of his ancestors and never weary of telling about his father and maternal grandfather, should have heard so little from his father about old Obadiah. A single story remains, and it indicates a certain shrewd humor and cynicism. A neighbor of Obadiah's complained bitterly one day that his three sons were all born under unlucky planets, one to be a beggar, one a thief, and one a murderer. "What in the world do you worry about them for?" asked Obadiah. "It is not worth your while to grieve away your life about them. . . . If you will take my advice your sons will all go through the world respectably. The one that is born to be a beggar, make a minister of him; and the one that is born to be a thief, make a lawyer of him and he will pick people's pockets and they will have the desire for it; and the one that is born to be a murderer, make a doctor of him." [7]

Until he was of age in 1776, Peter Cooper's father, John, seemed destined to lead the quiet and prosperous life of his own father. He had set up in business as a hatter in Fishkill, and was wealthy enough before the Revolution to keep some of the slaves who were then driven about in the country for sale like flocks of sheep. John remembers as a boy throwing corn to some of these poor starved creatures and watching them scramble for it. He told his son that he kept one black servant just to make wampum for trading with the Indians, who had a passion for the white-and-blue clamshells strung on wires.[8]

The Revolution temporarily disrupted John Cooper's life. One of the first to enlist, he served as a Minute Man and then in the militia for a total of six years, and gave a good account of himself. According to Peter, who was firmly convinced that the conduct of one's ancestors is as important as inherited tendencies, his father set 'a glowing example of patriotism and devotion to humanity.'

John Cooper's first service was as sergeant in the company of Captain James Weeks in Colonel Bailey's regiment of General Swarthout's Brigade of Minute Men. Formed hastily from among the New York country people, who left their grain to perish for want of the sickle, these Minute Men were rushed to New York City to help Washington's feeble army of some ten thousand men hold the town. John Cooper's regiment built entrenchments on Governor's Island against the British, whose ships were already in the harbor and had landed troops on Staten Island. 'They had to dig themselves underground before morning to get out of the way of the grapeshot they might send at them from the English vessels in the harbor. He [John Cooper] said that they worked all that night, next day and the end of the next night, and then they were presented with a tub of rum and water and some raw pork.' [9]

But two regiments, all that could be spared, were hardly enough to hold the island, and Cooper's regiment abandoned it and fled through New York back into Westchester County. During the next year Cooper served at White Plains and at West Point defending Fort Constitution, and was present in October, 1777, at the fall of Fort Montgomery, which Sir Henry Clinton engineered as part of a diversion on the lower Hudson to help the desperate Burgoyne. Having no transportation across the river, Cooper and his men were forced to watch the four assaults on the fort from the east bank, from which they could hear the mingled hurrahs for King George and Congress.[10] His son Peter heard how dead bodies were piled up almost to the top of the cannon, and later saw for himself cartloads of the bones of those who had been buried in the riverbank.

When, after two years, Cooper was drafted for four months' service outside the state, he availed himself of a New York State law which permitted him to get a substitute for sixty dollars, and retired to Fishkill. But not for long. In 1778 he voluntarily joined as a second lieutenant Captain Richard Van Wyck's company of Colonel Abraham Brinkerhoff's regiment of the Dutchess County militia,[11] and served for four years at West Point, at Highland under Governor George Clinton, and, as commander of his own detachment, at Fishkill. The regular job of the militia was to protect Dutchess County inhabitants and the public stores and munitions, located on the farm of Captain Van Wyck, from enemy depredations. As Cooper said, in presenting a memorial to Congress in 1838 asking for a pension to cover his last four years of service (he finally received an eighty-dollar-a-year pension in 1826 for his earlier enlistment), the duties of the officers of militia were more 'arduous, harassing and more constant than those of many officers and regiments of the continental line of the army,' and yet they had no 'claim to the pay and rations to which daily the continental troops were justly entitled.'

Like so many soldiers, Cooper was seized in the course of the war by a desire to marry, and on May 4, 1777, was wedded to a twenty-year-old girl named Martha Pinfold. Scarcely a year later, on September 18, 1778, she died, leaving him with an infant son, John. The young widower did not long stay bereft. On Governor's Island one of his companions had been a young man from New York City named Thomas Campbell, who, not so fortunate as John Cooper, had escaped from the British only by hiding in a cave for several days with no sustenance but the water that flowed through the cave. After the evacuation of New York City Thomas' older brother, John Campbell,[12] fled with his wife and children north to Fishkill. On December 21, 1779, John Cooper married the latter's seventeen-year-old daughter, Margaret, at Fishkill.[13]

This alliance was a step up in the world for John Cooper, and may well have been unwelcome to his wife's family.[14] Margaret's parents, John and Sarah (Oakley) Campbell, were old New Yorkers, both having been born in New York City, and John Campbell was one of the town's more important citizens. Owner of a tile- and pottery-making establishment, and of a number of houses on Broadway on the old Duane property, he was a man of considerable wealth. Before the Revolution he had been a major in the old state militia. When war broke out he was appointed by Washington deputy quartermaster general in the Continental Army and entrusted with the protection of the citizens of lower New York State. He was a very remarkable man and the great hero of his grandson. Though Peter met him only once, when as a boy of six or seven he took a brief ride in his grandfather's gig on the latter's visit to Peter's father in Peekskill, memory of the short, thickset old man haunted his grandson's thoughts for the rest of his life.

John Campbell had most of the qualities that Peter Cooper

—by imitation or otherwise—came to admire. At the very beginning of the war he loaned all his ready money, eleven hundred guineas, to the Revolutionary government. When the time
for the evacuation of New York came in 1776, Campbell was
put in charge of the operation, and, sending away his family
and all they could carry in two wagons 'with the directions to
fly before the enemy as long as they could find roads to carry
them,' stayed loyally behind to help his poor neighbors escape.
Remaining too long, he was caught by the English press gang,
which started to lead him to one of the ships in the harbor. At
this point fate intervened in the form of a friend, evidently a
man of influence. As Peter Cooper wrote in words of Biblical
tinge, the friend told them 'to have no business with that man,
let him go, and they let him go.' Escaping north to Fishkill,
Campbell helped to establish the lines which hemmed in the
British in the vicinity of New York. When the French Army
landed he was given the task of finding a place for their encamp-
ment, and selected, over the protests of its owner, the home of
an old Tory as the most available site. Fearful that these 'foreigners' would steal his corn, the latter demanded a guard at
the 'length of every fence.' The indignant French general, insisting that 'my soldier no teef,' peremptorily refused, but did
put a guard around the field. When the farmer came down early
next morning, fearing the worst, he found that not an ear of
corn had been stolen, and was greeted by the French general
gleefully shouting "I told you my soldier no teef." Much, one
imagines, to the satisfaction of John Campbell, the old Tory
told him, when the army left, that the French had paid whatever their owner demanded for every chicken wing they had
taken.

Much of John Campbell's work was hazardous in the extreme.
He owned a favorite stud horse imported from England, for
which he was once offered three thousand dollars, and during
the seven years of the war he rode this horse numerous times
through enemy-infested territory on important missions. On one

occasion he had to carry $500,000 of Continental money to pay the army. To insure its not being discovered, he wrapped it around the body of his small son. Evidently not even his son was as important to him as his country.

His country did not, when the war was over, recompense him even to the extent of paying what was due him. Having placed his papers in the proper hands, he waited long and vainly for a settlement, and then journeyed numbers of times to Philadelphia to induce the impoverished and politics-ridden government to reimburse him. Finally, being unable to get his papers back, he demanded them (according to his grandson) of Alexander Hamilton at the point of a gun. He did not get the money but he got the papers, which were discovered by his grandson thirty-four years after his death. Indignant at such treatment of his hero by the Federalist enemy of all good Jeffersonians, Peter Cooper journeyed to Washington during Jackson's administration, determined to retrieve the money even at this late date. Finding in the office two of the very men who had examined the account and signed the papers so many years before, he demanded the money, which amounted to $7800. Though, according to Peter, his claim was immediately acted upon, $1300 was still owed in 1842 when Peter wrote to James Roosevelt in Washington on behalf of a man than whom even 'General Washington himself could not have obtained more unqualified evidence of character for honesty and faithful service during the war.' [15] In 1846 there was still talk of pushing John Campbell's claims in Congress.[16]

When the war was over John Campbell took charge of the troops at West Point until they were disbanded and then returned to his prosperous pottery, which he removed uptown to Duane (then Barley) Street. One of the first chairmen of the General Society of Mechanics and Tradesmen, in 1787,[17] and alderman in 1792, he died in 1798 as a result of another of those actions that so impressed his grandson. In 1795 the yellow fever paid one of the more violent of its sporadic visits to New York.

Having sent his family north, John Campbell remained at his post in New York and came down with the fever, which, though it did not kill him, so weakened him that he succumbed three years later at the age of fifty-nine.

His widow lived on a good many years and was the only one of his grandparents whom Peter really knew. As a boy he visited her frequently, and when he came to New York as an apprentice she let him use the back room of one of her Broadway houses. The kindly dispenser of small presents and soothing words, she became for Peter the symbol of security in a rough-and-tumble world. Peter remembers that she had a particularly beautiful cow, for whose welfare she was so concerned that she ordered its feed warmed in winter, and personally supervised the carrying-out of her instructions.[18] She also offered security of a more tangible kind. Always the owner of property, she helped John Cooper financially on more than one occasion, and gave him the use of one of her houses at Duane Street and Broadway as a shop. After her death John and Margaret got a much-needed share of the $30,000 obtained from the sale of some of her holdings.

Margaret Campbell Cooper appears to have been a worthy daughter of a worthy couple. Though, as is not infrequent in nineteenth-century family annals, the women receive only the scantest attention and that of the most conventional type, there is enough information to make it plain that Peter's mother was the real mainstay of the Cooper family. Born in 1762 on the site of the future St. Paul's Church, where the pottery then stood, she well remembered the old *cheval de frise* placed as a bulwark against the Indians across the whole island at Duane Street.[19] Her father and mother were or became Moravians,[20] and Margaret was educated at the Moravian School at Bethlehem, Pennsylvania, one of the best of early schools. Besides a better-than-usual education, she possessed a strong character, well fitted to keep her impetuous husband in tow and to get him out of scrapes. It is reported that once, when he had been imprisoned in the guardhouse for some unnamed offense, she got him released in twenty-four hours by her persistent petitioning. She was evidently imperturbable. When a neighbor's child ran in to announce that young Peter was climbing the ridgepole, she said calmly, "Then he will not be drowned in the Hudson River"; when she heard that he was swimming in the river, she was glad to know he was in no danger of falling off the roof. Family tradition reports that she was gentle and tender and beautiful as well, and so short that when she went to get a cake from the cupboard she needed a footstool to reach the chair on which she stood to open the top shelf.[21] Though Peter Cooper never showed that he preferred her to his father, and limited his specific praise to the somewhat formal remark that she was an 'excellent woman,' it is evident that hers was the greater energy and moral force.[22] One writer who knew Cooper avers that she was the source of all that was superior in him.[23]

She needed all the superior qualities she possessed to keep the family's head above water during most of the years of her married life. At the end of the Revolution, postwar restlessness infected John Cooper and made the quiet Fishkill life of his ancestors unpalatable to him. Or perhaps it is unfair to blame the war. John Cooper seems to have been inherently bold and impulsive and endowed with a roving and restless spirit. Unfortunately, he did not match those qualites with the worldly judgment or the patience and hardness necessary for success in the life he had marked out for himself. A big bear of a man who could lift a barrel of cider from the ground and put it in a wagon, and who, in an encounter with a bull from whom he could not escape, is reported to have seized the beast by the nose with one hand and so battered him about the head with a stone that the brute was glad to turn and fly, he had all the kindness and easygoing amiability that so often accompanies size. He sold his watch for thirty dollars to help feed his destitute comrades during the war,[24] and in his later business life extended credit to almost anyone who appealed to his generosity. As a consequence, though he was able to make money and even to prosper at times—his son referred to him at one point as a 'flourishing manufacturer of hats'—, he never seemed able either to settle down in one place or to hold onto the money that he had made. Peter Cooper got not only a 'glowing example of patriotism' from his father but a 'warning against business carelessness and getting into debt.' [25] Fortunately for his relations with his father and for his own development, the former impression was not eradicated by the latter, strong as it was. With all his faults and weaknesses John Cooper offered to his son a not uninspiring model of behavior. The concluding words of John Cooper's plea for a pension, written in the last year of his life, reflect the sturdy pride that a long life of wrong turns and misfortune had not destroyed: 'Straitened as may be the pecuniary circumstances of your memorialist yet he is conscious that his revolutionary services were not at that time tendered with a view to recompense of reward in dollars and cents—and his sense of self-respect will not permit him as one of his last acts of the few remaining years of his life to solicit that from his country as a favour which he might, and which he would only wish to ask as a right.' [26]

For a time after the war John Cooper apparently lived on in Fishkill, but around 1785, perhaps at the solicitation of John Campbell and his wife, who had returned to town, he moved his hat business and his growing family to the town with which his son's history was to be so intimately related. This move, part of a general migration from upper New York State to the city in the 1780's, was the wisest of the many that John Cooper was to make. New York was beginning for the first time to offer those opportunities for self-improvement which have attracted successive and ever-increasing waves of immigration from all over the world, and which in such a relatively brief time have made a metropolis out of a tiny Dutch hamlet.

Immediately after the war the outlook for New York was not promising. Its prewar population of 21,863 had been almost cut in half by emigration during the occupation, and the twelve thousand remaining inhabitants were rent by political division and discouragement. As late as 1789 New York presented to the casual eye the spectacle of a half-grown and dilapidated village. Pigs and dogs roamed its poorly paved streets between ragged rows of wooden or brick-faced houses and the blackened ruins of the great fire of 1778. Its wharves were dirty, Fort George was used as a stable, and the Battery was nothing but a filthy earthwork. There were two thousand slaves in the city and a large pauper population living in crowded quarters full of pallid, barefoot women. Nearly the most prominent features of the town were the gallows, enshrined in a Chinese pagoda between the almshouse and the jail, and the stocks and whipping post nearby in a grove where the City Hall now stands.[27]

But life was stirring under the surface. Each year John Cooper could see hosts of eager new faces in the narrow streets of the town, whose population nearly tripled in seven years. By 1790, when the number of its inhabitants reached 33,131, New York had already become the nation's greatest port and largest city. Among the new residents were enterprising foreigners such as John Jacob Astor and his brother Henry, and politicians like Jay and Hamilton and Burr. With growth came prosperity, unbroken from 1786 to 1791. John Cooper could watch great houses rising on Bowling Green, the Battery, and lower Broadway. The famed City Hotel on Broadway and the Tontine Coffee House at Wall and Water Streets were built in 1792, and the College of Physicians and Surgeons, the American Museum, and New York's first bank, Hamilton's Bank of New York, were founded in 1791. By 1789, when Richard Varick became mayor, bitterness against Tories was nearly dissipated, and lively political warfare had begun to develop between Jay's and Hamilton's Federalist aristocracy and artisans and shopkeepers like John Cooper, led by the recently formed Tammany Hall. And

· (17) ·

this same year New York had its moment of glory as the federal capital. For a few months John Cooper could observe Washington progress in state from his home at No. 1 Cherry Street to Wall and Broad Streets, where stood Federal Hall, the nation's capital, its grand vestibule paved with marble and in its Senate Chamber an azure ceiling resplendent with sun and thirteen stars.

John Cooper did not move into the most fashionable part of town, but set up his shop in the business district on Little Dock Street, now Water Street, two or three doors from Coenties Slip, where gloomy warehouses today loom over the last of New York's elevated railways. All accounts agree that he prospered. Credit had been eased in 1786 by the issuance of two hundred thousand pounds in paper money, to be lent on real estate, and shopkeepers and artisans benefited. Peter Cooper, who later strongly favored exactly such a measure, may have heard of its beneficent effects from his father. True, rents were high and there were corporate restrictions on both voting and shopkeeping, which were limited to 'freemen.' But John Cooper evidently had enough money to buy this privilege, which could be obtained by paying a fee, and business was good. In 1790 the young fur trader John Jacob Astor, who had been looking for a shop, finally found one at 40 Little Dock Street, having 'very likely' heard of it, says Astor's biographer, 'through a hatter named Cooper, who dwelt not far from No. 40.' [28] Cooper was a good customer of Astor, buying the beaver skins which the latter secured from western Indians and Hudson River boatmen. There is a record in Cooper's ledger book of selling bearskins to Astor in return for muskrat and gray fox skins. John Cooper's chief business was in beaver, castor, and felt hats, for which there was a ready market. If, owing to lack of currency, there was no cash available, he took payment in 'hay, buggy-hire, bricks, firewood, tobacco, wool, sugar, flour, honey, old sheepskins, casks of rum, three days' work of a negro, and so on.' [29] He thus soon found himself in the grocery as well as the hat business, and continued to sell groceries and other items for many years.

By 1790 he was well established in New York and is listed in the census of that year as possessing a household of five white males over sixteen, three under sixteen, and four females.[30] Whether the fourth female and the white males were boarders or servants and helpers we do not know. But the others were his rapidly expanding family: two girls, Sarah and Martha, now eight and seven respectively; and three boys—John, his son by Martha Pinfold, born in 1778, James, born in 1786, and Thomas, who died on August 20, 1789, at the age of eleven months.[31] And his wife was once more pregnant. On February 12, 1791, she was delivered of her third son,[32] Peter, who was thus born within three years of the birth of the new nation.

Chapter 2

A ROLLING STONE

THE naming of a great hero is always of the first importance and John Cooper, who had a special feeling about this son, took his obligation very seriously. Perplexed about what he should call the boy, he was walking up Broadway 'in the dark hours of the night' shortly after the birth when it seemed 'as though a voice had spoken saying call his name Peter and he will do a work for the world as important as that done by Peter of old.' [1] This 'waking vision' confirmed John Cooper's impression that the boy 'would some day have more than ordinary fame,' and would 'be of great good in some way.' He accepted the recommendation on the spot.

The most interesting part of this story is Peter Cooper's reaction to it. Never did he admit believing in the supernatural manifestation, which he was quite prepared to grant might be the 'mere wanderings of a disordered mind.' He was well aware that his father 'was a man who tried to make all the acts of his life a part of his religion,' the surest way to encourage visions. He ought to have known, too, that, though Peter was not as usual a name in the family as Obadiah or John or James, John Cooper had had a baby stepbrother named Pieter, so that it required no occult visitor to think up the name. Yet—whether he believed the story or not—it 'made an impression I have never been able to forget,' and he repeated it in public and in his writings on numerous occasions. It 'has stimulated me,' he asserted, 'to an effort to give the world an equivalent in some form of useful labour for all I may consume in life,' or, as he wrote at another time, 'to do something towards fulfilling the wishes and aspirations of my father and mother concerning me.' Memory is a tricky thing, and it is notorious that old men tend to fasten on such incidents as explanations for later behavior. Yet there is no reason seriously to doubt the importance of this episode to Peter Cooper. And what surely impressed him most was this confidence in him entertained by his parents, who were perhaps influenced by the hopefulness that swept over the new nation, itself born so recently. Peter Cooper had that prime essential of a successful beginning in life: parents who believed in him.

Other influences of his early years were of a more ambiguous kind, especially the atmosphere of instability and insecurity in which Peter grew up. When Peter was three years old his father packed up his family and moved up the river to Peekskill, where he bought some land, put up a store, and became a grocer. Since he had been highly successful as a hatter, there seems to have been no reason for the move except wanderlust; as Peter phrased it, he 'became enamoured of the country life.' Disaster followed quickly. Business was brisk enough, and John Cooper's ledgers show extensive sales of molasses, rum, and sugar, as well as such items as penknives, buttons, oilcloth, and bridle bits. But Cooper made the mistake of taking his religion a trifle too seriously. He not only helped his Methodist brothers build a chapel, but, forgetting, as his son said, that hospitality could only be supported by an ample fortune, made his house a home for the traveling clergy and gave them carte blanche at his store. As a consequence, 'the visiting clergy ate up the profits of the store, while the Church, being consigned to religion, naturally failed to make up the deficit or stored the payments too high in the next world to be of any use in this.' [2] John Cooper also, in his goodnatured way, extended credit far too widely, since he found 'plenty of persons who would buy' on these terms. It was 'not more than two or three years before he found that nearly all of his property was in the hands of other people, and that it was impossible for him to collect it.' [3]

Until Peter Cooper was a grown man and could help his father in a substantial way the family were never again in really comfortable circumstances. For the next decade or more John Cooper wandered with his growing family—three more children, Thomas (1794), William (1799), and Edward (1803) were born to him—up and down the Hudson from New York City to Catskill, looking for success in half a dozen callings including farming, making bricks, and brewing, which he supplemented by vending wild honey and netting and selling pigeons. We cannot follow these wanderings with any accuracy, not because Peter Cooper was not explicit about them, but because he flatly contradicted himself in the several versions that he has left us. We know that John Cooper moved back to New York before the last year of the century and took up hat-making again, and that he lived either in Brooklyn—he had a home there at some time between 1796 and 1808—or in one of the Duane Street houses of his mother-in-law, where Peter remembers living as a boy. His ledgers show sales of hats in all the years from 1796 to the end of the century, and indicate that he took rum, wood, and food in exchange. This Duane Street hatshop he sold eventually to Peter's half-brother, John. We know also that he moved back to Peekskill some time between 1800 and 1803 and built a brewery there, and that he later built another in Newburgh, where he lived at some time before 1808 and where he was residing in 1814. He also lived for a period at Catskill, where he made bricks, and may have returned to New York once more before 1808. He died—to complete the record—in 1838 in New York at 33rd Street and Third Avenue on one of Peter Cooper's properties. His son's help plus some money he inherited from his mother-in-law relieved somewhat his later years. [4]

The unsettled life of the Coopers had one unqualified advantage for Peter: from his earliest years he was free to wander, unhampered by parental restrictions, through the fields and woods of half a dozen townships, and to acquire the familiarity with new experience that breeds self-reliance. Like other lower Hudson Valley boys he swam in the river or climbed prickly-pear trees for birds' nests, cherry trees for fruit, and tall pines just for the pleasure of sailing back and forth as the wind rocked them. Peter knew old Pierre Van Cortlandt, New York's first lieutenant-governor, who used to give him peaches from his Croton estate four miles from Peter's Peekskill home. His beautiful wife, Joanna, Peter often saw in the church John Cooper had built, but never the old gentleman.[5] Sometimes Peter went with his father long distances up Fishkill Creek to Methodist meetings. More fun, however, must have been excursions after the honey to be found in hollow trees, which involved attracting the bees by burning honey and then chasing wildly after them to their hiding places.[6]

Peter showed initiative and daring from his earliest days, whether in climbing ridgepoles or swinging from the tops of tall trees. At the age of nine he was the leader of a gang of 'progressive' youths, who, according to Peter, sometimes engaged in ventures that 'may shock the moral sense,' though he never specified what they were.[7] Accidents were inevitable, and Peter suffered more than his share. He got his first scar at the age of four or five when he tried to step from one beam to another of a house his father was building and fell on a sharp iron pot, cutting his forehead to the bone. He got another lifelong scar when he hit his axe on a clothesline and the axe flew back and hit him in the head. A little boy who was building a sandpile with him provided a third: as they were getting up, the boy—accidentally, one assumes—struck Peter in the cheek with a knife he had in his hand, the knife passing right through his cheek into his mouth. Peter lost one of his teeth when he fell from a high tree holding an iron hook with which he had been reaching for cherry-bearing branches. The hook, being a little longer than Peter, struck the ground first and caught one of his teeth, 'but for which it would have torn my cheek open.' These mishaps were but the prelude to dozens more, which occurred at all stages of Peter's life, making it often seem a miracle that he survived even to middle age. No wonder that his mother gave up any attempt to protect him. She apparently found out early that Peter was determined to try anything and everything no matter what the physical consequences.

Even when he was a boy some of these efforts took a constructive direction. Peter was a born inventor. He had that inquisitiveness and reluctance to do more manual labor than necessary which, together with the scarcity of labor, has made America the home of the labor-saving device; and he had the talent to implement his preferences. 'In my early boyhood,' he wrote later, 'I recollect helping my mother in doing the family washing by pounding the clothes. The soiled clothes were put in a barrel with soapy water enough to saturate them, when a wooden pounder with a long wooden handle was used. It was a tiresome way, and I thought I could make an improvement, which I did in the following manner: I constructed a wheel about half the size of the diameter of the barrel. On each side of this wheel I attached a handle for a pounder—resembling two handles to a pump—by which I could keep the pounder in operation. To work them more conveniently I made a double lever, as it might be called, fastened by a wheel on each side of it. A post in the top of this wheel, connected with this double lever, enabled me to take hold of a handle with its opposite end fastened to the wheel in the pounding barrel, and thus work both pounders at once, and by means of a ratchet attachment I caused them to strike in a new place every time. This was about the first improvement on anything I ever attempted with success.' [8] It was also typical of the many he later made: involving no new principle, it was a triumph of observation, trial and error, and ingenuity.

His other notable work as a boy was making a pair of shoes. With characteristic curiosity he carefully opened an old shoe to understand how it was put together. 'When I saw the mode of its construction I made a last, and got my mother to give me money to buy leather, awls, and shoe thread, when I went to work making shoes, as well as slippers for myself and other members of the family, especially for my sisters; and they were said to compare favorably with the shoes manufactured in those days.' [9]

Though for the most part country-bred—he retained all his life the simplicity and earthiness of a country boy—, young Peter knew the little city of New York too. Before the first move to Peekskill he was too young to remember anything except the alley next to his father's store where he scratched out mortar between bricks into a little paper box and pretended it was snuff. But when he returned at the turn of the century the city, now grown to over fifty thousand, gradually opened up to him. He knew best the region where his grandfather's houses were, upper Broadway around Chambers Street, with its rail fence on the east side and the grove with the whipping post in City Hall Park, once a cabbage garden of the poorhouse. At Chambers Street and Broadway, where later A. T. Stewart's great store would go up, was, Cooper remembers, the Negro burying ground. To the north toward Canal Street were fields where Peter recalls watching from a cart a man and woman hunting. Here too was the excavation made by the Manhattan Company and the log pipes that supplied much of the city water. The city waterpump, with its sun and planet wheel made of cogs inside of a crank, was at Chatham and Pearl Streets, and the water it pumped up, Peter says, was too often salt water which had percolated through the sand from suction. At Canal Street a log with a rail for balancing was the only bridge across the stream emptying out of the Collect, a large pond where Centre Street now runs between Canal and Pearl Streets. Cooper also remembers the old wooden fortification forming a kind of fence around the Battery and the fine houses on the street to the east. Way off to the north between Union Square and the North River lived Aaron Burr, in a house that Cooper recalls as one of the most extravagant in the city. Far to the east, on Brandy Moody Point, was old Colonel Rutgers' farm, to which Peter walked one night as a boy.

Life was perhaps not as much fun as in the country but there were always gangs of boys for Peter to lead, rivers to swim, and ferryboats to ride. As was to be expected, he almost drowned several times. Once, swimming in the Hudson, he missed a plank his brother put out to him and, losing his presence of mind, went right to the bottom. At another time, crossing to Brooklyn on the ferry, he was swept overboard by hitting the taut line of a privateer that the ferry was trying to avoid. Peter had seen the line and, to no avail, had warned the boatman that he was going to hit the privateer. On a third occasion—though Cooper's recollection of the time of this occurrence may be inaccurate—he drove across the Hudson on the ice with a horse and sleigh and nearly fell through, as the ice was melting rapidly. 'But I drove on, keeping the line of the road that had been made over the ice, and got safely across. In looking back, however, I saw two other sleighs and horses which had followed in the same track, had broken through the ice, and I ran with others to help them.' To get one horse out it was necessary to fasten a rope so tightly around its neck that it would choke and turn over on its side, enabling it to be dragged out.[10] The greatest sport—and the most dangerous—was jumping from log to log on the rafts that came down the Hudson River and were moored opposite Trinity Church and up as far as Washington Market. Naturally he fell in the river. At least once.

New York, moreover, offered more sights than the country. The most solemn of these occurred in 1799. Standing in front of St. Paul's Church, Peter saw the mock-funeral procession of George Washington that New York, like many other towns, arranged as a tribute to their leader, buried at Mt. Vernon. What surprised him especially was the 'peculiar way in which his boots were reversed in the stirrups of the charger that followed the hearse.'

More indelibly impressed on Cooper's imagination were, however, three less edifying spectacles. In Washington Square, then the Potter's Field but occasionally used for punishment, he once saw a man hanged for theft. "The recollection has chased me through life like a nightmare," he told Lloyd Bryce, "and whenever I look up I see him hanging, his head bent over on one side. There he remained for several hours, with the jeering crowd about him." Another time, near the same spot on the northeast corner of Fifth Avenue and the Square, he saw two Negroes forced to flog one another, to the even greater enjoyment of the crowd. "At first, as may be supposed, the punishment was light; the culprits mutually agreed to spare each other as much as possible. At last, however, one hit a little harder than he intended; the other retaliated, and each, becoming angry, laid on his blows in a manner that made the punishment greater than the severest taskmaster could well have inflicted. Young as I was, I tried to stop the proceedings, but without success." [11]

A third incident that was seared on Cooper's heart took place in City Hall Park. 'There I stood by and saw two men whipped at the whipping post, one a white man and the other a black man. The white man's back resembled, from his shoulders to his hip, just a bloody blister. The screams of that man will always remain in my memory. The scream of that man was perfectly frightful. He would scream, get a little lower down, and it seemed as if it was beyond his endurance.' [12] Even at an early age Peter showed himself innately tender and sensitive to cruelty. As the years passed, such feelings were transmuted into the desire to relieve suffering and to help humanize the world.

There is no suggestion in this fragmentary record of Peter's childhood or anywhere else that he was seriously harmed by the lack of security or stability in his home life. A slim, somewhat frail youth, he would have benefited had the family been better provided for. 'When I was twenty-one,' he wrote later, 'my hand trembled so that I could hardly put a cup of tea to my lips. I did not think I would become an old man.' [13] Emotionally, too, he would perhaps have been better off had his childhood been less haunted by family anxiety, as his later reference to a 'want of confidence in myself' suggests.[14] But there is little evidence that he really lacked confidence to any degree; on the contrary, few boys have seemed as able as was Peter to face life with robust equanimity. Much of this strength was undoubtedly supplied by his mother, who early learned to appreciate the gentle and kindly boy, always so ready to help her in her duties and so capable of taking burdens off her hands. She gave him a love that conquered fear, confirmed the sweetness of his nature, and made him ready to tackle any problem in life with an assurance that seldom took no for an answer. The peregrinations of the Cooper family exhilarated rather than depressed Peter, and their troubles were but a challenge to be eagerly accepted.

Yet the precariousness of affairs at home left their mark on Peter nonetheless. From the days when he first became aware of the cause of the family predicament almost until his death he was haunted by a near-obsessive fear of debt. There were, of course, sufficient rational grounds for this fear. The debts that John Cooper was constantly piling up might mean jail in the eighteenth century. Peter himself remembered seeing the jail in New York 'literally filled with persons confined there for the payment of debt, even after they had given up all their property.' He also heard, when young, of the Connecticut law that had permitted the sale, possibly for life if they couldn't work off the debt sooner, of insolvent debtors. And as a boy he visited with his father a shoemaker named McClain, a poor old man with one crooked leg, whose household furniture had been removed for a debt he could not possibly pay.[15] It is strong testimony to Peter's basic sanity that the spectre of debt never tempted him to hoard money, or made him anything but contemptuous of old misers he knew who kept boxes of gold under their beds or in their cellars until they died.[16] His attitude about debt was nevertheless more that of a fanatic than of a rational man. Not content to praise staying away from lenders as sound policy, he insisted over and over again that most of his success could be credited to this policy; and he refused for many years even to keep money in a bank or to have any accounts outstanding at the end of a year. Moreover, his repeated references to the subject and anecdotes about it, many of which were quite pointless, show how it preyed on his mind.[17] Debts were evidently the objects of basic fears in Cooper's youth.

These fears—and perhaps others—were accentuated by the religion to which Peter was subjected as a boy. The Methodism which John Cooper professed had many virtues. It was democratic in its emphasis on informality, the inner life, the personal, and the separation of church and state, attitudes that Peter Cooper was himself staunchly to adhere to all his life. And it gave Peter a sound pattern of moral values on which to base his life. As he wrote years later, he had parents who 'taught me that it was always safe for me to do what I knew to be right and always dangerous to do what I knew to be wrong—guided by that course I have gone through a long life with comparative competence and comfort.' [18] And with benefit to his fellowmen as well, since when later he came to see that doing right meant helping others he was prepared to act instantly on that conviction. Yet Methodism was a grim religion. In Peter's words, 'My father's religion was of that kind that he feared everybody would go tumbling into hell,' and he frequently held meetings, which young Peter attended, to warn of sin and damnation.[19]

For many years Peter was unable either to accept or entirely to reject this stern religion,[20] however much he may have disliked the clergymen who sponged on his father. He has stated his deep perplexity in one of the more moving passages of the *Reminiscences:* 'It fell to my lot to have been led like one of old by ways

· (29) ·

that I had not known and paths that I had not trodden. I was led not only forty days and forty nights but for more than forty years up into and through the tangled maze of creeds and systems of human device, where I found myself longing and hoping to find something that would satisfy the cravings of a rational and moral mind. In my anxiety to find a place of rest for my anxious mind, after I had been taught to fear that there was such a thing as a state of endless misery after the pleasure that was possible for mankind, as I had heard that there had even been a war in Heaven, a picture was drawn to my mind that the angels who had been cast out were banished to a place of endless punishment where the worm dieth not and the fire is not quenched. In this state of anxiety I heard and went to hear all the different "Lo, here's" and "Lo, there's," all professing to show me the way to safety to escape from the terrible circumstances that caused me so much dread.' [21]

Peter also suffered in a more tangible way from the family difficulties. The worst of these occurred just when Peter should have been starting to school, with the result that he was 'the only one of the family' to receive virtually no education. He went to school at Peekskill but 'three or four quarters,' and then for only half a day, and that was all the schooling he had. Ill health and a lack of interest in studies have been advanced as further reasons for the meagerness of Peter's education, but, as he says himself, the chief cause was that 'my father's misfortunes in business left no opportunity for me to attend school.' [22] Despite what democratic sentimentalizers of the school of hard knocks have said or implied, Peter Cooper was almost fatally handicapped by his lack of education. His writing was never skillful enough to earn him the hearing he deserved; his scientific work was always that of the amateur, deficient both on the technical and the theoretical side; and his political and social thinking remained to the end somewhat crude and inflexible. Peter himself was the first to deplore the limitations imposed by his lack of education, and made it his life's work to see that the same thing did not happen to others. 'If I could have had such advantages as we can give the poorest boy now,' he wrote years later, 'how much more could I have done.' [23]

By the time Peter Cooper was ten or eleven, sport no less than education was becoming a thing of the past. Even before that, at the age when his head just reached the level of the table, he had started to help his father in his work, and he was to continue to do so until, wearied of Newburgh or his father's ineptitudes or just of life at home, he struck out at the age of seventeen on his own. 'Among my earliest recollections was the pulling the hair and cutting the fur from skins and carding the wool to be used in the manufacture of hats.' [24] By the time he was fifteen he could make every part of a good beaver hat, an elaborate and imposing structure. When his father turned to brick-making Peter was made useful in carrying and handling the bricks for the drying process. When he took up brewing Peter learned that business as well. He helped build both of his father's small breweries, and for a twelve- or thirteen-year-old boy who was supposed to be sickly did a prodigious amount of work. He helped drag the dirt out of the excavation for the Peekskill brewery. And he carted the stone for the foundations of the Newburgh brewery for more than a mile, a neighbor having given permission to take from his field all the stone needed. 'I picked up these stones, many of them being all I could poessibly lift.' [25] When the breweries were functioning, Peter had to help in the manufacturing and to deliver the kegs of beer to the customers around the countryside. For this purpose he had to make use of a horse whose vagaries almost caused his death on at least three occasions.

Such a training had one disadvantage besides preventing Peter from going to school. It made him a jack-of-all-trades rather than a master of any one, and encouraged a tendency to shift from trade to trade for many years of his adult life. Fortunately Peter Cooper did not live in the days of specialization, and was not severely handicapped by being a rolling stone. And there were compensations. His early training brought out his innate mechanical genius and made him, in true pioneer fashion, a competent if not a master craftsman in a dozen fields. It endowed him, too, with the sort of healthy pragmatic attitude that even in later life caused him on occasion to cut through fruitless theoretical arguments with the sharp reminder that results were what counted.[26] Above all, it gave a bent to his mind that education often stultifies; compelled to find solutions for practical problems, Peter Cooper learned to think for himself, and to have infinite faith in his ability to tackle the knottiest problems in mechanics or economics or politics or religion. The world remained as fresh as on its first morning to one whose mind had never been fitted into a mold or tamed by doubt or sicklied o'er with the pale cast of thought.

All this was not without its obvious dangers. Peter Cooper was often banal and occasionally absurd, and was seldom aware of being either; loath to admit mistakes or to question his own beliefs or motives, he defended his most ridiculous notions with the same pertinacity as his finest insights. Yet he never made a disastrous failure. Idealism, pertinacity, blind stubbornness, lack of a critical sense—call it what you will—might make him cling forever to the strangest ideas, but commonsense and native shrewdness always prevented him from staking his fortune on an absurdity even while he was defending it in words. In Peter Cooper, optimistic idealism was nicely blended with down-to-earth practicality. He was as well prepared to be a businessman as to be a pioneer, an inventor, or a philanthropist. He could be all of them at once, and they never got in each other's way.

There was one thing, however, that he was not going to be, as he discovered by means of an incident that he considered one of the most fortunate events in his life. 'When quite a small boy,' he wrote, 'I made a little waggon. In giving one of my little brothers a ride in it one day, a friend of my father's came along and offered me six dollars for it, which I was very glad to take, although I had spent a great deal of time and labour on it with the few tools I had. In some way, which I scarcely now remember, I succeeded in adding four dollars to the amount, and I used the ten dollars in buying lottery tickets.[27] My uncle persuaded me to do this, as it was his business, and he was authorized by the state to sell lottery tickets. I had the "good luck" to draw nothing but blanks, which I consider one of the best investments of my life, for I then learned that it was not my forte to make money at games of chance.'

No, it was indeed not Cooper's forte, and he was always convinced that the 'wheel of fortune is only turned by common sense applied to common events.' Like Andrew Carnegie after him, he deplored stock-market gambling and determined to earn his fortune the hard way, through creative efforts in business enterprise. Success or even establishment in business was thus long in coming. It must have seemed far off to him indeed, when, some time in 1808, he set out from Newburgh for the big city to earn his living on his own.

Chapter 3

COACHMAKER'S APPRENTICE

To an energetic and talented young man the little Hudson River towns of the turn of the century seemed stifling. Peter recalled the suspicions aroused by his neighbors when a successful Peekskill lawyer, wishing to 'keep up with the improvements of the age . . . indulged in the extravagance of having a carpet for his stairway. Not long after this his poor wife had the misfortune of catching her toe at the top of the stairs, when she fell headlong and broke her neck, and I recollect hearing it remarked that it was a terrible judgment on such extravagance. In those days people thought they were well enough off if they had clean floors, with Rockaway sand, nicely ornamented with the broom, with which they marked different figures on the floors.' [1] Peter inevitably succumbed to the lure of independence, which for a century and a half has been drawing boys off the farms of America to Broadway.

Not that New York was yet by any definition the big city. Its modern industrial and commercial development was to start only a dozen years later when—as if it were waiting for him— Peter Cooper was ready to participate as a leading manufacturer. The closely packed houses, which must have impressed young Peter, away from New York for so long, reached little above Chambers Street on Broadway (only recently laid out to the future Union Square) ,[2] and only to Bond Street on the Bowery, the main traffic artery north to Boston. It probably did not seem strange to Peter that the north side of the beautiful new City Hall had been built of freestone instead of marble, since few, surely, would ever see it from that side. The Post Office took up one room forty feet long in the house of General Theodorus Bailey at William and Garden Streets, and the few letters from the south that braved the high postal rates could be brought across the Hudson in two bags in a rowboat each day. There were only two hotels for Peter to stare at, the City on Broadway and the Union on William near Cedar and Pearl; half a dozen taverns—the Bull's Head in the Bowery and the Tontine Coffee House being the most famous; three banks; and one theatre, the famous Park Theatre built in 1798. The upper Bowery, where Peter was to settle a dozen years later, was farms and country residences; the whole area west of Broadway both north and south of Canal Street was known as Lispenard Meadows, and was swampy ground; Manhattanville, Harlem, and Greenwich were independent villages, the last of which served as a haven for New Yorkers in the yellow fever epidemics that crippled the city every few years.

Though he saw fine new houses around the Battery, on Lower Broadway and Greenwich Streets, Peter must have found much that was familiar to him in the still primitive little city. New York in 1808 was ill-paved, poorly lit by a few smoky oil lamps that often went out before morning, and without adequate garbage disposal. The inhabitants swept their own housefronts, and twice a week the garbage was picked up by a cart, announced by a bellman, unless one was rich enough to hire a Negro to carry it away in buckets on his head. Often the cart did not come and the poor simply threw refuse in the streets for the goats and pigs. Peter probably accepted such conditions as normal, but even he must have wondered about the way the water tasted. Both the wells dug by Aaron Burr's Manhattan Company,[3] which supplied water to the city through bored wooden logs leading from a reservoir in Chambers Street, and the tea-water pump in Chatham Street, whose water was sold from wooden tanks with tea water on their sides, were already becoming contaminated. So was the Collect, whose days fortunately were numbered. Discharges of the Nassau and Fulton Street tanners, dead cats and dogs, mingled there with the dirt from the town's washing, and it is somewhat of a miracle that New York was not wiped out instead of being merely inconvenienced by various epidemics.

There were other pleasanter reminders that New York was not the city of today. The air was filled with woodsmoke from the hickory that was burned in the town's fireplaces; at daybreak the cry of "Sweep ho" from the little Negro chimney sweeps woke the soundest sleeper. Farmers carrying tins suspended by yokes over their shoulders delivered milk in the early morning hours. Oblong wagons brought bread from door to door in tall round baskets; peddlers sold tea rusk, hot cross-buns, and gingerbread in the streets. Mr. Bogart, the biscuit maker, sat on his stoop at Broadway and Cortlandt every afternoon with pipe in mouth. 'Dressed in small clothes, and woolen stockings; buckles at the knees and in his shoes; body-coat, with large pockets and buttons; a white stock, buckled behind; a plain, neat shirt, with sleeve buttons; his hair powdered; a long queue, and broad brimmed beaver hat,' he was a symbolic figure, model of the comfortable burgomaster in an eighteenth-century world.[4]

Already, however, many signs pointed to the future. The population of 80,000, small by European standards of over a half a million for both Paris and London, was two and a half times larger than when Peter was born. New York was already the commercial center of the nation, and when Jefferson's disastrous Embargo Act of 1807 was repealed in 1809, New York's commerce equaled that of Philadelphia and Boston combined.[5] The year before Peter's arrival Fulton ran his famous steamboat on the Hudson to predictions of dire disaster by those who accompanied him. 'But the horrible monster steamed on, breathing fire and smoke. Pine wood was used for fuel, and the blaze often shot up into the air considerably above the tall smoke-stack and whenever the fire was replenished immense columns of black smoke issued forth mingled with sparks and ashes. The terrific spectacle, particularly after dark, appalled the crews of other vessels, who saw it approaching in spite of adverse winds and tide.' [6] There were many new sights for Peter to see: the filling-in of the Collect with earth taken from another old landmark, Bunker Hill; the completion of the City Hall, started in 1803; big buildings on Wall Street, already becoming the financial center of the nation; the first public school, founded by De Witt Clinton's Free School Society, at Madison and Pearl Streets. Peter could read, if he wished and was able to, five morning and three evening papers, including Coleman's *Evening Post,* founded in 1801, as well as some ten weeklies. He could become a man of elegance by employing a barber who advertised himself as 'proficient not only in embellishing the head and beautifying the countenance divine, but in all the accomplishments of a *finished* gentleman'; he had, however, better stay away from the barber's rival, 'a mere *jaw scavenger,* employed to remove the rubbish.' [7]

Less pleasant though equally characteristic developments were also taking place. Peter found the housing problem already endemic. A traveler from Philadelphia in 1806 noted what he considered the absurd custom of changing one's abode the first of every May because the landlord was always increasing the rent.[8] For the new Irish immigrants and others who couldn't pay the rents in better-class districts there were already—south and east of the Collect—slums with low frame houses half-buried by erosion from the hills and backyards and cellars sunk in pools of slimy green water. The 'Five Points' at Mulberry and Worth Streets, the most notorious of all fetid areas, was the scene—on Christmas Eve, 1806—of the first riot caused by native-foreign hostility. With the growth of a foreign population and the letting-down of voting bars for alderman to $25-a-year rent payers in 1804, city politics was already assuming its modern form. Corruption, that hardy perennial of American city governments, was very much present: Benjamin Romaine was removed as controller for malfeasance in 1806; William Mooney, a founder of Tammany, spent four to ten times his allowance as superintendent of the Alms House in 1809.[9] In short, New York was beginning to be New York. In 1807 a commission was appointed to plan the city's expansion, and, as evidence of their confidence in the future, laid out as far as 155th Street the rectangular grid of streets that has both blessed and cursed the city.

When Peter Cooper arrived in New York, he signalized his new freedom by deserting both the trades he had been brought up to,[10] and apprenticing himself to the firm of Burtis and Woodward, leading coachmakers,[11] at Broadway and Chambers Street. Peter's first interview with John Woodward was to the point and satisfactory. His employer discovered that, though Peter knew nothing about the business, he had worked all his life, was permitted by his father to choose any trade he desired, and would stay his time, four years. Peter went to work at $25 a year, and so much did his employer learn to trust him that he never asked him to be indentured in writing, assuming—quite correctly—that he would serve the full term without being bound.

Peter's perseverance is perhaps more to be applauded at this time than his instinct for profitable employment. Coach-making, though carried on in New York from 1750, did not hold the prospect of a fortune. Private carriages had not become general until just before the Revolution, and even in 1808 the upper classes, the only ones to use them, tended to import French and English coaches.[12] There was really very little use for private carriages except to transport the aristocracy to their country homes, especially along the East River, or to make the dusty, hilly fourteen-mile drive up the Bowery to McGowan's Pass at 108th Street, across to the Bloomingdale road and down. In the city, though there were horsecarts, most of the carrying was handled by porters with handcarts and leather straps over their shoulders who, for 12½¢—18¾¢ for distances above Chambers Street—would carry loads anywhere in town.

It took Peter Cooper four years to learn the lesson, but he learned it thoroughly. When his apprenticeship came to an end his employer showed his confidence in Peter by offering to set him up in business. Peter refused, and allowed all he had learned to go with his knowledge of hats and brewing into his storehouse of temporarily useless information. 'I had thought the matter over, and was about to accept his generous offer, when an incident occurred which changed my decision. Mr. Woodward had just completed one of the finest coaches that had ever been built in New York. The gentleman for whom it was made was supposed to be one of the richest men in the city. But a day or two before the coach was to be delivered the gentleman died, when he was found to be entirely insolvent. This made me hesitate. If I should accept my employer's kind offer, and have such a misfortune happen to me in the sale of an elegant and expensive coach, I should consider myself a slave for life.' [13] Later, when John Woodward went bankrupt, Peter must have shivered at his narrow escape.[14]

In the meantime he thoroughly learned the business of carriage-making and performed faithfully the tasks imposed on apprentices in these later years of the apprenticeship system. Up at daybreak, the apprentice was supposed to clean the office, fetch water from the pump, sprinkle the sidewalk, push the rubbish into the street for the Negro's cart, trim the lamps, carry in wood, and make fires. He also ran errands (in Peter's case to the waterfront for lumber or to the upholsterer), and sometimes accompanied his master when he went to talk to customers. The work was varied, but hard for a not altogether robust boy. And it offered little pay or excitement, and no opportunities for quick advancement.

In his leisure moments Peter must have been lonely. He knew none of the leading figures of the town, and his puritanism excluded him from the company of his fellow apprentices. Freed from their long hours of labor, they spent their time in the numerous drinking places and houses of ill fame that sprouted in nearly every street. Despite their jeers, Peter neither drank nor smoked nor followed them 'in their rounds of lewd company,' which, Peter later affirmed, 'brought them all to premature graves,' though he cited specifically only one boy who 'literally rotted and died of the bad disorder before he was sixteen years of age.' [15] So Peter walked the muddy streets of the town, or found refuge in Savage's Museum at Cortlandt Street, where he admired the stuffed bearskin, the suwarrow root of colossal size, the electric battery for shocking visitors, and other objects of interest which, along with later discoveries at Scudder's and Barnum's Museums, so impressed him as to influence his plans for Cooper Union. Once he went to hear the great Thomas Addis Emmet[16] talk for three hours in Federal Hall and win a case by his eloquence that he had no business to win, particularly after the judge had warned the jury that "lawyers are paid for talking." Above all, he drowned his loneliness in work. His grandmother allowed him to use a little furnished garret in one of the houses she owned on Broadway, and there, deep into the night, the young apprentice labored to improve himself.

He first taught himself ornamental wood-carving, selling the pieces he made to his master and to other coachbuilders to supplement his meager earnings. He also, inevitably, dabbled in mechanics, and shortly produced a machine for mortising the hubs of carriages (up to that time done by hand), which he sold to Burtis and Woodward. Though he never took out a patent on his method, it was still, he wrote in 1879, 'mortising all the hubs in the country.' From mortising hubs he went on to more ambitious projects, for, as he said, he was 'always fussing and contriving' and 'was never satisfied unless I was doing something difficult—something that had never been done before, if possible.' [17]

The most ambitious of Peter's projects at that time, an attempt

· (40) ·

to harness the East River currents for power, illustrates his amazing ingenuity and self-confident belief in his unaided powers no less than his inevitable limitations as an inventor. Noticing that the tide ran violently around a point of rocks where the Fulton ferry later landed, Peter decided that he could use this current for power by extending a frame with wheel and belts out over the water from a building to be erected on the point of rocks. Employing a complicated system of cogwork, trannel head, and gearing that suggests a Rube Goldberg cartoon, he accounted for the rise and fall of the tide and enabled his waterwheel to use the flow of the current. Then, to show that by his scheme he could generate the power to move machinery, he erected a model sawmill as a test. His real purpose, however, was to use his power to compress air in a reservoir on the dock in order to propel ferries from bank to bank. This compressed air— Peter had to add some more complicated gearing to transfer his power to machinery for compressing air—was to be transported when ferries landed to cylinders supporting the decks of the ferries through flexible tubes extending from the reservoir on the dock to the hulls of the boats. The compressed air would then, as in a steam engine, drive the paddlewheels of the boat.

'After I had completed this machine,' Cooper wrote, 'Robert Fulton came to witness its experimental working. But, as I was only an apprentice boy, Mr. Fulton merely looked at it without making any comment.' Peter was bitterly disappointed at this rebuff and never quite forgave the great inventor, who had himself been so brilliantly successful only two or three years before. He records with great glee a rebuff that Fulton was supposed to have received from John Watts when, at a dinner celebrating the launching of one of Fulton's boats, Fulton insisted it was "the perfection of steamboats." Said Watts, "Mr. Fulton, I shouldn't wonder if some Yankee should make some little improvement even on this boat." Fulton, offended, replied, "That's all you know about it, sir." 'This boat that Mr. Fulton considered the very perfection of steamboats,' Cooper added, 'went at the monstrous pace of six miles an hour.' [18] Cooper never relinquished a wistful fondness for his invention. He 'carried the wreck of that model' with him 'in moving from one home to another,' and preserved it until his dying day. If this was characteristic of Peter, it was equally characteristic that, swallowing his pride, he quietly desisted from any attempt to bring it into practical use. Fulton's disdain had undoubtedly confirmed his own doubts.

It was this experience, perhaps, that crystallized Peter's dissatisfaction with himself. Mere manual skill, he became thoroughly convinced during his apprentice days, was the skill of a beaver, not of a man. Even inventive genius was not enough without knowledge of techniques and scientific theories, and life was barren without the wisdom to be gained from books. He looked around for some institution to which he could go to fill up the great voids in his education, but found nothing. He then tried to read books, but there were few of the elementary kind and he was more puzzled than enlightened by those he did read. Finally, he got a teacher to teach him arithmetic and other things for a small compensation in the evenings. For the rest he had to be content to read and reread the few books he knew, especially the Bible.

Chapter 4

A TASTE OF INDEPENDENCE

WHEN his apprenticeship ended, probably late in 1811, there was for many years to be little time for more education. Having decided to 'earn my first dollar by day's work rather than incur so heavy a debt,' Peter accepted an invitation from one of his brothers—either James or Thomas[1]—to visit him in Hempstead, Long Island, and was almost immediately persuaded by a 'gentleman of that town . . . to go to work for him in an establishment for making machines for shearing cloth.' Now only a few miles from the Brooklyn city limits, Hempstead was in the early nineteenth century a thriving independent village reached by horse ferry[2] from Catherine Slip or Fly Market at the foot of Maiden Lane, and then by long coach ride in overcrowded coaches from Brooklyn Heights. Situated in the midst of the 'Great Plain,' it was bounded, as a contemporary traveler has written, by thick woods on the west, by a chain of hills on the north, and by the horizon on the east; the surrounding country was fertile and full of pastures, orchards, and fields of corn and grain, intersected by meandering rivulets.[3] There Peter settled down once again as a mechanic in the sort of small town he had known as a youth. The conquest of the big city was postponed.

According to his own oft-repeated statement, which both

Hughes and Nevins accept without demur, Peter worked for nearly three years at the then very large wage of $1.50 a day,[4] and then bought the rights for the State of New York to a machine for shearing cloth. But there is no room for these three years in the chronology of Cooper's life. If we accept his assertion that he worked for Burtis and Woodward from the time he was seventeen until he was twenty-one—and this specific statement he made over and over again and never contradicted—his insistence that he worked for nearly three years *before* he bought the rights to the machine must constitute one of those lapses of memory of which he is often guilty. The time was nearer one year, and this is the figure Peter himself gives in one small fragment of autobiography started some ten years before the statements that Zachos and others quote. For the agreement to purchase the rights is dated November 28, 1812, when Peter was still twenty-one years old. On this date he and William and Gideon Nichols paid $375 to Jesse Mollenoux of Hempstead for the joint right to sell the machine in all of New York State except Suffolk County. Somewhat over ten months later, on October 1, 1813, Peter, now considerably wealthier, bought out his partners for $750 and obtained complete New York rights to the machine. The rights for New England and Maine he took over on August 28, 1816, from the Nichols', John Tredwell, and John Lefferts. But by 1816 the machine was a drug on the market, and Peter paid only $100 for the final rights.[5]

Peter was now in business for himself, and never again in the seventy years that remained to him was he to work for anyone else. From these small beginnings he was to go on, with hardly a setback, to become a rich man within less than twenty years. But there were to be no spectacular gains, no reckless gambling of all on the throw of the dice. From these first days of meager earnings to the end, he was to play the game carefully, following his instincts boldly but never allowing them to lead him into recklessness or to be a substitute for calm calculation or hard work. We are fortunate in being able to watch his procedures in some detail in these crucial years when the pattern was being set.[6]

Though Peter was in no position in 1812 to open a coaching business, he had already saved some money during his apprenticeship and managed to save a good deal more out of the high wages he received in Hempstead. As early as May, 1812, he wrote his mother that should his father fail in Newburgh, which he showed more than the usual likelihood of doing, she should not worry: he would 'strive to have a home for you and the family'; in the meantime he hoped 'to be so situated before a great while' as to have his sisters at least come and live with him.[7] The question was, how could he most profitably use his savings? For a moment he flirted with investment in what was soon to be one of the great basic industries of the country, but was turned aside by a piece of superstition. 'Just before I purchased the patent right of the shearing machine I had heard of a very cheap property in Pennsylvania in a coal mine, and I bought a horse and offered to go there and, singular as it happened, the horse fell three times before I got to Brooklyn and so I turned around and came back to my business again, for I thought the fates were against going there. I took it as a hint.'[8] Though the coal mine might have been successful, it would have been a great strain on his resources. The shearing machine fitted Cooper's situation at the time much better, as he must have seen. Since he was permitted to pay his part of the $375 out of sales, he could use his savings to start his business. And the immediate possibilities in the textile field in New York were abundant in 1812.

Ever since the War of Independence the government had heavily subsidized American manufacturers in an effort to build up a branch of the economy stifled by Britain. As a consequence, even before the War of 1812 the manufacture of textiles—no less than of iron, paper, liquors, gunpowder, window glass, and hats—was flourishing, and Albert Gallatin reported in 1810 that two-thirds of the clothing worn in America was homemade. New York led the field with 9,000,000 yards of cloth, as against 4,100,-

ooo for Massachusetts and 6,400,000 for Pennsylvania. Then, when war broke out in June, 1812, and English manufactures were cut off, textiles boomed. Every power site in New York, particularly in Oneida, Dutchess, and Columbia Counties, was put to use, and machinery such as Peter Cooper offered was in demand everywhere.[9]

There was just one slight hitch in Peter Cooper's plans. Early in 1813 a British force appeared off New York and there was a frantic burst of recruiting activities. Along with many others, Peter was drafted as a militiaman and 'brought down to Brooklyn,' where he was stationed on a high piece of ground and set to drilling. This he found 'very tedious, for there was no enemy in sight, and no telling when they would come.' Fortunately for Peter, the draft of 1812 was not the draft of 1942, and he soon found a substitute whom he could pay to take his place. The patriotic fervor which he had imbibed from his father and grandfather did not prevent him from being 'very glad to go home and attend to my own business.' The most curious part of the whole affair is the way he made his military career sound when, fifty-six years later, he wrote to Horatio Seymour, then Democratic candidate for President. He felt, he told Seymour, that he had a 'right to plead with my countrymen' to follow his advice because 'I . . . served my country in person and by substitute from the commencement of the war with England to its close.' [10]

It is hard, however, to blame Peter for wanting to get back to his business. When he was drafted he was just beginning 'to do a good business' after months of dogged unaided labor, and here was the reward about to be snatched from him. Those early days had been very difficult indeed. Hiring a shop and purchasing materials with his savings, he built three machines which he valued at $150 apiece. Then, like so many early businessmen, he went out personally to peddle his wares. Hiring a horse and wagon, he started north in the dead of winter toward Hudson, from which had come his only inquiry for a machine. On his way he left one off on trial at a factory on the Saw Mill River and another at Poughkeepsie. When, however, Peter went to find the person living back of Hudson who had shown interest, he found that the latter had failed. Undismayed, he started to cross the river on the ice to look for factories on the west bank. But 'the snow fell so deep that I was compelled to turn back and make my way as far as Poughkeepsie on the ice.'

Then, when he was most discouraged, 'my fortune turned.' Matthew Vassar, who was then running an ale-and-oyster house in the basement of the Poughkeepsie County Court House, liked his machine so well that he not only bought it for $150 but purchased the rights for the county for an additional $250.[11] 'This put me in possession of so large an amount of money, according to my ideas at the time, that I was very elated, and rejoiced at what I considered my good fortune.'

Peter always considered this a landmark in his life. As he told the Vassar students many years later, he could never recall the incident without a thrill of grateful pleasure. Seeing Matthew Vassar at his home in 1863—Peter had met him only once in fifty years—moved Peter deeply; and the picturing of Cooper Union on the same page of a monthly periodical as the proposed Vassar College pleased him greatly.[12]

Actually, Peter got no immediate use from the $400. After leaving Poughkeepsie he deposited his last machine at a factory owned by Governor Lewis and then stopped at Newburgh to see his father on the way home. 'I found my Father required nearly all the money I had received to meet the pressing wants of the family.' Despite his ambitions, there was no hesitation in Peter's response. He not only gave his father all but what he needed to get him home and purchase a small amount of material, but endorsed a note for $400 'to save the family from being broken up.' When that note was due it 'required all that I had made to discharge the debt, which I did, leaving me a very small amount of material with which to again commence my work.'[13] Peter Cooper always put first things first. He did not wait until

· (47) ·

he was comfortably fixed to pay his filial obligations, but, firmly resolving that his father should never suffer the, to Peter, terrible ignominy of bankruptcy, saved him when he most needed to be saved. Nor did he now feel that he owed nothing further. Before many years he was helping his whole family in one way or another, and his later charities seem but a gradual extension to the larger family of mankind of his tenderness for his own family. In Peter Cooper striving and loving always seemed perfectly balanced. That is probably his greatest appeal to our distracted age.

The immediate price that he paid for his generosity was great. He had hardly the money to make any new machines. Worse, he soon found that he couldn't extend his business much without improving his machine. Peter consulted with the inventor, who agreed that something must be done to keep the machine from shearing the 'list of the cloth' or else manufacturers would be unable 'to imitate the imported cloth.' Much thought on the subject was, however, to no avail. Then Peter put his own inventive mind to work, and 'after much consideration I thought I had discovered a plan by which that result could be obtained. After spending about all that I had made I succeeded in producing a machine that answered the purpose.' [14]

As a consequence of this invention, Peter's situation was much improved by the fall of 1813, a year after his original purchase. A part of the New York rights to the machine now brought twice the 1812 price of the whole. Business was coming in to him, making his trips north less necessary; he was having a hard time fulfilling contracts within the time promised; and he was beginning to treat customers for his old narrow machines somewhat cavalierly, since he was making broad ones for broadcloth, which were more profitable.[15] He was also now in a position to hire selling agents in upper New York State. On November 10, 1813, he made Aaron Dennis his agent for Rensselaer, Washington, Warren, Essex, Clinton, Franklin, Saratoga, and Montgomery Counties, and the next day gave the agency for the rest of the state to his friend Henry Trowbridge. Dennis was to pay $110 for the single, or narrow, machine, which he must sell for $150; and $250 for the double, or broadcloth, machine, with no selling price stipulated.

Peter's troubles were, however, by no means over. Right up to the end of the war there were complaints about the machines, and Peter had to make many more improvements to satisfy his customers. Purchasers were not unnaturally annoyed when in a season of huge demand they had to shear one piece of cloth twelve to eighteen times, worrying constantly that the machine would damage the cloth.[16] Moreover, despite Peter's later claim that he sold machines 'as fast [as] I could get them made,' [17] sales were not uniformly good, and pay was not always forthcoming. In March, 1814, Dennis wrote that he was unable to make 'conclusive contracts' because manufacturers thought the prices too high and wanted the machines warranted to shear as well as any in America, not merely as well as any of their kind.

In the course of the spring and summer Dennis sold several machines, but between difficulties in collecting money and the necessity of giving discounts because of imperfections, he made little profit and gave up the agency.[18] Trowbridge had as little luck as did Dennis. On June 18, 1814, he wrote Cooper sadly that he had had eight applications for machines, 'but none of them that suited me. Some were not ready to pay for them, others would wait a while.' Though by July customers were expressing themselves as better satisfied, some were complaining as late as May, 1815, that the machines fed too fast and cut holes, and that new improvements were unsatisfactory. The really surprising thing is that, with all his difficulties, Peter made a go of his business at all. But make a go of it he did. Through the greater part of the war he was earning, by his own estimate, '$250 per month which at that time seemed a rapid mode of making a fortune.' [19]

If Hempstead saw the start of Cooper's success, it also witnessed his social blossoming. Despite his intense efforts to succeed, Peter was not at Hempstead the industrious recluse that he had been as an apprentice in New York. In the congenial atmosphere of a small town he permitted himself to relax and to share in the pleasures of his contemporaries. These were simple enough. There were gatherings at home or in a hotel, where the young men would engage a black fiddler to have a dance—a cheap method, as Peter wrote, of bringing the young people together. Or there would be parties for surf-bathing in the ocean. Peter threw himself with the zest of a young colt into these activities, and under the inspiration of female company his old recklessness returned. On at least two occasions his tendency to show off nearly proved disastrous. One day, driving a young lady back from the beach in a gig behind a very fast trotting horse that he had purchased, he was careening along at breakneck speed over a little wooden bridge when there was a sudden jar. Much to his amazement Peter suddenly saw one of his wheels running alongside of him. Before he could stop, the wheel and the gig had run along some fifty yards side by side, and only by the most dexterous management was Peter able to slow the gig down on one wheel. The lady, remarks Cooper, was somewhat agitated. Another time, when there was a large company on the beach, the men started a competition as to who could get through the breakers, which were running very high. Peter proved himself the only successful competitor, and was floating along lazily beyond the breakers, exulting in his male prowess, when he became aware that all the company were frantically waving to him with their hats. Looking around, he saw with a shock that he had been swept far out to sea by the falling tide. 'A little frightened,' he started for shore, alternately fighting desperately with head down and feet up against the backwash, and then letting the next breaker carry him in. He was finally thrown on the beach, almost buried in the sand and unable to move another yard.

All this male bumptiousness was not long without a specific and suitable audience. Either before or just after he moved to Hempstead he met a young lady named Sarah Bedell. A particular friend of the unfortunate occupant of the gig the day the wheel came off, she was a frequenter of the parties Peter attended, and shortly Peter was calling on her at her father's house. By the late spring of 1813 she was known among Peter's friends as his 'favorite,' as indicated by several letters from Cooper's friend Weekes, who was trying to arrange a joint beach party of Hempsteaders and New Yorkers. The New Yorkers were to come to Hempstead by chair or coach and go to the beach the next day. 'Sally B.,' as Weekes calls her, had the measles in New York and was unable to come. 'I shall expect you to be one of the Party,' wrote Weekes, 'even if the one half of your Heart is in Town. I saw her yesterday afternoon. She is rather better so that she was sitting up but she appears very weak yet. You talk of coming down this week, if you should I would advise you to put shelving on as I think you may possibly get a full load of live stock, for I think that I know of a stage load agoing up myself.' For some reason Weekes asked Peter to 'commit this to the flames' after reading, and it is amusing that it is, on the contrary, one of the few early personal letters Peter has preserved. By November, Peter was looking for a house and farm with mill privileges, and consulted his friend Weekes about one he had located in Hempstead.

He had not yet found a suitable home, however, when, in December, he led his 'Sally' to the altar in her father's house in Hempstead. Though both his parents were Methodists, Peter usually attended St. George's Episcopal Church in Hempstead, and his marriage is recorded in the register of that Church on December 22, 1813.[20] Not until over two weeks after his marriage did he inform his family of the great event. Then on January 7, 1814, he wrote laconically to his father, 'I would inform you that you have another Daughter-in-law.' Just in case this might worry his debt-pressed parent, he added: 'I have been about entering into the cotton business which has engrossed the great part of my attention. You must not be uneasy, I shall have a way provided for you and the family before the time that you have to move from Newburgh.'[21]

The Bedells were among the earliest settlers in Hempstead, having come over from France in the middle of the seventeenth century. Sarah's father, Benjamin Bedell, who was born in 1753, belonged to the fifth American generation of a family that had spread far and wide but left a numerous clan still in Hempstead.[22] He and his wife, Mary Raynor,[23] worked a farm and raised eleven children, of whom Sarah, born in 1793, was the seventh.[24] Trained to the spinning wheel and the loom so that she soon was capable of supplying her family with linens and woolens, she made just the sort of wife a rising young businessman required. There were to be long years of struggle ahead, and Sarah Cooper was well fortified to endure them. She expected neither luxury nor sophistication nor a career: Puritan and Huguenot in spirit, she knew, as Dr. Bellows said at her funeral, no 'modern discontent with woman's sphere.' The place that Providence gave her was enough, and that place was by Peter's side. For half a century she was his helpmate, keeping his home economically, raising his children, and bolstering his spirits when he was dejected.

What she was like as an individual it is impossible to discover. In Peter's generation as in his father's, wives seldom led an independent existence. She has left no letters whatever, and the comments of those who knew her are of the conventional laudatory sort. But that she deserved these generalities of praise there is no reason to doubt. Peter's success and happiness in life were largely dependent on having a wife whose character balanced and supplemented his own. Sarah Cooper had, on the one hand, a prudence and hatred of self-indulgence that were invaluable to a struggling young man; on the other, she brought to his fireside a genial kindliness and informality that banished strife and won the affection of friend and stranger alike. Her good sense steadied Cooper's judgment and kept his prosperity unpretentious; her tenderness gave support and meaning to his life. Nor have we cause to question his lifelong affection for her. Always a puritan whose excess energies were turned into business and philanthropic pursuit, Peter Cooper never found another woman's attractions even worthy of comment. For fifty-six years his wife was, as he wrote after her death, his 'day star, the solace and the inspiration of his life.' The years did not diminish their romance, and 'to old age he never sat near her without holding her hand in his. He never spoke to her nor of her without some tender epithet.' [25] When she was dead the old man saw her at least once a week in dreams; and once, at the funeral of a friend, when he was awake, 'She looked just as if the sun was shining upon her and she looked just like she had in her best days. She gradually faded away.' [26]

About three months after their marriage the young couple found the home Peter had been seeking in November. On March 14, 1814, he bought a half-acre of land with a house on it in the country near Hempstead from his friends William and Gideon Nichols for $762.50, paid in cash. The land is described as bounded on the south by the highway leading from the Episcopal Church east to the east meadow brook, on the east and north by fences and common land, and on the west by the highway from the plains by Laurence Seaman's north to the place of beginning. He also bought a quarter of an acre of ground and a workshop across the road to the south of his home. Here Sarah and Peter settled down comfortably to a life of domesticity.

Though the days of parties and racing behind fast trotters were over, for a short time the young couple were still free to roam the country after work or to take trips to New York. On one of these latter trips they witnessed a phenomenon that haunted Peter's memory all his life: 'three water spouts, all in sight at on time,' the largest of which looked like a solid black marble column a hundred feet high.[27] But the days of freedom soon ended. Their first child, named John Campbell after Peter's grandfather, was born on September 5, 1814, and a week after the second anniversary of their marriage he was joined by a brother, named Benjamin Bedell after Sarah's father. Since the Coopers had no servants, the children confined them pretty much to their home, and when Peter returned from work in the evening he usually found his wife rocking the cradle. This task he invariably took out of her hands, feeling that she had done enough work during the day. He did not, however, enjoy the monotonous labor, and it soon stimulated him to one of his most ingenious and certainly most amusing inventions: a self-rocking cradle.

Hempstead life had left him little time so far for tinkering, and he had made only one previous invention while there. This was a machine for mowing grass, constructed on the principle of his shearing machine. An Episcopal clergyman had put the thought into Peter's head and had offered to pay him to make a model. 'I made him an operative model, with all the parts necessary to show how grass could be cut with it. That model was on the same principle as those now in use, having a great number of blades which were almost identical in shape, form and movement with the present mowers. My model had even the guards, similar to those they now have, to prevent the points of the blades from being injured in going over stones. The same machine I then constructed was in existence some thirty-five years ago, hanging up in a stable, I was told, in Hempstead.' [28] But it was never found, and Peter got neither credit nor money for it. The cradle, on the other hand, brought him for the first time a very small taste of both.

The essence of Cooper's cradle was a pendulum arrangement that would, when wound up, rock the cradle mechanically. In the exuberance of his inventive zest Peter added to it 'a musical instrument that would sing the child to sleep' and a cloth which, when the cradle rocked, 'would keep the flies off the little one.' The pendulum had a weight on a cord attached to a crown wheel, capable of running for nearly a half-hour before rewinding. Later Cooper substituted springs for the weight, but the movement was not as good. The cradle was housed in a simple frame made of three uprights connected by bars at top and bottom and two boards at right angles as a base. The pendulum was between two of the uprights, the cradle between the other two.[29]

Peter felt that his invention was a 'beautiful piece of furniture,' and immediately—on March 27, 1815—took out a patent on it, the first that he had applied for. The patent is signed, as was the custom until after Jackson's time, by the President, then James Madison. A few days earlier Peter's family were informed of the event by a Brooklyn friend of Peter's sister Sarah. 'I suppose before this,' she wrote Sarah, 'you have heard that Peter has got a patent for a machine he has invented. I hope success may crown his steady industry.' [30] Peter evidently felt that it would, for he advertised his 'Pendulous & Musical Cradle' in the New York *Mercantile Advertiser,* and secured at least one offer to purchase.[31] A much better offer, to buy the right to manufacture the cradles in the State of Connecticut, was made by a Yankee peddler who came along one day. 'I asked him how much he would offer. "I'll give you my horse and wagon and all there is in it." On that we concluded a bargain. Among its contents was a hurdy-gurdy. I had heard one played before on a steamboat trip, and I thought it the sweetest music I had ever heard.' [32] The peddler made a few of the cradles, but Peter claimed they were 'nothing like as good as mine.' [33] In 1883 Peter's attention was called to an old lady of eighty-seven—younger sister of one of his brother James's wives—who said that her daughter was rocked in her infancy in one of Peter's musical cradles.[34]

Chapter 5

GROCER AND INVENTOR

IN 1814 it must have appeared to Peter as if he were settled comfortably, profitably, and permanently in Hempstead as a manufacturer of shearing machines. But suddenly, on Christmas Day, the war ceased and the bottom fell out of his business. Superior British goods began to pour once again into American markets and the hundreds of little American textile manufacturers were unable to compete. The British were willing to sell at a loss 'to stifle in the cradle,' as Lord Brougham put it, 'those rising manufactures in the United States which the war has forced into existence contrary to the natural course of things.' Three-quarters of American factory owners went out of business.[1] The $12,000,000 woolen business and the makers of fine broadcloth were particularly hurt. Peter Cooper was too busy at the time to search deeply into the causes of the catastrophe, but he took note and was not long in discovering the answer. All his life he remained an enemy of free trade, and in his *War of Commerce* many years later centered his bitterest attacks on British attempts in the early nineteenth century to crush colonial and foreign business. Peter Cooper's philosophy came less from books than from experience.

With his natural resilience Peter did not despair at the new turn of events. He also did not act as promptly as his own oft-repeated words would suggest. According to Peter, when the war with England ended he could not sell another machine and immediately 'turned my work shop into the manufacture of cabinet furniture, as I could make almost anything that was made with wood or iron. This I found a slow business in the town of Hempstead where I had purchased and paid for my house and factory which I sold, taking what I could get for it,' and 'removed to New York.' Actually he went on living in Hempstead for at least two more years, persisting in a desperate effort to sell his machines. In April, 1815, he called on Mr. John Drake and offered him a narrow machine for $100 and a broad one for $300. 'You may have a broad and narrow one,' he wrote, 'for four hundred dollars delivered at your factory and warranted to equal any shears frame that is to be found, and if after you have had a fair trial of them you should find them not to answer your purpose you need not feel yourself under any kind of obligation to keep them after they are delivered.'

Trowbridge was still selling an occasional machine in Albany, as was Lewis B. Slocum, who had taken over Dennis' agency, but business was very slow. On April 21, 1816, Slocum wrote that he had made no sales, though Mr. Barrett wanted another machine and claimed that Cooper had given him the right to build them himself. Though as late as September, 1816, Cooper was planning to send Slocum ten machines, by April of the following year the game was about played out. Slocum owed Cooper money on a note and was having a hard time paying it. 'I have had very bad luck in selling machines for you as I sold but one and that I was obliged to take back.' Peter had already decided by the fall of 1816 to try his hand at cabinet-making, as indicated by his ordering a lathe built for him in Hackensack, New Jersey.[2]

Peter gave up his Hempstead house and moved back to New York sometime between the spring of 1817 and the summer of 1818. His brother-in-law, Benjamin Bedell, who was a grocer in the city,[3] urged him to come to town and open a store.

Though Peter admittedly 'had had no previous experience in that branch of business,' he readily acceded. The firm of Bedell and Cooper set up shop in 1818 on the Bowery near Stuyvesant Street.[4] After several years[5] Peter decided to go into business for himself, and bought a lease of the nearby property from the Stuyvesants. The lease, which was for twenty years, entitled him to six lots and two houses where the American Bible House now stands opposite Cooper Union. On these lots he built four more frame houses and kept a grocery store on the corner, at Stuyvesant Street and the Bowery.[6]

Peter's grocery store was located a mile or more out of town. The city in 1818 reached only to Houston Street (then North Street) on the Bowery, though on the west it was stretching toward Greenwich Lane and Astor Place (then Art Street). Bowery Village, just to the east and south of Peter's grocery, still had somewhat the aspect of a country town with its village square and town pump and its tavern where Cooper Square now is. Reached only by the stages that rumbled up the Bowery each day for Harlem and Manhattanville, it was still used, along with the village of Greenwich, as a resort and refuge in time of fever. To the west, between Broadway and the Bowery and the future 7th and 10th Streets, was Captain Randall's farm; and north of that, where Grace Church now is, was Brevoort's garden. To the south, stretching from the Bowery to Broadway just below Astor Place, was the famous pleasure resort, Vauxhall, with its graveled walks, flowerbeds, and pavilion for music; and near it Sperry's garden and greenhouse. The Peter Stuyvesant property on which Cooper built was fenced pasture and garden, and as late as 1853, when the whole block was bought by the Bible House, most of the directors of that institution thought it was too far uptown. Above 10th Street, Broadway was a country road, and the houses on Bowery Hill (Union Square) were still considered country homes in 1824. In 1821, when it was decided to open the recently surveyed Third Avenue from 4th Street north, it was agreed in the Common Council that the country around it 'has been, and for a long time to come can only be valuable as lands for the purposes of agriculture or country residences.' Peter Cooper had not made a drastic change in leaving Hempstead, and for another fifteen or twenty years he was to contrive to keep himself outside the fast-growing city.[7]

There are a few pleasant glimpses of Peter as a grocer. One of his neighbors, at 21 Stuyvesant Street, was the future statesman, Hamilton Fish, who was a boy of ten in 1818. He remembers how the kids of the neighborhood loved the kindly grocer for his lively encouragement of their sports and amusements.[8] Another old New Yorker wrote of Peter's store, 'More than one quart of blackberries have I exchanged there for the seductive taffy or bunch of raisins.' [9] Everybody was Peter's friend, including the old man in charge of the potter's field at Washington Square, who showed him the eight-foot trenches into which they piled coffins three or four deep as they came in.[10] Peter's moral force was evidently great. One day a small boy, the child of a poor and dissipated family, received from Peter a dollar too much in change; fifteen years later his acceptance of it still haunted him, and, meeting Peter on the street, he insisted on returning the money.[11]

By his own testimony, Peter did well at this new business and increased his savings from the shearing machine. He was able, as early as 1819, to begin investing modestly in New York real estate, his first purchase being a 100 x 25-foot lot at Third Avenue and 126th Street, obtained for $150 from the estate of John S. Sickels of Harlem.[12] But being a grocer was a hard and, Peter felt, an unrewarding and somewhat tedious occupation. He never gained, as did Richard Bulerd on Broadway and James Geary on Mulberry Street, the reputation of being a fine grocer, and he never liked the business.

For Sarah Cooper this was a particularly difficult time. Peter had merely to tend to the store and buy groceries from the wholesalers on Broad, Water, and Front Streets. She had to be up to give Peter a hot breakfast at six, and do the family wash-ing and other household chores by noon. In the afternoon she was at her oven, baking what Cooper called the 'best bread in New York.' She often thought at the time that 'if her arms would ever stop aching and she did not have to get up at three o'clock in the morning it would be Paradise.' [13] To make matters worse, the winter of 1820-1821 was the coldest on record; people walked from Brooklyn to Staten Island, and food was high in price and hard to get.

During these years, too, Sarah Cooper had to endure the first two of the four tragedies that haunted the attempts of the Coopers to raise a family. Her second son, Benjamin Bedell, fell on his head and died of 'dropsy of the brain' when he was three and a half, on June 1, 1819. A year later, on June 7, 1820, when she was three months gone with her daughter Sarah Amanda, she lost her older boy, John Campbell, of the croup. 'I recollect about the last struggle,' wrote Cooper with Heming-way-like starkness many years later. 'He put his hand down his throat and drew it up with blood on it and said, "Papa, I can't stand it." He was about five years old. This was John; and died a few moments after that utterance. That was the last he said.' [14] Her daughter Sarah Amanda was born on December 18th, and two years later, on December 20, 1822, a third son, Peter William.

In the meantime, out of kindness, Peter had taken into his house the first of a long series of relations whom he was to har-bor under his roof. In 1818 Sarah's sister Mary died, and shortly afterward her husband, Benjamin Clowes. Their orphan daugh-ter Martha became virtually an adopted daughter of the Coop-ers. In 1826 she was married in Cooper's house to Peter's good friend Daniel F. Tiemann, soon to be the owner of a large paint business and later mayor of New York with a fine home in Manhattanville at 125th Street. It was probably also at this time that Peter took his two sisters to live in his house. They never married, and both lived to old age under Peter's hospitable roof.

According to Peter's grandson, one of them had been engaged to a mate on one of John Jacob Astor's ships, which sailed around the Horn and never came back; all through her life she kept a lamp burning for him in her window.

To relieve the tedium of keeping a grocery Peter threw himself more eagerly than ever into tinkering with mechanical devices, and produced two of his most ambitious efforts. The more valuable of these two efforts and the one which gained him his first slight recognition in high places was a method of propelling canalboats by an endless chain moved by the power from the water elevated in the locks. Reading with the intense interest of all New Yorkers of the progress of the Erie Canal, then nearly completed, Peter decided that he could provide speedier transportation by his method than that supplied by horses on a towpath. Never one to hesitate when he had an idea, he immediately built a flatbottomed scow and, taking a couple of helpers with him, rowed out into the East River to discover the most advantageous place for a trial of his idea. Finding this in the mile stretch of nearly straight river between Bellevue and Brandy Moody Point (somewhat north of 8th Street), he proceeded to drive posts into the mud two hundred feet apart. On these posts he fastened two two-inch grooved rollers twelve inches in diameter, made of block-tin and zinc, which Peter cast in a mahogany mold, whitewashed so it wouldn't burn. 'It was no small job I can tell you,' he wrote later. These rollers carried the two lines of chain, made of eight-inch links of twisted iron wire, which were to propel the boat up and down the river. At the Bellevue dock—and one supposes at the other end also—there was a wooden wheel five feet in diameter with a crotched surface, around which the chain ran and was thus made endless. The next problem was power, and again Peter did all the work himself, at great expenditure of time and energy. He constructed an overshot waterwheel nine feet in diameter at Bellevue, to whose shaft he attached his crotched wheel, and built a reservoir twelve feet square and three feet deep on the dock, into which he pumped the river water that was to turn the wheel. On the canal there would not, he believed, be any necessity for pumping, since the elevation of the water would supply the power.[15]

When all was ready, he took his scow out into the river, fastened his towline to the chain by a hook, and started his waterwheel. Everything worked as planned. On January 24, 1820, he patented his invention and a few months later invited Governor Clinton and some other gentlemen to a trial run. The minutes of the Common Council for June 26, 1820, record the fact that the 'Common Council accepts an invitation from Peter Cooper to visit an Experiment of an Hydraulic Boat Propelling Machine at Bellevue to-morrow.' [16] A houseboat was hired to transport the council from Catherine Ferry to Bellevue and back.

On the great day itself Peter was down early inspecting his system. At the last minute 'I thought my chain was a little too slack. I went to tighten it and pulled up the end post. I had all that was possible to do to get stone enough to anchor it before the time for him [Clinton] to come. I had just succeeded in getting it fixed and was coming up to the dock when I saw him coming down in his carriage to witness the experiment, and I had to ask him to get into the boat before I had a chance to go around it myself.' But everything turned out more successfully than even the sanguine Peter expected. Governor Clinton and the others, who included the twelve-year-old Hamilton Fish and his father, got into the boat and were propelled the two miles down and back in eleven minutes. This included the loss of about a minute in taking the hook from one chain to the other at the end of the run. 'De Witt Clinton was so well pleased with it that he gave me eight hundred dollars for the privilege of the patent right to that invention to be used on the Erie Canal.' [17]

The sequel was not so fortunate. A few days later Clinton had to inform Peter that the chain could not be used on the Canal. He had 'had great difficulty in getting the farmers on the line of the canal to give him the right of way, and in order to induce them to grant it had held out to them the great advantages that would arise to them of selling their oats, corn, hay, and other produce to the canal men for the use of the horses. . . . If the endless chain was used, these promises would be broken, as there would be no horses to feed.' The farmers had also been led to expect they could sell their horses to the canal men and their food and lodging to travelers forced to spend the nights en route. So the whole idea came to nought. Peter ran the chain on the river ten days 'during which I carried nearly a thousand people in the boats to show how conveniently practical such a plan could be,' and charged not a cent for the privilege. Then the project was abandoned, all that survived being a few rusty links of the chain which Cooper kept in a drawer and showed to anyone who evinced the slightest interest in the subject.

The matter was not, however, allowed to sleep. Fifty-six years later a newspaper reporter, trying to dig up something to discredit Cooper when he was running for the Presidency, got hold of the story of the abandonment of the experiment and rushed eagerly to the conclusion that the 'sheriff had pounced down on' all his possessions. This was hitting the old man in his sorest spot, and he immediately sent for a representative of the paper, and, after telling him in no uncertain terms that he had never 'made a failure,' gave the true account of what had happened. The idea was essentially sound, he insisted to the reporter. About 1870 the president of the Camden & Amboy Canal Company 'hit upon the endless-chain plan for getting his boats through the locks. He tried it, and it worked well. So he went to Washington to take out a patent, and found, on searching the records, that I had taken out a patent on the very same invention fifty years before. Of course my patent had run out, so the invention was free to all.' [18]

Peter himself never abandoned either the endless chain idea or his fascination with locomotive problems on the Erie and other canals, and both appear as characteristically recurrent themes in his later life. Two of his very last efforts, made when he was over eighty, were to apply the endless-chain principle to New York's elevated railway problem and to win a bounty offered by the state to anyone who would operate a steam canal-boat successfully on the Erie Canal.

One of the devices by which Peter expected to earn this bounty was a rotary steam engine. His interest in rotary engines had its origin in the same year as the endless chain, when he himself invented such an engine, and he cherished the idea for a half-century with a warmth and persistence not even exceeded by his devotion to the endless chain. He took out two patents on the subject, one in 1820—a scheme for changing alternate to rotary motion—and the other in 1828—a perfected plan for transforming rectilinear to rotary motion in the steam engine. It was Peter's contention that there was great loss of power in the steam engine occasioned by the use of the crank in turning the rectilinear motion of the piston-rod into the rotary motion of the axle, and he was confident he could build an engine that would eliminate this difficulty. He first experimented with two machines, one made to go by the application of the power of a suspended weight, the other by some arrangement involving alternate motion. Through this means he proved to his own satisfaction (and, according to Peter, to that of the city engineer) that there was considerable loss in power caused by the two dead points in the crank.[19]

He then decided to build an experimental steam engine. 'I described the method as well as I could to a young engineer of the Sterling Iron Works . . . and he seemed to understand how to do it. I agreed with him to get me up a little engine, and he did so.' Peter describes it as follows: 'Just imagine a steam cylinder, with a pison-rod going entirely through it. Imagine a chain at each end connected with the piston-rod, and the chain passing around a wheel at the top, and another wheel at the bottom. With the piston-rod this made the chain endless. Then imagine the chain bolted to the top and bottom wheels. Then I put a chain upon the other two wheels, and crossed the chains so that one was loose at the top and the other fast at the bottom. When the engine made its stroke it made alternate motions. There was a catch that caught on the edge of the flange. These catches were borne up by a spring behind them, and as it made this motion one way the catch was perfectly free to slip, and the instant it stopped the other was ready to take it up and carry it on. In this way the rotary motion was kept up about as perfectly as you can imagine.'

When this wonderful contraption was finished, Peter asked permission to attach it 'to the boiler of an engine three times the size of mine. They were boring a steam cylinder with it, and doing nothing else. One dropped the work and the other took it up, while the safety valve was balanced exactly, and it did not take two minutes to perform the operation. To the astonishment of all who saw it, the *little* engine did the work. I remember the remarks of an English engineer who was there at the time. He looked at it with astonishment, and then said: "If any man had told me that that engine would do that work, I would have told him that he knew nothing about mechanics. I now see that we will yet cross the ocean in six days." ' [20] The only trouble was that the edges of the cogs wore easily and the strain caused slipping. 'This discouraged me from making a larger one.' But he kept the original in his factory grinding chalk for a year or two until he made his great experiment with locomotives in Baltimore. He then transported it there and, with 'some old wheels that I got at the railroad shops,' turned it into a locomotive. It was suitable, his 1828 patent application had said, both for canalboats and for 'land carriages, in consequence of its lightness and smallness of bulk.'

Though this engine thus became the basis for one of Cooper's most memorable exploits, the principle which it had been built to demonstrate was not established by Cooper, nor has it ever been by anyone else. Far from being simpler than Watt's great invention, as Cooper contended, the new transforming mechanism was a cumbersome apparatus of rods clawing at endless chains, which only an infatuated fanatic would have thought an improvement over the crank.[21] Moreover, no improvement was really needed. Cooper's observations notwithstanding, there is no loss of energy caused by the crank, as he would have discovered had he known about the laws of acceleration and work.

Such things were, however, just what he didn't know. Like so many Americans of his generation he had to trust to experience, ingenuity, and luck for his achievements. When these failed him there was nothing to do but to call reluctantly on his commonsense to blow the signal for retreat. The rotary engine was never discarded as was the tide machine, but when this particular engine failed to function well he refused to let it interfere with the running of his locomotive. 'I took that same little cylinder, put it on a cross-head with a bottom-bar, piston-rod, and a couple of little shackle-bars, with a crank and a cog-wheel, and put the locomotive on the road.' And he did this despite the fact that one of his two motives for building the locomotive was to show that he could get rotary motion without the use of a crank. The only salve he administered to his pride was to insist that he was forced to make the substitution because the engine 'was so unskilfully handled by some meddlesome persons that it broke twice.' [22] In 1875 he still believed that 'the day will come when the principle embodied in that engine will be successfully demonstrated as correct.'

The Baltimore failure did not occur until a decade after he began working on his idea with such high hopes. In 1820 there must have been great temptation to stake his future on his inventive powers, which were flowering so beneficently. He had never been 'well pleased with the business' of grocer and was constantly searching to 'see what change I could make for the better.' After three years in his store this need for a change was ripe to bursting. Though the grocery kept him from want and even allowed him to save, its possibilities were distinctly limited. Peter was now thirty years old and had tried his hand at four trades without achieving distinction in any of them. He was in danger, despite all his talents and ambitions, of ending his days as an ordinary middleclass tradesman, indistinguishable from thousands of others. His lack of education shut to him cultural and scientific doors and his financial position limited his acquaintanceship among the rising businessmen of New York. At the dawn of the third decade of the nineteenth century, Peter Cooper's was a name as little known to the Aspinwalls and Astors and Howlands as to the older ruling class of Livingstons, Schuylers, Stuyvesants, and Van Cortlandts.

Yet there is no evidence that Peter Cooper ever contemplated throwing in his lot with those thousands of young men of his generation who puttered away their lives hoping—not always vainly—to achieve the one great success and make a fortune, and who wasted untold energy proving the unnecessary and scaling the impossible. He was too canny and too little given to speculation for that. Though in a long career he made more inventions 'than I have time to remember,' he never made discovery the central business of his life. When he was rich and could afford the luxury, he indulged his fancies and those of others in endless experiments, but he went about acquiring riches by more deliberate means. Even in 1820 he was well aware that his doggedness, shrewdness, and imagination, strengthened by a dozen or more years of rich experience in handling the world, were tremendous business assets. All they required was opportunity to make them flower into success.

That opportunity walked into his grocery one day in 1821. 'One of my customers informed me that a man by the name of Vreeland had set his son up in the manufacture of glue at Kipps Bay—and that the son had become so dissipated that he had determined to sell it out.[23] This Mr. Vreeland I knew from having been sent to his store for the purchase of hardware when I was an apprentice. On the same day I saw Mr. Vreeland pass my door. I asked him if it was true that he wanted to sell his factory. He said that he did. I started with him at once to look at the place. And after examining the buildings and stock, he named his price which I at once agreed to give. I went with him to town and had the contract drawn.[24] . . . What I made by building machines and in the grocery business had enabled me to pay for the glue factory on the day of the purchase.' [25]

Though the event did not occur in quite this way, Peter had by 1822 come into possession of the glue factory. He was a rolling stone no longer. The second of the three periods into which, in 1882, he divided his life had begun. In the first he had been 'engaged in getting a start in life'; now he was to be 'occupied in getting means for carrying out the modest plans which I had long formed for the benefit of my fellowmen.' For the next seven years he worked exclusively at the glue business until he had built up a modest fortune and was able to expand into other activities. And for the rest of his business life the making of glue remained the core of his activity and the basis of his ever-increasing fortune. The meeting with John Vreeland was the great event of Peter Cooper's early life.

Chapter 6

A SMALL PRIVATE BUSINESS

THE agreement to purchase the glue factory is dated October 3, 1821. It states that John Vreeland has leased from the City of New York two and 12/100 acres of land, in the Ninth Ward on the west side of the Middle Road adjoining Schieffelin's land [1] and near the United States Arsenal,[2] for twenty-one years beginning May 1, 1820, at a rental of thirty-five dollars a year and taxes. On this land are several buildings, a glue factory, and a stable. Vreeland agrees to sell to Peter Cooper the buildings and all materials, stock in trade, fixtures, utensils, goods and chattels on the premises except oil and bone on hand, and to transfer to him the lease of the land. The price is $2200, one thousand dollars down and the rest by mortgage on the property or as may be agreed; five hundred dollars plus interest is to be paid May 1, 1822, seven hundred dollars plus interest May 1, 1823. Cooper is to be subject to a fifteen-hundred-dollar penalty if he fails to meet the payments.[3]

By paying cash Peter evidently lopped two hundred dollars off the purchase price.[4] He could not, however, consummate the deal as speedily as he said he did. The City Council had yet to be consulted, and they were foresighted enough to demur at establishing a glue factory for twenty years at what might soon become part of the city. On October 29th the request of John

Vreeland to assign the lease of the so-called 'Powder House Lots' to Peter Cooper was reported favorably by the Finance Committee, which could find no reason not to permit the transfer. But it should not be inferred, the committee insisted, that such permission was tantamount to legalizing the continuance of a glue factory on the premises; if in the future it was deemed 'expedient for the public health or convenience, that the same should be removed,' [5] Cooper was to remove it. Within less than twenty years that time would come.

In 1821, however, the glue factory disturbed no one. It was on the south edge of the village of Kipps Bay, far from the built-up part of town. The Middle Road began at Fourth Avenue between 28th and 29th Streets, ran northwest over the crags of Inklangbergh (Murray) Hill, crossed Madison Avenue [6] between 35th and 36th Streets and met Fifth Avenue at 42nd Street. The glue factory, on the west side of the Middle Road between 31st and 34th Streets, was set amid fields of clover and surrounded by large buttonwood trees. Adjoining it was a small lake, Sunfish Pond, which extended from Lexington Avenue across Fourth Avenue and from 31st almost to 33rd Streets. Peter drew some water from this lake for his factory, and the local inhabitants fished for eels and skated there. One quiet sunny day Peter saw a strange and beautiful sight. The skins that were manufactured into glue were drying on a shed when suddenly they all began turning in one direction. A small whirlwind had arisen. Passing over his field, almost tearing up the clover, it collected leaves and straw until it formed a column of dust some two hundred feet high. Then the whirlwind crossed the Middle Road to where a neighboring factory was drying hair on a flat rock some half an acre in extent, and, picking up the hair, formed it into a huge round column of dazzling loveliness.

Almost immediately after buying the glue factory Peter moved out in the country to be near it. He first rented the country home of John Thompson, a seventeen-acre tract on Murray

Hill between 32nd and 36th Streets.[7] This property, which extended across Fifth Avenue and included the site of the old Waldorf-Astoria, was later one of the chief sources of William Astor's fortune.[8] Then on May 3, 1826, Peter purchased a piece of property at 28th Street and Fourth Avenue, which was to be his home for nearly a quarter of a century. The land, belonging in 1826 to Ann Rogers, was part of the great Rose Hill farm of Nicholas Cruger, most of which lay south and east of Cooper's site. Peter's original purchase was a modest one, consisting of two corner lots, each fronting 24 ft. 8⅛ in. on the east side of Fourth Avenue and reaching back 100 ft. The price for the two was $800. Nine years later he bought the adjoining six lots at public auction for $11,825, or at a price per lot approximately five times that of his original purchase. This gave him all but one of the eight lots fronting on Fourth Avenue in the block running south from 28th Street, and a depth of nearly 125 ft. through half the block and 100 ft. through the rest.[9]

When Peter bought his first lots neither Fourth Avenue nor 28th Street existed, and it was necessary to find the location by means of the stones and iron bolts that in 1826 marked future street intersections. Until 1833, when Fourth Avenue was opened to 28th Street (which became a thoroughfare the following year), Peter obtained access to his home by the Old Eastern Post Road, which, branching from the Bloomingdale Road (Broadway) to Albany at 23rd Street and Fifth Avenue, wandered northeast and crossed Fourth Avenue between 28th and 29th Streets. Until 1822 this had been the main road to Boston, and the corner on which Peter lived, where the Middle Road to the center of the island began, was still an important intersection. Third Avenue, however, had now been opened and paved and was a much straighter road to Harlem and Boston than the old route via the Bowery,[10] the Bloomingdale Road, and the Eastern Post Road. The Post Road soon became a backwater, and was finally closed in 1839.

The tradition in the Cooper family, as stated by his son-in-law, Abram Hewitt, in 1897 and repeated to me by Peter's grandson as heard from Cooper's lips, is that when Peter moved to 28th Street he took his Stuyvesant Street house with him, moving it by oxcart.[11] According to several writers, he personally 'directed the taking down of the structure, and the marking of each essential part, so that it might be put in its proper place in the progress of the reconstruction.' [12] The only trouble with this story is that Cooper himself never mentions it anywhere, and in his *Reminiscences* he several times remarks specifically that he *built* his house at 28th Street and Fourth Avenue.[13] As Peter devised it, it was a roomy and comfortable affair with three windows in front and ample stairs and large parlors and bedrooms, though in the pictures of it taken not long before it was torn down in 1909 there is little to remind one of its gracious earlier days. Peter himself 'made a great many improvements' in the place. He apparently carved much of the ornamental woodwork, including two wooden mantelpieces preserved at Ringwood, and invented a large drum fitted upon the stovepipe to heat the upper rooms.

The garden too was spacious, and contained 'many luxuries . . . in the way of fruit, having cherries, apricots, figs and apples and plums. . . . I remember on one occasion . . . taking home one of the most beautiful peaches I had ever seen and gave it to my wife who, after eating it, raised up the sash of the basement window and reached her arm out and stuck the pit of the peach in the ground, which pit grew to be the most magnificent tree, and for many years bore us loads of peaches, so that I believe in its time it must have borne us carloads of peaches.' Peter also planted elms some fifty feet apart, which grew to be enormous trees, 'the finest, I think, that could be found on the island.' About four hundred feet from his house there were, when he bought the place, two enormous elms, which guarded the entrance to the lane leading to the old Cruger mansion near the East River, occupied from 1790 until his death in 1806 by General Horatio Gates.[14]

The country around his new house was still beautiful. The city, whose closely packed houses now reached to 8th Street, had not yet encroached on the farms that dotted the Post Road above and below 28th Street, and from the high rocky ground on which his house was built he could look north over fields and meadows and Sunfish Pond toward Murray Hill, and south over groves of trees and wheatfields where New Yorkers were wont to picnic and hold turkey shoots. Beyond, his vision was blocked by the crags just below Union Square, which rose far above the street. To the west was the little Gramercy Pond, in the present Madison Square, and Buck's Horn Tavern on the Bloomingdale Road, surrounded by gardens and apple orchards. Only to the southeast was there the beginning of what promised to mar the countryside. In 1825 the Bull's Head Tavern, the principal cattle mart of the city, moved from near Chatham Square on the Bowery to 26th Street and Third Avenue, where it throve under Dan Drew's crafty management. Around it, between Second and Fourth Avenues and 23rd and 27th Streets, grew a whole village, known as 'Bull's Head Village,' which contained the city's principal cattleyards and slaughterhouses.[15] Since this development made the carrying-on of Peter's glue business much easier, he probably looked on it with mixed feelings.

Peter's location had one unqualified disadvantage. Being near the city and yet not in it, the region above 14th Street offered temptations to the town's lawless element, which took advantage of the absence of even the meager police protection afforded farther south. In 1831 the Common Council voted to put fourteen streetlamps on Third Avenue between 14th and 28th Streets, because, although the district was outside the area for lamps, the nearness of the new Bridewell at Bellevue made it dangerous.[16] Once when Peter was riding with his wife at dusk along the Bloomingdale Road through the future Madison Square, a man tried to grab the reins of his horse. Peter gave his horse a cut with the whip as he went by and thought he had gotten away. But when he shoved back the rear curtain, there was the man's face close to his. Dashing madly ahead, Peter succeeded in finally throwing the robber off before the carriage reached 28th Street.

During the first half-dozen years after he bought his glue factory Peter devoted his days to almost continuous labor. Up before it was light, he was at his factory—only a step across the fields from his Murray Hill home and less than a quarter of a mile up the Middle Road from his Fourth Avenue house—at dawn to light the fires. From then until evening he was hard at work, either at 33rd Street or in the city, where he drove in his horse and buggy to order supplies or make sales. For many years he was his own bookkeeper, manager, salesman, agent, and even handyman, and as late as the 'forties he knew every detail of his business and carried on most of the then vast correspondence. At the factory he labored side by side with his men, lending a hand to anything and everything from getting materials off a ship to hoisting machinery.

Naturally he was almost killed several times. Once, when he went aboard a large ship to inspect some chalk he was importing from England, he narrowly missed dropping fifteen to twenty feet into the hold through an open hatch. Shortly thereafter he was climbing a stepladder to inspect some glue stock that was drying, when the 'foot of the stairs slid away' and he fell a whole flight. 'I broke one or more of my ribs. This was after all the men had gone from the factory, and I lay there some time stunned by the fall until I was finally able to get up and go home.' At about the same time he escaped by inches almost sure death in 'the most terrific form that could well be imagined.' In order to get a large pump into a well, it was first necessary to hoist a thirty- or forty-foot log by means of a perpendicular beam and guy-ropes. Just as they got the end 'entered into the well' the log slid and broke the guy-ropes. The big beam fell and, catching Peter hemmed in by the building, came within a hair's breadth of crushing him. On a fourth occasion a part of his factory blew down in a storm just after he had gone home to a sick child. It is little wonder that Peter began to accept the view, held, he tells us, by the Arabians, that two guardian angels follow us through life.

Late in the afternoon, after everyone else was gone, Peter trudged home to his wife and children, who often watched for him from the window. In the evening, though he sometimes busied himself once more with glue-factory affairs, poring over accountbooks or handling correspondence, he found time for talking or reading with his family. But there was little joy in the Cooper family circle in these years. In 1824, while they were still living on Murray Hill, the Coopers had their third and fourth children snatched from them, as their first two had been. Sarah Amanda died of an infection of the throat early in her fifth year; Peter William died suddenly in his second year of acute bronchitis, caught, Peter says, watching for his father from the window. Worse, perhaps, than the deaths themselves was an ordeal to which Sarah Amanda was subjected when she was a baby. Her father's bald, detached description of the event does nothing to lessen the horror:

'Sarah Amanda when born was a beautiful child, one of the prettiest we ever had. . . . The nurse who had charge when she was born in wintertime placed her on a pillow with her face to the bright, blazing fire. It brought on cataracts in both eyes. She became entirely blind. Dr. Mott was employed to operate on her for the cataract. When he came he brought half a dozen of medical students to witness the operation. He found he had forgotten an instrument to do it with, so he made a temporary instrument to hold the eye, and when he attempted to hold the eye with it it was too large and it went right over the eye. Then he tried to bend it more, trying three times before he could hold the eye, and ruined the eye entirely and caused the child intense suffering. . . . I was so overcome with the screams of the child that it made me almost frantic. The child's mother could not stand it to see the sufferings of the child.' Though a Dr. Delafield eventually saved one eye, the other 'was a different color and was terrible to look at, as well as being totally blind.' [17]

With the deaths of Sarah Amanda and Peter William, the Coopers were left, after so many years of struggle and heartache, childless. Or almost. Less than two months before Sarah Amanda's death, on October 26, 1824, Sarah Cooper gave birth to her fifth child, Edward Cooper. At last their luck changed, and this boy lived, to become his father's staunchest business support and mayor of New York City. Then, for many years, there were no more children. Finally, in 1830, came their last child, Sarah Amelia, who became her father's darling and a compensation for much earlier sorrow.

Disease seemed to hover about the Cooper household—Peter himself almost died in the early 'twenties of yellow fever contracted when buying hides from a ship in Brooklyn—, and it is characteristic of Peter that he soon grew interested in patent cures for various diseases. His very early business notebooks contain, amusingly scrawled on the covers or even between pages of figures, remedies for most of the physical ills of man: cancer, consumption, disease of the 'prostrate gland,' and dropsy no less than colds, bruises, cuts, rheumatism, cramp, whooping cough, croup, vomiting, piles, and the bite of a rattlesnake. Eating chalk 'as long as it is found to give relief' was recommended for the 'prostrate gland'; for rheumatism one 'kian' pepper boiled in water and drunk before going to bed was prescribed. The 'cure for the cancer' was more elaborate: 'Use a strong potash made of the lye of the ashes [of] red oak bark boiled down to the consistence of molasses to cover the cancer . . . and in about an [h]our after cover this with tar which must be removed after a few days and if any protuberances remain in the wound apply more of the potash and plaster of tar until they all disappear.'

Despite his preoccupation with his family and his absorption in work, Peter was still freer in these days to devote time to his inventions than when he became an important figure with a dozen conflicting responsibilities. Indeed, not only did his inventiveness not flag but—to anticipate somewhat—reached its greatest fruitfulness in the late 'twenties and early 'thirties. Besides perfecting the rotary engine, Peter had by 1831 discovered a way of laying waterpipes under rivers, made an important improvement in glue-manufacturing, and created his *Tom Thumb* locomotive. He had also taken out several patents for relatively minor efforts—a new method for making salt (1824), an improvement in the construction of steam boilers—and had made bold and ingenious attempts both to navigate the air and to launch torpedoes.

In 1824 America, like England, was suddenly electrified with enthusiastic sympathy for the Greeks. While Lord Byron was sailing to his death at Missolonghi, Henry Clay was stumping America, begging cheering crowds at great public meetings to help stop the Turk before it was too late. Peter Cooper, who heard Clay speak in New York, 'partook,' as he says, 'of the common fervour.' Clay 'was a very inspiring man. For a person who had so heartfelt a horror and detestation of war, I became very much excited at the time.' A large ship was fitting out in New York harbor with supplies, and Peter determined, 'after his own fashion,' to make his contribution to this ship.

He had apparently heard of David Bushnell's plan to blow up the British fleet in New York harbor, and he set to work to perfect Bushnell's idea. He constructed a small, tube-shaped vessel equipped with one of his favorite rotary steam engines, with a screw wheel to guide it. 'My plan was to have this boat carry its torpedo on a crooked iron placed in the bow of the vessel, so as to strike the vessel to be blown up from a distance below the surface of the water, and have it explode by the actual contact in striking the vessel at the point aimed at.' Peter had no intention, however, of losing his vessel each time a torpedo exploded. 'When the explosion should take place, it would bend the iron holding the torpedo, and this would reverse the action of the steam engine, and cause it to go right back to the place from which it started.' The vessel itself was under the complete guidance and control of the person directing it from the shore, who held in his hands two steel wires fastened to the tiller of the boat, with which he guided the vessel as one drove a horse. Peter thought of everything. In the darkness the operator could see the boat by a light which it carried, whose bright side was toward himself and whose dark side was toward the object to be demolished. The boat had two rudders, one to guide it and one to make it dive under the water. Various gases or compressed air could be substituted for steam as a motive power, though as Peter planned things red-hot cannonballs in the boiler were to generate steam.

Though Peter was in no position to test the effectiveness of his boat as a torpedo, he took it down to the Narrows to see if he could guide it successfully for the ten miles his wires stretched. Placing the reels on the dock, he employed a little steamer to carry the wire as far as it would reach. 'After making about six miles, a sail vessel crossed our track and broke our wire, and I could not tell how far we might have gone on successfully.' Before Peter could demonstrate the practicability of his scheme, 'the ship sailed which bore provisions to the struggling Greeks.' The boat and all its attachments were stored in the glue factory, where eventually they were burned to ashes in a fire that destroyed the factory. Peter 'never renewed the experiment.' But, once again, he did not really admit defeat. In 1856 there was talk of war with England, and Peter, whose patriotism exceeded his sense of humor, offered his scheme to the *Journal of Commerce* as a 'peacemaker.' Years later he wrote: 'I had the satisfaction of believing that I had something to do in bringing that unfortunate threat of hostilities on the part of England to a peaceful termination.' Peter could be fatuous.[18]

He did little exulting, however, over his experiment in flying, which nearly cost him his life. With his sanguine belief in his ability to do anything, Peter had decided, like most inventors before and since, that 'it was possible to navigate the air' if one could find a gas of sufficient power. Inquiry brought forth the suggestion to try the gas of chloride of nitrogen, and Peter went confidently ahead, with the assistance of his youngest brother, Edward, a doctor, to experiment with the gas. A flying apparatus of 'very cheap material' was constructed and the material for making the gas was collected. 'Everything went well at first— till it came to heating the gas to the required temperature. Then we made the water a little too hot, which caused such an explosion as blew our apparatus to pieces. One piece of glass cut me in the left eye, entirely across the cornea, and somewhat in two directions. At first a portion of the vitreous humour of the eye protruded to about the size of a large pea; but fortunately, as soon as the contraction of the muscle took place it was drawn in again; but for that the humours would have run out.'

Though his brother put the cornea back in place, Peter had to remain in a dark room for five months. After ten days of restless and painful tossing on his bed, he made matters worse by carelessly thrusting his thumb into the wounded eye, necessitating 'a course of cupping, leeching, and other medical treatment.' Eventually Peter was 'able to see with it nearly as well as with the other, although there has always been an apparent mist before it.' This experience achieved what no amount of discouragement had ever been able to do. 'I have never,' he wrote laconically, 'renewed the experiment of air navigation.' [19]

The central fact of Peter Cooper's life in the 'twenties is, of course, the success of the glue business. Unfortunately, the details of the growth of that business are denied to us. No balance sheets or earnings statements were ever published or made. With his ingrained individualism and secrecy Peter shared neither his business nor its affairs with anyone for some twenty years, keeping the key figures in his head. As his grandson says, 'He always knew what the cash balance was and what the bills payable were approximately, so he knew that the bank balance was profits.' Even after he moved the factory to Brooklyn and gave over its management to his brother, William, he allowed little to be divulged.[20] As late as 1884 the compilers of a history of Brooklyn complained that of 5200 manufacturers in Kings County the managers of the Peter Cooper Glue Factory were the only ones 'who have persistently and peremptorily' refused 'any information whatever concerning their business.' [21]

It is not hard to tell, however, that the business grew rapidly. Though there are no earnings statements there are numerous ledgers showing the accounts with various customers, which increase rapidly in number and size. John Vreeland, to whom Peter sold glue after buying his business, owed Peter $1756.34 for glue in 1825, $2836.98 in 1826, and $2994.37 in 1827. Gideon Lee's account in 1826—Lee was Peter's banker, his customer for neat's-foot oil, and, as partner in a $60,000 tannery, a source of supply—showed a balance of about $1200, in 1827 of $2650. All the other early accounts—with men like Daniel F. Tiemann and Henry Schieffelin, paint manufacturers, Edwin Post, and William E. Dodge, a drygoods merchant, men who were soon to become friends—were small throughout the period, but their number grew from a few dozen to hundreds, and by the turn of the 'thirties included out-of-town customers as well as New Yorkers. Before he moved out of Manhattan Peter was doing a large business in Philadelphia, Baltimore, New Haven, Albany, and Boston. And he had long since expanded his business to include not only glue but gelatin, isinglass, neat's-foot oil, prepared chalk, and whiting (pulverized chalk cleansed of impurities); later he also ground white lead and did the milling for the manufacture of buckskin leather. In 1833 the stock in his factory was valued at $15,000, and the factory and lease of the ground at $10,000. Cooper himself admits that he 'had made a good deal of money' by 1828. His grandson, who says that the glue factory 'was much more profitable than anyone knew,' estimates that he made $10,000 to $20,000 a year from it while it was in New York.[22] Peter's little brown notebook shows his assets in the middle 'thirties as $123,459.

How did Peter Cooper make this money? In an expanding economy it is not too difficult to increase one's capital, and there is little mystery about the growth of Cooper's fortune later on. The $400,000 that he had in the middle 'forties, the $1,000,000 or more that he possessed in the middle 'fifties, and the $2,000,-000 of the middle 'sixties are of far less interest than his first $100,000. The theory current in Cooper's day and voiced in dozens of eulogistic biographies was that success was the reward of virtue and that all the early industrialists gained their fortunes solely by earnestness, honesty, prudence, and hard work. The industrialists themselves contributed to this mythology. As Peter's friend Cyrus Field, who made a fortune in the paper business and retired at thirty-four after paying all the debts of an earlier bankrupt firm, wrote modestly, 'There was no luck about my success, which was remarkable'; it was not due to large capital or the help of friends or speculations or fortunate turns of events but to 'constant labor and with the ambition to be a successful merchant.' [23] Peter too, in some of the interminable speeches an aging founder inevitably makes to the beneficiaries of his largesse, was not free from the cant of his day. 'Whatever of wealth I have achieved,' he said at eighty, 'has been due primarily to habits of patient industry formed at the outset of my career'; he early learned that 'waste makes want' and saved himself by taking 'stitches in time' and seeing that intemperance was the parent of poverty, vice, and crime.[24]

In reaction against this theory the radical muckrakers of the early twentieth century have gone to the opposite extreme, asserting that only by luck, chicanery, and the brutal exploitation of their fellowmen could any of the great fortunes of the nineteenth century have been made. As Gustavus Myers,[25] the boldest and most painstaking of the group, put it, these fortunes, far from being the result of industry and ability, were merely the logical outcome of a system bound to despoil the many for the benefit of the few. Myers contended that the law favored property as against labor power, and that the Astors and Vanderbilts and Lorillards and Rhinelanders twisted the law to secure city property and important franchises for a song. Industrialists swindled labor, the Indians, and the public in general, he said, and the bankers worked hand in glove with them. Vanderbilt, whose steamship fortune grew out of $30,000 made just when Cooper was earning his first money from glue, built up the largest pile, according to Myers, by combining all methods of exploitation, driving out competitors by underselling and then charging exorbitant rates, and corrupting officials to get mail subsidies and dock privileges. Though Myers actually cites only a dozen or so examples of exploiters, he insists that his few illustrate the practices of all capitalists.

Myers admits, however, that the beginning of the worst of capitalist practices came in only in the late 'thirties and 'forties with the railroad boom. Moreover, the great industrial—as against banking or land or steamship or railroad—fortunes belong just before and particularly after the Civil War, and Myers has very little to say about—or against, which is the same thing —the early manufacturers. He has nothing whatever to say about Peter Cooper, though he names him as one of five New Yorkers with over a million dollars before the Civil War.

Surely he was wise to leave him out. Not the most careful scrutiny can discover a trace of dishonesty or sharp practice or brutality in any of Peter's behavior as a manufacturer. True, he was not tempted to engage in many of the more questionable practices: he wanted no favors from the government, either in the form of franchises or land grants. But in the highly competitive industrial world of the 'twenties and 'thirties there was plenty of opportunity for vicious dog-eat-dog tactics. The worst that was ever said of Cooper was that, like all men whose 'acquisitiveness' was 'strongly developed,' he exhibited a certain 'strictness in bargaining.' [26] When he lent money, too, Cooper expected as prompt return as he would make himself, and in later life he who was usually so generous would in a business transaction often haggle irrationally over the smallest detail.

But there is no evidence that he ever tried to ruin a competitor by deliberate underselling, however often various new firms tried to gain his market by price-cutting.[27] His agents were worried, but Cooper was always confident that quality would tell in the end. Moreover, he never believed in charging exorbitant prices when he had a monopoly. On one occasion, later on in the iron business, he was disturbed over the amount of money he was making on an article on which, because of a patent, he had a monopoly, and deliberately lowered the price. 'The world needs this thing,' he told Lester, 'and we are making them pay too high for it; if it were a mere matter of fancy, or luxury, or taste, I should feel differently about it; but as it is a very necessary article I must do something about it.'[28]

Though he was no friend to militant labor unions or to laws reducing hours, his relations with his employees were always of the friendliest, and there were never any strikes in the glue factory. Having few employees, Peter knew and was friendly to all of them. One employee of thirty years' standing, Patrick Taafe, reportedly died of shock on hearing the news of Peter's death.[29] Another worked for Cooper for fifty years and was given $3000 by him when he retired. When this man was a small boy running out the glue on nets for drying, the other boys teased him by telling him his mother was a Yank and his uncle a Dutchman, and, Peter wrote, 'he thought that was so terrible that it almost broke his heart. So he came to me at the office one morning with his heart almost breaking. . . . It took me some time to satisfy him that a good Yank mother was an honorable thing,' as was an uncle who was a Dutch clergyman.[30] Peter paid good wages. In 1847, when his son wanted to reduce wages of iron puddlers to $4, Peter made things difficult by telling a number of them that he'd employ them at $4.50.[31] It was Cooper's proudest boast that, though he later employed in various businesses as many as two thousand men, he was 'unable to remember any week or month when all the men that worked for me did not get their pay at the regular time desired.'[32]

The positive contribution of these moral virtues to Peter's success may be somewhat problematical. There is less doubt—whatever the muckrakers have said—about the effect of other familiar attitudes and abilities: shrewdness, self-reliance, care about money, dogged industry and earnestness, enterprise, ingenuity, and decisiveness. These were the basic elements out of which his success, like that of many other young manufacturers of his day, was fashioned. All of his successful friends, Dodge, Lee, Field, Tiemann, exhibit the same traits, from doggedness to being, as Dodge's biographer wrote, 'as careful of their credit as a woman of her honor.' [33]

The manufacturer of the 1820's was in many ways a phenomenon quite distinct from the other businessmen of his day. Even as late as the 'seventies, as has been frequently pointed out, the great industries of the country were typically founded, not by the old merchant class, but by country boys with a bent for tinkering over crude machines. Carnegie's father was a country weaver, Rockefeller's an itinerant peddler, Frick's a farmer. Even more was this true in the 1820's. Owners of private fortunes or of capital from commerce invested mostly in banks or large corporations. The manufacturer was usually a laborer who had put his savings in a small business, which he then continued to support out of earnings. 'Manufacturing operatives, owners of small shops and water mills, invested their accumulations in extending their business, and thus became the founders of large enterprises, catering to local markets and managed directly by their proprietors.' [34] It was this common background that gave Cooper and his friends the characteristic traits that accounted so largely for their success. It was also this background, together with the nature of their occupations, that explained their attitudes toward other groups in the 'twenties. Industrialists like Peter Cooper had more in common with the farmer and the laborer than they did with the distributing, lending, and speculating classes. For many years they were as opposed as were the workers to the great capitalists and to the philosophy of Hamilton. After they had made a good deal of money and had become owners of great concerns many of them managed to forget their origins and to change their points of view. Peter Cooper never did.

Neither moral virtue nor other desirable traits can, however, alone explain Peter Cooper's rise any more than can chicanery or brutality. The truth of the matter is that before the rise of large industry, requiring great accumulations of capital and a good deal of ruthlessness, it was easier to make money by simple, straightforward methods than it ever was to be again. Never had opportunity been so great for so many people. The small manufacturer was in a particularly enviable position. Though there were great risks—from fire, price fluctuations, tariff charges, currency insecurity—and thousands of businesses failed, manufacturing enterprises in which the owners worked in their factories were, as Samuel Slater of the Pawtucket Cotton Mill averred in 1831, less likely to fail than was any other kind of business. Given a little capital, a little shrewdness, and a great capacity for work, the future was virtually unlimited. Peter Cooper had these things, as well as inventive genius and an uncanny instinct about when to be bold. His success was the perfect meeting of the man and the moment. It is at least arguable that, had he had to start from scratch in the 'seventies or even in the 'forties, he might not have become a millionaire. By then, however, he had capital to work for him and subordinates to handle the details and to grapple with mid-nineteenth-century men and conditions.

Peter bought his glue business at an especially propitious moment: the bottom of a severe depression that was to be followed by the first great industrial expansion that the new nation experienced. This was not by any means entirely chance. The depression was precipitated by the action of the Second Bank of the United States, whose behavior in 1817 and 1818 Peter had watched with misgivings. The new bank, chartered in 1816 to check the excessive note issuance indulged in by the state banks, soon began itself to overextend both note circulation and loans. As Peter saw it later, this was inevitable: you couldn't give so much power to a private corporation, even when managed by a good man, without having it abused. 'As it was made his duty to loan out this money and take the best security for its return that he could obtain, this good man would very naturally see that as soon as he commenced loaning this money out to the people that all the property of the country would commence to rise,' and he would see nothing wrong in borrowing himself to buy property. Everyone, including the presidents of the branch banks, would behave in the same way, and for a time property would increase in value and people would grow more extravagant. Then would come the crash. The president of the mother bank, 'this good man,' would find it his duty to curtail the accommodations of other banks, the presidents of other banks would sell their property and curtail their loans to their people, and the people who were dependent on banks for business operations would have 'to make all sacrifices to pay the banks.' [35]

This is just what occurred in 1819. Finding that, despite a reduction of credits, demand liabilities exceeded specie by $100,-000 and that one branch in Baltimore had already crashed with a loss of $3,000,000, the Second Bank in March called in Langdon Cheves of South Carolina to save the situation. As Peter Cooper tells it, 'they held a council for five days to ascertain whether it was possible to save the bank from an entire failure' and determined that the only method was drastic curtailment of loans and circulation. From 1818 to 1820 loans dropped from $41,181,000 to $31,401,000, and circulation from $8,339,000 to $3,589,000. The results were ruinous. 'Nearly all the manufacturing establishments of the country were broken up, their owners ruined, and their property sold at enormous sacrifices.' Peter Cooper said that he saw in Baltimore and Philadelphia 'whole rows of houses' given up to escape ground rents agreed on during inflation. William Cobbett, in *The Curse of Paper*

Money and Banking, a book with which Cooper was familiar, says very much the same thing: In 1822, at the bottom of the depression, 'houses of four stories, with marble steps and copper spouts, were in great number sold for a dollar apiece' on Market Street in Philadelphia.[36]

'The sight of such ruin . . . brought upon the country . . . about the time of the commencement of my business life' taught him, Cooper said, a great lesson: 'To do what business I should ever be able to do on such means as I could have of my own so as not to be dependent upon the tender mercies of banks.' [37] Reinforced a dozen years afterward by the theories of the leaders of the Jacksonian revolution, this experience formed the basis of Cooper's war in later life on the National Banking Act. But Peter did not need the experience of 1819 to know that 'debt and demoralization are always near' or to be suspicious of banks. He had long believed that, even when no prospect of a crash was in sight, it was foolish to discount notes at the exorbitant rates banks charged. To illustrate this, Peter Cooper once offered to lend a merchant money for three years by discounting his $10,000 note at the three-percent-a-month rate that the merchant was willing to pay a bank for a six-month loan. As quickly became evident even to the somewhat credulous merchant, not only would he get no money on the discounted note, but he would begin by owing Peter $800, since the three-percent interest for three years amounted to $10,800.

As a consequence of what he had learned in his youth, Peter was not caught in the 1819 crash, any more than he was to be caught in the even more serious panic of 1837 or the eight other 'panics in the money market, that I have myself witnessed.' When money was scarce, those were the times when things could be bought cheapest. Those were also the times when 'I was most easy in my own money affairs.' No, it was not chance that Peter Cooper was able to buy the glue factory for a song in the year 1821.[33]

Peter Cooper could hardly, however, have foreseen the great

development that was to follow. Ever since the Revolution the opportunity had been there, since there were no entrenched classes holding it back and a whole continent needed development. But progress had been slow for various reasons before the War of 1812, and was checked by the postwar depression. Now, however, manufacturing establishments were springing up everywhere, and, with the development of inland waterways, were able to distribute their products far and wide. Between 1820 and 1840 capital invested in manufacturing rose from fifty million to two hundred and fifty million, and the movement from the farm to the city, which has been such a marked feature of American life, was on in full force. In these twenty years those engaged in manufacturing increased 127 per cent, those in agriculture only 79 per cent; in 1820 only one-twentieth of the nation was living in cities of over eight thousand, in 1840 one-ninth. The depression of 1819-1822 was followed between 1825 and 1828 by America's first great boom.

New York profited by the new developments more than any city in the country. The opening of the Erie Canal on October 26, 1825, accompanied by ten days of banquets and bonfires as the *Chancellor Livingston,* towing a flotilla of boats, proceeded to New York, where Clinton poured a keg of lake water into the sea, gave the trade of a continent to the metropolis. Before the opening of the Erie Canal it took three weeks and cost one hundred dollars to transport a ton of freight from New York to Buffalo; after the opening it took eight days and cost fifteen dollars. Imports in New York rose from $34,000,000 in 1821 to $50,000,000 in 1825.[39] People poured into the city, whose population rose from 120,000 in the early eighteen-twenties to 168,000 in 1825. In anticipation, three thousand new houses were built in 1824. Yet in 1825 houses were unobtainable; said the *Evening Post:* 'Shops and stores command double rents to what they did the last season, and still the demand cannot be supplied; the streets are so obstructed by the great number of buildings going up and pulling down, that they have become almost impassable, and a scene of bustle, noise and confusion prevails that no pen can describe nor any but an eyewitness imagine.' [40] Business of all kinds prospered, and though manufacturing did not at first keep pace with trade and commerce, a description of New York in 1826 [41] lists smelters, sawmills, iron and porcelain works, coal, oil and copper companies, and manufacturers of cotton, linen, and wool goods.

As New York grew into a city it gained in dignity and impressiveness. In May, 1825, the first gas pipes for the city south of 14th Street were laid by the New York Gas Company, and in 1830 contracts were let to illuminate the northern part as well; in 1827 a great new Merchants' Exchange for $230,000 was built in Wall Street; the buildings in Pine Street were so tall, wrote a contemporary, the sun was seldom seen; omnibuses began running in Broadway in 1830; in the same year Scudder's American Museum, of which Cooper was so fond, opened in a marble building on Broadway opposite St. Paul's, having moved from 20 Chatham Street. The wealthy were being pushed out of lower Broadway, and Cedar, Liberty, John, and Fulton were all given over to business. Though there were still fine houses downtown, the fashionable were moving to Leonard, Franklin, and White Streets, to St. John's Park and even to Second Avenue near Stuyvesant Square and to Washington Square, which had ceased to be a burial ground and from which Fifth Avenue was opened by 1830 as far as 21st Street. In 1826 Lafayette Place was cut through from Astor Place South, and Colonnade Row, in which both Washington Irving and John Jacob Astor had homes, became the most desirable place in town to live. Broadway, which lay 'at nearly an equal distance from the noble streams which lave the commercial metropolis of the United States,' wrote a contemporary, was 'the most elegant and spacious street we now have.' It was lined with retail shops, bookstores, hotels, churches, and fine houses, and had sidewalks of flagstone and brick; most of the houses had doorsteps, windowsills, and lintels of fine freestone or white marble and boasted plates and ornaments of pure silver. New Yorkers, who ignored the slums that were developing as fast as the elegance and grandeur, were mightily impressed with their city, and there were two lengthy guidebooks to the town published in 1827 and 1828 alone.[42]

The atmosphere of progress and hopefulness in which Peter Cooper passed the early years of his business life had a profound effect on him. Always an optimist, he now became so firmly convinced that anything was possible in America that even the darkest times and the most changed conditions could not shake his faith. When he bought the glue business, his natural carefulness and business conservatism made him wary, and the most he would say was that if others could succeed in making glue, so could he. By 1830 he was convinced that it was easy to make money, and he never changed his opinion.

It was his firm belief, also confirmed in this period, that it was right to make money in industry. His inherited beliefs had included a glorification of work as a duty and had justified success as the reward for labor. In the 1820's production was the need of the times, and even Northern farmers were persuaded that America's infant manufacturing concerns were a boon to the country. The New York County Agricultural Society, of which Cooper became a member in 1823, had as its purpose the promotion of domestic manufactures as well as horticulture. In the early days of his career Peter Cooper had every reason to feel that he was performing a public service in manufacturing glue. Unless we understand this we will not realize fully the moral implications of his statement, echoed by many in his day, that he was 'determined to give the world an equivalent in some form of useful labor for all that I consumed in it.'

There is no intention in the foregoing to explain away Peter's success. When everything else has been taken into account— Peter's determination, his optimism, his possession of certain appropriate abilities, the propitiousness of the times—there still remains some special talent or genius which no explanation can cover. Peter's business was in many ways peculiar, requiring skill and originality of a high order. In part, at least, it was because Peter brought such gifts to the solution of difficult problems that he outstripped so many of his contemporaries.

The main problem in the glue business was not one of competition in selling. The field was very small when Peter Cooper started, and, except for a few manufacturers, most of the glue was made by tanners who boiled up their own stock in open kettles. Even in 1850, when statistics first appear, the census lists only forty-seven glue establishments in the country, with capital of $519,950; not until the 'eighties, by which time there were eighty-two establishments with a capital of $3,916,250, did glue-making became a great industry. In the meantime there was an increasing demand for good glues for furniture, books, and many other articles.

Nor were costs a serious factor. The only materials necessary were the glue stock, lime, a little sulphuric acid, some scrap zinc, coal, and water. The glue stock, which came from what had been considered waste material, cost Peter, according to his grandson, only 1/4 to 1 1/2 cents a pound. Since labor costs were small, Peter could manufacture glue for around 6 cents a pound. He could sell it for from 10 to as high as 60 cents a pound, producing a nice margin of profit.

The real problem was to get the glue stock. Peter's solution of this difficulty was simple and thorough, and went far toward insuring his success at the outset. He took all the glue stock that the tanners and butchers in New York had to offer, thus freeing himself for many years—until the great packing houses arose in the West—from all local competition. From the tanners he got the 'roundings,' 'skivings,' and 'trimmings' from hides of deer, goat, sheep, and cattle; from the butchers he got cattle and calves' feet and pates. For a while he personally canvassed his sources, and his wagon could be seen loading scraps every morning at the establishment of Henry Astor, largest slaughterer in the city, conveniently located in the Bowery near Daniel Drew's large cattleyards. In 1830 he made an agreement with one John Hornby—an agreement that lasted or was renewed for at least fifteen years—to pay him to collect feet from the more than two dozen butchers in New York.

Cooper's relations with his sources and selling agents were always of the best, and this also contributed mightily to his success. In an address to the tanners in 1877 Peter said that for fifty years he had had nothing but the pleasantest dealings with them, and couldn't remember one difficulty settling an account. The same applied to such agents as C. Sigourney & Son in Hartford, Field Fowler and Amos Cummings in Boston, and English and Mix in New Haven. It was Peter's policy to be generous with defaulting agents, and he would sue only if there was theft involved. Nothing is more characteristic of him than his hatred of a quarrel and his willingness to make concessions or to abide by the word of a third party. When his friend E. W. Upton of Boston and Danvers, a glue manufacturer from whom Peter bought materials and whom he often visited, sent him some hide-cuttings that were not up to par, Peter agreed to pay part of the cost of retrimming rather than allow a misunderstanding to develop. When he had a disagreement with John Hornby, he agreed to pay for the feet delivered pending a settlement, adding: 'I should still be pleased to settle the difficulty between us in relation to the agreement by referring it to disinterested persons as has been previously proposed and urged by myself.' To his customers Peter typically gave six to nine months' credit, or five to eight per cent off for cash. His own payments were prompt. Averse to banks, he usually went to Gideon Lee, who acted as his banker, for money, though occasionally he borrowed for short periods from customers, repaying the loans in glue delivered. 'I have made it a rule to pay everything as I go. If, in the course of business, anything is due from me to anyone, and the money is not called for, I make it my business on the last Saturday before Christmas to take it to his business place.' [43]

Cooper's other great problems were technical ones, and he

solved these, partly through his own inventive talent, with equal skill. When Peter took over the glue business, most glue came from Ireland, England, and France, whose output even at high prices and with a tariff of five cents a pound was preferred to the American article. Within a few years Peter was turning out glues that could compete with the foreign product at one-third the price. But cheapness was never Peter's aim so much as quality. As he told Susan Carter, 'I have always tried to do the *best* I knew how . . . and then people have wanted what I made. I determined to make the *best* glue, and found out every method and ingredient looking to that end, and so it has always been in demand.' [44] He refused to give discounts, except for cash, as at least one disgruntled customer discovered, and was averse to cutting prices even in bad times or when customers complained they were being taken advantage of. In 1892 a compiler of statistics on glue prices wrote of Peter's firm that 'the conservative methods of this old establishment in the past have sometimes made them slow to respond to the temporary fluctuations of the glue market in either direction.' [45] Peter's three highest grades of glue did not vary one cent in price, for example, from 1844 through 1857, being forty, thirty-four, and thirty cents a pound respectively.

His glue won its way through quality, and his agents were constantly assuring him that even when business was bad they could make sales 'from the favorable character your glue has acquired.' Moreover, it became the standard by which other glues were measured. For Peter learned to test his glue and produce it in uniform and unvarying grades, of which by 1844 there were ten. His grandson says that as a young chemist in Berlin he examined Peter's method and found that he had solved a difficult problem in organic chemistry without, of course, any technical knowledge of chemistry. So jealous was he about his grading system that he was deeply concerned when anyone used one of his numbers; an inferior glue might be mistaken for his and hurt his 'reputation for quality and exactness.' Today Peter's system of grading is still being used, though many manufacturers prefer the newer method devised by the National Association of Glue Manufacturers.[46]

Glue-making in these early days was full of vexatious technical difficulties. The essence of the process is simple enough: If various animal substances are boiled in water and the solution cooled and dried, the result will be a light-yellow to black-brown, brittle, glossy solid known as glue. But there are many glue-yielding substances, from the sinews of calves' feet and shin-bones—Peter's staple—to fish scales, scraps of parchment, and old gloves, and each of these has its own properties and must be treated differently, presenting problems at every stage. Before being boiled, calves' feet have to be freed of blood and flesh and separated from the fatty matter. Peter did this, according to a plan preserved among his papers, by introducing limewater under a pressure of fifty pounds into a vessel and drawing it off several times until the skin and sinews were thoroughly penetrated.[47] Then came the boiling, done by Peter in shallow cylinders lined with slate or made of metal to keep the feet free from taste or smell and with heat from without.

The resulting 'foot-water' had next to be evaporated in such a way as to produce a clear, consistent product of proper strength. Here once again Peter's inventive genius came to his aid, and in 1830 he took out a patent, signed by President Jackson and Secretary of State Martin Van Buren, for an 'improvement in the art of making Glue, by evaporating the water commonly called the foot-water, or the liquor after boiling the bones of all kinds of animals, to a proper consistence for cutting, drying, and making into Glue, by means of a double-floored evaporating basin.' Peter's plan was to run water into a basin built on a flue extending from the furnace, and thus, rather than in an open boiler, heat the foot-water, which was placed in an upper basin. The concentrated liquor, run off in sheets, congealed into jelly, and cut into large cakes, had now to be dried—the most precarious process of all, since too much heat meant cracking and too-slow drying meant putrefaction. Peter, with no access to modern methods of artificial drying, apparently dried his jelly when frozen. For preserving he used sulphate of zinc, still the best preserver of glue.

From the very beginning Peter made neat's-foot oil (which rises to the top when calves' feet are boiled), and later isinglass and gelatin—all products closely allied to glue. Isinglass, in great demand in Peter's day for clarifying wines, manufacturing ink, court plaster, and household cement, making jelly, ice cream, and candy, and giving luster to textiles, was largely imported from Russia at four dollars a pound. Peter never produced a substitute for the Russian product, which came mainly from the air-bladders of sturgeons and was the finest of animal glues. He did, however, make from the bladders of hake a darker, less soluble, and on the whole inferior product at less than a quarter of the price. To do this necessitated a great deal of care if not much skill: the bladders had to be carefully cleaned, macerated in water, cut open, and pressured between iron rollers.

To produce gelatin—so similar to glue that Abram Hewitt said, 'Where glue ends and gelatin begins no man can tell' [48]— calves' feet were made to yield a pure bone glue, carefully cleansed, freed from fat, and strained. Peter took great pains to get his gelatin tasteless by careful preparation of the feet and drying of the jelly. So as to know the proper weather for freezing the gelatin before drying, he built a gelatin eagle, whose wings stood erect in dry weather when the gelatin, which absorbs moisture, shrank. The result of his efforts was unqualified success. Peter Cooper produced the first widely used packaged table gelatin in America. Mrs. Cooper wrote the recipes printed on the packets, and housewives soon were using his gelatin rather than making their own calves'-foot jelly.

The obscure grocer was becoming a name in households all

over America. By 1829 he had rented property in Yonkers to increase his supply of glue, and the following year bought an office downtown at 20 Ferry Street to carry on his expanding activities. The times, a spirit in tune with them, and a touch of genius were producing one of America's early successful manufacturers.

PART TWO

A Man of Affairs and Dreams

(1828-1859)

Chapter 7

THE TOM THUMB

EIGHTEEN twenty-eight was a key year in Peter Cooper's life. Thirty-seven years old and an established glue manufacturer in New York, he made his first large scale foray into outside fields of business enterprise, acquiring, almost inadvertently, a measure of national fame. And, elected to the Common Council of the City of New York, he began the long career of public service and philanthropy which brought him less spectacular but more lasting recognition. In the years immediately following 1828 he was also to acquire most of the basic ideas that were to guide his life and to flower much later in a series of remarkable and unexpected pamphlets and speeches. With the decade of the 'thirties the mechanic and craftsman of an almost pioneer society was to expand into a citizen of the larger world of America's ripening manhood.

When Peter embarked in 1828 on his daring land venture in Baltimore, he had already had some experience investing in real estate. He early realized, with his usual shrewdness, that New York City property was bound to increase rapidly in value, and 'as fast as I obtained money I purchased houses that would bring me in some revenue.' By 1828 he held, he said, twelve houses on Third Avenue and on the Bowery. These included, besides his Stuyvesant Street and Bowery purchases, two houses, a schoolhouse, two stables, and several other buildings on Sandy Hill—a low hill that extended west from the Bowery at 8th Street—, bought in 1826 for $1300 from the Sailor's Snug Harbor, inheritors of old Captain Randall's property. Peter was also buying land in these years: a $550, twenty-acre farm in Mamaroneck in 1827, a $1000 tract of eight lots on the Hudson River between 113th and 114th Streets in 1828, and a piece of land 172 x 194 feet on 33rd Street and Third Avenue, purchased in 1824 for $2600. This Third Avenue land, on which he established a wire mill in 1837, he began to sell off in 1844; when the last piece was disposed of, in 1851, Peter had taken in $26,-227.71, or ten times the purchase price.

Peter did not, however, make the fortune out of New York real estate that the Astors, Rhinelanders, Peter Goelet, the Lorillards, and the Schermerhorns did. He was never tempted, as some people were, to buy up city-owned land secured at cheap prices by questionable methods. Nor would he speculate in real estate, but bought only what he had the cash to purchase. Thus in 1824 he had to refuse an $11,000 offer of eighteen acres of ground between Fifth and Eighth Avenues at 21st Street: he had just bought the 33rd Street property and had used 'all the money that I could spare from my business to do so.' Henry Eckford bought the property, and soon after sold a part of it for $400,000; in 1879 the whole was worth some $5,000,000.

The Baltimore project was far more ambitious than anything Peter had heretofore undertaken. In 1828 Baltimore was in the throes of the country's first railroad boom. Railroads, which were to spread everywhere within a dozen years, were then in their infancy. Though both the Mohawk & Hudson and the Delaware & Hudson had been chartered in 1826, the ground for the former was not broken until 1830 and the latter was only thought of as an accessory to the Delaware & Hudson Canal. But the subject was very much in the air in 1825 and 1826, and travelers returning from England reported on the cumbrous pre-Stephenson engines they had seen drawing coal trains. Moreover, the citizens of Baltimore were desperate. Though nearer to the fertile lands of the West, Baltimore was rapidly losing trade to New York's Erie Canal, and found to her dismay that a canal on the route of either the Potomac or the Susquehanna would be prohibitively costly. So a town meeting was called in 1826, and in 1827 a charter for a railroad was pushed through the legislature, authorizing the city and the State of Maryland to purchase stock. There was an immediate and almost unprecedented wave of enthusiasm. One excited participant, William Patterson, made such extravagant calculations of future profits that he told Peter Cooper that they 'could afford to make the rails out of silver.' [1] Everyone wanted stock and set about getting proxies for the limited amount available; parents subscribed for their children, paying down the dollar specified in the regulations. 'Before a survey had been made—before common sense had been consulted, even, the possession of stock in any quantity was regarded as a provision for old age.' [2] The climax came on July 4, 1828, when Charles Carroll of Carrollton, the last surviving signer of the Declaration of Independence, lifted the sod for the first stone of the Baltimore & Ohio Railroad amid picturesque floats, fireworks, and speeches. Peter Cooper, watching from New York, was caught up in the excitement and induced to plunge deeper than his caution had ever before permitted.

Two New Yorkers of Peter's acquaintance conceived the idea of profiting by the rise in real estate values sure to accompany the successful laying of the roads, and asked Peter to join them in purchasing 3000 acres of land at Lazeretto Point. The men said they had large means and the speculation sounded good; within the city limits of Baltimore just southeast across the bay from Fort McHenry, the land extended three miles along the shore and included the best shipping water in the harbor. Peter went to see the property and, finding that it equaled their representation, consulted Gideon Lee, on whose advice in politics and philanthropy no less than in business Peter was coming more and more to lean. Lee, who had walked over the property and knew all about it, said that in his opinion it was worth nearly $500,000 whether the railroad was finished or not. This decided Peter, and he put down the $20,000—some of it borrowed from Lee—demanded as his initial payment on one-third of the land, the total purchase price of which was $105,000. The Canton Company[3] was chartered in 1829[4] to hold land up to ten thousand acres, to improve it by erecting wharves, warehouses, buildings, and by laying out streets and canals, and to sell or lease portions of it.

Peter's ordinary prejudice against going into business with partners was soon considerably increased. As he tells the story in his *Reminiscences,* he went down to Baltimore again at the end of a year, having in the meantime been drawn on 'every little while for taxes,' and found that 'neither of my partners had paid a cent on the purchase, and that I had been sending down money to pay their board!' Seeing that 'I was caught . . . I bought my swindling partners out—paying one of them $10,000 and the other $8000.[5] The surgery was unfortunately not as quick or relatively painless as Peter here suggests. Peter had more than the two New York partners to consider, a Baltimore paper listing as his associates (besides Gideon Lee) Francis Pease, Ely Moore, and James Ramsey of New York, and W. Patterson, Columbus O'Donnell, Ebenezer Z. Finley, and W. Gwynn, the first president of the company, of Baltimore.[6] In April and again in July of 1829 the Canton Company offered capital stock to the public under the sponsorship of Peter Cooper (listed as a director), Gideon Lee, Elisha Tibbits, and Gilbert Coutant.[7] Peter Cooper scrupulously avoided mentioning the names of his two swindling partners, but his papers refer in 1829 to the obstinacy and mismanagement of a Mr. Price, which were doing great harm to the company, and to the bankruptcy of Moore, who ought to dispose of part of his interest in the company to meet exigencies. Peter made the mistake, too, of lending money to one Charles McCully to buy stock, taking the stock as security, and then was sued by McCully for selling him out at less than McCully thought the stock worth. 'Can it be possible,' Cooper wrote in anguished amazement, 'that you have been playing a trick on me—*can it be* possible Mr. McCully that you can be guilty of such black ingratitude?' It was more than possible: Cooper ended by having to pay the $6050 cost of the suit.

With the disappearance of his two chief associates Peter was left with what he called an 'elephant' on his hands. He began leveling hills and draining swamps and cutting firewood, employing his usual ingenuity in the process. To fill one creek he rigged up an endless-chain device for transporting the sand, which was nearby on higher ground. It consisted of a frame containing an upper and lower set of rails and a set of boxes hinged together to form a chain resting on the rails. A hopper just over the upper train permitted sand to be shoveled in at the top. Gravity then carried the heavy cars down until they dumped their sand into the creek, after which they were carried up again on the under set of rails.

His lands could not, however, possibly yield him a profit for some years no matter how rapidly he developed them, and taxes and assessments were draining his resources. Peter met this challenge in his usual way. He surveyed the situation and discovered that there was both iron ore and wood to make charcoal on his land. Without a moment's hesitation he determined to become an iron manufacturer. In 1830 this was by no means the undertaking it would have been even a dozen years later. The American iron industry was still in the primitive condition of small furnaces, forges, and bloomeries near sources of charcoal supply, the use of anthracite for smelting in blast furnaces, which revolutionized the industry, being all through the 'thirties in the experimental stage. Yet only some one with Peter's confidence and resourcefulness would have undertaken a new venture in an unknown field at this doubtful juncture of his affairs.

Peter first built large brick kilns, twenty-five feet in diameter, twelve feet high, and circular in form, around the top of which he put an iron hoop, and arched the whole over with brick. In these kilns, which contained small openings for the admission of air, he burned the wood into charcoal. He then had forty-five thousand tons of ore dug, which he proceeded to smelt into iron. Just what process he used or what forms of iron he made cannot be stated with any certainty. He did not have a modern blast furnace, as futile negotiations to erect one later indicate. He either smelted pig iron in a charcoal furnace or made cast or wrought iron direct from the ore, as was common practice in early days. The principal equipment of what he calls his foundry[8] was a forge built for him by one George Johnson in 1831 in a building erected for that purpose. Under the agreement Johnson was to 'set in operation a forge for making iron' and a steam engine with two cylinders to drive it, made to work from the same boiler, the one to work a blowing cylinder and stampers for pounding, the other to drive the hammers for drawing the iron. Though the agreement called for a price of $3500, by July of 1831 Peter had already paid out $4195.04, and by the end of the year had spent $6457.39, not counting the $2609.55 that the building cost. On this forge Peter hammered out bars and other kinds of wrought iron during the year or more that he operated the ironworks.

His iron business was a source of new stimulation and excitement to both himself and his family, who frequently accompanied him to Baltimore between 1829 and 1833. In Baltimore they stayed at Barnum's Hotel, where on one occasion in the spring of 1830 they had the room adjoining that of the great John Randolph of Roanoke, whose singular squeaking voice they could hear through the partition; the old man, Cooper said, looked more like one going to his grave than to Russia where he was bound as United States Minister.[9] They also saw the beautiful home of Jerome Bonaparte on the Delaware, and once viewed him ride through the city on horseback with his bride.[10] The trip from New York to Baltimore was itself in those days an ever-varying novelty. In winter the whole journey was made by great lumbering coaches carrying nine inside and one or two outside, with four good fast horses changed every ten or twelve miles. In summer there was a break at Trenton, whence a steamer carried the passengers to Philadelphia to pick up another coach for Baltimore. The ride was very comfortable, Peter said, after they 'had suspended the bodies on long leather braces, which allowed them to roll about very easily.'

Mishaps and perils but added to the fun. Once, Peter said, the coach got stuck in the mud and the passengers 'had to get out and pull a fence down that we might use the rails to pry the stage out of the mud with.' On another occasion—this on a trip from Washington—a bridal couple, who were coming East, had their luggage on top of the coach: 'It so happened that the jolting of the stage opened the cover of one of the bride's trunks, and the consequence was that the articles of clothing which it contained dropped out one by one and were scattered along the road for some distance before the accident was discovered, so that the finery of the bride was nearly all out on the highway.' The passengers inevitably found this more amusing than tragic, much to the annoyance of the husband, who vented his anger vainly on the stolid coachman. A third mishap was caused by a swollen river. Peter's stage got over the bridge, guided by the rails on the side, but the next one missed the bridge and was carried downstream, the ladies having to be pulled out through the windows. One summer Peter chartered a coach to take him, his family, a servant, and $10,000 in silver to Trenton to pick up the steamer. In transferring the silver, carried in ten-gallon kegs, to the boat one of the kegs dropped and broke open, scattering the silver in the sand. Peter remembered that he lost only $1.50.

(Though not blessed with much of a sense of humor, Peter dearly loved practical jokes, particularly one that occurred on a trip from Albany to New York one winter in a horse sleigh. 'The weather was very cold and we were sitting with straw up to our knees. We had no sleigh bells, and were quietly gliding at a rapid speed over the frozen snow when the party was suddenly startled by what appeared to be a fierce fight, accompanied by prolonged and angry squeaks of rats under the straw. In an instant the staid Quakers of our party jumped up on the seats and commenced to punch the straw vigorously, which, as it appeared to hurt the rats, only caused the squeaks to increase.' The shrewd Peter quickly became suspicious, and was not long in discovering that they had a ventriloquist on board.) [11]

Accidents were not the only danger in the still half-domesticated countryside, and Peter once came very near losing his life, so often in jeopardy from so many causes, at the hands of robbers. Returning home from a five-hundred-mile trip in a one-horse wagon through New Jersey, he stopped at the house of a manufacturer of large iron screws and other machinery. Fortunately the man induced Peter to load the pistols that he carried with him but 'never felt fear enough' to load. It was just before sundown, and Peter wanted to go another twelve miles so as to get home the next day. About an hour after leaving the man's house, when it was 'coming on' so dark that 'I could not tell a white man from a negro,' Peter saw three men standing right in the middle of the road in front of him. The road was so narrow and 'at such a point of a hill' that he could not turn around and had nothing to do but meet them as well as he could. 'I took my pistols out at once, laid one of them on the seat and took one of them in my hand, with the lines in one hand and the whip and the pistol in the other I drove slowly up to the first man and then gave the horse a severe cut of the whip and he sprung with such violence that he knocked the man down and ran over him.' One of the other two men tried to stop the flying horse by grabbing hold of the shaft, the other the front of the wagon. 'I did not get too far when the wheel ran right over him, nearly throwing me out of the wagon. I do not know what became of the third man.' [12]

A far worse fate almost overtook Peter at the very outset of his career as an iron maker. As was his custom he personally supervised the first burning of wood into charcoal in his kilns. When he thought the fire had done its work, he plastered up the openings for air, and, after waiting a number of days for the fire to go out, had his men start removing the charcoal. The job was half-finished when suddenly the coal itself burst into a blaze that refused to succumb to the ministrations of the exhausted and despairing men. At this point Peter himself went 'just to the door of the kiln and looked at it to see if anything more could be done, and at that instant the gas itself took fire. . . . I was blown by its force some eight or ten feet. Fortunately for me, the flame went up and I went down,' so that he was thrown beyond the reach of the fire. 'I found that the flame had burnt my whiskers and eyebrows,' had scorched his forehead, blistered his face, and burned his coat. He told a *Herald* reporter in 1879, 'Had I taken one breath . . . while I was surrounded by the flame, I should not be here today.' [13]

Before he had actually made any iron, Peter was threatened by disaster from another quarter. The railroad, on which all his hopes and those of thousands of others were based, was in deep trouble by the fall of 1829, only a little over a year after its exuberant inauguration. Much time had been lost in planning a level route from Baltimore to the Potomac, with inclined planes to take the horses—the expected mode of locomotion—up and down the grades. In Baltimore there were difficulties about getting down to the wharves, as the city at first ordained that the railroad had to come into the city sixty-six feet above high tide. The work on the first thirteen miles to Ellicott's Mills was interrupted by numerous quarrels among the workmen and by cave-ins, and the first permanent tracks were not laid until October, 1829. These proved far more expensive to set down than had been anticipated, as most of the long metal strips used for rails[14] were placed on expensive granite slabs instead of on wood cross-pieces. Most of the cash in hand had been spent and there was little to show for it.

Despite discouragement the work proceeded, and by May, 1830, the thirteen miles to Ellicott's Mills was opened. Already in January, when the mile and a half west of Mount Clare was laid, the enthusiastic directors had had built for themselves a car like an open market cart to draw them back and forth behind a single horse. When the whole thirteen miles was finished the public was allowed to go thundering along in 'brigades of cars' at fifteen miles an hour over the unyielding iron and stone. But those in the know were worried. The astonishing success of George Stephenson's *Rocket* at the trials on the Liverpool & Manchester Railway in the fall of 1829 had confirmed what the commissioners sent to England by the B. & O. had begun to suspect: not horses, on foot or on a treadmill, not Evan Thomas' curious sailing vessel,[15] but steam was the future form of locomotion for railways. Moreover, English locomotives appeared to be the best. This opinion was confirmed by the successful trial of George Stephenson's *Stourbridge Lion,* imported by Horatio Allen, on the tracks of the Delaware & Hudson Railway at Honesdale, Pennsylvania, on August 8, 1829. Stephenson and others insisted, however, that no locomotive could go around a curve with a radius less than three hundred feet, and the Baltimore & Ohio, to save the cost of deep cuts, had built or planned curves with radii of one hundred fifty to two hundred feet. The company were plunged into despair, and there was even talk that the stockholders would no longer pay up the assessments on their stock.[16]

At this fatal juncture Peter Cooper rode into the lists. 'In the abandonment of that road,' he writes, 'I saw the defeat of my enterprise. It would have been a terrible defeat to me, for I saw that the growth of the city of Baltimore depended upon the success of that road, and I had purchased that tract with a view of taking advantage of the rapid growth of the city which was anticipated.' So Peter went to Philip Thomas, the president, and to a few of the directors who were principally interested, and told them that if they would hold on for a little while 'I would put a small locomotive on, which, I thought, could pull a train around those short curves. So I got up a little locomotive.' [17]

Thus began one of the most inspiriting and romantic events of Peter's career, one that brought him a fame equaled only by the founding of Cooper Union. The whole episode was characteristic of him in a dozen ways. He entered it partly, as he says, as a purely business proposition to save his investment, partly to test out his favorite scheme for changing rectilinear to rotary motion, and partly, in the spirit of adventure, to see if he couldn't solve a practical problem that was baffling others. He carried it out almost entirely by himself, pitting his ingenuity— he calls it his 'knack of contriving'—and his craftsmanship against established theories and routine practice. And he remained the amateur to the end: his locomotive was frankly an experiment, never intended to be run as a working engine on the line. This amateur quality of his effort has led Stewart Holbrook in his recent book on railroads to deny any great importance to the 'much-heralded, much-pictured race between Peter Cooper's *Tom Thumb* engine and a gray horse, the horse winning hands down.' But the fact remains that Cooper's was the first American locomotive to be run on a regular railroad in America; he did solve the problem of short curves, or rather showed that it was no great problem; and he did convince not only the directors of the B.&O. but the whole riding and investing public that American steam engines and American railroads were here to stay. Even on the day Holbrook refers to the horse did not win because he was faster. And he was never to win again anywhere.

When William H. Brown began in 1869 to compile his history of early American locomotives, the first book of its kind to appear and an indication that railroads had come of age, he wrote to Cooper and asked him whether he had built his locomotive in 1829 or 1830. Peter put on his 'thinking cap,' and came out with the positive statement that the year was 1829. Brown took him at his word, and stated that though the great trial was in the summer of 1830—everyone agrees about that—Peter built and experimented with his engine in the previous year. W. S. Wright in his *Romance of American Railroads* goes one step farther and says that Cooper ran his engine in the summer of 1829, while Hungerford, the historian of the B.&O., avers that Cooper carried Philip E. Thomas, the president of the road, a 'few feet' in the fall of 1829.[18] The matter is, perhaps, of no great importance. But if Cooper built his engine in the summer of 1829, that is, before the English trials or even the importation of the *Stourbridge Lion,* it makes him much more farsighted than he was—or could have been. The demand for English locomotives and the problem of radii only arose in the fall of 1829.

Actually, all the evidence points the other way. The most conclusive is a bill for shipping a steam engine—undoubtedly the little bit of a brass engine that Cooper had had built on the rotary principle—from New York to Baltimore on June 15, 1830. There are also bills in the summer of 1830 for work done on the engine amounting to $171.92, of which the largest item is one of $109.60 for construction of a steam boiler. Moreover, in all the accounts that Cooper gives of building his locomotive, the story is presented as a continuous one, extending over a few weeks and ending with a trial in the summer of 1830. Finally, whenever Cooper mentions the subject, the assumption is that the railroad has been built the thirteen miles to Ellicott's Mills, a feat accomplished only on May 24, 1830.[19] Though Peter may have spoken to the directors in the late fall of 1829, he almost surely did not build his locomotive until the summer of 1830.

Peter worked on his rotary engine at the Mount Clare Railroad Shop, which he calls in one place a coachmaker's shop. He found there 'some old wheels,' with which he rigged up a platform, and then had a boiler made for him. Here arose his first difficulty: how to attach the engine to the boiler. 'I couldn't find any iron pipes. The fact is that there were none for sale in this country. So I took two muskets and broke off the wood part, and used the barrels for tubing to the boiler, using one on one side and the other on the other.' [20] Another difficulty, caused by the smallness of the boiler, was that no natural draught was sufficient to keep up steam. So the ingenious Peter rigged up a 'blowing apparatus, driven by a drum attached to one of the car wheels, over which passed a cord that in its turn worked a pulley on the shaft of the blower . . . I found that I had sufficient power to draw the shavings right through the boiler.' Increasing the speed was also a problem, and to solve it Peter placed a spurwheel on the crankshaft on the frame of the car, which he geared with a pinion to the forward road-wheels. To insure elimination of the problem of curves—attended to later by movable trucks—Peter used, besides a shorter wheelbase than English engines, the 'coned' wheels invented by Jonathan Wright, chief engineer of the B.&O.

By these devices Cooper finally assembled his makeshift engine, which, as he said, was 'about as temporary as any you ever saw.' Peter called it the *Tom Thumb*, and occasionally 'Teapot,' because it was so insignificant. 'The boiler of Mr. Cooper's engine,' said John H. B. Latrobe, lawyer for the B.&O. for many years, 'was not as large as the kitchen boiler attached to many a range in modern mansions. It was of about the same diameter, but not much more than half as high. It stood upright in the car, and was filled, above the furnace, which occupied the lower section, with vertical tubes.' 'It was difficult to imagine,' said Latrobe, after he had looked years later at the boiler found among old rubbish at Mount Clare, 'that it had ever generated steam enough to drive a coffee mill.' Ross Winans gave the height of the boiler as 5 or 6 feet and the diameter as 20 inches; the engine, he said, was a one-cylinder, one-horsepower affair with a cylinder $3\frac{1}{4}$ inches in diameter and a $14\frac{1}{4}$-inch stroke; the road wheels were $2\frac{1}{2}$ feet in diameter. The whole machine, wrote Latrobe, was 'not larger than the hand cars used by workmen to transfer themselves from place to place; and as the speaker now recalls its appearance, the only wonder is, that so apparently insignificant a contrivance should ever have been regarded as competent to the smallest results. But Mr. Cooper was wiser than many of the wisest around him. His engine could not have weighed a ton; but he saw in it a principle which the forty-ton engines of today [1868] have but served to develop and demonstrate.' [21]

When the engine was finished, Cooper invited the president and directors for a ride. There was a track in the car shop with a turntable, on which Cooper could run the engine back and forth. Here, one day, various people watched 'Mr. Cooper, as with his own hands he opened the throttle, admitted the steam into the cylinder and saw his crank-substitute operate successfully with a clacking noise, while the machine moved slowly forward, with some of the by-standers, who had stepped on it.' [22]

All was now ready for the trial run. But this was not to take place before a series of misfortunes had occurred that would have exhausted the patience of almost anyone but Peter Cooper. 'While I was away for a little while, after I had got it all ready to go on the road, somebody ran it backward and forward on this temporary track, and not understanding the operation, ran it so hard that they broke a piece out of one of the wheels. It was a good deal of trouble to get another; but I did get another, and put it on, got it into the railroad house, and got up steam overnight, ready to make a start in the morning. The president and two other gentlemen stepped on the locomotive, and we went out a little way and came back. I felt confident that the next day we would go on with it and have a fair trial.' But again someone ran it and broke off another piece of the wheel. 'I had another one made. I was standing by the man watching him as he was finishing it off, and thought we would soon be ready for a start; but as bad luck would have it, when he was putting the last touches upon it, it slipped out of his hand and broke another

piece off. Thought I, the fates are against me.' [23] It was at this
point that Peter gave up his crank-substitute. Even so, he had
one more cross to bear. Arriving on the day set for the trial, he
found to 'my grief and chagrin . . . that some scamp had been
there and chopped off the copper from the engine and carried it
off—doubtless to sell to some junk dealer! The copper pipes
that conveyed the steam to the piston were gone.' It took Peter a
week to repair the damage. [24]

One fine August day the great event finally came off. Peter
carried six men on the engine and 'thirty-six on the car which I
took in tow.' 'The curves were passed without difficulty,' said
Latrobe, who was aboard, 'at a speed of fifteen miles an hour;
the grades were ascended with comparative ease; the day was
fine, the company in the highest spirits, and some excited gentlemen of the party pulled out memorandum books, and when at
the highest speed, which was eighteen miles an hour, wrote their
names and some connected sentences to prove that even at great
velocity it was possible to do so.' [25] The only one for whom pleasure was mixed with painful labor, no less than anxiety, was
Peter himself, who was his own engineer. When he was about
to start, he set his safety valve at the amount of steam he wished
to carry, only to find that 'the steam blew off too fast. The safety
valves would discharge the steam so rapidly that I thought all
of the water would go out of the boiler. I could not conveniently
alter the safety valves, and I knew that the boiler was strong; so
I put my hand on them and held them down.' [26]

The reward was worth the suffering. Ascending an average
grade of eighteen feet to the mile, the little engine made the
passage to Ellicott's Mills in an hour and twelve minutes and
returned in fifty-seven minutes. Ross Winans and the editor of
the Baltimore *Gazette*, who were both on the trip, estimated the
coal and water used and the number of passengers and reported
that 'we did better than any English road did for four years after
that.' Peter could write proudly that he had done what he set
out to do. 'The result of that experiment was that the bonds of

the road were sold at once, and there was no longer any doubt as to the success of the line.' [27]

For those not convinced by this first trip, the little locomotive ran back and forth to Ellicott's Mills a score of times in the course of the summer, and in September carried a number of Baltimore gentlemen to a dinner at Donghoregan Manor to celebrate the ninety-third birthday of Charles Carroll. On one of these trips, on August 28th, when the *Tom Thumb* carried the president and directors to the celebration of the opening of the Oliver Viaduct—a massive granite structure of three arches over the Frederick Turnpike—someone made an exact calculation of the engine's performance. There were, this time, 26 men on the open car, which was pushed ahead of the engine, and the total load was between 4 and $4\frac{1}{2}$ tons. On the early miles the train did a mile in from $4\frac{1}{2}$ to $6\frac{5}{8}$ minutes, and on the last four, where the curves were bad and the grades steep, in from $6\frac{1}{2}$ to $7\frac{1}{2}$ minutes. Four minutes or so were lost changing tracks, and the total, not counting the four minutes, was 1 hour and 15 minutes.[28] Returning, with four more passengers and with four minutes lost taking on water, the train made it in 61 minutes. One mile was done in $3\frac{5}{8}$ minutes, and none took over 5 minutes. *Niles Weekly Register* for September 4th reported that Mr. Winans, 'who witnessed the performance of Mr. Cooper's engine, speaks very highly of it.' [29]

The fame of Cooper's locomotive did not go unchallenged. Not long after his first success the leading stage proprietors of Baltimore, Stockton & Stokes, decided that they had better explode Mr. Cooper's bubble before people began taking the new craze for steam seriously. So they resolved to meet the *Tom Thumb* one day on its return from Ellicott's Mills at the Relay House, eight miles out, where the coaches from Baltimore first changed horses. 'A gallant gray of great beauty and power was driven by them from town' and attached to a car on the second track of the double-tracked road that the company had started to build. On the arrival of the *Tom Thumb* the match was made, engine and horse were put side by side, and on the given signal started for Baltimore.

'Away went horse and engine,' said Mr. Latrobe, 'the snort of the one and the puff of the other keeping time and time. At first the gray had the best of it, for *his* steam would be applied to the greatest advantage on the instant, while the engine had to wait until the rotation of the wheels set the blower to work. The horse was perhaps a quarter of a mile ahead when the safety valve of the engine lifted and the thin blue vapor issuing from it showed an excess of steam. The blower whistled, the steam blew off in vapory clouds, the pace increased, the passengers shouted, the engine gained on the horse, soon it lapped him—the silk was plied—the race was neck and neck, nose and nose—then the engine passed the horse, and a great hurrah hailed the victory. But it was not repeated.' For Peter's ingenious blowing device failed him at a crucial moment. 'Just at this time, when the gray's master was about giving up, the band which drove the pulley which drove the blower, slipped from the drum, the safety valve ceased to scream, and the engine for want of breath began to wheeze and pant. In vain Mr. Cooper, who was his own engineman and fireman, lacerated his hands in attempting to replace the band upon the wheel: in vain he tried to urge the fire with light wood; the horse gained on the machine, and passed it; and although the band was presently replaced, and steam again did its best, the horse was too far ahead to be overtaken, and came in the winner of the race.' [30]

Peter Cooper did not like to be beaten and was even more averse to admitting that he had been. In the lengthy account of the *Tom Thumb* episode in the *Reminiscences* there is no mention of the event. When, years later, a representative of the press hinted at the tradition that the *Tom Thumb* had been beaten, Peter replied: 'Yes—no—not exactly; they tried a little race one day, but it didn't amount to anything. It was some time after our first experiment; we had been out several times, when the men, whose horses had been out there, came on the track to try paces with us, but it didn't amount to anything. It was rather funny, and the locomotive got out of gear.' [31] Cooper need not have been ashamed. As Latrobe wrote, 'the real victory was with Mr. Cooper. . . . He had held fast to the faith that was in him, and had demonstrated its truth beyond peradventure. All honor to his name.'

The Baltimore & Ohio directors were so convinced by what Mr. Cooper had done that, less than a year later, on June 1, 1831, they offered $4000 for the best locomotive delivered for trial in six months. This competition was won by the *York,* built by Phineas Davis, a watchmaker, at the Pennsylvania town of that name. It was followed in short order by the *Atlantic,* the first that could take the grades with ease, the *Traveller,* the *Arabian,* and the *Mercury.* By 1834 the Baltimore & Ohio had seven locomotives, thirty-four passenger cars, and one thousand freight cars; and the gaudily painted coaches with leathern braces that succeeded the market carts had given way to eight-wheeled cars with aisles in the middle. In the meantime other roads were also importing or building locomotives. In 1831, Horatio Allen, whom Cooper was to know as assistant engineer on the Croton water project, built the *Best Friend* and the *West Point* for the South Carolina Railroad at the West Point Foundry, and these were considered by many the real beginning of successful locomotive-building in America; in August of 1831 New York's first home-manufactured engine, the *DeWitt Clinton,* made its much-heralded appearance on the Mohawk & Hudson Railroad (between Albany and Schenectady) , the first link of the future New York Central.

Peter Cooper, however, took no part in all this, except perhaps, as Hungerford says, to give advice on the construction of the *Atlantic.* He had met an exciting challenge, proved his point, and inspirited a failing cause. He was content to return to making glue and iron and to leave locomotive-building to the professionals. Only once again, a half-century later, was his exploit with the *Tom Thumb* to come back forcibly to his memory. In 1880, when Baltimore celebrated its 150th anniversary, Cooper was sent a special invitation by the mayor, and had the president's private car *Maryland* put at his disposal at Jersey City. Baltimore, which had not forgotten that it was Peter Cooper who had dispelled the prejudice that had almost stopped the building of its road, was disposed to award him the credit of being the 'pioneer in the application of steam to American railways.' Peter accepted the invitation and was deeply moved by his reception. 'In the vast procession . . . Mr. Cooper and his little *Tom Thumb* locomotive [a model of the original] were the two most conspicuous objects, and received all the honours which could be paid by a quarter of a million of enthusiastic people.' [32]

Peter saved the railroad and the future of his land, but he could not turn his ironworks into an immediate success or ease the burden of tending to the affairs of the Canton Company. So, even while he was building his forge in 1831, he was contemplating selling out and returning home, where the glue factory demanded his attention. The Canton property he sold in 1832 to Amos Binney, Edmund Monroe, and Pliny Cutler of Boston. Though he had to take a portion of the price in $100 par stock, which was worth only $44 at the time, the stock went up, as Cooper wrote, 'like a balloon,' and he sold the last of it at $235 a share.[33] The ironworks, which he reserved at the time, he sold in 1847 to Horace Abbott, a Massachusetts blacksmith, who made a very good thing of them. It was at the Canton Iron Works in 1841—when Abbott was renting them from Cooper—that the first heavy engine forgings (as against castings) were made; and the Abbott Iron Works had cordial relations with Cooper's Trenton works all through the 'forties, 'fifties, and 'sixties, when Hewitt called on them to help him turn out mortar-beds for the Ordnance Bureau.[34] It sounded, in Professor Nevins' words, as if Cooper had 'landed, as usual, squarely on his feet.' And, indeed, he eventually did. Not, however, without much time, anguish, and loss, which Cooper characteristically omits from the story but which are as much part of his life as was his astonishing success.

Cooper's first thought had been to hold on to the Canton property and possibly accept a $400,000 loan offered him by a Mr. Jacobsen. But Cooper's Baltimore agent, Henry Fitz, urged Peter to let him go to Boston and try to sell it, and Peter was perfectly willing, desiring only to be relieved of all responsibility and to get out 'without much loss.' Fitz made a satisfactory arrangement, but it was binding only if the place was found to be healthy. When Munroe and his partners thought they discovered that the land bred 'bilious and intermittent fevers' they broke the agreement, and Peter had to renegotiate, giving a $35,000 bonus in stock to the purchasers and remaining in the company as a large stockholder. In 1842 he wrote to Fitz: 'I came out of the concern . . . with a loss as you well know of more than $20,000—a loss possibly more than I should have sustained by selling the whole property at auction for the most that it would have brought and have saved myself the years of harrowing anxiety and loss that I have since encountered.' Gideon Lee's partner, Shepard Knapp, confirmed Peter's statement: 'Mr. Cooper from my own knowledge has had more trouble and loss growing out of his connection with that company than I would endure to own the whole.'

Not the least of Peter's troubles were with the ironworks. In June, 1833, he leased them to Joel and Eleazer Johnson for ten years at a rental of $450 a year, but they did not stay their time and in the early 'forties Horace Abbott was occupying the works. In January, 1843, Abbott asked if he could renew his lease for fifteen years, and Peter was more than willing. But the deal fell through, even though Peter eventually offered Abbott

$4000 of the $6000 the latter requested to build a blast furnace to make pig iron. Alfred Munson, president of the Canton Company, refused to renew Abbott's lease of ore lands, and the suspicion arose that he intended to build his own furnace and compete with Abbott. Though Peter urged Abbott to forget about a blast furnace and to lease the forge, buying his pig iron for the present in the market, Abbott was wary of the whole proposition and stepped out. Peter then had the problem of collecting back rent from Abbott, of preserving his foundry from decay, and getting a new tenant. He took the rest of Abbott's rent in pig iron for his New York factory, and in September rented the ironworks to Thomas Smith, an employee of Abbott, and Henry Thompson for $450 a year for five years, less expenses for the repair of the machinery and the engine, from which all the copper and brass had been stolen. It was not until October, 1847, when Abbott bought the ironworks, that Peter's troubles were over.

Peter might have saved himself much annoyance had he written off small matters, but that was not his way, and it was perhaps why he kept the money he made. Not even the most minor problems about the several houses he owned in Baltimore or the little carpenter shop escaped his notice.[35] To climax the petty difficulties, Peter had a nasty misunderstanding with Henry Fitz, which illustrates both Peter's dogged insistence on the letter of the law in money matters and his essential decency.

Fitz had been working for Cooper off and on for ten years when suddenly he sat down and wrote to Cooper's friend George Dodge in Baltimore, and to Tiemann, William E. Dodge, and Knapp in New York, trying to persuade them, as Peter put it, 'that you had performed great and important services for me and had received little or nothing in return for such services.' Peter had made the fatal mistake in 1840 of lending money to Fitz which Fitz was unable to pay, and nothing so irks a man, as Peter ought to have known. In April, 1841, Cooper had extended the loan, but in January of 1842, when Fitz again begged him not to call for payment, Peter demurred. This produced Fitz's outburst, in which he raked up all his past wounds.

Peter would have done well, perhaps, to have dropped the whole matter, which amounted at the time to only $700. Instead he sat down and wrote Fitz a nice fatherly letter, in which he pointed out that he, Peter, had lost money at Canton and that, as he demonstrated in great detail,[36] he owed Fitz nothing. 'I name these facts not to add to the troubles that now oppress you but to show how strangely you have forgotten and misrepresent the merits of the services that passed between us. I regret exceedingly that you should be involved in such pecuniary embarrassments at your time of life. And instead of feeling a disposition to oppress or injure you I have endeavored to serve you whenever it was at all convenient.' Times were now very bad, and yet Cooper would help Fitz again: he would await Fitz's convenience on the principal and give Fitz $200 in addition if he gave Peter a deed on his property, to be returned in three years if principal and interest were paid.

Naturally, this arrangement when carried out merely involved Fitz in greater difficulties and increased his resentment, which exploded violently again half a dozen years later in a letter that Fitz, who was now unable to use his right arm, had George Dodge write for him. Peter was disturbed and perplexed, and could only assume that Fitz's mind had suffered. 'I cannot account for his ingratitude to me,' he wrote Dodge in April, 1848, 'as shown by the course that he has adopted on any other principle.' [37] He refused to see or communicate with Fitz, which drew down on him a half-pleading, half-scurrilous letter from another friend of Fitz, Lewis Andoun, who told Peter he'd relent if he could see Fitz screaming with agony. This attempt to dragoon Peter was futile, because it outraged his sense of justice. Eventually, when Andoun, Dodge, and Fitz had all apologized, Peter relented to the extent of writing to Fitz but made a point of disregarding the latter's reference to himself as an old, sick, suffering friend mistreated by a rich man. Fitz's letter was ungenerous and erroneous; Peter had inconvenienced himself greatly and had been very forbearing. No, he would not extend the loan to 1852: he would sell the property and Fitz could have the balance over the cost of the houses plus interest. Peter was through.[38]

And so ended Peter's Baltimore connections twenty years after their commencement, though he still held a few lots there in his name and some in the name of nieces and nephews. The last years, inglorious as they were, cannot, however, either dim or detract from the inspiring and even heroic tale of the earlier years, when Peter Cooper's faith, ingenuity, and doggedness helped inaugurate a new era.

Chapter 8

THE EDUCATION OF PETER COOPER

It WAS on November 7, 1828, at almost the exact moment when Peter plunged into his Baltimore venture, that Peter Cooper and Gideon Lee were elected respectively assistant alderman and alderman of the Twelfth Ward of New York City, which included the whole of the large and thinly populated part of Manhattan Island north of 14th Street. The concurrence of these two events was symbolic. The rest of Peter Cooper's life was to be divided almost equally between his ventures as an entrepreneur and his work as a public servant and philanthropist. The climax of his career came in the 'fifties when, on the one hand, he was helping to finance the great Atlantic Cable project and on the other was founding Cooper Union.

To Peter there was never any conflict between the two roles. His charities were not, as they were for some, guilt money paid to compensate for the dollars wrested from an exploited public. Producing, making money, and accumulating property were for the general good; public activity and philanthropy were simply other ways of serving the world. Some things needed to be done for which there was no direct monetary compensation; vicious men occasionally distorted God's purposes either as thieving politicians or as parasitic bankers, and they had to be stopped; some men through character defects or unfortunate circumstance required help to help themselves. It was man's duty to devote some of his efforts to such things as well as to business. Moreover, by doing so he was, just as much as when he provided for his family, serving his own self-interest and achieving happiness, 'the universal involuntary desire of all intelligent life.' The 'experience of a long life,' he told the notables of New York who came out to do him honor in 1874, 'enables me to say that money and efforts expended for the general good are a better-paying investment than any possible expenditure for personal gratification.' [1]

In 1828, when he began his career of public service, it is unlikely that Cooper had formulated these or any other theories. Still largely uneducated and not much given to thinking along any but practical lines, he made his debut in politics, the harbinger of so many things, for no well-planned reason. Successful young businessmen frequently served a term or two in the Common Council, and Peter happened to have in Gideon Lee a good friend able to win for him the nomination as assistant alderman in the ward for which Lee was to be alderman. His interest in philanthropy and education arose in the same casual manner. He needed no theory of the duty or pleasure of civic and charitable endeavor to propel him into these fields any more than he required a justification for making money. At thirty-seven Peter was still responding for the most part unconsciously to the forces in American life that accorded with his temper and upbringing. Early environment and family inheritance had marked him an individualist, an optimist, and a democrat. And a loving nature made it inevitable that he would respond to the humanitarianism that was as much a part of America's heritage as self-reliance and materialism. As Peter wrote years later, 'I have lived from my early recollection under a strong conviction that some way would open by which I should in some way become the instrument of good to my fellow men—the bare hope of which has stimulated my efforts and formed the brightest prospect of my life.'

In the next ten years, however, Peter was to come of age intellectually. He was to read, to talk to people, and to gain wider experience of the world. As a consequence he was gradually to become aware of ideas in a way that he never had been before, and to develop conscious theories about the world and his place in it as well as about specific problems in politics, economics, education, and philanthropy. It is no exaggeration to say that all of Peter Cooper's basic views stem from the 1830's. Chief Justice Charles P. Daly of the Court of Common Pleas, who loved him well, said at Cooper's death that he had known him for forty years and that what impressed him most was the 'uniformity' of his character: 'He was always the same man in mind, character and to me even in personal appearance.' [2] The same might be said of his ideas. This implied no stagnation. As Peter asserted truthfully at eighty-three, he didn't feel old because 'I have always given a friendly welcome to new ideas, and I have endeavored not to feel too old to learn.' Most of Peter's ideas were not put into writing until later life, and by then he had both acquired new ones and modified old ones to suit changed conditions. But the pattern of fundamental belief was woven in the first years of his public life.

Peter chose a good moment in American history to be educated. The dozen years following Jackson's first election in 1828 witnessed both a great democratic and equalitarian movement in politics and a renascence of humanitarian and religious feeling. Jefferson's efforts, in the first years of the century, to make the artisan and small farmer the center of the American economy, had by the 'twenties given way to compromise with the inheritors of Hamilton's system of favoring the commercial and banking classes. True, Federalism with its frank espousal of political control by the propertied classes was dead,[3] though to Jeffersonians like Peter Cooper, Hamilton's supposed remark, 'Man must have an idol'—an indication, they thought, that he intended to set up a monarchy—was still a living memory.[4] But in its place had arisen a scheme to give control to business through economic means: Henry Clay's 'American System,' which, evolving out of Hamilton's views, tied the government to the banks and to a protective tariff by encouragement of funded debt and internal improvements.

Clay and Nicholas Biddle, the head of the Second United States Bank, like Hamilton wanted power to rest with property, not, as Biddle said, with those who have 'no property to assess and no character to lose.' Workers and farmers in both east and west were becoming increasingly restive, as they saw their proud inheritance of independence melting away in factories and being crushed by the monopolistic power of the Second United States Bank. In Jackson and his able band of lieutenants the common man found leaders to fight for him, and for a decade the onward march of special privilege was checked. There was to be nothing like the Jacksonian movement again for four decades, until industrialism had entrenched itself firmly in power under cover of the Civil War. Then, when it was almost too late, farmers and workers rose once more and attempted, this time with little success, to reassert the principles of Jacksonian democracy. That they made the aged Peter Cooper, one of the few survivors from the days of Jackson, their titular leader was no mere chance.

The struggle of the 'thirties centered principally around the question of the re-chartering of the Second Bank of the United States, whose charter expired in 1836, and later around Van Buren's Sub-Treasury, set up as a repository for government funds in place of private banks. At first the fight was merely against the power of one particular corporation; but by the mid-'thirties it had developed into an attempt by hard-money men to curtail the right of all banks to issue currency. That this seemed merely a technical question blinded no one to its import. The able men with whom Jackson surrounded himself—Amos Kendall, whom Peter Cooper was later to know well in the telegraph business; Senator Thomas Hart Benton of Missouri; Martin Van Buren, the 'Red Fox of Kinderhook' (whence, a century before, had come Peter's ancestor); Silas Wright, the astute leader with

Van Buren of the Albany Regency; and others like Polk, Benjamin Butler, and Roger B. Taney—were well aware that they were carrying on a fundamental struggle for economic equality against entrenched privilege. As William M. Gouge, the Philadelphia editor and economist who was the chief theorist of the hard-money group, put it, the power to issue currency and to expand and contract credit not only caused depressions but created a moneyed aristocracy with a stranglehold over the economy. Both Benton and Samuel Clesson Allen, the leader of the Massachusetts farmers and workers, saw the issue as a straight duel between the productive people and the unproductive rich: bankers, in contrast to labor, which created wealth, were nonproducers, 'who render no equivalent to society for what they consume.' Other issues besides the currency and banking privileges also were drawn into the discussion in the course of the 'thirties—free trade, cheap western land, debt laws, education, technological unemployment, political corruption, hours of labor, the separation of church and state, and the issuing of special monopolistic charters—but the bank and currency issue was the heart of the fight, which before it was over had taken on the proportions of an economic and social revolution.[5]

Peter Cooper took no active part in the Jacksonian revolution either as politician or propagandist, and with parts of it, its agitation against a high tariff and for shorter hours of labor, he had no sympathy. Peter's high-tariff views, which as a manufacturer he came by naturally enough, later found their theoretical support in one of the chief opponents of Jacksonian democracy, Henry Carey. Low tariffs were not, however, at first basic to the Jacksonian revolution, and in the early years were not even a part of the radical creed. Northern radical Democrats like Van Buren and Silas Wright were for the tariff of 1824, were not opposed to that of 1828, the highest prior to the Civil War, and straddled on the 1832 tariff. Even Jackson was in the 'twenties a believer in the home-market idea, opposed chiefly by the shippers, who were mostly Federalists. Shorter hours for labor were a

later addition to the creed of the Jacksonians, who only reluctantly added the industrial proletariat to their ranks along with
farmers and small producers. Though Ben Butler and others
agitated for shorter hours and Van Buren tried to pass a ten-
hour bill for government workers in 1840, little was done in the
'thirties on this score.

With the basic Jacksonian creed Peter Cooper was in full
sympathy. As an artisan and manufacturer he was as suspicious
of banks, as worried by the factory system, and as opposed to the
Whig policy of chartering vast corporations as were the farmers.
And being at heart a Democrat he did not retreat from these positions when he became rich. He was therefore not only not driven
from the party in the 'thirties, as were other Jeffersonian industrialists, by its free-trade views, but rather confirmed in his allegiance. This allegiance in turn brought him contacts with
people and books that widened his outlook and supplied intellectual support for his inclinations.

He knew the New York leaders of the Jacksonian revolution,
Samuel Tilden, John A. Dix, and Martin Van Buren. When Van
Buren returned to New York in 1841, after his defeat for the
Presidency, Peter Cooper, charged by the Common Council to
pay him the proper respect, entertained him at his house.[6] The
two men were in perfect agreement about Van Buren's loudly
criticized Sub-Treasury scheme, which Cooper said caused his
defeat. He probably also knew Benton and Silas Wright, and he
read what they had to say and quoted from them copiously in his
later writings. Silas M. Stilwell, who started on his career as a
Jacksonian member of the State Assembly from 1829-33 and in
the 'sixties sponsored a legal-tender bill, was a friend of Cooper;
Albert Gallatin, Jefferson's now-aging Secretary of the Treasury,
who, though no Jacksonian and originally a supporter of the
Bank, later fought against its recharter and for hard money, was
an acquaintance of Cooper and the acknowledged source of his
views on finance. Peter perhaps read, too, some of the men who
influenced the Jacksonians: Adam Smith, enemy of mercantil-

ism; William Cobbett, whose *Paper Against Gold* was reprinted in New York in 1834; and William Gouge, whose *A Short History of Paper Money and Banking in the United States* Cooper's friend William Cullen Bryant serialized in his Jacksonian *Evening Post* in 1833.

Jackson himself Cooper met several times, being received at the White House 'with great kindness' when he went to Washington about John Campbell's pension. On one occasion he was present when Jackson, surrounded by a group of ladies who were listening to Senator Van Plank's ideas about fixing up the grounds of the White House, suddenly jumped up 'as though someone had stuck a pin in him' and said, ' "I came near forgetting to say I had a present today." ' A moment later the servants brought in a beautiful, lifesize white bust of Jackson, which the President proceeded to examine with a candle in each hand, and asked the company to express an opinion on what kind of marble it was made of. Senator Van Plank, much to everyone's amusement, put his fingers in his mouth and reported that the answer was sugar.[7]

By 1840, when Peter told a lawyer named Murray on a train to Philadelphia 'that money should be issued to represent only work actually done,' he had become master of the chief Jacksonian doctrines. His hatred of bank paper supported by an inadequate specie base, of bankers as monopolists tyrannizing over the people through their power of note issuance, and of commerce and banking as unproductive activities compared to farming, labor, and manufacturing, was second only to theirs. He shared with them, as well, other specific beliefs: in universal free education, which was a fundamental Locofoco[8] tenet; in cheap land in the West, opposed by Eastern industry that wanted to keep a plentiful supply of labor on hand and therefore not secured till the Homestead Act of 1862; and in the rigorous separation of church and state, which was sponsored by Jacksonians in opposition to the pressure of the clergy, mostly Whigs, for a state religion to keep labor in its place. He had also acquired the general Jacksonian interpretation of laissez-faire—taken over later by monopolists and big business as a slogan with a very different meaning—as a free society to be achieved if necessary by government interference to protect the rights of the small producer. The Jacksonians were not socialists but Jeffersonians trying in a new world of big business to protect the free enterprise of all the citizens. Beyond all this, Cooper was confirmed forever in his optimistic political faith: belief in self-reliance and the free, non-determined individual, in the integrity and perfectability of man and his ability to operate a democratic government, and in the right of men, guided by reason and conscience, to overthrow or change any government that interfered with their liberties.

These last ideas, fundamentals of the democratic creed since the days of the Founding Fathers, could hardly be traced directly to Peter's Jacksonian friends. Stemming from Locke and the Deists via Jefferson, the idea that men were reasonable and moral creatures who could be trusted to manage their own affairs and who were a court of appeal against the governments they had created, permeated the very air of the 'twenties and 'thirties. The same can be said of Peter's other most basic beliefs: in philanthropy as both a duty and the highest self-interest, and in education as a right and as a practical and moral necessity.

Part of the age's interest in education had a purely practical origin. In a time of great business and scientific advance it was inevitable that, sooner or later, mechanics and artisans would begin to agitate for more educational opportunity and that some manufacturers like Abbott Lawrence would see the desirability of more technological knowledge. Benjamin Franklin and others had urged scientific and utilitarian training a half-century before, but now the demand became irresistible. In 1825 Stephen Van Rensselaer founded the Rensselaer Polytechnic School in Troy, to teach—in words that Peter Cooper was later virtually to copy—the 'application of science to the common purposes of life.' The first school of its kind, it was, like the Lowell Institute of 1836, an inspiration for Cooper Union. Lyceums and mechanic's institutes, featuring lectures on science and other subjects, sprang up quickly everywhere after the founding of the first lyceum by Josiah Holbrook in 1826. By 1834 three thousand communities had lyceums.

The impulse toward education had, however, more profound sources that linked it to the great philanthropic and reformist movement sweeping across America in the 'thirties. The age of Jackson witnessed a great expansion in popular free education under the leadership of Henry Barnard and Horace Mann; it beheld, in the ten years between 1830 and 1840, the founding of sixty-seven colleges, including Oberlin, the first coeducational college, and various female colleges under the inspiration of Emma Willard, Catherine Beecher, and Mary Lyon; and it saw the birth of movements for temperance reform, for improvement in the lot of women, and for the founding of hospitals and other institutions for the care of the poor. Though Barnard and even Mann later appealed to businessmen to support such undertakings on the basis that they had a money value, making the residue of property more secure and more valuable,[9] the reformers themselves were moved chiefly by a set of philosophic beliefs born of deep spiritual forces.

Peter Cooper shared or acquired, in the 'thirties, the most basic of these beliefs. Above all he held, with most of the thinkers of the age,[10] that there existed a moral and beneficent order in the universe, which supports human society and which is apprehendable by man's reason and conscience. To Cooper, as to the romantics and transcendentalists, this itself suggested that the individual reached his highest potentialities and greatest happiness through being a social reformer. For by helping to realize a society 'whose individual members should participate in the best life,' a man was acting in accordance with God's law, was becoming a co-worker with God. The worthy self, as Emerson put it, was one which through devotion to all men's good was predisposed to social and cosmic harmony. Horace Mann's 'Be ashamed to die until you have won some victory for humanity' became the watchword of the enlightened spirits of the age. Moreover, work for education was the most useful sort of reforming zeal. Since evil was a mere accident in the scheme of things, it could be exorcized by knowledge. Man had reason and conscience and free will and therefore needed only the truth about himself and the universe to act in accordance with right and thus secure his own happinesss and the welfare of society. This implied, of course, that education would be more than technological instruction, the aim of the practical educators. It would be a thorough liberal education, giving its recipients a deep awareness of the essential nature of things. It would be truly scientific, as the age employed that much-abused word, in that it would show from a study of nature and society God's pattern of order and justice in the universe. If Peter Cooper's ideas for his Union have a breadth and sweep not usually associated with plans for vocational schools, it was because he acquired his ideas before the heavy hand of a narrow materialism had settled over the land.

However diffused the sources of Peter's general ideas about education, the first inspiration for Cooper Union itself came from a specific individual. In 1830 or 1831 Dr. David Rodgers, a fellow member of the Common Council, gave Peter 'an account,' as Peter wrote, 'of the great advantage he had derived from a short course of study in the Politechnique Institute [the *École Polytechnique*] of Paris.

'He stated that the consummate ability of the instructors with their perfect appliances for illustration had enabled him to obtain as much valuable information in a few months as he had done in as many years of previous study.

'What made the deepest impression on my mind was the fact

as stated by him that he found hundreds of young men from all parts of France living on a bare crust of bread in order to get the benefit of those lectures.

'I then thought how glad I should have been to have found such an institution in the City of New York when I was myself an apprentice at a mechanical trade.

'I then determined to do what I could to secure to the youth of my native city and country the benefits of such an institution . . . and throw its doors open at night so that the boys and girls of this city, who had no better opportunity than I had to enjoy means of information, would be enabled to improve and better their condition, fitting them for all the various and useful purposes of life.'

Not for nearly a quarter of a century was the cornerstone of Cooper Union to be laid. But from that day it was ever in Peter's mind as the goal of his efforts, and in 1839 he purchased the first piece of the property that was eventually to be the site of his beloved institute.

Peter's first impulse toward philanthropy in general can also be traced to an individual, his friend Joseph Curtis. Curtis, a gentle and farseeing humanitarian, is one of the most attractive and yet pathetic figures of his time. Too much interested in the poor and the weak to give wholehearted attention to business, he engaged with only partial success in half a dozen occupations, from selling hardware, manufacturing iron, and making jewel-cases to acting—in his impoverished later years—as Custom House inspector.[11] Peter may have dealt with Curtis' hardware firm when he was an apprentice, and certainly knew him in Hempstead. Curtis, who had married a Quaker girl from Hempstead, participated in the beach outing of 1813. The two men were friends all their lives, Peter regarding the older man (who was nine years his senior) 'as the best and truest pattern of a perfect man that it has ever fallen to my lot to know.' [12]

One would have to follow Curtis through his whole life, Peter said, to know his devotion to humanity, and one would have to do the same to track down the 'many ideas in regard to doing good' that Peter says Curtis gave him.[13] Curtis' influence was first strongly exerted in 1825 when he got Peter to visit the House of Refuge for vagrants and petty criminals every Sunday, talk to the inmates, and ply them with gifts of food. Curtis headed this institution, which he had gotten a group of friends to organize in the buildings of the old United States Arsenal at 23rd Street and Fifth Avenue. There he put into practice his idea, advanced for the time, that the object of a house of refuge was not to discipline delinquents but to rehabilitate them through trust and love. Peter was deeply impressed by the mutual confidence that he saw growing between director and inmates. The other trustees, mostly businessmen with little love of and no faith in Curtis' ways, were, however, shocked, and Peter soon learned a very different sort of lesson. It was bad enough, the trustees felt, to serve molasses beer and molasses cake to inmates carrying hods of bricks in the summer sun. But their wrath knew no bounds when Curtis refused to use the prescribed cat-o'-nine-tails on a runaway boy, and, according to Peter, they sent a committee to see that Curtis carried out the punishment. He refused—the other boys had brought back the runaway, trusting Curtis to do the right thing, and the delinquent had acknowledged his fault —, and handed in his keys to make room for an ex-schoolmaster who had practice in using the rod.[14]

From his earliest days in New York at the turn of the century, when he had gone over to Flatbush every Sunday to tutor a class of Negroes, using letters that he made out of pasteboard and held up before the class as his only means of instruction, Curtis had been interested in education; and his influence upon Peter in this field was undoubtedly felt when he sat with the latter as a trustee of the Public School Society from 1839 to 1853. Firmly believing that the best sort of education was that which taught people to help themselves, Curtis formed in his own business a 'little republic' of apprentices, whom he instructed and encouraged to make inventions of their own.

After Curtis' death his influence was continued through his daughter, Ann, who taught in the School of Design at Cooper Union until she was retired with a $400-a-year pension. Ann Curtis made the fallen women on Blackwell's Island her particular concern, and Cooper helped her and her associates in carrying on the Women's Home[15] for their care. Later he also contributed to the Working Women's Protective Union, which protected working women from being given starvation wages or no wages at all by their employers. The problems of women, treated like inferiors in the nineteenth century, always had a special interest for Peter Cooper.

Between such specific influences as Curtis and the general atmosphere of the age impelling Cooper toward good works, was his religion. For Jefferson and many others of the Founding Fathers, reason, the Constitution, and the law of nature had been sufficient guides to conduct. But not for the early nineteenth century, which, under the influence of a great religious revival in both England and America, had returned to a belief in the prime necessity of faith in God as the basis of action. Though opposed to a state church, most of the Jacksonian radicals were nevertheless religious men for whom Christianity offered the prime sanction for reform. Peter Cooper, brought up as a believer, was inevitably drawn early in his life into the search for a satisfactory religious belief. This he found, midway through the 'thirties, in Unitarianism.

One of the two men to whom Cooper acknowledges indebtedness for his religious beliefs was Elias Hicks, a Foxite Quaker. Born in 1748 in Hempstead, Hicks became one of the two or three most effective Quaker preachers, and was admired in his old age by the very youthful Walt Whitman. A pleader all his life for the rights of the underprivileged, he scorned outward authority and historical revelation and placed salvation within the soul of man. He was accused by many in his later years of being a Unitarian, and, though the accusation was unjust, his radicalism precipitated a Quaker separation in 1827.

The other religious influence was William Ellery Channing, the great Unitarian opponent of revelation and original sin, who converted so many by his eloquence. Channing's first sermon in New York was in 1819, two years before the Unitarians were given, in the teeth of Episcopalian and Presbyterian opposition, a site for a church by the College of Physicians and Surgeons. He spoke there often afterward, his most famous sermon being on December 7, 1826, at the dedication of Dr. Orville Dewey's Second Unitarian Church at Prince and Mercer Streets.[16] On one of these occasions Peter Cooper heard him, and the burden of fears and doubts that had intermittently oppressed him since he began to question his father's faith was immediately lifted. 'I well recollect how he unveiled the almighty power and beauty of goodness and showed me that *God is love* all-embracing and love eternal—and that it was from this fountain of ever flowing light and life that we derived a being formed in the likeness and image of our creator.'

Peter did not immediately join any church. It was not until 1838 that he became a member of Dr. Dewey's congregation, and then almost by chance. In 1837 the Mercer Street Church burned down and services were held for a year or two in Stuyvesant Hall, before the New Church of the Messiah was built on Broadway. Cooper and Curtis were strolling down Broadway one Sunday as the congregation was entering the hall. ' "Let us go in here, and see what *this* is," ' Dr. Dewey quotes one of them as saying. 'When they came out, as they both told me, they said to one another, "This is the place for us." And they immediately connected themselves with the Congregation, to be among its most valued members.' When the new church was finished Cooper bought a pew (No. 36) for $400, and for fifteen years or more was a faithful attendant at Dr. Dewey's services.[17] Around 1855 he moved to Dr. Bellows' All Souls' Church at

Fourth Avenue and 20th Street, which was closer to his new Lexington Avenue home. But he remained, along with Bryant, near whom he had a pew, a Unitarian all his life.

The choice of faiths was an appropriate, nearly an inevitable one. Indeed, one wonders here, as one so often does in dealing with a man's life, whether what he learned as a Unitarian could possibly be as important as the forces that made him one in the first place. Deeply religious by nature, Cooper could not possibly have been a Calvinist, a Roman Catholic, or an Episcopalian. He was too kindly and optimistic for the first, having no trace of what we call today a tragic sense of life; and he was too individualistically opposed to an authoritarian clergy for the other two. On the other hand, he was neither sophisticated nor mystic enough for Emerson's brand of transcendentalism, of which he had probably not heard in the 'thirties. His poetic tastes no less than his philosophic beliefs were, like those of so many Americans, anchored in the eighteenth century. Around 1830 he bought from a Methodist clergyman a copy of Pope's *Essay on Man* for ninepence, and, as he said a half-century later, 'it has been a treasure to me ever since.' [18] He quotes from it almost *ad nauseum,* and family tradition asserts that at ninety he recited the whole *Essay* by heart, a fearful ordeal for the listeners. Together with Young's *Night Thoughts* and some of Dryden this poem composed nearly the whole of Cooper's visible poetic knowledge. The thoughts he derived from the eighteenth-century poets and from the works of America's Founding Fathers were, along with strange gleanings from the Bible, the staples of Peter's philosophic equipment.

An attempt to reconcile religion and reason, Unitarianism came closest of all the early-nineteenth-century faiths to answering Cooper's emotional and intellectual needs, and where it did not he was always free to strike out for himself, as he inevitably would and did. The somewhat vague and glittering generalities of the Unitarian creed satisfied Peter emotionally, without, as a more sharply edged religion might have, stirring him to self-questionings or impossible longings. They assured him that the universe was fundamentally good, that the love and hope and desire to do good that animated him had their origin and support in the nature of things, and that all men—not just a chosen few—could be saved through love and the practice of the good life. They denied the necessity for priestly intercessors in the search for truth, which could be pursued through scientific reason and the imitation of Jesus' example. By advocating reform, not defense of the current social order, they freed Peter to fulfill his tasks in the world with confidence and ease. "Love and duty I have ever found to be the 'pass words' of all that is true and noble in life," Cooper once said with the childlike fervor that touched everyone who heard him, "and when they are separated the fires on the family altar die out, and life loses all its charms, never to be compensated by the false jewels which are often worn in the public gaze." If such sentiments suggest no profound contemplation of reality, they provide a good working basis for the highly useful work that Peter Cooper was to do in the world.

Chapter 9

CITIZEN OF NEW YORK

THE Common Council on which Peter took his seat in the winter of 1828-9 was in a transition stage. By the Constitution of 1823 and a law of 1826, property qualifications for Charter elections had been abolished, making the Council a democratic body, subject to control by the already dominant Tammany Hall. In 1828 nominees were still chosen, however, by ward committees of respectable citizens, so that the Council was made up of business and professional men who served without compensation, rather than of the professional politicians of a decade or more later. Peter Cooper, who claimed in 1879 that he remembered distinctly all but one of his colleagues, lists some dozen or more of the twenty-eight, all of whom were bankers or businessmen, except General Henry Arcularius, and Samuel Stevens, son of the Revolutionary general, who was a wealthy lawyer. Gideon Lee and David Bryson were tanners; John Lozier was head of the Manhattan Water Works; John R. Peter owned a hotel at Wall and Pearl Streets; Thomas Jeremiah was president of the Bowery Savings Bank; Benjamin M. Brown was a shipbuilder; James N. Wells was a wealthy carpenter; William S. Coe was a banker; and William Seaman, William W. Mott, and John Yates Cebra were merchants.[1]

This collection of respectable citizens met as one body in a large room, aldermen and assistant aldermen sitting facing one another in opposite semicircles separated by the mayor at one end and the clerk and recorder, Richard Riker, at the other. At these meetings, held once a week and in the evening to permit the members to attend to their private concerns, aldermen and assistant aldermen had an equal voice and worked jointly. They were a powerful body, much more powerful than any common councils have been since. They, not the people, elected the mayor. They could make assessments, order improvements, and dispose of public property at will, giving no account of expenditures. They established ferries, laid out streets, created markets, inspected food, erected prisons and almshouses, granted liquor licenses, and appointed the few executive officers like the police captain. They also sat as justices of the peace and presided with the mayor at the trial of criminals, which meant that they were often trying offenses against laws that they had themselves made.

Such a system was subject to abuses even when run by the most exemplary citizens, and though corruption did not perhaps become a truly fine art until a generation later, there was much chicanery and even occasional large-scale robbery in the 'twenties. Contracts were given to relatives; city land was sold to cover up squandering and bought in for a rise by insiders; bank charters and franchises were given with little compensation to the city; contractors put up buildings and then cheated the laborers out of their pay. As a consequence there occurred, during Cooper's years on the Council, one of the waves of reform agitation that have periodically swept over the city. A reluctant Tammany was forced to abolish imprisonment for debt, to sponsor a bill to insure a laborer's pay, and to vote for a tax of four-eightieths of one per cent on real estate to run public schools, thus—though the amount was only $14,000 a year—establishing the principle of tax-supported education for the city. In 1831 the city voted itself a new charter, the first of many vain attempts to prevent swindling by taking legal power from those who were abusing it. The new charter gave the mayor, now to be elected by the people, veto power over the actions of the Common Council, which had formerly appointed him; the two chambers of the Council were divided so that one could check on the other; and executive departments, appointed by the Council, were set up to administer city affairs.

Peter Cooper sat in the Common Council for two and a half years, being reelected in 1829 and remaining in his seat, because of the change in the election law, until May of 1831. His record is disappointing to anyone expecting to find in him a great leader of liberalism and reform. He was elected as a Tammany Democrat in a ward with a scattered population in 1825 of only 7938 people and 409 electors,[2] and he voted consistently as a regular party man. Where Tammany was forced to be liberal—on the school-tax issue, for example—Cooper voted with them. But he also voted with them against applying to the legislature to alter the charter of the city to permit the people to elect the mayor.[3] And he was passively a party to the somewhat mysterious proceedings by which the hardware merchant, Walter Bowne, was reelected mayor in January, 1830, in spite of the fact that the opposition produced affidavits from half the members stating that they had voted for Thomas R. Smith.[4] Only once—though the action was prophetic—did he vote against Tammany on a social issue: he did not agree with the majority that helping the Union Emigrant Society would but induce paupers to stay in the city.

Moreover, Peter seemed happily ignorant of what was going on around him. Fifty years later he told a *World* reporter that when he was assistant alderman, and for a decade afterward, councilmen were uniformly respectable and intelligent because they got no salaries and had the job thrust on them. He then astonishingly added that in the whole ten-year period from 1830 to 1840, 'he recalls but one instance in which a member proved unfaithful to his trust. This man attempted to push a measure from which he would derive personal benefit, although but to an insignificant extent. The measure was voted down, and the

Alderman, despite the fact that no suspicion was directed against him except implicitly, vacated his seat at the first decent opportunity and until his death, years afterwards, always hung his head when he appeared upon the streets.' [5] The scandals over the chartering of the Seventh Ward Bank, which involved Cooper's friend James R. Whiting, let alone the Harlem Railroad franchise bribery affair, ought to have been enough to silence Peter. But the only scandal that he could recollect was the practice of the aldermen, who often worked from five to midnight, of stealing up to a large room above the aldermanic chamber and eating oysters and bread against the protests of outraged taxpayers. When the protests got too loud, the councilmen were 'forced to vote in effect that in an official capacity they never dreamed of a stomach,' and to forbid the lunching 'alleged to be carried on within these walls contrary to the self-evident principles of economy and good government.'

The truth is that Peter Cooper in 1830 was excessively naive politically. All his life he exhibited a strange duality: shrewd and careful in his business, he was often as trusting and optimistic as a baby when dealing with politicians, inventors, or beggars. And in 1830 he had had no experience to temper his wide-eyed confidence. Not until the early 'fifties, when the Tammany stench became overpowering, did he wake up to the need of local political reform. In national affairs his education as a Jacksonian radical was just beginning in 1830.

The party leaders must have realized, however, that Peter Cooper, though naive, would be no party tool. So they carefully excluded him from important policy-making committees, giving him instead positions on committees with practical non-political tasks to perform: the regular committees on Arts and Sciences, and on Lands and Places, and the special committees on Water and on Blackwell's Island and Bellevue. Most of the earnest, effective work he did on these committees has no great interest, involving such matters as installing pumps and wells on different blocks, the purchase of a new map of New York, the removal of oyster stands around the Park and the Battery, the setting-up of a machine to inspect flour. Or sometimes—as with the attempts to get stone wharves for the city, to purchase Great Barn Island for an almshouse, to enlarge Blackwell's Island prison to separate the 'vicious' from the 'respectable' poor—the work was important but the results inconclusive. Only one minor job did Peter plan and see through to a finish himself: the installation of a lighted clock in the cupola of City Hall. Peter's proposal, made on November 16, 1829, involved 'raising up' what was then called the pepperbox top on the cupola and putting in an octagonal section fitted to receive a clock with four dials. The Council voted Peter $600 to have the work done, and later $650 to make the clock strike, $1500 for a bell, and $1000 for dials of glass in copper frames. In February, 1831, the clock was in operation.[6]

Peter's great work as a member of the Common Council was his contribution to securing for New York its modern water supply. This work he began in his two terms as an assistant alderman between 1829 and 1831, and concluded when he was elected as an alderman for one year in the spring of 1840, his only other period of service on the Council. During his year as alderman he helped keep public education free from religious influence, his other most notable achievement as a city politician.

The city's water, still supplied by the Manhattan Company's wells and by springs, had been dangerously impure for a generation; by the 'twenties even sentimentalists were beginning to realize that the pleasant meetings of girls and their beaux around the town pumps were a poor substitute for pure water. In 1830 the head of the Manhattan Company admitted to Peter Cooper (who received the information with surprisingly little indignation) that the reason the water tasted brackish that summer was because, the season being dry and the wells having given out, 'he had been giving the people surface water pumped from the river.'[7] In warm weather the water became 'offensive in a few hours,' and was impure at all times, partly, it was thought, because of graveyard seepage and partly because of the excrement that crept into the sandbank under the city to such an extent as to be 'assumed to be incredible . . . were it not susceptible of demonstration.'[8] Reasonably well-to-do citizens imported water from the country. Of even impure water there was not enough for fire protection, especially with the primitive apparatus in use. When the alarm bell back of City Hall started booming and the lantern pointed toward the fire for those who could see it, all good citizens threw the leathern buckets with which each house was provided into the street and the Common Council marched out bearing wands as insignia of authority. But the only method of fighting fires was to pass the buckets from hand to hand between the nearest pump and the twenty-man hand-engines which pumped the water onto the fire. By the late 'twenties the famous gangs of Bowery Boys had added their help, but pumping water by hand from the river was an exhausting and unsatisfactory arrangement.

Though since 1815 there had been dozens of committees formed in the Common Council on the water situation, public apathy and rivalry between different plans and between the city and private companies had thwarted all of their schemes. But in 1828 a $600,000 fire loss finally moved the city to action. In March, 1829, Alderman Samuel Stevens got through the Council a proposal to build a large reservoir at 13th Street and the Bowery, equipped with a steam pump and supplying water through iron pipes leading to city hydrants, a scheme that impressed the public with what could be done. And on December 14th the Council gave permission and $200 to the Fire and Water Committee to visit Croton and other possible sources of water in company with an engineer.[9] The committee, of which Peter Cooper was a prominent member, first went to Philadelphia to observe the reservoir that collected water from the Schuylkill River, and then visited the Croton River. There they constructed a low dam of planks to see how much water was running at the time. 'It was a very dry season of the year,' Peter wrote, 'when all the streams of the region were very low, and, as I expected, the quantity was so small that I began to despair of our getting a supply from that quarter.'

So the committee, or Peter alone, took a look at the Bronx River, which was found even more inadequate. Then Peter extended his researches to northern New Jersey, and hit upon a plan of his own to use the water from Paterson Falls on the Passaic River. Even before he was a member of the Council—in June, 1828—he had invented what he considered an improvement on the method of conveying water in aqueducts across and upon the beds of rivers. His scheme included the use of cylinders that revolved longitudinally and could therefore be put together joint-by-joint in a furrow plowed in the river to avoid the anchors of ships.[10] Peter offered this idea to the Common Council for conveying the water of the Passaic River from above Paterson across the North River or—if they preferred—across the Harlem River from Croton. That such a scheme was feasible and desirable we now know, and Peter himself saw it used later in taking water across the Hackensack River. Had it been adopted in bringing water from Croton, Peter said, it would have avoided the obstruction to navigation of High Bridge, and 'what is of greater importance, our water supply would have been free from the dangerous possibility of being blown up by a single keg of powder, or a ball of dynamite no larger than one can carry in his pocket.'[11]

Such rare foresight was too revolutionary for the committee in 1830. So, for that matter, was the scheme of using Croton, which would have necessitated the construction of a huge dam. Peter's committee was satisfied merely to lay before the Council all the possible plans—to use the Croton River, Rye Pond, and the Bronx River; the Passaic River, as Peter wished; or merely the wells of Manhattan. It was left to a new committee to bring in, in December, 1831, the first concrete recommendation. Discarding the scheme of wells as inadequate and the Croton project as too expensive, they concluded that the waters of the Bronx River would supply a population of 450,000, which seemed in 1831, when New York had about 200,000 inhabitants, a great many people. 'No individual after examining the subject,' reported the committee, 'will . . . doubt the efficiency of the supply of the Bronx . . . the water of the Croton will not for centuries ever be required.' [12] Fortunately for Peter's temper, he was no longer a member of the Common Council when this report came in. Nor did he have anything to do with the whole water project again for nine years, until it was within two years of completion. The credit for drawing up plans, submitting them to the people, and carrying out the project belongs to a state-sponsored commission and not to the Common Council.[13]

What happened, briefly, after the 1831 report was that the State Legislature, sensibly doubting the wisdom of the Bronx River plan, sent out a number of engineers of its own, who all agreed that the Croton project was the only feasible one. In April, 1835, this project was submitted to the people, who voted 17,330 to 5963 to borrow $4,250,000 to build a dam at Croton and a closed aqueduct to bring the water to a reservoir on Murray Hill. The work began immediately, under the supervision of a state commission headed by Stephen Allen. Despite opposition by Westchester landowners and occasional strikes, this commission had by the spring of 1840 brought Croton water to the Harlem; they had started constructing High Bridge in accordance with the recommendation of the chief engineer, John B. Jervis, whose scheme had been preferred to Cooper's idea of a tunnel under the river; and they were laying pipes to the reservoir on Murray Hill at 42nd Street and Fifth Avenue.[14]

In the meantime the city began to take measures of its own for the reception of the water. But by the spring of 1840, a year after the work had been started, only 35 of the 160 to 165 miles of pipe needed south of Murray Hill had been put down. Moreover, a sharp controversy had arisen with the new state commissioners, appointed in March by the recently elected Whig government at Albany, the latter claiming that it was their and not the city's job to lay these pipes. It was at this juncture that Peter Cooper came back into the picture, having been chosen alderman for the Sixteenth Ward in the April, 1840, elections. On May 18th, six days after he was sworn in, he offered a resolution to set up a special joint committee of the Common Council to manage the Croton Aqueduct, and was immediately made chairman of this committee.[15] For the next two years, until New York's fountains were spouting with the clean waters of the distant mountains, it was Peter Cooper's hand that chiefly guided the work of laying the pipe and of winning for the city control of its own water supply.

On June 29th Peter Cooper's committee presented a masterly report to the Common Council. Peter had gone with three others to Philadelphia to get the latest information on the laying of pipes from a Mr. Graff, the agent of that city's waterworks, and had discovered that the greatest error came from 'attempting to pass the water through mains and pipes of too small a size,' friction being greater than expected. He had found that if good pipe was correctly laid in New York and the water sold at Philadelphia rates, so that it cost the citizen only five dollars a year, the system would pay for itself even if only half of the estimated revenue was forthcoming. The committee urged haste in making contracts for pipes, since at the present rate not half the city would be covered by the time the aqueduct was finished. It also suggested that records be kept in order to avoid the necessity of digging up the streets to see what was there, a request that few modern New Yorkers will believe was acted on.[16]

After delaying a month, the Council acted favorably on the committee's petition. The Croton Aqueduct Department was organized, composed of the committee, a commissioner, and a water purveyor, and there was a rush of activity. $249,176.64 was spent on pipes in 1840, as against $68,474.44 in 1839.[17] But Cooper, who continued to be impressed by the 'importance of urging this work to a rapid completion,' was having his troubles. As soon as advertisement was made for pipes every iron founder in the city, of course, put in a bid, but at such prices that 'I had about concluded that the undertaking would involve an exorbitant outlay.' Then came a bid from a Philadelphia founder, Stephen Colwell, who later became one of Peter's close friends, offering to do the work for one-quarter to one-third less than would anyone else, which meant a saving of around $200,000 on the approximately $1,000,000 of pipe needed. Colwell could do this because he cast his pipes direct from the blast furnace and thus saved the cost of transporting to another furnace and remelting.

Immediately there was an outcry from the New York founders. Colwell was a 'foreigner,' and besides, casting direct from the furnace was inferior to remelting in a cupola furnace. The help of the state commissioners was elicited, and they promptly reasserted their claims to the right of laying the pipe, denouncing the city as incompetent to do the job. The excitement ran so high that Peter feared he would be unable to carry his point. But he 'had the good fortune at that time' to get support for his views from the report of a government committee 'sent to Europe to ascertain the best means for getting great strength of iron for cannon.' The committee stated that Swedish iron, cast direct from the furnace, was less brittle, freer from dross, and of more even texture and uniform thickness. Backed by this eminent authority, Cooper hit back at his enemies in March, 1841, in a fifty-seven-page report to the Common Council. He was, he said, 'surprised and astonished at the pretensions of the Water Commissioners who claim for themselves the power to take from the people of this city all control over the laying down of water pipes,' and urged the Council to fight the state's efforts to give the commissioners, because they were of the 'right party,' a power to which they had no claim. Perhaps the commissioners were sincere, but one of their number, to whom the city had already paid an exorbitant price for pipe, was now applying for the contract to lay the large mains. Far from being incompetent, the Aqueduct Department had cut costs as much as thirty per cent where it had been given a free hand.[18] The Council, solidly backing Cooper, authorized the arrangement with Colwell.

Peter supervised the whole job of pipe-laying himself. 'I made it my business, as fast as the pipes began to arrive,' he wrote later, 'to be very particular that a process of testing the strength of each pipe should be made, to be sure that it was perfect. This was done by closing the ends of each pipe, and then bringing hydraulic pressure to bear, equal to three hundred pounds to every square inch: thus no weak or imperfect pipe was allowed to pass into use.' [19] Peter also concerned himself with the difficult problem of getting hydrants that could be conveniently drained of water 'so that when wanted they would not be found frozen in winter.' Nothing was beyond his prying attention. When there was difficulty about finishing High Bridge on time, he tried once more to induce the Common Council to accept his tunneling plan of 1828. Temporary pipes in the form of an inverted siphon, he told the Council in March, 1841, could be sunk in the river below navigation by means of a scow built especially to carry boiler iron; the upturned ends of the pipes, which should be long enough to be above water, could be attached to the pipes on the temporary bridge.[20]

Though no longer an active politician after May, 1841, Peter was consulted at every move by those engaged in fighting the commissioners in the Legislature. On May 16th Solamen Townsend wrote him frantically from Albany that he was ready to vote against the whole Croton bill, since it gave such outrageous powers to the commissioners, but was afraid New Yorkers would be angry unless the city could raise the money itself. Cooper's answer was unflinching: 'In the event of the bill passing in accordance with the wishes of the Water Commissioners it will be the signal for an entire suspension of the work—I think the Legislature will hesitate before they make such a course absolutely necessary in defense of the homes and interests of our city.' By June the danger was over, and R. M. Stratton wrote Cooper jubilantly that the proposed new laws were satisfactory and would, he hoped, 'end that crusade that both you and I have so sedulously laboured to put an end to.' The bill that finally passed on July 26th confirmed entirely the city's contention, requiring merely that the city take over contracts already made by the commission.[21]

Cooper's final contribution to the Croton project was a long and earnest letter to Alderman Davies, who had sent him in July, 1842, his proposed law for the organization of a department to manage the distribution of Croton water. Handling the city's vast new water supply, Peter wrote, would be an important trust requiring all the safeguards 'that it is possible for the Corporation to throw around it. . . . It appears to me that the corporate authorities of our city should approach the subject of the distribution of the Croton water as the Fathers of our City—bound by everything that should stimulate honorable men to act independent of every selfish personal or party consideration.' Since all property was bound for payment of the debt, it 'becomes a question of the most absorbing interest to determine how' most to benefit those who must bear the taxes. Everyone ought to be induced to use the water, and everyone who benefited from it ought to be taxed.[22] In the course of a long life Peter was to address many such letters of practical advice and moral exhortation to politicians and others. His faith in the people, if only their leaders could be made honest, was never seriously shaken.

His practical connection with New York's water supply was now finished, and he refused, because of pressure of business, to sit on the new Croton Board. But he had seen the construction job through. On June 27, 1842, the water was let into the receiving reservoir in the future Central Park and, on July 4th, into the 42nd Street distributing reservoir. New Yorkers of all descriptions traveled on foot, by horse, in carriages, and on trains to Yorkville to drink a tumbler of the 'sweet, soft, clear water' which ex-Mayor Philip Hone described as forming two 'limpid, placid Mediterranean Seas' of wholesome temperance

· (149) ·

beverage, well calculated to cool the palates and quench the thirst of New Yorkers.[23] The huge project, which had saddled the city with a $12,000,000 debt, was finished, and on October 14th the event was celebrated in characteristic New York fashion with a five-mile procession and noisy jubilation. Peter Cooper could well feel, as he looked at the spouting fountains in City Hall Park and at Union Square, that he had begun to pay some of the debt he felt he owed to his native city.

Never really able to drop any subject that had once interested him, Peter continued for the rest of his life to bombard the Common Council and others with ingenious schemes for improving New York's water supply, especially as it related to fires. In 1854 he suggested that a thirty-foot-high boiler-iron tank be placed on the top of the reservoir on Murray Hill and kept full by a small steam engine; the City Hall should be raised a story and covered with an iron tank holding ten feet of water, the 'outside of this tank to be made to represent a cornice around the building'; in every street there should be a cart with a three-hundred-foot hose, which could be rushed to the nearest hydrant in case of fire, and thus save the time and health of the young men who had to go to fires. In 1865 he was one of those who helped introduce steam fire-engines and a paid fire-fighting force in the teeth of longstanding opposition from the strongly entrenched groups of volunteer fire fighters. Even in his eighties he was still speculating on how to get enough water to supply all commercial firms, which too often used methods of getting power that increased the danger of fire. The Croton dam and reservoir could, he said, be greatly enlarged to include the water from surrounding lakes and streams. When, in 1882, the city contemplated such a project at an expense of $15,000,000, to take five to eight years, Peter averred that in the meantime the city might burn down, and offered a scheme of his own, which could go into effect immediately and would cost only about two million dollars. This was to build a dam enclosing ten to fifteen acres in Central Park on a level with the Harlem flats, one assumes where the lake now is at 108th Street. This area could be kept full of water for emergency use by means of a steam pump drawing water out of the ground. A pipe running down the center of the city would then supply fire engines with a column of water two hundred feet high. When the water was not wanted for fires—Peter never forgot anything—it could be used for manufacturing purposes, and, on its way to the rivers, would also clean the streets.[24]

Getting enough water was not, Peter realized, the whole problem in fighting fires, and even while he was working on the Croton project in the Common Council he was contemplating an ingenious scheme to cut fire losses through a more efficient use of the police. In 1840 New York had no day police at all. At night it was guarded by the watch, which served under a captain of the watch for four hours a night at so much an hour, and whose only uniforms were varnished firemen's hats, from which the front helmet-piece had been removed. It was the duty of the watch to call the hours of the night and give fire alarms by crying out the street, ringing a bell, and hanging a lantern on a pole to indicate the site. Though some improvement in police efficiency had been made in recent years by enlarging the watch, setting penalties for neglect, and creating constables appointed by the mayor for emergencies, the police force was hopelessly inadequate to control either theft or fire. Peter Cooper decided that the chief trouble was that the watch had insufficient incentive to do its job, and on December 16, 1840, read to the Common Council a long communication containing a plan which he was convinced would remedy the difficulty.[25]

The loss and damage from fire were to be averaged for forty or fifty years and the pay of the watch was to be docked at a rate of two shillings a day at the end of any year that fire losses exceeded the average. Peter also hoped that the insurance companies would give the watch a percentage of the saving if losses fell below the average. In order to frighten incendiaries, the watch was to be given the right to arrest loiterers, and, under Peter's scheme, it would be their *'immediate interest* as well as their *duty* to do so.' Finally, to insure a good police force, Peter wanted to make the captain of the watch take an oath and give security in the sum of $5000 that he would choose watchmen only on the basis of fitness and not allow 'the *political* or *religious* opinions of any man to be called in question.' [26]

This curious scheme, with its mixture of businesslike realism and political naivete, fell on completely deaf ears, and was laid permanently on the table by the Common Council. Peter was by no means discouraged, however, and the events of the next few years but increased his sense of the need for some such plan as his, and fortified his belief in the efficacy of his particular scheme. In February, 1841, Peter served on a committee of the Council to inquire into the expediency of abolishing the watch and creating a corps of twelve hundred policemen to be trained as officers, watchmen, firemen, and lamplighters.[27] Nothing came of this, but in 1844 the State Legislature finally created a regular day and night police force of eight hundred men under a chief of police nominated by the Common Council and appointed by the mayor. When, after a year of wrangling,[28] this force came into being under Mayor William F. Havemeyer, all Peter's fears of a 'political' police seemed about to be realized, and he wrote to the Common Council warning of the danger. 'I saw at once,' Peter wrote later, 'that it would not be long before the most corrupt party would bid the highest for the spoils of office—I well remember that I became horrified with the prospect of a Political Police—I had just before that been reading an account of the Police or janissaries of Tripoli—where they had become such an unbearable scourge to the people that there seemed no other relief but to do as they did and kill the whole body of men.' Fortunately, says Peter, his friend Mayor Havemeyer was an honest man, and this staved off the difficulty for a while. He assured Peter that he was so impressed with his responsibility that he intended to appoint a political opponent as head of the police department, so that the two might check up on one another. His appointee, George W. Matsell, long outlasted the mayor, however, and in a few years was on the payroll of Madame Restelle, the notorious abortionist. Particularly under the unscrupulous Fernando Wood were Peter's fears realized. The people, after attempting other remedies, finally resorted in 1857 to a state police force.

Peter Cooper thought his old plan was better, and in 1854 presented it in refurbished form as a substitute.[29] Punishment was now wisely changed to reward, the two shillings a day being paid as a bonus for reducing fire losses below a ten-year average rather than deducting them for failure to maintain the average; in place of the captain of the watch or the mayor, Peter proposed that fire commissioners, chosen by the Legislature, appoint police officers and that they be made to take the oath and pay the $5000 penalty for failure to choose underlings on the basis of merit. The bonus would be enough to pay the rent of policemen, thus making them want good government; they would also learn the 'elevating satisfaction' of saving fifty dollars while they earned one dollar for doing it, and better men would be attracted to the force. Three-quarters of the duties of the voluntary fire department would disappear and private watchmen would no longer have to be retained.

Again, no one paid any attention to Peter, but he was still undaunted. In the 'sixties, in the 'seventies, and finally in 1882 he again brought forth his scheme. The three-quarters figure seemed to fascinate Peter, and in the 'seventies he gave this as the percentage of property that would be saved and of officers who would do their duty, as well as of fire department responsibilities that would lapse. If his scheme had been adopted earlier it would have saved, he estimated, $100,000,000. Peter Cooper was a good citizen, an ingenious schemer, and tenacious as a terrier. He was also blindly and stubbornly and naively over-confident of his own remedies.

Peter Cooper did not become for a second time a member of the Common Council in 1840 in order to work on the Croton project or on behalf of bonuses to policemen. He did not in fact take his seat willingly at all. Not only was he reluctant to neglect his business and his family, but local politics were becoming increasingly distasteful to him. From 1834, when the mayor was first elected by popular vote, politics became more and more a game played by professional vote getters. The increase of immigration stirred the seeds of anti-foreignism, and there was constant violence between foreigners and natives, radical Locofoco Democrats and conservatives, Abolitionists and States Righters. By 1842, with the coming of Mike Walsh and his ward heelers and the systematic cultivation by Tammany of the recent immigrants, the days of the respectable ward committees and of Peter Coopers on the Common Council were about over.

It was one of the last of these delegations of better citizens that in 1840 waited on Peter Cooper to persuade him to stand as alderman for upper New York City, now the Sixteenth Ward. He refused on the grounds that he was in no respect fitted for public life and was immersed in business. ' "Very well," they said, "we have come here to board and lodge with you until you accept the nomination, and we intend to stay." ' Peter offered them $5000 to go away, 'but instead they made a concerted movement as though preparing for bed. . . . Of course . . . there was nothing to do but as they wished.' [30] Actually there had been opposition to Cooper in the nominating committee, several electors preferring James Ryan, but the Locofoco general committee had finally approved Cooper as successor to

Daniel F. Tiemann. On April 16th, in a smashing Locofoco victory, he was chosen alderman by 302 votes, winning the *Herald's* accolade as a 'simon pure.' [31]

The reason that Cooper, though reluctant, was willing to serve was that he wanted to defeat his rival, who was not, he said, sound on the 'school question.' After his term was over he was glad that he had served, not primarily because of his work for the Croton project, but because he 'was able to keep the school question out of official discussion.' Free non-sectarian education for the common man had been a cause dear to his heart for a decade, since his memorable interview with Dr. Rogers and his vote, at about the same time, 'to tax myself and all the real and personal property of the City for an amount sufficient to maintain a system of public and general education.' From the day in the spring of 1838 when he became a trustee of the Public School Society until he climbed the stairs of his beloved Cooper Union for the last time in 1883, he devoted more time and effort and thought to its accomplishment than to any single work of his life. In 1840 when the Catholics made a dramatic bid for public funds, he was deeply fearful that the whole free education movement was about to take a wrong turn, and he fought tenaciously and successfully to see that this did not happen.

The Public School Society was in a flourishing condition when Peter joined it. The first and for many years virtually the only organization devoted to giving free non-sectarian education to the masses in New York City, it had been founded in 1805 to cure vice and sloth by giving to those poor not provided for by denominational charity schools 'sufficient knowledge to enable them to understand and pursue their best interests.' When DeWitt Clinton, president of the Society until 1828, opened the first school in 1806, a small apartment in the present Madison Street easily accommodated the handful of children. By 1838 the Society was expending nearly $130,000 annually on some 20,000 pupils.[32] The chief problems with which Peter, who was immediately put on the five-man executive committee, had at first to deal were how to make more children go to school and how to raise enough money, both perennial problems. Not until the city made education compulsory, which the Public School Society demanded and the city shied away from doing, could the first problem be disposed of; the second has never been solved by any charitable institution, but it was made especially difficult for the Public School Society in 1838 because its tax allotment was still based on 1831 land valuations. Moreover, the teachers were demanding salary increases, which a committee on which Peter Cooper sat granted them to the extent of ten per cent in August, 1839. When the city refused further funds in 1839, the Society had to borrow $5000 to meet current expenses and $32,000 to build a new building.

Besides serving on the executive committee, Peter's chief duty was to pay weekly and quarterly visits of inspection to the seventeen schools run by the Society. This was a time-consuming and onerous task, and for Cooper had nearly as disastrous results as some of his more daring exploits. In these examinations he often had to sit three or four hours on wooden benches without backs. 'Being thin in flesh at that time I hurt the seat bone, the end of the thigh bone, bringing on inflammation which has continued from that time to this.' When he returned from a school he for a long time kept hot cloths on all night, and to the end of his life could lie only on his back in bed. His salvation was the discovery of an India-rubber air cushion, which he carried with him wherever he went. To those who knew Peter Cooper in later years this air cushion became one of the eccentric trademarks of the beloved old man.

The Catholic bombshell burst early in 1840 in the midst of the Society's worst financial troubles. William H. Seward had been elected governor the previous year, in the Whig revival presaging the national results in 1840, and, looking around for an issue to win popular support for the reputedly silk-stocking party, suddenly discovered the foreign population. In his annual message, after deploring the condition of the children of foreigners deprived of education in consequence of 'prejudices arising from difference of language or religion,' he made the following plain incitement to action: 'I do not hesitate, therefore, to recommend the establishment of schools in which they may be instructed by teachers speaking the same language with themselves, and professing the same faith.'

The Catholics, who lost no time in taking up this challenge, immediately demanded of the Common Council a pro-rata share of the school funds for their schools. The Public School Society, scenting the danger at once, appointed Peter Cooper one of a committee of seven to remonstrate and, if necessary, to fight the Catholic pretensions before the Common Council. The 'Remonstrance,' which appeared on March 20th, called the Catholic claim both unconstitutional and inexpedient. It was unconstitutional because no school in which the 'peculiar tenets' of a faith were taught was entitled to public funds. Such funds would be in effect tithes or forced payments to an institution in which the public did not participate and of which it morally disapproved. It was inexpedient because the public schools, now flourishing, would be crippled by sharing their funds. 'Of such great importance,' the committee added, 'do they consider the subject, that, unless the Common Council are prepared, on a mere statement of these objections, to deny the application, your remonstrants respectfully request that they may be heard, in defense of their positions, before a joint meeting of your two boards.'

The application was not denied out of hand, and the controversy raged for over two years with increasing acrimony. Indeed, though the question was eventually settled temporarily, it continued to agitate American minds through the rest of the century, Peter Cooper himself presiding at a mass meeting called at Cooper Union in 1870 to prevent Catholics from securing state funds for education.[33] The issue is very much with us at the moment, and it is very doubtful whether there can ever be a real meeting of minds on the subject. The Catholic contention, which involves for Catholics basic premises, challenges equally fundamental American notions. To Catholics morality is part of education and must be taught in schools; morality in turn cannot be separated from religious doctrine, which in turn implies the authoritarian precepts of a revealed religion. They have always demanded, therefore, where they are unable to control public schools themselves, that they be given the same privileges in schools of their own choosing as others receive in their schools. Though this sounds reasonable enough, it strikes straight across the basic American concept of the separation of church and state: no religious doctrine shall be promulgated in institutions using money belonging to the people of the United States. This principle, referred to with little regard for euphony as 'unsectarianism,' had been established in New York City only after two bitter trials of strength—in 1824 and 1831—between the Public School Society and several denominational institutions. Peter Cooper, who had imbibed the doctrine from his Jacksonian associates, was willing to fight for it through all eternity.

There was much to win one's sympathy in the Catholic position in 1840. Though cries of persecution come with better grace from those less willing when in power to censor the thoughts and beliefs of others, the Catholics were then a persecuted minority. In 1834 fanatics burned the Ursuline Convent in Charlestown, Massachusetts, and a few years later the great Samuel Morse wrote a book accusing the Catholics of a plot to make America a Catholic monarchy. 1841, the very year of the height of the school controversy, saw the birth of the Native American movement, a political party designed solely to keep down foreigners and powerful enough in 1844 to elect James Harper, the publisher, mayor of New York.

Moreover, the Catholics did have an educational grievance, which even Peter Cooper, fairminded as he usually was, failed to see. The Public School Society, though it had been designated by the Common Council in 1824 as the chief beneficiary of public educational funds, was actually a private corporation offering free education (it was originally named the Free School Society) to the poor, not a public body charged with the training of all the citizens. Controlled almost wholly by Protestants, it could not, even if it acted with strict impartiality, meet the charge that Catholics were excluded from control over institutions for which they paid taxes. Nor were the trustees of the Society likely to be entirely unbiased. All of them believed, in characteristic nineteenth-century fashion, that morality ought to be taught in schools and the Scriptures read. The textbooks used were naturally all Protestant and were full of anti-Catholic propaganda; and the King James version of the Bible was of course objectionable to Catholics. From the Catholic point of view the Public School Society, while claiming to be non-sectarian, was in effect teaching false religion. No wonder Bishop John Hughes, the indefatigable defender of the Catholic cause, felt called upon, in the fall of 1840, to voice his objections in a speech before the Common Council lasting nearly three and one-half hours.

Few reading the testimony before the Council will accuse the representatives of the Public School Society of joining the prejudiced hue and cry against the Catholics. Unlike some of the representatives of Protestant churches, who even dragged out the ancient charge that Catholics taught it to be legitimate to kill heretics, Hiram Ketchum and Theodore Sedgwick did everything they could to mollify Bishop Hughes. Unfair Catholic charges[34]—such as that Quakers controlled the Society and taught disobedience—were temperately answered, and Catholics were vainly urged to cooperate with the Society in eliminating objectionable matter from school texts.[35] On the main point, however, Peter Cooper and his colleagues would not concede an inch, agreeing with their president, Robert C. Cornell, that some principles were 'so dear, so deeply rooted, that honest men of every party will lose sight of inferior objects and unite in their support.'

So long as the controversy was merely over admitting Catholic schools to a share of the funds awarded the Public School Society, the Catholics could not win. Though they had their hearing—Peter Cooper succeeded once in having it postponed [36]—they were beaten fifteen to one in January, 1841, when a vote was taken in the Common Council. But in February the Catholics appealed to the Legislature in Albany, and the grounds of the controversy suddenly shifted, leaving the Public School Society no longer fighting for exclusion of Catholics from state money but for its very existence. Secretary of State John C. Spencer (who, like the governor, was sympathetic to the Catholic cause) claimed in a lengthy report issued in April that it was wrong to give public funds to a private corporation over which the state had no control.[37] No wonder, he said, not half the population sent their children to school. 'Such a system is foreign to the feelings, habits and usages of our citizens,' and should be replaced by one that was truly public.

However sound Spencer's views may have been, it is understandable that Peter Cooper and his colleagues should have fought him bitterly. They had been working together successfully for many years and were deeply wedded to their system. A suggestion of Spencer's about local option on the religious question brought before their minds, with some justice, the picture of a district in which a Catholic majority forced a Protestant minority to subscribe to Catholic doctrine. And, with the increasing corruption of local politics, they were also deeply worried about a politically run school system.

Their fight on this issue was, however, a losing one. Spencer's program was defeated in 1841, despite three days of almost continuous talking by Bishop Hughes; but nemesis was approaching. The subject became a political issue in the fall elections of 1841, and the Catholics terrified the politicians by acting as a body and putting ten members in the Legislature pledged to Spencer's ideas. Despite Cooper's efforts as a member of a lobbying committee sent to Albany, a bill introduced by the Jacksonian Democrat William B. Maclay and embodying Spencer's ideas passed the Assembly on March 22nd by a four to one majority.[38] Peter Cooper wrote desperately to Isaac L. Varian, who had been mayor when Cooper was in the Council, begging him to get the bill thrown out by the Senate, to secure submission of the question 'to the whole people of the city,' or at least to have the bill 'so amended as to make it as harmless as possible.' [39] It was no use. The bill passed the Senate and became law, though there were near-riots when the action became known.[40]

The bill provided that the common schools already in existence should remain under the government of the Society, but set up a locally elected board of education to control the whole system and to start new city-owned schools. The Catholics, however, lost their main point too, as it was specifically forbidden to teach any sectarian doctrine in schools belonging to the City of New York, and only such schools were to receive public funds. Bishop Hughes's biographer says that the 'compromise was a failure and has never satisfied Catholics,' who believe that education must be religious and belongs to parents, not to the state, which by assuming the task usurps parental rights, assumes spiritual functions, and interferes with conscience.[41]

The discomfiture of the Catholics was, unfortunately, no balm to Peter Cooper and his colleagues, who bewailed their fate as loudly as if they had not won the point they claimed they had been making all along. Their 'noble institution,' said the Annual Report of 1842, was to be subjected to the 'blighting influence of party strife and sectarian animosity. . . . The glory of their system—its uniformity, its equality of privilege and action, its freedom from all that could greatly offend, its peculiar adaptation to a floating population . . . is dimmed. . . . The boast of our city, that in her public schools the children of the rich and the poor, of the American and the for-eigner, all mingled as a band of brothers . . . is overthrown.'

Having delivered themselves of this mournful epitaph, they nevertheless proceeded to carry on in their limited sphere for another eleven years. Peter Cooper played an active role through all these years and, when it became evident that the citizens of New York preferred the new schools with their relatively high salaries to the old ones,[42] helped bring about the liquidation of the Public School Society. He served on a committee of three which negotiated the 'merger' of the two systems in 1852, when the Board of Education forced the issue by refusing funds to meet a deficit. He chaired the meeting on January 19, 1853, at which the Society signed its own death warrant, 'not from a con-viction of their best judgment' but from the 'necessity of the case.' He went with four others to Albany a month later and returned with a bill that ended the Society's existence but of-fered a few sops to its dignity: for a few years the Society was to have fifteen commissioners of the common schools and three trustees for each ward. And he then passed with the others over to the Board of Education, where he served as a commissioner until January 1, 1855, over a year after he had laid the corner-stone of the Cooper Union.

Peter Cooper gave the valedictory of the Society at the July meeting, and it was a characteristic performance. Others might repine and allow the bitterness of 1842 to prolong itself into the next decade, but not Peter Cooper. In fact it is evident from an unpublished fragment in his papers that he had intended to be somewhat severe on his colleagues. The Society's system, he contemplated saying, 'had not kept up to the Spirit of the Times, to the growing wants of this great community'; the com-mon schools had started as a system of charity schools and 'the odor of that system has not entirely left us to this day.' The So-ciety was accused of caring for the ragged and destitute and neglecting those able to pay for private schools; if they had used the law that levied a tax on all property to educate all and had popularized the system by 'introducing into our body some few members elected by the people,' the ward schools would not now have superseded them.

What he actually said was more innocuous and emphasized the positive rather than the negative, the duties of the future that followed the past stewardship. To anyone who looked around the world these duties would appear, Peter said, onerous enough to stifle repining for the past. Despotism in Europe was trampling on freedom everywhere, and it was a question whether even America could save her dearly won privileges. For here too—and Peter must have had the Catholics at least partly in mind—'the combined influences of pride, of selfishness, of bigotry and superstition' were 'all uniting to undermine the virtues, and misdirect the energy and intelligence of our people.' Only knowledge could save us by showing us the truth. This being so, ought we not assume that our new associates on the Board of Education are as devoted to the cause as we are and welcome them? 'It will be our duty to be slow to find fault or condemn what may at first appear less desirable than the customary rules and practices that have prevailed within our own Society. It will better become us to look to those motes that may by possibility float unperceived in our own eyes.'

Peter Cooper was never at home in a futile wrangle over dead issues. When, appropriately, he was asked by the Society to welcome the new, elected board members, he talked not of the past but of model schools for teachers and other proposals for the future. Indeed, his mind was never fuller of the future than it was in the middle 'fifties, when his thoughts were turning more and more toward the myriad possibilities of his new Union. To show that he had no hard feelings toward the Board of Education, he would, before the Union opened, offer the board the opportunity to take it over and manage it.

Chapter 10

A MAN'S CASTLE

THE year that Peter Cooper served as alderman he passed his fiftieth birthday. No longer was there any outward sign of the callow youth who had come wonderingly to New York thirty-odd years before, or even of the mechanic and tradesman of the 1820's. The associate of important politicians and businessmen, he was a well-known, respected, and substantial citizen, and he began to look the part. He had been lanky and somewhat frail as a youth, but now he had filled out into a robust, solid figure with a long, sharply featured face, massive forehead, almost ascetic lips, and a strong chin. His hair he wore down almost to his shoulders and curled over his ears; around his chin he grew a fringe of hair like a ruff. His gold-rimmed spectacles, the most striking aspect of his appearance, had two octagonal lenses on the side as well as the ordinary ones in front, not unlike the blinders on a horse except that they were transparent. The long black coat, the spotless stiff shirtfront and high-standing stiff collar, and the neatly folded broad satin stock covered up any traces of the workingman of an earlier day.

Yet the old Peter Cooper was still there. At heart Alderman Cooper remained the self-reliant craftsman of frontier days, ready to tinker with a machine or tenaciously carry through an experiment, impatient of the academic and ever willing to experiment, both shrewd and kindly in a simple, earthy way. His granddaughter has recorded that he loved to quote frontier wisdom to his guests, such as that building a house too near the woods meant dampness and the danger of forest fire. He advised his listeners to give a man money rather than endorse his note, a maxim he did not to his regret always follow himself. Despite much reading, he was still semi-illiterate and without some of the more fashionable niceties of manner. He was also completely without the ostentation that the rich were beginning to exhibit, and to the end of his days lived in the simplest manner compatible with comfort and hospitality. For many years he kept only one woman servant to look after the house, and a man to do the rough work and look after his horse and buggy. Even later on only the least expensive vehicles were permitted in the Cooper household, as his wife and daughter once discovered. Though Peter wished his wife to have a carriage, when he saw the landau that she and Amelia had purchased, 'he thought it entirely too fashionable and exchanged it for an old-fashioned clarence with a glass front which he thought more in keeping with his democratic ideas. He had to pay the dealer a large bonus to take the other one back.' [1]

He felt the same way about clothes. 'He always had a fine broadcloth frock coat and high black satin stock for evening wear,' and when his son grew up he bought him two 'French Cloth Frock Coats' (at $28 each), two 'Black Silk Vests' ($6 each), a velvet vest ($8), and a pair of 'Black French Car Pants' ($12). But his 'republican principles would never permit him to wear a dress coat, which he considered the livery of fashion. So, when he was made chairman for the ball given in New York to the Prince of Wales, afterward King Edward VII, and by common consent of the community his was the only name on the card of invitation, it was with great difficulty that he was persuaded to wear a dress suit. The argument which finally made him yield was that he would not be honoring the Queen of England and she would be annoyed. He said that he would never do anything to displease a lady, and ordered a suit, but that was the one and only time he wore it.' [2]

In another man this might have been mere affectation. But Peter Cooper's ideas and behavior in larger matters squared with his eccentricities of dress and equipage. While many of his friends succumbed to the lure of the new Whiggery, with its palaver about the workingman's best interests coinciding with the wealth of the capitalist, he remained a Jacksonian Democrat, ready all his life to side with labor against the mere accumulators of riches. And by a thousand acts of kindness he showed that his own wealth had not spoiled the simple heart with which nature had endowed him. So widely was he known as a 'man of philanthropy' even before he founded Cooper Union, that people would ask his help on matters as unrelated to his concerns as securing damages from the Water Power Company for harm to their property.

Though thus basically unchanged, Peter had grown to meet the new circumstances with which his life was inevitably surrounded. His great resources and the vastness of the enterprises in which he now participated no longer permitted him, except on rare occasions, to tend to details as he had when he was a small glue manufacturer on the Middle Road. He had to learn to delegate authority, to inspire others to carry out efficiently and happily the plans that he initiated. And he did. He possessed, as many have testified, a mixture of benevolence and sternness, of power and persuasiveness, that made him the 'central pivot around which everything moved within the reach of his influence.' [3] Cooper Union no less than business enterprises like the Atlantic Cable were organized and operated by others, Peter supplying the vision and the faith. Fortunately his vision was seldom clouded. Able now to take the chances that he firmly believed it to be the capitalist's function to take, he often indulged his faith in the infinite possibilities of science by backing doubtful enterprises. But, though he threw away many small sums, he seldom lost large ones. His investments paid off with amazing regularity. Peter Cooper was as much at home in the world of mid-nineteenth-century capitalism as he had been in the days when New York was a small town and he and his wife managed the corner grocery store.

A good deal of Peter's time and energy from the 'thirties on was devoted to his family. This included nephews and nieces and their children, and even friends and acquaintances who drifted under his benign influence and who, before long, were as dependent on his guidance as were his own children. Typical of the latter was a certain Captain Benjamin Savary, to whom in October, 1838, he leased a farm he had bought in East Wareham, Massachusetts, with the hope that Savary would one day buy it. Savary not only never collected the necessary $2000, but he and his relatives were for the rest of their lives a constant drain on Peter's time, pocketbook, and patience. In 1852, when Savary wrote Peter in utter discouragement that he could no longer work the place as his sons would not stay there and he had thrown his arm out of joint, Peter simply kept him on doing what odd jobs he could manage. On Savary's death his brother (or son) John took over the farm, and the old round of unpaid debts, fires in the cranberry bog, and attempts to sell crops, fruit, and wood continued. In 1878 John's two sisters, who, when John got married, had begged Peter to let them keep 'the old place,' were still lamenting that the farm 'has not been in any way remunerative to you.' One of Peter's strictest injunctions in his will was not to sell the farm until the Savary sisters had lived out their lives there. In 1897 at least one of them was still alive.

Another example of Cooper's fatherly benevolence was his treatment of a young man, Lewis Schofield, who was suspected of theft in 1854. Instead of turning him over to the authorities, Peter pleaded with him to restore the money and not to destroy all his 'future prospects in life for any paltry considerations' of monetary gain. Though 'every real friend you have would gladly cover up anything that would blast your future and bring disgrace on your family,' the boy should remember 'that we must be the companion of our own conscience not only for this life but for that which is to come.' One did not violate God's fundamental law, the 'law of retribution,' with impunity. 'The present is now answering for the past and the future must answer for the present.' [4]

With all his brothers and sisters except his stepbrother, John, Peter kept up close relations. Only his brother Thomas, who worked with Peter in Baltimore and later in the iron business, shared Peter's gifts as either an inventor or a businessman, with the result that Peter was forced into the role of *paterfamilias* to the rest of them. His two sisters lived with him, one dying January 21, 1850, at his Fourth Avenue home, and his brother William for a time in the 'forties resided in a house on one of Peter's Fourth Avenue lots. William, the rolling stone of the family, had been captain of a brick schooner on the Hudson until some time in the 'forties, when Peter handed over to him supervision of the glue factory. He and his sons made so good at this that at one time Peter was paying them together some $19,000 a year, and in the 'sixties he gave them one-third of the business. When William died his estate contributed a surprisingly large sum to Cooper Union.[5]

James became a storekeeper in Baltimore, helped Cooper with his iron business there, and later acted as his agent for collecting rents. But he did not do well, and in 1841 told Peter that he was 'so tired of the grocery I think of purchasing a place within a few miles of Baltimore and occupying myself on the land which was always pleasing to me.' [6] When his wife died in 1846 he despaired of being able to manage his home—a farm twelve miles from Baltimore with a $2000 stone house on it—or to care for his two children. In 1864 Peter gave James's son-in-law, Anthony Cline, some of his Canton lots in trust for his five children. Most of these grandchildren were begging Peter for money for the rest of his life, and he provided for each of them in his will.

Peter's relations with his youngest brother, Edward, the doctor who had saved his eye after the explosion, were the saddest and the most complex. Twelve years younger than Peter, Edward had been like a son to the older brother, who had educated Edward at his own expense. By 1824, before the years when Peter could afford it, he had spent $846.25 on his brother, for whom he secured the sort of education he himself had longed to have. When in 1828 Edward married a Miss Maria Cropsey of Brooklyn[7] and settled down into the practice of medicine, Peter's efforts seemed repaid. Unfortunately the vision and idealism in Peter's nature had, by one of those quirks of nature and early experience, been transmitted in grotesquely exaggerated form to his brother, who soon showed signs of a fanaticism suggesting serious inner disturbance. Already in 1833 he had been neglecting his practice for other pursuits, and in 1834 Peter had to buy his home at 22nd Street and Third Avenue for $9000 to pay his debts. The climax came in 1837 when Edward used money Peter had given him for his profession to issue handbills and a book setting forth his philosophic theory.

The ensuing tragic controversy, which dragged on for over a year, might well be left to oblivion did it not throw such revealing light on the character of the older brother, who on no other occasion in his life was placed in such a perplexing dilemma. Edward was plainly crazy, no matter how one defines the term. His poor tortured mind had convinced itself that he was the 'personal development of the true and proper SPIRIT OF TRUTH of the Christian faith and expectancy,' and evidently he was encouraged in this delusion by some clergymen and literary hangers-on. It was only because of the 'moral fear of the present enslaved state of society,' he was sure, that no one reviewed and not a soul bought his book, though it contained the 'first published discovery of the origin of the alphabet of all language and the source of knowledge to all moral truth.' Convinced that he was divinely inspired, he naturally expected—with the inexorable logic of the insane—that Peter would support him at any cost, and alternately begged and commanded his brother to do so. He had, too, his moments of lucidity, when he would make reasonable promises to desist if the next attempt failed, and to remove to another town and take up his practice. Then, when the next attempt did fail, he would charge Peter with trying to prevent his mission and keep him in poverty, a martyr to a truth that Peter was incapable of understanding. If Peter then made concessions, this was taken as proof of his guilt, for if he were not guilty he would not have been reconciled to one who called him a 'damned rascal' to his face. If Peter refused concessions, Edward raved with all the irrational venom of the paranoiac that he undoubtedly was. Peter's life, Edward wrote on one occasion, would end in 'loathsome infamy unless you choose to make proper acknowledgements for your past cruelties and tyranny and violated faith to your Brother. . . . ENVY and GUILT have stained your conduct and character in your exertions to destroy your brother by Poverty and insult.'

Poor Peter was bewildered by such behavior. There was no room in his world of commonsense and reason and benevolence for this character out of a Dostoevsky novel, and he had no idea either what he was facing or what to do about it. It would be ludicrous if it were not so pathetic to watch this kindly practical man trying to cope with a raving madman as if he were simply a somewhat unreasonable fellow adult. When Edward begged, Peter tried to play the benevolent brother, forgiving him for all the accusations against his character and motives. On August 22, 1837,—not two weeks after Peter had broken with Edward for the latest of his tirades—Peter offered him $500. And he did so despite his grave doubts as to the propriety 'of depending for support on so uncertain and untried an experiment . . . as authorship.' In September he paid some of this amount, though it was impossible to collect money because of the panic, but could not resist a friendly warning. Peter had, he told Edward, 'heard the opinion of seven different persons who have all read your book in whole or in part, and have all given their opinion that it is a work from which there is no chance of your gaining pecuniary advantage—I give you this information in the hope that you will profit by it knowing as I do how few there are that feel sufficient interest in your welfare to induce them to communicate to you in person such unwelcome opinion.'

It never seemed to occur to Peter that frankness was just what his brother didn't want or that the emphasis on pecuniary standards was bound rather to infuriate him than to bring him to his senses. The shock when his brother did not keep his promise to return to work if the book failed was correspondingly great. Peter was driven to say that in future he would not 'part with the little property that I have obtained by a life of incessant toil—to be expended in a pursuit that to *me appears so perfectly hopeless,*' but only to advance Edward's practice. The book, he said baldly, deserved to fail: it was 'unintelligible,' and 'a perfect gorgon if not a pernicious theory.' When this brought wrath and denunciation showering down on him, Peter simply refused in sorrow to have more to do with his brother. 'I have at last come to the conclusion,' he wrote his brother-in-law, James Cropsey, in January, 'that all my past efforts to aid him have been worse than lost. . . . My mind is now deliberately and unalterably made up—and no threats, or violence that he can offer, will ever cause me to make any other or different proposition.' Peter didn't of course cling to his original sternness, and when in February Edward, in a moment of lucidity, was contrite, he acceded to the pleas of his sister and offered him $200 and then $800 in weekly installments. 'After this,' he added, 'your sympathies and entreaties in behalf of your Brother will never draw another dollar from me on his account.'

Despite the happier omens, Edward eventually had to be sent away to the Bloomingdale Asylum. To the very end there is no evidence that Peter ever understood that his brother was mad. When Edward wrote that he had voluntarily made himself insane and gone into a madhouse 'to complete his knowledge of HUMAN VILLAINY,' Peter took him at his word. Even later on, though he sorrowed for his brother's condition, he persisted in acting as if the whole thing were but a temporary and unfortunate episode. His one extant letter to his brother after his second confinement is devoted almost entirely to denying Edward's charge that he was responsible for having him committed. 'You know . . . that all that I have done in relation to your confinement after hearing that you had been committed was to go and obligate myself to pay your board to prevent you from being a publick charge and to furnish money to the doctors with an urgent request that they would see that you did not want for anything that would add to your comfort—At the same time stating to them that it was my wish that you should be liberated as soon as it could be done with safety to yourself and family.' A noble nature, Peter Cooper's. He did not resent Edward's 'loading' him 'with every charge that your imagination could invent that you thought would inflict a wound upon my feeling,' and continued for the rest of Edward's life to help support him both in the outside world in the few moments he was free and during the long darkness that ensued. But he seemed incapable of accepting the irretrievable collapse of a human being, or of the profound pity that arises from such acceptance of the tragic mystery of life.

Peter's relations with his two children were fortunately happier. In 1841 Edward was seventeen and Amelia eleven, and they both gave promise of providing Peter with the outlet for his love that he was denied in his first four children and in his brother Edward. Peter brought them up with a good deal of oldfashioned strictness, believing, as he used to say, that 'you must teach children to mind before they can walk.' When as a boy the painter Thomas Snell tracked mud into Cooper's house Peter looked at the tracks disapprovingly. 'Son,' he said, 'you must always be more careful of other people's property than of your own,' and sent him out to the garden to weed cabbages as a lesson.[8] Peter's children were both given 'vocational' training at home, the old craftsman being convinced that everyone should have a trade as a resource. Edward learned handicrafts and Amelia housekeeping, cooking, washing, and sewing. They both received the formal education denied to their father. Amelia and Edward at first attended Public School 15 at 27th Street and Third Avenue—the section assigned to Peter as a member of the Public School Society. Then Amelia went to Miss Meer's Select Classes at 10th Street and Broadway, and occasionally took dancing lessons in Howard Street from the Italian exile Ferrero. By 1850 the little girl in pigtails had become a tall woman and was attending Miss Kirkland's School, where she and a young cousin, Julia, another addition to Peter's house, delved into the mysteries of logic. Edward, on the other hand, had gone on from school to Columbia, from which he graduated in 1843 at nineteen.

There was relaxation too. Amelia in later years particularly recalled shopping with her mother at William Constable's in Canal Street and at A. T. Stewart's at Chambers Street and Broadway; going for long walks up the Boston Post Road or east to General Gates' house or northwest to the reservoir on the edge of town at 42nd Street; riding in her mother's new clarence up to the Tiemanns' in Manhattanville, overlooking the Hudson; and catching crabs in Bushwick, which they cooked by plugging up one of the hot exhaust pipes at the recently removed glue factory. Edward's early recreations are not known, but in the summer of 1843 he took a walking trip through the White Mountains, and in the following spring an extended tour of England, France, Germany, and Italy.

His companion on these trips was a college friend named Abram Hewitt, who was to play a key role in both his and his father's life. The son of a furniture maker whose profitable business had been wiped out four years before Abram's birth, Hewitt had struggled up from poverty to a scholarship at Columbia, where he ran away with all the honors the place had to give. After graduating in October, 1842, the brilliant and ambitious lad threw himself so vigorously into several pursuits at once—teaching in the grammar school of Columbia College, studying law, and tutoring—that his eyes failed him in little over a year and he had to take a complete rest. Among his private pupils was Edward Cooper, two years his junior, whom he had met in college and who now needed help to finish his college career. Peter Cooper's records show that he paid Hewitt $34. for thirty-four lessons from October 24 to December 7, 1842, and another $33.33 from December 8 to January 16, 1843, at the rate of $70. for twelve weeks. The boys became fast friends and remained so the rest of their lives, though there was always something of the older-younger-boy attitude in their relationship.

Abram became Edward's companion on the White Mountains and European trips. On their return in the fall of 1844, Peter Cooper took both boys in with him in his new business venture in iron-manufacturing in Trenton, and from then until the end of his life Hewitt was an integral part of Peter Cooper's life, managing his business, tending to his personal affairs, and running Cooper Union. In 1855, after a long and decorous courtship, Hewitt married Amelia, whom he had admired from the time she was a girl of twelve, and became as much a member of the family as any son could be.

In the diary which he kept of the White Mountains trip Hewitt drew a pen portrait of Edward Cooper that reveals as much about the narrator as it does about his subject. Good-natured, of a kind heart and modest to a fault, Edward was, wrote Hewitt, wanting in boldness, 'talented—yet wanting perseverance—neat personally—yet awfully given to keeping his trunk and room in disorder—ever in a hurry yet always behind —so that there is not the slightest prospect of his getting a respectable meal on the routes—patient of reproof and never repining—sadly given to making excuses for every unfortunate event—and withal very compliant to every humor—appearance decidedly prepossessing—and I sadly fear that he will make awful havoc among the chambermaids and factory girls of New England.' [9] The description was strictly accurate. With much of his father's kindness and practicality, Edward lacked entirely the latter's power and sureness, being so ready to see both sides of a question that he was unable to make decisions, and so indifferent to acclaim that he seldom followed an idea through.

But what of the author, the young man of twenty-one who could so coldly appraise a companion and friend amid the green hills of New Hampshire? Professor Nevins has done full justice to Peter Cooper's son-in-law in his *Abram S. Hewitt,* and there can be no question but that he was a capable man and a useful citizen. Without him Peter Cooper might have made a great deal less money and given away a great deal too much, and New York might have had Henry George for its mayor and learned to like socialism. Brisk, intelligent, well-informed, decisive, and determined, Abram Hewitt was not only an efficient and effective person but a thoroughly honest and decent and public-spirited one as well. If he was shy, intense, irritable, and so sharp-tongued that he often deeply wounded his best friends, he was frank, occasionally witty, and even voluble, and quick to apologize. As he wrote to his angry brother Charley in 1859, 'It is a source of inexpressible regret to me that my quickness of speech is so apt to give offence where none is intended.' [10]

But he lacked Peter Cooper's vision, in business matters no less than in politics and philanthropy. And not even Professor Nevins can make us love him. There is a formality, an acidity, a lack of spontaneous warmth in Hewitt that often makes his kindest and noblest deeds slightly distasteful. To Hewitt's credit, neither Peter Cooper nor his son nor his daughter ever, as far as we know, felt this. And, in all fairness, it must be said that living for so many years under the shadow even of Peter Cooper might have soured a more naturally genial man. Hewitt had grown up in a poverty-stricken household, where he learned to face life with realistic grimness, and he was boundlessly ambitious. Peter Cooper gave him the great chance of his life. Hewitt, who jumped at the chance, made good in a spectacular way. But not until he was well past middle age could he really call his soul his own; to the end of his life he was known to most people as Peter Cooper's son-in-law. In 1882, when Hewitt was in Congress, he suddenly 'let out' in the middle of a debate 'that the greatest ambition of his life' was, 'instead of his being introduced to strangers as the son-in-law of Mr. Peter Cooper,' for 'that eminent philanthropist' to 'be introduced to them as his father-in-law.' [11]

The trip to Europe in 1844, which ended with a shipwreck and hours of mortal peril in an open boat, cemented the friendship between Abram and Edward. And it won Peter Cooper's confidence in his son's friend, who had safely chaperoned Edward through a long journey. How dear his son was to him is evident from a series of letters—virtually the only ones of their kind that we have—that Peter wrote to him abroad. Writing personal letters was a laborious procedure for Peter, who had no gift for small talk, for easy, warm, inconsequential chatter about the passing scene or his own feelings. After a few perfunctory comments about Edward's plans and the activities of the family, he gravitated inevitably to the ponderous and the eternal. 'To you my dearest son,[11] he wrote in one characteristic letter, 'we look for our sources of comfort to cheer us through the downhill of life to our final rest—I know you will not willingly deprive us of the pleasure we anticipate—O then my son be careful of your health—and above all things preserve that purity of heart that is the pearl of great price, the richest treasure that earth or heaven can give—O my son let me beseech you with a Father's love to continue to remember thy creator in the days of thy youth and when you are old he will not leave nor forsake you—Life is short at best and will soon pass away and leave nothing of value but the triumphs of virtue.'

Peter was not, as we are, restrained from taking a high line out of embarrassment or humor or what you will, and his letters are full of moral exhortation. 'In youth such are the boiling passions of our nature,' he warned his son, 'that we need constantly to remember that we live in the immediate all surrounding all embracing presence of "our heavenly father who will have all men to be saved and come to the knowledge of the truth." ' When his daughter went abroad a few years later, Peter wrote her in similar vein, though for references to 'boiling passions' he substituted more philosophic reflections on life as an 'unexplored ocean on whose bosom' we sought the 'true, the good and the beautiful . . . anchors reaching out to immortality.' Such stilted moralizing and unabashed sentimentality were natural to Peter, evidences of his love and sincerity, not, as we so often suspect, of the reverse.

Both Peter Cooper's children grew up in the 28th Street house, but as mid-century approached it was becoming evident that the family would have to move. It was not that commerce or slums or business had yet encroached on them. New York was growing by leaps and bounds, its population approaching the half-million mark, and the value of its real estate rising above $200,000,000; from 1840 to 1849, 1,161,564 immigrants, many of whom stayed in New York, entered the country, as against 343,517 in the previous decade. But the closely packed, narrow, high buildings of the business center and the noise and crowds of a great city were still confined to Chambers Street or below. In 1850, 42nd Street marked the outer limit of the city, and there were no buildings above 34th Street. One could still pick blackberries in 1845 by the side of the old Middle Road where it crossed Madison Avenue at 35th Street. It was perhaps a sign of the times, however, that the sidewalk on the south side of 28th Street between Third and Fourth Avenues was ordered paved with flagstones in 1841.

What finally drove Peter Cooper out of his dearly loved home was the proximity of the New York & Harlem Railroad, 'the noise of which disturbed me so much that I could not get the needed rest.' [12] How he held his ground so long is somewhat of a mystery. The New York & Harlem had been chartered in 1831 to run up the Bowery and Fourth Avenue, and on November 26, 1832, the *John Mason,* the first coach-like streetcar, made its initial passage from Prince to 14th Street with thirty passengers inside and on the roof.[13] For a time horsecars were used exclusively, but from 1834 to 1837, as the railroad was built under Murray Hill to Harlem and beyond, there were attempts to use steam, and in 1839 a steam train was drawn as far south as 14th Street, where the boiler of the engine exploded, killing the engineer and injuring twenty passengers. The New York & Harlem had established offices and stables in the block between 26th and 27th Streets, 'which presently became the southern terminal for locomotives when large station buildings were erected there.' [14]

Though steam trains ran as far south as 26th Street for only a few years,[15] Peter Cooper and his family must have suffered greatly while they did. The sound and smoke of the locomotives were perhaps no worse than what occurred at the station a block from his house: fifteen minutes before leaving the starter seized an iron bolt about a foot long and banged violently on an iron plate set in the door of the waiting room; and for five minutes before starting a bell hung in the roof of the train shed was struck once every minute. Even after locomotives no longer passed Peter's house, long trains of horsedrawn cars did. Moreover, within a block of his house were John Stephenson's car shops and the railroad's market depot, where the cattle were run into the sheds, awaiting slaughter. 'The cattle cars,' wrote Peter's daughter Amelia, 'would often be left all night on the tracks in the front of our house, and the lowing of the animals disturbed my father.' [16] Despite all this, it was not until 1850 that Peter decided to move. A stubborn man, Peter Cooper; but the railroad finally won, and in 1852 he acknowledged the victory by renting his eight Fourth Avenue lots to the railroad company for twenty years at seven per cent—$2250 in 1852— of their value.

Where to move was the next question. Peter no longer felt the need to be in open country, but he was equally averse to settling among the fashionable and the new-rich on Fifth Avenue, where elegant houses were being erected whose interiors dazzled the eye and revolted good taste with their gold-velvet carpets, crystal chandeliers, gilded mirrors, marble mantels, and their masses of heavy hangings and lambrequins. Bond Street, St. Mark's Place, East Broadway, or Union Square with its handsome houses, its trees and benches and flowers, was possible. But when Samuel Ruggles, or one of the trustees to whom Ruggles had in 1844 deeded Gramercy Park, suggested Cooper buy near the park, he jumped at the opportunity. Ruggles had bought fifty acres of land in 1831 from the heirs of James Duane, dumped much of Bowery Hill into the morass north of it, and created the Gramercy Park area, which he divided into one hundred and two lots, forty-two for the park and the rest for houses. By 1850 comfortable brick houses with white-trimmed doors and brass knobs and knockers and set among grass and trees dotted the neighborhood. Conveniently near the city, Gramercy Park was then—and remains to some extent even today—a quiet and restful retreat.[17]

Peter Cooper did not buy on the park but within a block of it, on the southeast corner of Lexington Avenue and 22nd Street. His deed, dated September 20, 1850, records that he purchased from Thomas Ward for $10,000 a plot 105 feet wide on 22nd Street and 74 ft. 3/4 in. on Lexington Avenue. He was, however, in the Gramercy Park area, was entitled to a key to the park, and was subject to the area's restrictions, recorded at length in his deed: he promised not to erect 'any buildings within forty feet of the front of said lot except of brick or stone with roofs of slate or metal and will not erect or permit *upon any part of the said* lot any slaughterhouse smith shop forge furnace steam engine brass foundry nail or other iron factory or any manufactory of gunpowder glue varnish vitriol ink or turpentine or for the tanning dressing or preparing skins hides or leather or any brewery distillery or any other noxious or dangerous trade or business.'

Peter wasted no time in getting his house started, and by October 4th had a complete and careful set of carpenter's specifications. Building the house must have been no easy task. A little stream called the Crummarsie-Vly or 'Winding Creek'—the origin, probably, of the name Gramercy—had its origins in springs between Fifth and Sixth Avenues and 21st and 27th Streets, flowed into a pond at Madison Square, and then wound its way through Peter Cooper's property to the East River at around 18th Street. Peter's house had to be built on heavy piles. When the house was finished it was a big, square, red-brick building with a high stoop and lintels of cast-iron. Peter's study and bedroom were at the right of the front door, which for years he used personally to answer, thus subjecting himself to the importuning of beggars. But as he said, 'You never could tell—it might be someone in a hurry.' To the left of the door were the parlor, library, and dining room, the schoolroom, kitchen, laundry, and servants' dining room being on the street level. Behind were a yard and stables, and a garden which Peter arranged himself. His papers contain a plan for this garden, to be laid out 'in the center of a mound or circle to represent the great garden of the world,' with figures of 'our first parents' in the center. 'They are represented as looking round and listening to the voice of good saying through all that He has made behold I have given you everything upon all the face of the earth.'

Peter was now located at the heart of a social life different from any he had known at 28th Street. His next-door neighbor was Cyrus Field, with whom he was to have such intimate relations; and nearby were Cyrus' brilliant brother, David Dudley, who contributed so much to Jacksonian legal ideas before he ended as counsel for Jay Gould, Jim Fisk, and Tweed; and also a third brother, the kindly minister Henry Field, whose wife, Henrietta, was the notorious heroine of Rachel Field's *All This and Heaven Too*. John Bigelow and Samuel Tilden were but

the most famous of a host of other well-known neighbors. Peter
Cooper once insisted that he spent most of his life with ordinary men. But he also said, which was equally true, 'I have met
most of the prominent men of the country, the famous states-
men; I have seen all the great actors and actresses, and heard all
the great singers.' [18] In later years everyone of importance dined
at Peter Cooper's house—William Cullen Bryant, Joseph
Choate, Whitelaw Reid, Charles Dudley Warner—and it was a
feather in a young man's cap to be invited there. At Cyrus Field's
he met such men as the publishers George Putnam and Charles
Scribner, the politician William Evarts, the scientist Edward
Youmans, President Hopkins of Dartmouth, and Harriet Beecher Stowe.

Peter collected his family around him at 9 Lexington Avenue
and kept them there. In these days, when an almost compulsive
desire for independence and an over-consciousness of Oedipus
complexes send offspring scurrying from the parental roof at
an early age, we look with some suspicion on family relationships that bind children to their progenitors through the whole
of their adult lives. There is no doubt that Hewitt for one chafed
under the bondage. As he told his brother Charles with some
bitterness in 1863, he had never had a 'separate establishment'
except Ringwood, and even that he shared with others.[19] But
Amelia—and to some extent Edward—was quite unselfcon-
sciously devoted and tied to her father, and it never occurred
to Peter, who had himself left home so early, that there was anything wrong in accepting the proffered homage. When Amelia
was married in 1855, Abram took her for a year to Trenton,
where their first daughter was born, and then moved to Ringwood in New Jersey, which Amelia loved at first sight. But her
father wanted her near him, and for the rest of Peter's life
Amelia and Abram spent the winters at 9 Lexington Avenue.
The house was fitted up for two families, Hewitt occupying
the northern half and Peter the southern, with a common dining room. Though Edward was not taken into the house, Peter

· (181) ·

did the next best thing: when his son married Cornelia Redmond in 1853, Peter promptly bought him three lots across the street on Lexington Avenue for $13,100, where Edward settled down and brought up his children. Peter Cooper spent his latter years surrounded by his children and grandchildren, who subordinated their lives to his every wish. As he said proudly the year before his death, his son visited him every two or three nights and his daughter seldom went to bed without tending to his wants.

It is perhaps significant that the moment Peter died Abram had the whole Lexington Avenue house completely done over by Stanford White, who removed the stoop and redecorated the interior. In the ensuing years the house blossomed with the sort of luxury that Peter had never known: marble stairways, Moorish ceilings, walls of carved oak, stuffed peacocks, copper-lined bathtubs, a clock mounted on a bust of Napoleon, and thick tasseled red ropes on the balustrade. The Hewitts collected reliques ranging from green salad plates made to look like 'fatigué lettuce leaves' to allegorical murals picked up in Venice. In the 'nineties they added a music room, and in 1907 their daughters, using the house next door, built a ballroom half a block long with eleven full-length mirrors and ten large windows, which was last used in 1924 for the reception following the marriage of Peter's great-granddaughter to Prince Viggo of Denmark. The elder Hewitts kept fourteen servants, and a repair man who was constantly at work. In 1930, after the death of Peter's two maiden granddaughters, his grandson Erskine Hewitt took over the house, and its opulence began to fade. Living on the fourth floor, in the room he occupied as a boy, he seldom used the rest of the house. When he died in 1938 it was pulled down and most of its contents were sold at auction.[20] Today—though probably not for long—there is nothing but an empty space to mark the spot where Peter Cooper a century ago laid the foundation of so much pomp. But his more fitting memorial still stands amid the rumble of traffic fourteen blocks away.

Chapter 11

ENTREPRENEUR

IN THE nearly two decades between his fiftieth birthday
and the opening of Cooper Union, Peter Cooper had only one
real aim: to get enough money to build his long-planned institution. As he said many years later, he desired to 'carry it out as
soon as I thought I had the means to accomplish it, if I was compelled to live on bread and water for the remainder of my life.' [1]
Peter did not have to live on bread and water. In 1855 Beach,
who had not mentioned Cooper in his first edition in 1842, now
included him among the millionaires.[2] By his own estimate
he had increased the $383,500 he was worth in 1846 to $1,106,-
000 in 1856, exclusive of what he called 'paper' and the Cooper
Union property, carried at $500,000. 'I have at this time,' he
wrote in his notebook, 'notes and debts dew me. This $150,000
is more than sufficient to finish building on Astor and pay all
that I owe.' [3] To make this money he did, however, have to work
hard at a whole host of activities from glue-manufacturing to a
vast new undertaking in iron. And to complicate his life still
further in this period, he insisted on engaging in philanthropi-
cal and political activities that would alone have kept many men
busy. No wonder the little notebook that he kept in the 'fifties is
a chaotic jumble of heterogeneous material: thoughts on money,

· (183) ·

specifications for running a boat, reflections on God, glue and iron inventions, what to do about cholera, and so on.

The early 'forties—to take his activities outside of business first—were, it will be remembered, the time of his greatest effort on behalf of the water project, and the whole period saw him laboring for the Public School Society. To these tasks he added—in the philanthropic field—trusteeship of the Demilt Milk Dispensary, which Cooper and Joseph Curtis helped found in 1851; of the New York Juvenile Asylum for delinquents, of which he was one of the incorporators in 1851 (in 1882 he was vice-president); of the New York Gallery of Fine Arts, founded in 1845 to establish an art gallery with Luman Reed's collection as a base; and of the New York Sanitary Association, formed in the 'fifties to collect vital information leading to legislation. He also began in the 'forties to interest himself more and more in helping inventors get their ideas before the public.

Peter's own creative powers had begun noticeably to flag. The 'thirties and 'forties brought forth only three inventive efforts: 'A machine to grind and polish plate glass and all other substances that required a true perfect surface,' patented in 1835; a notable contribution to the iron industry in 1842, for which, however, his brother Thomas deserves much of the credit; and a scheme in 1835 to transport salt via the Erie Canal. This last, imparted to Gideon Lee, then in the Legislature, as Peter's contribution to the discussion over enlarging the canal, was the most bizarre that ever came from his brain. In the words of his highly amusing application for a patent, his 'improvement . . . consists in filling the Erie Canal with the most convenient brines that can be raised (by steam or other known powers) near the summit level of the canal and causing the same to flow, in sufficient quantity for all the purposes of canal transportation.' This would, he felt, have the double advantage of giving the canal a quarter again as much buoyancy and offering as well a convenient means of transporting salt, which could be recaptured by evaporation at Albany.[4] It would also secure 'the whole line' of the canal 'from the contaminating influence of fresh and stagnant water.' [5] Easy as it was to get a patent in those days, the petition was not granted and no patent was ever issued. 'It is hoped,' added the Franklin Institute, 'that it never may, as the plan proposed is one which caps the climax of absurdity.' [6]

Peter was as sanguine about the inventions of others as about his own efforts, and was seldom able to resist those who, as he grew wealthier, began to pursue him with their ingenious brain-children. In 1844 he gave E. F. Aldrich $2000 to experiment with a vessel propelled by submerged vertical paddlewheels. Though the inventor's claim that it would make one-thousand-percent profit in five years was not realized, the captain who sailed it during the Mexican War as a despatch boat asserted that it made fourteen miles an hour, and could put to sea when other boats couldn't. Peter long remained enthusiastic about this invention. In 1878 he financed the son of the inventor in an attempt to revive the idea, but insisted that the boat should have one paddlewheel of large diameter. At the trials Peter himself rang the starting bell, the engines whirred into motion, and the boat promptly sank: the paddle-box was not strong enough to stand the force of the water revolving in it and burst. Peter watched the disaster calmly: 'Well, I guess that experiment is a failure.' Four years later he was writing to Congress urging on them a thorough examination of the plan as the best way to increase American commerce. [7]

The 'fifties and 'sixties saw Peter interested in all sorts of inventions: electro-magnetic engines, refrigerators, punching machines, treatment of linseed oil to produce varnishes, use of the vapor of bi-sulphuret of carbon as a substitute for water vapor in steam engines, and dozens of attempts to improve iron and steel manufacture and glue- and gelatin-making. He also joined in attempts after 1845 to tighten the patent laws to punish infringers and to end the arbitrary handling of the 1839 clause giving commissioners the right to decide whether a patent was useful. In 1852 he was one of a committee of seven, formed at the suggestion of Henry Clay, that presented the ideas of inventors to Congress.[8]

It was in the 'forties and 'fifties, too, that Peter first began to present his ideas on public questions in writing. The oft-repeated suggestions about water, fire, and police were followed by other ideas for improving local affairs,[9] notably an ingenious plan to procure stone wharves for the city. This was first suggested to Mayor Wood at a time of unemployment in 1855. Peter recommended the purchase of marble quarries near Kingsbridge, to be worked by the unemployed at two-thirds the going rate for labor. The city would build them places to live, making sure that they worked hard and were not pampered. By these means beggary would be ended and the unemployed made independent, the city would get wharves, and private business would not suffer competition. It was a typical Peter Cooper plan, even down to the technical suggestion of having the less strong put rough stones and chips of marble in a box, to be cemented together for the parts of the bulkheads below the waterline.[10] As usual Peter never gave up this idea, presenting it a second time to the Dock Commissioners fifteen years later when a system of wharves had been voted by the Common Council. On this occasion he offered to contribute $50,000 to erect the buildings.[11] He repeated his plan a third time some years later when his advice was asked concerning a proposed poorhouse, a necessity to which 'we are driven . . . by the best sympathies of our nature.'

Peter Cooper never again held political office after 1841. In 1845 he was a candidate for mayor of the city, a circumstance for some reason never referred to by Peter.[12] Tammany was looking that year for a respectable candidate who could recapture the city from James Harper and his Native American party, which had won in the 1844 election. At the nominating convention on March 20th Cooper received the second-highest number of votes among eleven candidates, only to be defeated on the second ballot, 29 to 10, by William Havemeyer.[13] Once more, in 1855, he was offered local office, that of comptroller. But Peter had sense enough not to compromise himself by accepting office from Fernando Wood, even though the bait of opportunity to reform abuses was held out to him.[14]

For a dozen years after he gave up his seat on the Common Council, Peter showed no desire to reform abuses. A loyal Tammany man, he was as unconcerned about the political corruption that was daily growing worse as about the complicated struggles between factions within the party. As late as 1852 he presided at Tammany gatherings, making bland speeches about honesty and purity, and thus tacitly lending his support to a party that behind his back was feeding ever more gluttonously at the public trough.[15] In 1853, however, the smell became too strong to ignore, and Peter Cooper promptly made a complete turnabout. For the next two decades no one worked harder to help clean up the government of his native city than did he, and he did not desist even after Tweed had been put behind bars in the 'seventies.

Though New Yorkers have become so used to misgovernment and to measuring corruption by the more grandiose standards of the Tweed gang that they are not impressed by what seem the minor misdemeanors of pre-Civil-War politicians, the situation in 1853 was truly appalling. For a decade Tammany had been mastering the art of buying the foreign vote with favors and bribes and controlling elections with the gentle help of 'knuckle-dusters' and 'dirk men.' Only division within its own ranks had put brakes on its rapacity, and in 1852 there was relative harmony. The government of the 'forty thieves,' who set up an organization in the Common Council to distribute bribes, was the result. Their most notorious exploits were the purchase of sixty-nine acres on Ward's Island, worth $30,000, for $103,-450—top graft for the time; a $30,000 steal on chartering the Third Avenue Railroad; and the sale of the Gansevoort Market property for $60,000. The city had been offered $300,000 for this latter property, which it had to repurchase ten years later for $533,437.50.[16] When in February, 1853, a grand jury disclosed these facts (though corrupt judges refused to indict), the citizens of New York suddenly awakened to their predicament.

On January 12, 1853, some six hundred men met in the Stuyvesant Institute to organize for action, and on March 5th called a mass meeting which was presided over by Peter Cooper and attended by five thousand citizens. Accusing the city government of a whole catalogue of vices, the meeting appealed to the Legislature—as had the reform movement of 1830—to amend the city charter so as to clip the wings of the Common Council. In response the Legislature immediately proposed laws prohibiting sales or franchises except by public auction, requiring a two-thirds vote of the Council to override the mayor's veto, and taking away from the Council the right to sit as judges or to appoint policemen, a right given to the mayor, recorder, and city judge. Peter Cooper was made chairman of a city reform committee, formed to gain public support for these measures. At mass meetings on June 5th and 6th he led the denunciation of the city government, pointing out to his fellow citizens that under present conditions no one's money, health, or person was safe; debts were mounting, the city was unclean and unhealthy, and the police inefficient and corrupt.[17] The reformers not only got their proposals through but won the 1853 fall elections. Elated, they nominated Peter's friend Wilson G. Hunt for mayor, and prepared for the elections of 1854. Writing to the *Times* on November 3, 1854 (both as head of the committee and as a private citizen), Peter applauded the good work already accomplished by a minority of the Common Council, and pleaded with the citizenry to elect Hunt and permit the improvement to continue.[18]

The reformers quickly learned their first lesson: that the people can be momentarily swayed by the cries of reform, but that when they see no startling changes they are disappointed and relapse into indifference. Fernando Wood won the election over Hunt and two other candidates, with the help of a whispering campaign against Hunt, the support of gamblers, prostitutes, female abortionists, and the underworld in general, and a wholesale buying of votes. The Sixth Ward cast four hundred more votes for Wood than there were people in the district. Then the reformers learned their second lesson: not to trust a politician's pretensions. Wood, realizing how close the election had been, made a play for the support of honest men by instituting a few changes and championing the popular doctrine of self-government for the city. He hoodwinked the citizenry so successfully that in 1855 he had the representatives of $50,000,000—including Peter Cooper, Harper, Horace Greeley, Hunt, and Havemeyer—sitting on a platform at the Tabernacle and thanking him for fighting against control of the police force from Albany.[19] But disillusionment was speedy as Wood soon showed himself the most vicious mayor in the city's history. As one friend wrote to Cooper early in 1856, the administration 'just submits to enough reform to bring reform into disrepute.'[20]

The reformers made one more brave attempt, putting up James R. Whiting as mayor in the fall of 1856. Again Cooper chaired the meeting, to introduce Whiting and to see, as he put it, 'what can and what ought to be done to rescue our beautiful and beloved city from sinking overwhelmed in a vortex of corruption.' Honesty was not enough, he had found out, for the juggernaut of party organization simply rolled over mere honest men; there must be intelligence and the will to fight for the right. There must, too, be a greater separation of the legislative, executive, and judicial powers of the government—a favorite theme of Cooper's, for their union in the Common Council was 'what Thomas Jefferson called a despotism and . . . a fruitful source of demoralization of our Public men.' Every power and duty should be confined to an appropriate department, with each individual held to strictest accountability. Furthermore, the people should, before every election, assemble in every block and choose the proper officers to represent the ward and thus bring back democracy to the primary meetings. Whiting got the least number of votes of the five candidates.

Wood's second administration, which fortunately lasted only a year, was the worst up to that time in the city's history. It was necessary finally, in 1857, for the Legislature to create a metropolitan police force under a Board of Commissioners appointed by the governor. This time the people did not object, but Wood did, and his eight hundred officers refused to accept the new force until, after severe rioting, Wood was arrested. In the fall of 1857 Daniel F. Tiemann was successfully opposed to Wood, and it appeared that a better day might be dawning. Peter must have thought so when Tiemann made his son, Edward, street commissioner.[21] But Tiemann had owed his election to the rising power in Tammany, the future Boss Tweed, and threw most of the appointments to him. Then in 1859 Wood, who had broken with Tammany, came back into power and things went from bad to worse. No mere administrative or legislative changes could solve New York's problem, nor could a reform administration that merely promised purity and economy and offered the common people little of the real help that even the most corrupt Tammany administration gave them. Peter Cooper never found these things out, and when, toward the end of the Civil War, he once more took up the cudgels for good government he was to suffer another long series of disappointments and betrayals.

Cooper's active interest in national affairs was only in the incubating stage before the Civil War.[22] He did not, apparently, join his friends Bryant, Shepherd Knapp, Havemeyer, William E. Dodge, Whiting, Hiram Ketchum, and others in protest against the Kansas-Nebraska Bill in 1854. In 1856, however, the Democratic Presidential platform finally roused him to angry remonstrance. 'If I understand the platform,' he told his friend Nahum Capen of Boston, 'it seems to have for its highest object the perpetuation and extension of slavery over the unoccupied territory of our country—This I have regretted exceedingly.' To allow military forces from other states to control Kansas elections was, he felt, 'too monstrous to be tolerated by a civilized community.' The day was gone when two or three hundred thousand men with a pecuniary interest in slavery could be allowed to 'continue to control' the government; indeed, developments in Kansas had revealed 'such an unfathomable depth of demoralization in the people of Missouri' and in slavery advocates 'that I am confident the people of the north and west will from this time in future refuse to have anything to do in the creation of a slave state.' While slavery was viewed in the South as an 'evil only to be endured until some safe and rational mode of relief could be devised, it did not rapidly demoralize the white inhabitants. But just as soon as a community began to contend for slavery as being right in principle and show a determination to perpetuate and extend it, does it begin to destroy the better feelings of our nature.' There were signs now in the South of wanting to 'extend it at every hazard until like a dark cloud it shall spread itself over the future prospects of our country.'

All this was forthright enough, placing Cooper squarely with the Free Soilers and against the Fernando Woods and the majority of Tammany Democrats, who were pro-South. Moreover, though he did not cease to think of himself as a Democrat, Peter sponsored a meeting in September, 1856, called to further the election of the first Republican candidate for the Presidency, John C. Frémont, as the only way to solve the Kansas issue. But he was not yet ready in 1856 to give up hope for peace and union. How prayerfully he concentrated on these ends up to the very outbreak of the contest his plans for Cooper Union will indicate. In his letter to Capen he even suggested that if the South would throw itself on the mercy of the North and ask for jury trials for runaway slaves, the North would, he was confident, protect the South's constitutional rights. 'It would be almost impossible to find a jury that would take the oath required by the United States and then deliberately refuse in the face of unquestionable evidence to give up a slave.' Such a solution, however, was obviously a mere piece of wishful thinking, as Peter sus-

· (191) ·

pected it was. For the first time in his life he was frankly 'at a loss,' and asked Capen not to publish his letter. He could do more good, he felt, by not 'being drawn into the political conflicts of the day.' [23]

On his two favorite economic questions, the tariff and money, Peter did, however, break into print for the first time in this period.[24] In June, 1846,[25] in an open letter to Robert J. Walker, Polk's Secretary of the Treasury, he combined his ideas on the two subjects in clear and decisive form. Walker was at the time engaged in preparing his famous tariff bill, which lowered tariff rates in accordance with Jacksonian doctrine and which, except for minor changes, settled the tariff issue until after the Civil War. Peter could not resist giving him a little advice. Cooper and Hewitt were, as iron manufacturers, vitally interested in the subject, since the threatened lowering of the one-hundred-per-cent duty on bar and hammered iron and the possible raising of the low duty on railroad iron would affect them greatly. Peter's friend, Stephen Colwell, urged Peter to go to Washington in behalf of the iron manufacturers; since he was 'neither a politician nor an office-seeker,' his 'presence and explanations will avail with some senators more than those of any man.' [26] But Peter did not, consciously at any rate, offer his advice as an interested party; he thought of himself as a philosopher, not a lobbyist.

Though, as Hughes says, Peter's opinions in his letter to Walker directly contradict much that he wrote after the Civil War, the differences between his earlier and his later views are not as great as might at first appear. True, the high-tariff advocate of later years seemed content in 1846 with a moderate tariff on specific goods gradually to be reduced to a revenue tariff, emphasized the 'small amount of uniform bounty' that would be necessary, and insisted that between two countries 'starting in the race of political existence at the same time with the same natural advantages' no tariff at all was desirable or necessary.

But England and America were not equal in 1846—had they been so in 1870 Peter would have been a free trader then too—and it would therefore not 'answer . . . for this Government, at this moment, to aid the already overgrown capital of Great Britain, to break down the manufactures of our country.' Peter's moderation, indeed, came less from conviction than from a need to mollify Walker, whom he did not want 'blindly and hastily [to] uproot the very system, which we have for years been endeavoring to encourage.'

On the money question, which from 1840 on Peter considered the most important subject 'that can possibly be forced on the public attention,' his pre-Civil-War opinions were in one basic respect opposed to his later views. In his remarks to the lawyer on the way to Philadelphia,[27] in a letter to the *Times* in 1855, in an article in the *Banker's Magazine* in 1859 no less than in the Walker letter, Peter showed himself a hard-money man in the orthodox Jacksonian tradition. Only gold or silver—or else paper backed dollar-for-dollar by gold or silver—was a proper currency, since it alone had inherent value, the evidence of labor done. A country that issued paper money in excess of its gold reserve, Peter showed by an illustration, would suffer rising prices, an influx of foreign goods that no tariff could check, and a drain on its supply of gold; increasingly dependent on foreigners for goods and capital, the country was heading for disaster. In the 'seventies Peter completely lost this faith in gold and silver. His fundamental aims, however, had not changed. He still wanted above all a fixed, unfluctuating currency, not paper money that could be expanded and contracted at the will of the rich. But in a period of deflation, of an insufficiency of money, like that of the middle 'seventies, the problem was very different from what it had been under the inflationary conditions of the 'fifties. Peter thought it could be solved better by a managed currency backed by government credit than by gold, which he no longer saw as a necessary anchor for the monetary medium.[28]

Among Peter's various business activities the glue factory still held the center of the stage in the 'forties and 'fifties. It was his basic source of income, and he continued to devote a great deal of time to supervising and expanding its operations. By 1838, 33rd Street had ceased to be a tenable place for a glue factory, so Peter moved it across the river to Maspeth Avenue in Brooklyn, a region now occupied by small cheerless houses trailing off into dismal wastes filled with evil-smelling gas tanks and factories. On May 16, 1838, he bought five acres to the north of the 'Maspeth Turnpike Road' in the then town of Bushwick; in 1841 he added four adjacent acres bordering on Wood Point Road, and subsequently eight more to make a tract running all the way to Newtown Creek.[29] Here, on Maspeth Avenue just east of Kingsland, opposite where the small Cooper Park now marks the only spot of greenery in the landscape, he immediately erected three buildings to house his rapidly growing establishment.[30] Four years after he had set up his new factory, it burned down in the depths of an economic depression, with a loss of $40,000.[31] The story is that Peter left the fire still burning and went down to Wall Street where, without collateral, he obtained the money to rebuild it. Returning home he said to his wife, after telling her about the fire, 'The lumber will be on the ground in the morning.'[32]

The Cooper papers show that, almost up to the Civil War, Peter carried on a good deal of the firm's correspondence. He eagerly pursued all new ideas for gelatin and glue, and in 1845 took out a patent for a new form of gelatin. In 1849 he had Abram ask Edward, in Europe at the time, to find out how to manufacture a transparent French gelatin then selling in America almost as cheaply as his own, and to get the specifications for a celebrated German glue, made by a patent process near Cologne and brought to America in thick, opaque, whitish cakes. He also began milling the skins of deer, sheep, and goats for the manufacture of buckskin leather, a process that involved oiling the skins with fish oil and then beating them with heavy hammers until the oil penetrated every fiber.

After 1860 Peter took only the most casual interest in the glue factory, but by this time it no longer needed him and was expanding under its own momentum. By the early 'sixties it was selling high-grade glue through Osgood Field to London printers and manufacturers of straw goods, pianofortes, and furniture,[33] and was getting raw materials from as far away as South America. In 1869 Hewitt wrote that Cooper's glue works were the 'heaviest makers of Glue and Gelatine' in the world.[34] In 1880 its products were quoted as having an annual worth of $300,000 as against $4,324,075 for the whole country, and in the next decade it was employing two hundred and seventy people. In 1865 Peter formally retired, selling the glue factory to his son and daughter and to William and his children for $200,000; in 1866 the business was incorporated as the Peter Cooper Glue Factory, with Edward Cooper as president. As a result of protests by the City of Brooklyn, the factory was moved in 1878 to an eleven-acre tract on Smith Island in Newtown Creek near Gardner and Maspeth Avenues. In the twentieth century it left Brooklyn for good. Today its half-mile-long plant at Gowanda, New York, alone turns out 25,000,000 pounds of hide glue a year, and there are other plants for bone glue and gelatin in Chicago and Milwaukee. Peter Cooper's picture still adorns the packages of a company that claims to be the largest glue manufacturer in the world.

Other old interests, like his Baltimore venture and the New York real-estate market, continued to occupy Peter in the 'forties and after. He added to his land holdings on the east side of Third Avenue up to 7th Street, and he bought property at 46th Street and Eleventh Avenue, at Hester and Allen Streets, at 48th Street and Second Avenue, at 25th Street and Lexington Avenue, at 7th Street and Avenue A, at 31st Street and Madison Avenue, and at the Bowery and 2nd Street. He also, however, began to invest heavily in the new industries of the country. These were the years of the first great expansion of America's heavy industry and transportation system. Railroads and telegraph wires fanned out across the country, and the iron industry grew by unprecedented strides to keep pace with them. Accompanying these developments came capitalism in its modern form: the corporation rather than the small private business became the dominant form of industry. Peter Cooper, as ready for the new world as for the old, used his accumulated resources to the best possible advantage. At a time when great fortunes were made and lost in a day, when an investor had to know what he was doing and couldn't play relatively safe by buying General Motors or United States Steel or General Electric, Peter Cooper kept steadily increasing his fortune. Long before the Civil War he had become one of the great entrepreneurs of the period, and his new office at 17 Burling Slip, first occupied around 1840 and purchased in 1843 for $8000, became the center of a great network of activity.[35]

Peter Cooper's participation in the new industrialism took various forms. His major roles were as owner and builder of great ironworks in New Jersey, as a chief backer of ocean telegraphy, and as a key figure in the creation of the first great American telegraph monopoly in the late 'fifties. But he also played minor parts as initiator, director, and investor in many concerns and industries. Two of these minor parts deserve at least passing mention.

Peter Cooper was not a prime mover in the telegraph industry, which Samuel Morse, Amos Kendall, Alfred Vail, Joseph Henry, and others launched so dramatically between Baltimore and Washington in 1844. Though Samuel Morse had thought Cooper might be interested in telegraphy and had sent him in 1845 his 'Description of the American Electro Magnetic Telegraph,' Peter refused George Dodge's request as late as 1848 to invest in telegraph stocks, on the basis that his business required all his money. But in 1849, when his iron company began making telegraph wire in large quantities, he changed his mind.

Between 1844 and 1849 there had been unbridled competition

in the industry, which at length resolved itself into a war between the holders of Morse patents—Morse, Kendall, Vail, and F. O. J. Smith, the latter a greedy and disreputable politician who had early jumped on Morse's bandwagon—and a fighting Irishman, Henry O'Rielly, whom Smith had squeezed out of his rights to the patent and who proceeded to set up rival lines all over the West. In 1849 O'Rielly invaded the East with a new patent, Bain's chemical method of transmission,[36] and because he fought for small, democratically owned lines against what were considered monopolistic practices, the public was on his side. Edward Cooper and Hewitt backed O'Rielly's New York & New England Telegraph Company, which was to compete with Smith's line from New York to Boston; and in the fall of 1849 Peter Cooper and others helped set up the Merchant's State Telegraph Company, O'Rielly's rival to the Morse line from New York via Albany to Buffalo. Both the Cooper-backed lines disappeared in 1852, the former by amalgamation with Smith's line and the latter through purchase by the Rochester group, founders of Western Union. But Peter Cooper had gotten a taste for the telegraph business, which was to hear a great deal more of him.[37]

The other minor role was as one of a group pushing the establishment of a Hudson River Railroad, rivaling the already established New York & Harlem and Erie Railroads north from New York. Even this minor effort convinced him that there was too much politics involved in railroad promotion for his taste, and he never again tried it, though his son-in-law did. In 1841 the Erie, which had as yet opened no part of its line and was already in financial trouble, appealed to New Yorkers, for whose benefit it was being built, to subscribe to the road. Peter Cooper in his usual public-spirited way agreed to chair a meeting at Niblo's in behalf of the road, and to serve with committees nominated from the various wards to obtain subscriptions. That he had as alderman in 1840 served on a committee to push for the Hudson River, or New York & Albany, road, and had been one of the signers of a petition for a meeting on the subject, did not bother him in the least.[38] But his fellow workers for the Hudson River Road were aghast. How could he, a Democrat, associate himself with the Whig enemies of 'our Albany Rail Road, who only wanted Peter's name from sinister motives.' 'Stick to the ship now she floats,' wrote Charles Henry Hall, 'and let the enemies of our financial system smite alone without *one* Republican to join' in their efforts. Peter defended himself, claiming that he had been urged by his Democratic friends to do what he had done in order to effect a 'compromise by which both roads could be put through.'

To show his good faith Peter served on a committee of twelve appointed in March at a meeting in the mayor's office to investigate the property and available means of the New York & Albany in connection with trying to raise $1,000,000 for the road. But he already felt like washing his hands of both roads. 'I regret to say,' he told Josiah Rich, 'that a constant intercourse with the citizens of New York convinces me of the impossibility of getting subscriptions sufficient to complete the New York & Albany and the New York & Erie railroads while Mr. Delafield is at the head of the one [the New York & Albany] or those gentlemen who stand accused of a participation in the election frauds of our City are at the head of the other.' In August he refused a directorship of the reorganized Erie, giving the excuse[39] that he had no time to get acquainted with its 'complicated affairs.'

They were complicated, indeed, and though things began to straighten out when Horatio Allen took over the presidency in 1843, the whole property was sold in 1845 under foreclosure, and a $3,000,000 debt to the state canceled as a result of lobbying. The Albany road fared little better. Despite the efforts of Matthew Vassar and his Poughkeepsie and New York associates, the Hudson River Railroad was not chartered until 1847, though it was then rapidly pushed through to become, later, a key link in the New York Central System.[40] Cooper's friends were concerned in railroad projects which later touched his iron interests in New Jersey closely—the Morris & Essex, the Camden & Amboy of the Stevens' family, to which Cooper sold rails, and the Delaware & Lackawanna, in which William E. Dodge and Moses Taylor were interested—but Peter kept out of the endless intrigues and betrayals and blackmail that getting these roads started involved.

He was from the first, however, a heavy investor in railroads, many of whose stocks he took in exchange for iron rails sold to them by his ironworks. Of the Hudson River Railroad, as of the Baltimore & Ohio, he was one of the early stockholders, subscribing to two hundred shares of $100 stock in November, 1847. By 1859 or 1860 he had a portfolio full of the stocks and bonds of railroads, which included such Western roads as the Illinois Central, in which Hewitt was deeply involved, and a number of Eastern roads, most of them links in what were to be large systems: the Sussex (a small road carrying New Jersey iron ore to the Morris & Essex Railroad), the Stockbridge & Pittsfield, the Saratoga & Whitehall, the New York & Flushing, the Long Island. Shortly thereafter he purchased $100,000 worth of Morris & Essex and $30,000 of Pittsburgh, Ft. Wayne & Chicago stock, and subscribed to such new Western projects as the abortive Dubuque & Pacific and the Dubuque & Sioux.

Peter did not confine himself in his investments to railroads. Fire insurance stocks (Manhattan & Gebhard) and bank stocks (Fourth National, Hanover, New York Life & Trust, United Trust, United States Trust) were his favorites, despite his feeling about banks, and he also had money in such companies as the Ninth Avenue Railroad, the New York Kerosene Oil Company, and Horatio Allen's Novelty Iron Works. He was a director of the Manhattan Fire Insurance Company, the United States Trust Company, and the New York Life & Trust Company. In 1865 Peter Cooper had roughly a third of approximately $1,500,000 invested in the iron business, a third in telegraph stocks and bonds, and a third in outside investments. Real estate is listed but not valued. To his glue business also he gave no valuation, but it had been set down ten years before at $300,000.

Chapter 12

NEW JERSEY IRONMASTER

PETER COOPER drifted into iron-manufacturing in the same way that he had into the glue business. The Baltimore adventure, though it taught him a good deal about the subject, had not inspired him to become an ironmaster. When, therefore, he leased his 33rd Street and Third Avenue property in August, 1837, to George Peacock and John S. Gustin for a wire factory at $765 a year for fifteen years, it was probably with no thought of going into the business himself. But 1837 was a panic year and Peacock and Gustin, who invented a loom for weaving wire, owed Cooper $5000 which they couldn't pay. So in July, 1838, Peter took over the wire factory, and he and his brother Thomas decided to run it. Once more, as in 1821, Peter was starting a new project at the bottom of a depression because he had cash when others did not.

As soon as he had launched this business, Cooper became intensely interested in it. He had chosen a fortunate moment.[1] With railroads spreading their lines over the Eastern seaboard and groping toward the West, iron was coming more and more into demand, and was shortly to be recognized as the staple on which the country's industrial future rested. Moreover, just at this period the production of iron was being revolutionized by the introduction of anthracite instead of charcoal into the

· (200) ·

smelting of ore. Previously this had been difficult because no method had been found to get sufficient heat at the furnace mouth for complete combustion, but in the 'thirties various methods—notably David Thomas' in Scotland and Frederick W. Geissenhainer's in America[2]—of introducing a blast of hot rather than cold air and thus raising the temperature to 500° at the tunnel head were discovered. Even before the experiments were perfected, the production of iron was greatly stimulated in New York, Pennsylvania, and New Jersey. In 1825 New York City had only three iron corporations of any consequence—the Peru, Sterling, and New York Steel companies; in 1830 it had only nine furnaces making about 3160 tons of pig metal. By 1835 there were five additional works and the production of iron had become the city's most important industry. In 1840 its iron and steel products were valued at $2,373,100 and its factories employed 2362 people. There was a foundry for steam engines—James P. Allaire's works in Cherry Street—, for light castings, and for stationary engines; there were rolling and slitting mills, stove manufacturers, and even one steel plant.

Peter Cooper's ironworks was not a large undertaking, and is not listed among the principal ironworks in the city. In 1842, when Peter told Henry Fitz that he had some 'three hundred men women and children depending on my business for support,' he must have had in mind both his glue factory and ironworks. In 1843 John A. Roebling was looking for a capitalist interested in the manufacture of wire rope, and was referred to Peter Cooper as a 'gentleman . . . engaged in the manufacture of wire on a limited scale.' [3] The one record of the company, dated March 11, 1843, shows assets of only $26,938.90.[4] Cooper was engaged, moreover, only in the later stages of iron manufacture. His pig iron he had to buy through Horace Abbott in Baltimore or from other sources, which severely handicapped him as it was to handicap other manufacturers in a few years.

Yet Peter Cooper was fulfilling an important function. As late as 1834 there were only three wire mills in the country, with a total output of 4500 tons.[5] And Peter was not long satisfied with a wire mill alone; within a year or two he had built a small rolling mill for the manufacture of the rods to be made into wire and of other forms of bar iron, which he was selling in 1843 at $70 to $75 a ton. An amusing newspaper advertisement in 1840 lists all Cooper's activities together: he specifically advertised his neat's-foot oil, 'warranted equal to the best sperm oil for oiling machinery of all kinds, as well as for all the uses of softening and preserving leather,' but added that he also had 'an assortment of Glue, Iron and Wire.'[6] Moreover, he and his brother began almost immediately, as his letters to Horace Abbott indicate, to experiment with the new processes being developed around them. At one time he offered his works for a four-month experiment in making Russian sheet iron, with the idea that if the experiment was successful he would sell the factory, retaining only one-quarter interest and one-quarter profits. These efforts of Peter and Thomas were not long in producing important results in one direction. Experimenting with anthracite, they at first used it for heating, and then, after spending what Peter called a great deal of money, in February, 1839, found a successful method of puddling iron with it.[7]

The employment of anthracite for puddling was nearly as important a development as its use in smelting ore, for only when mills could puddle their own iron was there any possibility of keeping up with the ever-growing demand for rails. Puddling and rolling had been introduced for making wrought iron as early as 1817. But such wrought-iron bars were inferior to iron refined by the slower and more expensive process of forging on a charcoal forge, and would remain so until a mineral fuel could be effectively employed. Peter and Thomas Cooper were not the first to use anthracite in a puddling furnace—the honor has been claimed for Jonah and George Thompson, who used it at Phoenixville in 1827—but they were among the very earliest to employ the new fuel with undoubted success. If Peter's name 'has been,' as Swank says in his *History of the Manufacture of*

Iron, 'the most prominent and the most honored in the iron history of the state during the present century,' [8] it was as much for this achievement as for anything he did later.

The Cooper brothers took out two patents on the furnaces they invented—Thomas', dated August 25, 1840; and Peter's, which used an idea of Gustin's assigned to him by the latter, August 2, 1842. Their problem had been to find the best way of applying heat, and they solved it by substituting for an open forge a furnace in which a blast of hot air was forced by compression through a vertical descending flue around the sides of the furnace into a puddling or heating chamber under the fire and let out through apertures over the coal.[9] As early as the spring of 1840 Cooper's agent, William Serrell, was singing the virtues of anthracite and of the new furnace to Junius Smith in London,[10] and very soon Peter began to receive orders from ironworks in America for his furnace, the rights to which he sold for $200 and twenty-percent commission. By 1843 he had, he claimed, sold the rights to all the principal ironworks in New England, and the balance of the New England rights to Horace Gray of Boston for $3000.

In July, 1843, however, a cloud appeared on the horizon. Christian E. Detmold, working as the agent of one William Von Faber du Faur, for whom he had already taken out one patent in 1842, patented a furnace fitted with blowpipes through which jets of heated air were forced into combination with waste furnace gas, thus increasing the heat of the puddling furnace and saving fuel. Cooper had known about and been interested in Detmold's experiments, and had been introduced to him in November, 1842, by Horatio Allen, with whom Detmold [11] had worked on the Charleston Railroad. His enthusiasm, however, soon turned to worry. By June, 1843, he was urging on Detmold the wisdom of uniting their claims and, in case Detmold balked, pointing out that he, Cooper, had been first in the field and that Detmold's patent could easily be evaded.

This rather over-ingenuous double-edged sword moved Det-

South Trenton Iron Company, as the works were at first called, had been launched.

Peter Cooper did not, strictly speaking, take his son and his son-in-law into partnership with him. In 1884 Hewitt wrote that 'during his long life Mr. Cooper never had a partner in any business transaction whatever. So careful was he on this point, that even his own children were never admitted into partnership with him.' [14] Hewitt overstated his case: Peter had had partners in both the grocery business and the Baltimore affair. But he had not had very much luck with his associates, and was reluctant to enter into a similar arrangement even with his son. At first, therefore, he simply supplied the capital and Edward and Abram in effect worked for him. In 1847, however, when the business gave every indication of being permanent and successful, a more satisfactory arrangement was worked out. This involved, to begin with, the creation in February, 1847, of a corporation, the Trenton Iron Company, a concession to new business procedures that Peter made for the first time in one of his undertakings. The day when Peter could 'keep the particulars of his financial situation in his head,' as Raymond wrote later,[15] was over, and evidently Peter realized it: the new firm was to keep books and balance sheets and deal with banks in the ordinary way. Secondly, a company called Cooper & Hewitt, a partnership entered into by Edward Cooper and Abram Hewitt, was created to act as managing firm for the Trenton Iron Company and to hold $149,000 of the $300,000 of stock first issued. By this ingenious device Peter Cooper, who was president of the Trenton Iron Company and owned the other $151,000 of stock, remained nominally independent of and superior to his youthful lieutenants, thus avoiding a partnership at the same time that Edward and Abram had virtual charge of the ironworks.

During the first four or five years of the company's existence Peter was consulted on almost every detail by Edward and Abram, who wrote him long letters about technical problems,

sales of iron rails, labor relationships, and other matters as well
as about the finances of the company. And Peter himself, as
letters to his son in Europe early in 1850 indicate, retained a
lively interest in everything from the breaking of rails made for
the Camden & Amboy to the latest difficulty over getting the
proper heat in a blast furnace. There is a touch of the youthful
Peter in his personal interference in the operation of the Easton
blast furnaces. He went down there and found bad leaks in the
joints: 'These I corked and wrapt up . . . as quick as possible.
I had the masons set to work at once and built a chimney around
the descending hot blast pipe. I had by morning a strong fire
made at the foot of this pipe with coal which with a fire of resin
which I had burning in the main hot blast within an hour after
I arrived made a very sensible difference in the heat of the
blast.' Keeping the hot blast pipe covered was very important.
'I intend to arrange a cylinder in the archway connecting it with
the hot blast pipes. In this cylinder I intend to convert the rosin
into gas and let it pass into the furnace in that form and when
you return if you see any better way it will not be very expensive
to alter it.' A year or so later Hewitt wrote that Peter was going
to Easton to experiment with introducing finely ground coal in
the furnace for increasing the heat at will. Peter also watched
over his specially designed puddling and heating furnaces at
Trenton, whose operation he described in detail in the *Reminiscences*.

But Peter's interest in the iron business waned. From the beginning he thought of technical and managerial problems as
chiefly Abram's and Edward's responsibility, and in 1849 openly
informed a correspondent that he had 'entrusted all my interest
in the iron business to Messrs. Cooper & Hewitt.' During the
'fifties his two associates consulted him less and less, and long
before he resigned as president of the Trenton Iron Company
in 1860 he had ceased to concern himself about anything but
the most important financial matters. The growth and develop-

ment of the company are therefore as much if not more Abram's and to a lesser extent Edward's story than they are Peter's. Since Professor Nevins has told that story admirably and in detail in his *Abram S. Hewitt,* I will not repeat it here except in barest outlines and with emphasis on the relationship between Peter and his energetic and resourceful son-in-law.[16] That relationship is a fascinating one, illustrative of Peter Cooper's generosity and willingness to delegate authority to those he trusted, and at the same time of his curious unwillingness to offer the complete independence which he himself so much prized. Hewitt was never completely able to break the leading strings provided by his benevolent tyrant of a father-in-law, and both his own disposition and the iron business eventually suffered as a consequence.

The building-up of the iron business was a notable achievement. Within a month of the opening of the rolling mills in 1845, Hewitt had made a contract with the Stevens brothers of the Camden & Amboy for rails which virtually assured the new business of success at the start. From this followed other contracts for rails, as the railroad boom burst the bonds of the long depression of the late 'thirties and early 'forties and new lines swept up along the seaboard and out across the Alleghenies. By the spring of 1846 Hewitt could write Peter from Boston, 'You may rest assured of plenty of work for two or three years as I shall be able to show you when I return.' [17] On March 1, 1848, the Trenton Iron Company declared a dividend of twenty per cent on earnings in excess of $67,500, and by the beginning of 1849 it could roll twelve thousand tons of rails a year.

The business had been, in the meantime, growing in other directions. Both Hewitt and Peter Cooper realized that no large iron manufactory could succeed any longer unless it owned its own raw materials, and from the first Hewitt spent his free time among the hills of northern New Jersey looking for superior grades of ore that would not wear out and splinter, as did so much American ore when used for rails. Early in 1847 he dis-

*New York in 1808, the year Peter Cooper arrived there.
The built-up parts of the city (indicated by shaded areas)
extended, even at their farthest on Bowery Lane, only a block
above Grand Street. The houses belonging to Cooper's
grandmother, on Broadway, were within a short distance of
open country.*

Peter's 28th Street and Fourth Avenue home, in the last sad

REFERENCES

*New York in 1817, at about the time Peter Cooper estab-
lished his grocery store on the edge of town at the Bowery
and Stuyvesant Street (shown in the center of the map at the
edge of the shaded area). The triangular white space just
below is Vauxhall Gardens. Note the start of the Eastern
Post Road across the Parade at 23rd Street and Fifth Avenue
(top and center of the map).*

Peter Cooper, his wife Sarah, and their children Amelia and Edward, in the 1850's. From a daguerreotype.

*A drawing of Lincoln at Cooper Union on February 27, 1860,
making the speech that won him the East.*

*'Red Cloud at Cooper Institute'—a drawing by Reinhart in
Harper's Weekly, 1870.*

An early daguerreotype showing Abram S. Hewitt as a young New Yorker.

Hewitt in later years, from a hand-colored photograph by Napoleon Sarony.

'*Let Papa Cooper Show His Hand*'—*a* Puck *cartoon which appeared during Edward Cooper's storm-tossed mayoralty.*

Photo by Brown Brothers, New York

A photograph of Peter Cooper by the famous Civil War cameraman, Mathew Brady, probably taken in the early 1860's.

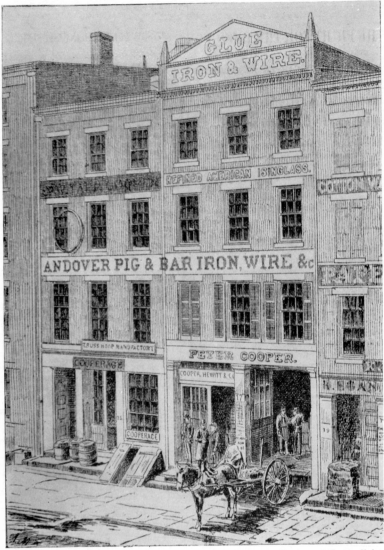

The office in Burling Slip where Cooper conducted his affairs for nearly forty years, shown as it appeared in 1883.

An unusual portrait of Cooper which was painted by Virginia Tucker some time after his death. It hangs in the home of Peter's great-grandson at Tuxedo Park, N. Y.

216,935.

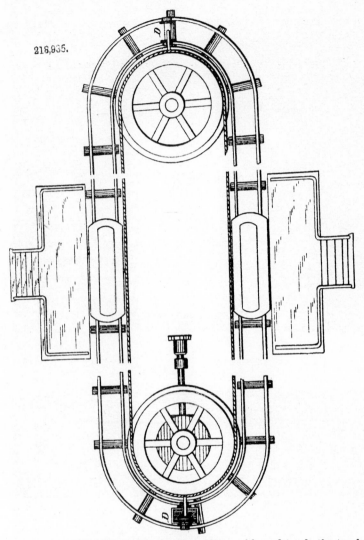

Claim.—1. In combination with the endless cable and track, the trucks D, substantially as and for the purposes set forth.

2. The arrangement and combination of the endless track, the stations equally distant apart, the endless traction-rope, and the cars secured thereto at distances corresponding to the distances of the stations, in the manner herein shown and described, so that all the cars on the circuit will simultaneously stop at and start from all the stations on the circuit.

From the Official Gazette, *U. S. Patent Office, August 26, 1879*

Cooper's design for an endless cable and track to be used on New York's elevated railways. This patent was filed in May, 1879.

Photo by Brown Brothers, New York

Two old friends: Peter Cooper and William Cullen Bryant.

Courtesy of the Frick Art Reference Library, New York

Christian Schussele's famous 'Men of Progress,' painted in 1861. Peter Cooper stands just behind Charles Goodyear, identified as a 'vulcanizer of gum elastic.' At the far left is Dr. Morton, the Boston dentist who first used ether; third and fourth from the left are Samuel Colt and Cyrus McCormick; while Morse, inventor of the telegraph, is shown seated in the right foreground.

*Henry Augustus Loop's painting of Cooper in extreme
old age.*

A Puck cartoon of 1883 entitled 'Three Monuments,' showing William H. Vanderbilt's Fifth Avenue house and Cooper's Union, with A. T. Stewart's Cathedral of the Incarnation in between. Stewart, the founder of Wanamaker's, bought the Long Island property which became Garden City as the site for low-cost model homes, and gave the money for the cathedral there.

Courtesy of the New York Public Library

Puck's *tribute to Peter Cooper the week after his death.*

Courtesy of Cooper Union

Cooper Union as it appeared in the 1870's.

covered and bought the famous Andover mines for just under $9500.[18] In 1853 the five-hundred-acre Rosehill mines nearby were added, and the great eleven-thousand-acre Ringwood estate. This vast tract, lying astride the New York-New Jersey line twenty miles west of the Hudson, was the most famous iron-ore property in the East, with a history going back a century and a half. In the 1760's a German known as Baron Hasenclever had spent 54,600 pounds to develop industry there on a scale heretofore unknown in the colonies. When Hasenclever went bankrupt, he was succeeded in 1771 by Robert Erskine, the most celebrated occupant of the place. Erskine turned out iron for the armies of Washington, and in 1777 became the first geographer and surveyor-general of the United States, the man who made it possible, by his maps of the land between the Hudson highlands and the Delaware, for Washington to outmaneuver the enemy there. An engineer of great capacity, he is a fitting ghost for the land on which is now located the Green Engineering Camp of Cooper Union. Peter Cooper acquired Ringwood from the thriftless sons of Martin J. Ryerson, who had made a great success of the mines in the early years of the nineteenth century.

The Ringwood property was of no great immediate use. It was too expensive to build a railway there or put up blast furnaces, and until Peter put in two blast furnaces, years later, all that was worked were two oldfashioned forges to earn the interest on the cost of the tract. To carry the ore from the mines to these forges Peter rigged up another of his endless-chain devices, six miles of wire—from which buckets of ore were to be suspended—run along a series of grooved wheels placed on the arms of large triangles two hundred feet apart.[19] But Ringwood did provide a home for the Hewitts, at which Peter Cooper was usually a summer-long visitor. Ryerson had erected a commodious three-story house of wood and brick close to the site of Hasenclever's and Erskine's residence, with latticed colonial windows, a heavy knocker and lock of English brass, fireplaces built on stone arches, and woodwork of finely carved mahogany. The Hewitts embellished the house, landscaped the gardens, dammed up a brook to form a lake, and added a greenhouse and a large stable, making Ringwood one of the finest estates in northern New Jersey.

After the first purchase of ore properties came blast furnaces. In 1847 the Trenton Iron Company bought forty acres of land at Phillipsburg, New Jersey, just across from Easton, where ore brought from Andover by the Morris Canal and later by the Sussex Railroad, built by Cooper, met Pennsylvania anthracite. Here the company erected two—later three—blast furnaces fifty-five feet high and twenty feet in diameter, which made pig iron for shipment by the Morris Canal and later by the Trenton & Belvidere-Delaware Railroad to the Trenton mills. Peter Cooper said that these furnaces, turning out twenty-five thousand tons of pigs a year, were the largest in the country at the time. In the meanwhile, Hewitt had been enlarging the Trenton plant, increasing the number of double puddling furnaces and heating furnaces, and erecting foundries, pattern shops, blacksmith shops, and machine shops. He was determined to have a large, well-rounded plant.

This meant that he could not depend at his mill entirely or even chiefly on rails, as he discovered early in 1849 when British competition suddenly cut the price of rails in half and, according to Hewitt, closed thirteen of fifteen American rail mills.[20] Hewitt immediately turned to Peter Cooper's old staple, wire, which the Trenton Company now began to produce in quantity for bridges, fences, and particularly for the fast-growing telegraph industry, most of whose wire the company supplied over a two-year period.[21] Then, five years later, when British competition and over-production helped cause a severe economic depression (the one that inspired Peter's wharf-building plan), the Trenton Company discovered an even more profitable staple. In 1854 it began to manufacture wrought-iron beams and girders for fireproof buildings, and thus made its greatest contribution to the American iron industry.

Peter Cooper's plan for Cooper Union in 1852 called for a huge and enduring fireproof building of five or more stories, which had heretofore meant a solid-stone structure of fabulous cost. Though cast-iron beams had been used on some buildings as early as 1827, and there had been some experimenting with wrought iron, no one had yet made beams long or deep enough for the construction of large buildings. Undeterred, Peter turned to the Trenton Iron Company. The company had been manufacturing railway bars four and one-half inches deep; why could it not, Peter wondered in characteristic fashion, roll beams seven inches deep? After two years of experiment and an outlay of $75,000 success was achieved, and it was not long before the company was turning out structural beams sixty feet long and fifteen inches deep.[22]

Cooper Union was not the first building completed with wrought-iron beams. Only two tiers of horizontal beams had been laid there when the Trenton Iron Company had a chance to do a piece of outside business. Harper & Brothers, whose whole establishment had been consumed by fire in December, 1853, were building their new building on Franklin Square, and Hewitt induced them to use his beams. Immediately work on Cooper Union was stopped, the machinery was put to work on the Harper office, and it was this building, finished in a record four months, which Peter called 'the first building, perhaps, ever completed in the world with iron beams.' Immediately the federal government turned to Hewitt to build the new Assay Office in New York, which was also completed before beams for Cooper Union were rolled in 1855. In the next year or two the Trenton Company received orders for more than a hundred state and federal projects, including the dome of the Capitol in Washington and the Mint in Philadelphia, and for many private buildings as well. No wonder Hewitt felt that making beams was a much better business than making rails and that it could absorb the company's whole time.

By 1854 Peter Cooper and his two lieutenants had reason to be proud of their accomplishment. At a time when Ohio and Pennsylvania were already topping the iron production on the seaboard they had created what an expert of the British government said 'may be looked upon as the leading establishment of the United States, not only in regard to its production but also in regard to its working arrangements.' [24] Production by the company's 2000-odd workers had reached 20,000 tons of wrought iron a year, a tremendous achievement when one considers that among some 2500 iron makers at the time only half a dozen could roll as much as 10,000 tons and none could come near the Trenton Company's total. Moreover, the company was one of only five American companies that combined the whole process of iron manufacture, from ore to finished product. Its constantly growing assets reflected this diversification: in 1854, of the $873,997.16 of fixed assets, $134,047.19 represented Ringwood, $226,933.91 blast furnaces, and $513,016.16 [25] the Trenton establishment, with its rolling, puddling, and wire mills. Profits varied from 9% in bad years like 1856-1857 to 17%—$173,790.06 on a capital of $950,000—in good years like 1855-1856. During the first ten years of its existence the company paid out 108% in dividends.[26]

Yet from the very beginning there had been serious difficulties. To maintain such a large business against vigorous competition in an era of swift technological advance required ever-renewed accessions of capital. The Trenton Company was chronically short of money, which either prevented expansion or meant a constant delay in expected returns of profit. As one reads Hewitt's reports as secretary of the company or his letters to Peter Cooper, one constantly has the sense that the company 'never Is, but always To Be bless'd.' In the fall of 1849, when the wire business was just starting, Hewitt urged Peter Cooper to accept an offer of a seven-percent mortgage loan from William B. Astor, because that was the only way, unless he was willing to be dependent on banks, that Cooper could both 'carry out the project [Cooper Union] to which I know you are more attached than any other' and keep the iron business on its feet. 'Nothing but the want of capital,' wrote Hewitt, 'can prevent [the Trenton property] from yielding from one to two hundred thousand dollars annually. You have carried a mighty enterprise almost to completion, and if we get through next winter without difficulty, the success is reduced to a mathematical certainty. . . . You have already made a great sacrifice of comfort—and I fear that unless we get matters into some easily manageable state, the anxiety of working things next winter will be more than you ought to suffer.'

Though the company weathered this crisis despite Peter's sensible refusal to put himself in the power of the acquisitive Astor, there was constant trouble. In 1853, in 1854, in 1857, and again in 1863 Hewitt complained that capital was inadequate, that improvements had drained profits, and that only the future —always seen in roseate hues—could justify present sacrifices.

The only source of capital in the beginning was Peter Cooper. He even guaranteed the loan at the bank—unbeknown to them —by which Edward and Abram were able to subscribe to their $149,000 of stock. Hewitt until his marriage had little of his own.[27] As late as 1863 he told his brother Charles that his 'command of personal means has never been large,' that Amelia's 'private income' from her father provided for the family, and that what funds he had were devoted to the business. Peter Cooper remained in effect the sole stockholder until 1853, and, though outside capital was then brought in, still controlled, in 1855, 4398 of the 8250 shares. Moreover he provided the chief source from which the company borrowed money, and was the guarantor of the loans for floating capital made by Cooper &

Hewitt to the company. He was also, as Hewitt wrote, the 'controlling power' though 'not a member' of the firm of Cooper & Hewitt, which owed him $200,000.[28]

Though Peter had always been willing enough to help his son and son-in-law, Hewitt did not, as he told the stockholders in 1858, 'like to see the Company reduced to taking favors of anyone.'[29] Such dependence depressed the stock, since Peter might suddenly enforce his rights, and if he died the loans would immediately become due. Funding the debt partially solved this latter problem, but it did not free Hewitt from the sense of personal dependence. It irritated him to think that stockholders joined the company only because of Peter Cooper's good name.[30] When, after twelve years of business, both Trenton banks still demanded Peter Cooper's guarantee on discounts of Trenton Iron Company drafts in favor of Cooper & Hewitt, Hewitt's cup ran over. 'A decent sense of self respect compels us to decide in the negative,' wrote Hewitt in refusing to accept the guarantee.[31] What made the situation even worse was that, though he helped Edward and Abram, Peter Cooper's heart was never wholly in the iron business and became less so as the years went on and money-making ceased to be the chief outlet for his energies. It must have been a shock to Abram when he learned —if he did—that in 1849 Peter urged his son in Europe to try to sell the rolling mills. Peter wanted, he told Edward, to be 'relieved from all but the blast furnace and the glue factory, which will always furnish business enough for comfort.'[32] No wonder that Abram acquiesced in—or encouraged—the attempt in 1853 to sell the whole business to Edwin Post. No wonder that in 1854 he wanted to retire from the management of the Trenton Iron Company. No wonder, finally, that rather than be dependent on Peter Cooper's bounty he preferred in 1858 to give up his ambitious project of developing Ringwood and to sell it back to Peter Cooper.[33]

Though the dependence of the iron business on an increasingly indifferent Peter Cooper may have irked Hewitt, it did not cause him to resign or produce a real crisis in the business until after the Civil War. In the meantime Hewitt worked with almost pathological intensity for the company, using the means at his disposal, and devoted his 'leisure' to studying technological problems in the industry, the results of which he published in scientific periodicals. And he did well for Peter, weathering the 'unparalleled financial distress and disaster' of 1856-1857 and the worse panic year that followed, and performing yeoman service during the war making gunmetal and gun carriages for mortars for the government. By 1865, however, makeshifts would no longer do. The age of iron was giving place to the age of steel, huge aggregations of capital and great new machines were being found to exploit the new processes, and Pittsburgh and the Great Lakes were witnessing the establishment of a new industry near the sources of the best ore. Hewitt had seen the change coming about even before the Civil War, and had thought of buying Lehigh ore beds. Now, certain that only a removal westward would save the Trenton Iron Company, he and Edward pleaded with Peter Cooper to permit it. There was even an offer by Carnegie to become his partner in Pittsburgh, the refusal of which the former 'was inclined to banter' Hewitt about in later years.[34]

But Peter was adamant. Cooper Union was in New York and it meant now a thousand times more to him than did the iron business. Besides, as he said—pouring salt into Edward's and Abram's wounds—, 'you young men lose so much money in the iron mill now that it takes all I make from the glue factory to pay your deficits.'[35] In 1868 he wrote with some asperity (and not, it would seem, with entire accuracy) to Herman J. Redfield: 'During a period of over thirty years, engaged in the manufacture of iron, the capital invested by me has not on the average yielded me four per cent per annum, and this with all the skill, energy and perseverance which I was able to command in promoting its profitable employment.'[36] What could Hewitt do? Amelia, who seems never in her life to have quite made the proper choice between father and husband, refused to leave New York. Hewitt could not go west on his own, as only Cooper's money was keeping the iron business alive as it was. He had no real choice except, as Amelia said in later years, to sacrifice himself for Peter and his daughter. Possibly, as Professor Nevins asserts, Abram did not really want to act independently. But he must have spent some wakeful hours in his bed at Ringwood.

Hewitt did the best for the iron company that was possible under the circumstances. Immediately after the war he bought the famous Durham Iron Works in Bucks County to compensate for the failure of the Andover mine; and he began making steel-topped rails by the Mushet-Heath process of fusing wrought iron and carburized Ringwood blooms in a high-temperature furnace. In 1867-1868 he brought the Siemens-Martin open-hearth method of making steel to this country, a process that later was to compete successfully with the Bessemer process. This was Hewitt's greatest achievement, though the Trenton Company was never itself able to turn out more than limited amounts of steel. By 1870 he was selling steel-topped rails to various railroads, in particular to Jay Gould's notorious Erie, and to the street railways of New York,[37] while he continued to furnish gunmetal to federal armories and wrought-iron girders for buildings.

The Trenton Company was, nevertheless, rapidly losing out in the competition with the new western giants. The stockholders had lost faith before Hewitt had, and early in 1866 Cooper & Hewitt bought the rolling mills from the company and set up a separate corporation to roll iron and steel, the New Jersey Steel & Iron Company. Then in August, 1867, Cooper & Hewitt bought the 7500 shares of the Trenton Iron Company stock at $70 a share, and the whole works passed back into the hands of the Cooper-Hewitt family.[38] At this point even Hewitt became doubtful. The business was in unsatisfactory shape, he told Charles in December, 1867, 'and I confess I do not think that we can continue to carry it on. The loss this year is very severe, and the prospect not encouraging in any direction. We have done a very magnanimous thing for the Trenton Iron Company and have probably crippled ourselves for years.' [39]

Hewitt did not actually lose money in the following years. But, as he said in 1900, 'in the thirty-five years since then [1865], the entire profit of the Trenton mills has not aggregated $600,-000.' By 1872 all-steel Bessemer rails—of which Hewitt remained sceptical for a fatally long time[40]—were being used on most American railways, forcing the New Jersey Iron & Steel Company to depend for survival on structural beams and the manufacture of car and locomotive axles. It henceforth played an increasingly minor role in the great industrial race, and Hewitt turned to politics as an outlet for his thwarted ambition. Peter Cooper's loss of interest had ultimately proved fatal to his greatest effort as an entrepreneur.

Chapter 13

WIRING OCEANS AND
CONTINENTS

Early in March, 1854, a memorable meeting took place at the Clarendon Hotel in New York City. Five of New York's most prominent capitalists—Cyrus Field, Moses Taylor, Peter Cooper, Chandler White, and Marshall O. Roberts—had gathered to determine whether they would buy a charter obtained by certain parties from the government of Newfoundland to connect the eastern end of that country with Canada by wire. The parties were unable to continue and wanted to sell out for enough to pay their debts, about $40,000.[1] The proposition seemed reasonable enough and the venture a moderate and sensible one. Though there was little chance of dazzling commercial success, the advantage of cutting the time of news transmission from Europe by intercepting steamers at Halifax made the small expenditure seem eminently worthwhile. All that appeared at first to be required was a land line across Newfoundland to a spot where fast steamers might pick up the news and carry it to Nova Scotia to be transmitted to the United States by telegraph. Possibly a cable might be constructed across the Gulf of St. Lawrence between Newfoundland and Cape Breton, though, according to Hewitt, no such suggestion was made at this meeting 'because it was doubtful at that time whether submarine communication of such length could be established and

· (218) ·

maintained.'[2] As for continuing the line east from Newfoundland across thousands of miles of ocean to Ireland—well, that too lurked, though only as a vision, in several minds that day in the Clarendon Hotel. But like so many visions dreamed by men of action, this one was soon to take command and transform the limited scheme of a Newfoundland-United States telegraph line into one of the most monumental achievements of the nineteenth century. The Clarendon Hotel was the birthplace of the Atlantic Cable.

Cable communications, though not to Europe, had certainly been in the minds of those who had secured the original charter.[3] The idea of underwater telegraph wires had been made possible by the discovery of gutta-percha for insulating, and as early as 1842 Samuel Morse had laid an experimental cable between Castle Garden and Governor's Island in New York harbor. In 1851 a successful cable was laid between Dover and Calais, and two years later between Ireland and England. It was Bishop Mullock of Newfoundland who in 1850 first suggested that Newfoundland was the nearest place to Europe, and that a telegraph line could be built four hundred miles across the island from St. John's west to Cape Ray, thence forty-odd miles to St. Paul's Island, and then twelve miles across to Cape North on Cape Breton Island. At the same time Frederick N. Gisborne, a telegraph operator, had a similar idea. In 1851 he surveyed the island and secured a charter from the Newfoundland government for the Newfoundland Electric Telegraph Company, which the following year stretched the first American cable from Cape Ray to Prince Edward Island and thence to New Brunswick.

After he had built thirty miles of road on Newfoundland, however, Gisborne's backers deserted him, he was sued by his creditors, and lost everything. Appearing in New York in January, 1854, he met Matthew D. Field, who immediately turned him over to his brother Cyrus, just returned from six months in the South American mountains. Having retired from business with a fortune made as a paper manufacturer, Field, still in his early thirties, was ripe for a new venture. Gisborne's talk inspired him, and as he turned the globe around in his hands a dream far transcending Gisborne's slowly came to birth. Morse had said ten years before that a cable to Europe was possible, and in February, 1854, M. F. Maury of the United States Navy had surveyed the bottom of the sea between England and Canada and reported that the whole sixteen hundred miles was an undulating plateau at an average depth of two and a half miles with no precipitous slopes and no current. Field determined to take the first step toward his dream, the building of the Newfoundland line, and immediately turned to his next-door neighbor, Peter Cooper, for assistance.

Peter did not rise immediately to the bait. As Henry Field, Cyrus' clergyman brother, wrote, Cooper at first evinced the 'indisposition which a man of large fortune—now well advanced in life—would naturally feel to embark in new enterprises.' [4] He had his iron business to think of, which had just begun manufacturing wrought-iron beams, he was leading the reform movement in New York politics that was soon to put up Wilson G. Hunt for mayor, and he was deeply absorbed in his Union slowly going up on Astor Place. Yet an enterprise that required daring and that involved scientific advance never left him unmoved. Electricity had an especial fascination, as it seemed the particular manifestation of God's power in the universe. And the way Field presented the project, it appeared to be less a speculation than a service to humanity, which made it irresistible. 'As they talked it over,' wrote Henry Field, 'the large heart of Mr. Cooper began to see that, if it were possible to accomplish such a work, it would be a great public benefit. This consideration prevailed, and what would not have been undertaken as a private speculation, was yielded to public interest.' [5]

Peter himself later wrote that the enterprise struck him 'as though it was the consummation of that great prophecy, that "knowledge shall cover the earth, as waters cover the deep." '

Many thought the scheme 'fitted those who engaged in it for an asylum where they might be taken care of as little short of lunatics. But believing, as I did, that it offered the possibility of a mighty power for the good of the world, I embarked on it.' [6]

To Cyrus Field belongs—and has been amply given—chief credit for the whole cable project. But among the other figures of the Atlantic Cable promoters who appear in Daniel Huntington's famous painting, none deserves a higher place than Peter Cooper. Once committed, he threw himself heart and soul into the planning and sustaining of the enterprise. Without his money and cooperation it could never have been carried through, for there were moments when 'no one else was willing to provide the means of keeping the company alive.' His faith and his faith alone never failed him over the twelve grim and discouraging years that ensued before a permanent cable to Europe was laid. Hewitt helped him but never shared his faith, and was 'agreeably disappointed' when the 1858 cable was successfully landed. 'I regarded the investment of so much money in a doubtful enterprise as a piece of folly. I am forced to acknowledge the superior wisdom of Mr. Cooper.' [7] Even Cyrus Field was once so discouraged he was ready to quit, and Cooper had to buck him up by telling him he owed it to himself and the world to continue. But never Peter. As Hewitt said truly, he was sustained by a faith characteristically based 'not so much upon scientific or mechanical knowledge, as upon the conviction that a scheme so desirable for the good of mankind must be possible.' [8]

The magic of Peter Cooper's name helped draw in Taylor, White, and Roberts. With the addition of David Dudley Field and, the following year, of Wilson G. Hunt, Samuel Morse, Robert W. Lowber, and the Englishman John W. Brett, this completed the group of promoters of the enterprise during its most difficult years. [9] Morse, Lowber, and Brett contributed little; White, a retired businessman and personal friend of Field, died within a year or so; and Hunt admittedly 'did not feel much interest in it.' Roberts and Taylor contributed their share at the beginning, but toward the end, Cooper said, it was 'like pulling teeth . . . to get more money from them.' Though willing investors and even speculators, these two were not idealists. Marshall O. Roberts became a notorious profiteer during the Civil War, making nearly $3,000,000 from a half-dozen steamers picked up for a song, and getting the Supreme Court to pay him $1,031,000 damages for losses after a brazen attempt to lobby the government into repaying him had failed.[10] Moses Taylor was an even more acquisitive sort, who for six decades allowed nothing to interfere with the singleminded pursuit of wealth.[11] The best that can be said for these men was that they were friends of Peter Cooper, who was seldom sullied by anything he touched, and that, however reluctantly, they aided Field and Cooper in the cable project.

The Clarendon Hotel meeting was followed by four others on successive evenings at Cyrus Field's Gramercy Park house. Without waiting for more adherents—Peter Cooper said that if ten men could carry out the project so could five—Cooper, Field, Taylor, White, and Roberts agreed to give White, Field, and his brother David Dudley up to $22,000 to send them to Newfoundland to get a charter. They returned shortly with their mission successfully accomplished, having obtained a charter which included provisions looking forward to a possible future establishment of telegraphic communication with Europe. The company was given a fifty-year monopoly to land cables on the island and a promise of a bonus of fifty square miles of land and $50,000 from the Newfoundland government when a cable was laid. At 6 A.M. on May 8th—'as the first rays of the morning sun streamed into the windows' of Dudley Field's house—the New York, Newfoundland & London Telegraph Company was born, with Peter Cooper as president—a post he held for the eighteen years of the company's existence. With its authorized capital of $1,500,000 the company planned to connect the eastern and western ends of Newfoundland by telegraph, and then, possibly by cable, to tie the western end to Nova Scotia. It was two years before the projectors dared look eastward from Newfoundland, and by then, if not long before, it had become evident that the New York Newfoundland Company was an inadequate vehicle for such aims.

The land line across four hundred miles of Newfoundland was a difficult enough undertaking. The interior of southern Newfoundland was mostly an uninhabited, largely unexplored country of rock, moor, lakes, mountains, and vast forests teeming with wolves and bears. In order to build a telegraph line, a road eight feet wide had to be cut through this wilderness. The poles had to be shipped from Nova Scotia and carried on the backs of mules to their destination. Often they had to be set in rock so hard that digging was impossible, the only feasible method being to support them by a stone embankment about each pole. Yet the work progressed during the summer and fall of 1854 under the guidance of Matthew Field, who worked with detachments of six hundred men supplied by sea. Back in New York the directors worked to raise money and paid the drafts drawn on them by White at St. John's. Nearly every evening during the autumn they met anxiously in Field's library, calculating costs and waiting with dread to hear of the first snow. It came before the work was finished, an augury of the difficulties, 'hardly possible to conceive,' as Peter later wrote, that were met at every step of the enterprise.

By December it seemed possible to plan for the more daring enterprise of laying a cable across the Gulf of St. Lawrence, and Cyrus Field was dispatched to England, on the first of forty trips, to secure a cable. There he met John W. Brett, the father of submarine telegraphy in Europe, who had stretched two lines across the English Channel and who proved to be the only Englishman to buy shares of Newfoundland stock. A cable of three copper wires surrounded by gutta-percha, iron wires, and tar was secured and shipped to Cape Ray by the sailing barge *Sarah L. Bryant* in August of 1855. Hearing of her imminent

· (223) ·

arrival, the directors of the company chartered a towing steamer, the *Thomas Adger,* for $750 a day, to help with the submerging, and formed a pleasure party to go and witness the great event. Field, Peter Cooper, Lowber, and Morse represented the company, and among the others present were Bayard Taylor and Dr. Gardiner Spring, minister of the Brick Church in New York.

The trip to Newfoundland, Peter's first journey beyond the borders of the United States, was a gay one. From the day the party sailed, August 7th, the sea was calm, and as the ship steamed north through the sunlit ocean Peter lay on deck and expounded his religious views at length to Dr. Spring, or watched the indefatigable Morse demonstrate the wonders of his telegraph instrument. At Halifax some of the passengers returned to New York, and the rest went on to Port au Basque near Cape Ray, full of happy anticipation.

But from the moment they arrived there things began to go wrong. The *Bryant* had not appeared, and there were several days of nervous waiting, which put a strain on everyone. The climax of irritation was reached when, according to Peter, Mr. Lowber put Dr. Spring and not the captain of the *Adger* at the head of the table, with the result that the captain was offended and 'became as stubborn as a mule thereafter.' Nerves were relieved by a trip to St. John's, where the party was warmly welcomed, and on their return the *Bryant* had arrived. But trouble had just begun, and the next few days were to witness a series of mishaps which accumulated at an almost farcical rate. Some of them, as Peter claimed, were probably the captain's fault, but the majority undoubtedly sprang from the attempt to use two boats to submerge the cable. Thereafter a single steamer carrying a cable would be used.

The first task was to carry the barge to a cove on Cape Ray, where a telegraph house to receive the end of the cable had been set up. It took four trials before the *Adger* could get hold of the cable ship, so that darkness had descended before they reached the cove. The end of the cable, however, was finally brought into the telegraph house, and the captain directed to take the *Bryant* in tow and start across the channel. Almost immediately, as Peter wrote, 'he ran his steamer into the vessel, carried away her shrouds and quarter-rail, and almost ruined our enterprise the first thing, dragging the cable over the stern of the vessel with such force as to break the connection; and we were obliged to cut the cable and splice it again. The captain of the steamer had failed entirely in trying to get hold of the vessel.'

The second effort was even less happy. The captain of the *Adger* succeeded in getting one of the two-hundred-foot, four-inch towing cables 'entangled in the steamer's wheel, and he halloed to the captain of the vessel to let his cable slip, in order to get this unentangled. At this, the captain of the vessel let go his cable and lost his anchor and one of our big [towing] cables, for we had to cut it, in order to disentangle it from the wheel. After that was got loose there was the vessel without an anchor, and she was going rapidly down upon a reef of rocks, with a strong wind against her. . . . We had to expostulate with the captain of the steamer until the vessel was within two or three hundred feet of the rocks, before he would consent to attempt her rescue; and by the merest good luck, we got out a rope to her and saved her from going on the rocks, when she was so close to the shore that we could almost have thrown a line there.'

By this time no one's humor was of the best. But on the third attempt the *Adger* made the necessary connection, and 'on a beautiful morning we started to lay the cable across the Gulf.' A flagstaff had been placed on the telegraph house, which the steamer as she crossed the gulf was to keep in line 'with a certain very excellent landmark on the top of a mountain some three, four, or five miles distant—a landmark which seemed to be made on purpose for our use.' The captain very soon began to get out of line with these marks. 'As President of the line, I called the matter to the attention of the captain. The answer I

got was: "I know how to steer my ship; I steer by my compass." '
Every few minutes, until the ship was eight to ten miles off the
course, Peter kept prodding the captain. Finally he said, "Captain, we shall have to hold you responsible for the loss of this
cable," and to show that this was not an idle gesture, he had a
lawyer on board draw up a legal paper setting forth the captain's liability. The captain immediately 'turned the course of
his ship, and went just as far from the line in the other direction.' He also kept running the ship faster than the cable could
be paid out, despite constant shouts of "Slower! Slower!," and
several times had to stop because a kink developed in the cable.
Eventually, late in the afternoon, a storm put an end to the
sorry business by making it necessary to cut the cable to save the
ship. It was subsequently found that though twenty-four miles
of cable had been laid they had gone only nine miles from
shore.[12]

Thus ended the first year's futile attempt. Peter's subsequent
comment sounds like a gross understatement of his feelings at
the time: 'We had spent so much money, and lost so much time,
that it was very vexatious to us to have our enterprise defeated
in the way it was, by the stupidity and obstinacy of one man.
This man was one of the rebels that fired the first guns upon
Fort Sumter. The poor fellow is now dead.' Undiscouraged,
however, the company went ahead the following year. With no
display and no party, a steamer successfully laid the cable. It
worked without a hitch for over nine years, when it was broken
by the anchor of a vessel. By that time two Atlantic cables had
been successfully laid and it was necessary for the company not
only to restore the first St. Lawrence cable but to lay a second.
The land lines through Newfoundland and Nova Scotia, finished in 1855 or 1856, had also to be supplemented by a second
line to complete the whole circuit.

Almost the whole burden of this enterprise had been borne
by Field, Cooper, Taylor, and Roberts, who for nearly ten years
made nothing whatever out of it. The unsuccessful effort of

1855 cost them $350,000, and by 1856 they had spent over $1,-000,000, Peter subscribing to at least $200,000 worth of the stock and $35,000 worth of bonds. Moreover, as Peter said, the Bank of Newfoundland would not trust the company and was constantly drawing drafts on him personally for as much as ten or twenty thousand dollars at a time. To lay their last St. Lawrence cable they issued more bonds, which the four of them had to take up at fifty cents on the dollar and later exchange for stock. Virtue was, however, well—some thought too well—rewarded in the end. In 1873 Field got the English Atlantic Cable company, the Anglo-American, to take over the 30,000 shares of New York, Newfoundland & London Telegraph Company stock at $90 a share. Peter Cooper, whose books in 1865 show that he held 5368 shares of stock and five bonds,[13] therefore eventually grossed nearly half a million dollars on his investment.[14]

With the successful laying of the St. Lawrence cable in 1856, the Newfoundland Company directors began finally to look beyond American shores, and in September sent Cyrus Field to England to negotiate about the Ireland-to-Newfoundland cable. As the result of further ocean soundings in the two preceding years, the feasibility of conducting electricity over so long a distance in deep water had been substantiated by Faraday, Robert Stephenson, and others. Field talked to Charles T. Bright and Dr. Edward O. Whitehouse, engineers and experimenters with electro-magnetism, as well as to the enthusiastic John W. Brett and others; and he sounded out Lord Clarendon at the Foreign Office. By December he, Bright, and Whitehouse had organized the Atlantic Telegraph Company, to which was handed over the Newfoundland Company's right to land cables in exchange for an exclusive connection.

Three-quarters of the three hundred £1000 shares were eagerly snapped up in England, and Field returned to America with the other eighty-eight. To his chagrin he found a lamentable lack of enthusiasm among his compatriots. Only twenty-seven shares was he able to dispose of in America, some of them to the ever-faithful Peter Cooper.[15] Cyrus Field, Peter Cooper, and other Americans had first thought of the idea and had carried on the enterprise alone for two years. Now it was to pass almost entirely into English hands. Englishmen controlled the company; the Englishman Bright was engineer and Whitehouse was electrician; Sir William Thomson, later Lord Kelvin, was a director of the company, and it was his system of electrical conduction that was used, not that of Morse, who resigned as electrician in 1858 when he was maneuvered off the board of directors and developed suspicions of the whole project. The cable was made in England by an English firm. Among Americans only Cyrus Field and to a lesser extent Peter Cooper played an important role in the better-known and more dramatic events that followed the completion of the St. John's-to-Nova Scotia part of the project.

The most important task that faced Cyrus Field and Peter Cooper in the spring of 1857 was to win for the project the co-operation of the American government. This was not easy, as, besides the opposition of special interests and of the chronic economizers, there was a general fear of giving England an advantage over America in some way; after all, both ends of the line were to be on English soil. But Field, Cooper, and Abram Hewitt worked manfully on Congress in person and by letter during February. Hewitt, using both his own and Cooper's name, bombarded Richard Brodhead and Stephen Douglas in the Senate and George Vail in the House with letters. The latter had told Cooper that the cable would harm his own telegraph interests, though when accused of this motive for voting against the telegraph bill he had claimed that his reason was opposition on principle to government subsidy of any private business. Hewitt pointed out to him that the bill merely authorized the President to grant money for value received; that is, it guaranteed $70,000 of government business a year to the cable. The bill finally passed the House by a small majority, the Senate by one vote, and was signed by President Pierce on March 3rd, a few hours before he left office.

Securing the two ships promised by the government, the *Niagara* and the *Susquehanna,* next engaged their attention. From March 14th until the *Niagara* sailed on April 22nd, Hewitt kept needling Isaac Toncey, Secretary of the Navy, to hurry her departure. The *Susquehanna,* the largest sidewheeler in the navy, arrived in New York disabled by yellow fever; fortunately —since there was no other boat available—she was eventually able to proceed.[16]

The 1857 plan of laying the cable was for the *Niagara* to start from Liverpool with half the cable, spooling it out as she progressed to mid-ocean, where she was to meet the British ship *Agamemnon* carrying the other half. But the *Niagara* never came near her destination. On August 11th, four days and 335 miles from Liverpool, the cable parted and sank into the ocean when Bright applied the brakes as the ship rose on a swell. So Peter was unable to have Field send over the 'chain,' as he asked him to do, his message of thanks to the 'Lord of heaven and earth' for all His 'demonstrations of power, wisdom, and goodness which the ages have developed in the rational and intellectual heart of man.'

But neither Field nor Cooper was discouraged, though the project had already cost $500,000 and had to be postponed a year. God's laws still guided them 'on this vast and ever-revolving ocean' and would eventually provide 'a means through which knowledge may yet cover the earth as the waters cover the great deep.'[17] As Peter wrote to Nahum Capen on August 31st, they had learned that the conducting power was not hurt by the pressure of two miles of water. 'This renders it certain that the work will be finally accomplished.'[18] In characteristic fashion, also, Peter decided that he had an improved plan for laying cable 'with (almost) a positive certainty of success and with a small part of the cost of the ordinary cable laying.' He proposed to drag after the ship steel wires held by gutta-percha in the form of a tube, smooth inside and ribbed outside to prevent the tube from twisting when drawn through the water, and long enough to reach the ocean bottom. The cable would pass through this tube and be deposited in the ocean without the usual wear and tear.

Unfortunately, Field came back to New York in the midst of the panic of 1857 when even Peter Cooper had to sell some shares of Atlantic Telegraph Stock. He was willing to sell as low as £250 a share, or at twenty-five cents on the dollar, though 'with my confidence in the ultimate success of the enterprise,' he told George Peabody in London, 'I hope to avoid serious loss.' [19] Even so, the money was raised. On March 9th the *Niagara* left New York once more, this time unaccompanied by the *Susquehanna,* which, despite Cooper's applications to the Navy Department, had to be left in the West Indies completely disabled by yellow fever.[20] The 1858 plan was to have the ships meet in mid-ocean with the cables, splice them, and then each sail for her respective shore laying the cable as she went. But the gods seemed again hostile. A storm at sea postponed the meeting for two weeks, and when the cable-laying finally commenced on June 25th it proceeded with little success. The cable broke three times, and after the last catastrophe, which occurred when two hundred miles separated the two ships, they were forced to repair to Ireland.

Undaunted by popular discouragement, they set out once more on July 17th. And once more the elements conspired against them, in the form of cable breaks, electrical failures, storms, near-collisions, and insulation defects. Yet to the astonishment of the civilized world, which had virtually written off the experiment, they succeeded. On August 5th the *Niagara* brought her end into the Bay of Bulls, Trinity Bay, Newfoundland, and shortly thereafter the *Agamemnon* steamed into Valentia harbor in Ireland, spanning the ocean with 1950 miles of wire. The excitement, in America in particular, knew no bounds, especially after the Queen's message was received on August 16th. The celebration lasted for two weeks in New York, and included lengthy ovations, a banquet, a procession from the Battery to the Crystal Palace, a torchlight parade by firemen, and illumination of the whole city, which caused the destruction of the cupola of the City Hall by fire on August 18th. The stock of the company reached a high of £910, and Cooper refused to sell at £850 what the year before he had been willing to let go for £250.[21]

Peter Cooper shared fully in all the celebrations. After the fireworks on the evening of August 17th he was serenaded at his home by a band led by a committee of the Common Council; on September 1st, the climactic day, a banner bearing his name flew from the west side of the City Hall; when he appeared with David Dudley Field in the great procession on that day, he was wildly cheered; he attended the ceremony at the Crystal Palace that followed the procession, and later in the evening the great municipal dinner, where he received—and gave—elaborate compliments.[22] Congratulatory letters from friends and enthusiasts poured in on him. A gentleman who called himself Baron William Spitzenafski sent him a sheaf of poems inspired by and dedicated to the Atlantic Telegraph Company, hoping that Peter would accept these poor verses, the 'true copies of my ideas,' from one who was formerly rich and belonged to 'some of the greatest vocal societies in New York,' but who lost a fortune 'during my great voyages in Europe, Africa and Asia.' [23] Another very 'humble friend' from Newark, one I. Dillex, wrote him that this enterprise was no common event but one guided by 'supernal intelligence,' as proved by the behavior of the heavens on the day of the celebration.[24]

Joy was, however, shortlived. The very day of the great celebration, September 1st, heard the last intelligible message from Valentia. For weeks afterward the cable was 'like a slowly dying person whose breathing is scarcely perceptible, whose lips at times move faintly, but form no intelligible words which those bending lovingly over the wasted form can detect.' [25] On October 20th it breathed its last. Immediately there was a popular revulsion, all those who had praised proceeding in their disappointment to damn. Lt. Francis Higginson, owner of £1000 of stock, claimed that the cable had broken on July 29th at 7:30 P.M. and all that followed was a deception. Men crossed the street when they saw Field approaching and accused him of selling stock at a profit in August, knowing the whole thing was a hoax. Now, if ever, was the time for courage and faith, and no one displayed them more conspicuously than did Peter Cooper. When even Field broke down and wept, Peter Cooper arose and said simply, "We will go on." And Field did. Peter helped refute accusations of deception and raised the money from his reluctant friends to send Field to England once more in May, 1859.

Clearing the company's good name was not too difficult. As Peter wrote, among the messages received over the cable in America was one which forestalled the sending of troops from Canada to the Chinese War, the news of the sudden termination of which had been received in London. One message received in London through Cyrus Field was the announcement of a collision between the *Europa* and the *Arabia* off Cape Race. One day, when a man denounced the cable as a humbug on the floor of the New York Chamber of Commerce, the shipowner Cunard arose, according to Peter, and 'said that "the gentleman did not know what he was talking about, and had no right to say what he had, and that he himself had sent messages and got the answers." Mr. Cunard was a positive witness; he had been on the spot; and the man must have felt "slim" at the result of his attempt to cast ridicule on men whose efforts, if unsuccessful, were at least not unworthy of praise.' [26] Getting money was, however, another story. When Field arrived in England people laughed at him, Cooper said. 'They thought the thing was dead enough, and buried deep enough in the ocean to satisfy anybody.' The British government refused to guarantee interest, thus preventing the raising of capital from private sources. Even the evident need of a cable, demonstrated in 1862 in the Trent affair, couldn't hurry matters, and in six years only £70,000 were secured in New York and little more in England.

It was not until 1864 that Field, in England, 'finally got hold,' according to Peter, 'of an old Quaker friend, who was a very rich man, and . . . so completely electrified him with the idea of the work, that he put three or four hundred thousand dollars into it immediately to lay another cable, and in fourteen days after Mr. Field had got that man's name, he had the whole amount of subscriptions made up.' [27] Peter was undoubtedly referring to Thomas Brassey, who, together with Sir John Pender, chairman of the Gutta Percha Company, and Glass Elliott & Company, makers of the cable, supplied most of the new £600,000 that was needed. By January, 1865, the money was finally raised and the huge new steamship *Great Eastern* began to load the cable into her three tanks, a task that was to take five months. On May 19th Cooper, Field, William E. Dodge, and A. A. Low, as honorary directors of the Atlantic Telegraph Company, forwarded to President Johnson a copy of an earlier letter of theirs to the recently assassinated Lincoln, and expressed their hope that the government would take the same interest in the project that Lincoln had given Field assurance of taking. A cordial union of England and America in this undertaking would be a happy augury of future good relations between countries so recently almost at swords'-points.[28]

There was to be one more disappointment. Six hundred miles from the goal the cable was lost bringing up an injured part, and after it had been grappled for four times the attempt had to be given up for one more year. But this time no one was discouraged. They knew that the *Great Eastern* was the answer to their cable-laying problems. Moreover, they had solved all the difficulties about cables, which had been successfully laid 1535 miles from Malta to Alexandria and 1400 miles in the Persian Gulf. They had learned the cause of the 1858 trouble, which was that the insulation had become thin when the cable had lain in the sun and the wires had sunk through the melting gutta percha.[29] They had also discovered that minute currents of electricity were all that were necessary and that the strong ones they had used endangered the conducting wire. The new cables had copper-wire centers three times the size of that of 1858, better insulation, less weight per pound, and two and one-half times the strength. The £600,000 of new capital was easily raised by creation of a new corporation, the Anglo-American Telegraph Company, which received what amounted to a preferred-stock dividend of 25%, or £125,000, on all earnings of the Atlantic Telegraph Company plus £25,000 a year from the earnings of the New York, Newfoundland & London Company.

The *Great Eastern* started this time on Friday the 13th of July, and landed at Heart's Content, Trinity Bay, on July 27th without a hitch. It then went out with six hundred miles of cable and fished successfully for the lost end of the 1865 cable. In Cooper's words, 'I do not think that feat is surpassed by any other human achievement. The cable was taken out of water, two and a half miles deep, in mid-ocean. It was pulled up three times, before it was saved. They got it up just far enough to see it, and it would go down again, and they would have to do the work over again. They used up all their coal, and spent ten or twelve days in "hooking" for the cable before it was finally caught.' [30] Actually, it took a month to get the cable, and it was not until the thirtieth try, on September 1st, that it was finally pulled up. On September 7th the amazed and delighted listeners at the Valentia end, who had been waiting hopefully for a year for sounds from the dead cable, suddenly got a message through it. The Atlantic had been spanned not by one but by two fully working cables.

At last there was no longer irony when Peter Cooper spoke of the cable as a proof that God rewards patient industry and minds that soar. His faith was at last justified, and he never enjoyed happier moments than at the great public banquet given for Field by the Chamber of Commerce on November 15, 1866, or when, as president of the Newfoundland Company, he in 1867 welcomed the Associated Press around the 'social board.' Fortunately, he did not live into the twentieth century. To him it was an axiom that the truth streaming around the world would make men happier. He had become, he felt, a co-worker with God in opening up the depths of the oceans to the light of truth and justice and civil liberty. And so perhaps he was, though it might have occurred even to Peter Cooper that copper wire makes no automatic selection in favor of truth.

From the idealist's point of view, the events that immediately followed the successful laying of the cable are somewhat anti-climactic. They are, however, very much part of the story. Though the cable was conceived as a great public service, it was also a business venture by private capitalists looking for financial reward, and all efforts after 1867 were turned toward consolidating monopolistic control of ocean communication. Peter Cooper abetted this aim in every way that he could. Unlike banks, which profited by laws granting them special privileges, the cable was, Peter told the government of Nova Scotia when it protested in 1858 against the fifty-year monopoly held by the Newfoundland Company, an 'invention' whose promoters deserved reward for work and risk. Far from being, as charged, a 'monstrous monopoly' gouging the public, the Newfoundland Company had not, he wrote in 1873,[31] made enough money for twelve of its sixteen years 'to keep the lines in repair,' and never paid more than eight per cent on invested capital. The promoters deserved at least freedom from competition.

The first competitive problem, which arose early in 1867, was the inevitable struggle between the three allies that had laid the cables, the Newfoundland, the Atlantic, and the Anglo-American Companies.[32] Though it was Field who eventually solved this problem in December, 1869,[33] getting the Anglo-American to absorb the Atlantic and share its revenue with the

Newfoundland (which it absorbed also in 1872),[34] Peter Cooper had done his bit to pour oil on troubled waters. The directors of the Newfoundland Company, he told Field in March, 1868, 'have more to gain than any other interest' from the failure of the Anglo-American and Atlantic Companies to agree, but they 'greatly prefer to endure the present subsidy [dividends on the preference shares held by Anglo-American] than to have a warfare between companies who have heretofore been associated together with so much advantage to mankind and so much honor to themselves.' [35]

'Advantage to mankind' had probably less to do with the final settlement, however, than the presence of a mutual danger, against which Hewitt, in vainly urging the three companies to unite, had warned against as early as May, 1867.[36] The prohibitive rates charged by the Newfoundland Company—a $48.60 minimum for a ten-word cablegram was in force through 1867 [37]—not only, as Peter complained to an understandably unsympathetic Horace Greeley, kept the public from using the cable[38] but encouraged aspiring rivals. In March, 1867, Congress granted the right to build a cable to the American Atlantic Cable Telegraph Company, a group of French and British and American promoters headed by Julius Reuter and Baron Emile d'Erlanger, who planned a cable from Brest to the island of St. Pierre and from thence to Duxbury, Massachusetts, a distance of 3333 miles or nearly twice as far as from Newfoundland to Ireland.

Assured by Hewitt that there was no immediate prospect of the French company's raising the necessary money (eventually, Hewitt said, the Newfoundland Company would have to extend one of its cables to Boston), Peter Cooper and his friends were slow to react to the prospect of a rival. Not until September 1, 1868, when they reduced their rates to a $16 minimum, did they make the first of many unavailing efforts to head off the new cable. On December 10, 1868, they presented a memorial to Congress protesting the grant to the new company, which, they said, was controlled by foreigners and a few Americans 'actively concerned in the late rebellion.' [39] When this appeal to anti-foreign feeling and waving of the bloody shirt failed, the Newfoundland tried a new tack. After Peter Cooper had innocently asked for and received assurance from the Attorney-General that no company could land a cable on the coast of the United States without the permission of Congress, he had Sumner introduce a bill into Congress early in 1869 giving the Newfoundland Company a twenty-year monopoly of landing privileges. The *Herald* was up in arms at once against this 'meanest swindle' of the 'British monopolists and those Americans who have sold themselves to the British telegraph line and British interests.' [40] The French cable was laid.

As happens so often in business affairs, the reality, however, was not as bad as anticipated. It was soon found that, despite the success of the French cable, the 'old cable will do the business,' [41] and Anglo-American shares soared. Within four years the Anglo-American had swallowed the French cable, to be itself eventually absorbed by Western Union. By 1892 there were ten cables spanning the Atlantic, all firmly in the hands of a single giant company.[42]

In 1866, when the successful landing of the Atlantic Cable precipitated a struggle for control, Peter Cooper had already had ample experience of the 'business' end of telegraphing. From 1854 to 1860 he was an important participant in the series of steps that brought order out of chaos in the domestic telegraph field and led eventually to the establishment of Western Union's great monopoly, the first of its kind in American history.

It was the cable project that precipitated Peter Cooper into more than the casual participation in the telegraph industry

which he had had in 1849. There was little use, Field and
Cooper quickly realized, in having a St. Lawrence cable unless
they had telegraphic outlets to New York and the South. At
first they tried peaceful means of securing these outlets: They
made Morse honorary electrician in return for the promise of
the free use of his patents from Nova Scotia to New York; and
then, when Morse's partner, Amos Kendall, objected—with
good reason—to Morse's giving away rights belonging to the
stockholders of other companies, they offered to lease the Kendall and Morse lines. But in September, 1855, Cooper and Field
made a discovery that they thought put rival telegraph companies at their mercy. This was a valuable telegraphic printing
instrument, the invention of a professor of music, David E.
Hughes, which transformed electrical impulses into letters at
a very rapid rate. They immediately bought the Hughes instrument for $100,000, withdrew the offer to lease the Morse lines,
and—on November 1, 1855—organized a new company, the
American Telegraph Company. The capital of this company was
$200,000, and its president Peter Cooper. A formidable power
had come into the telegraph field, which, after a four-year war
of nerves, was to control all the lines along the Atlantic seaboard.

During this war Peter Cooper consistently tried to play his
familiar role of peacemaker, but he was handicapped both by
the behavior of his associates and by his own mixed motives.
His first effort, made early in 1856 just after the American
Company had showed its hand by leasing all rival telegraph
lines from Nova Scotia to New York,[43] was in the form of a
letter to Morse, assuring him that the American Company had
no hostile motives in buying the Hughes patent and urging
him not to let 'petty questions of *meum* and *teum* dwarf the
noble enterprise' of world telegraphy.[44] Kendall, for one, was
not impressed, warning Morse that 'Field and Cooper are
shrewd business men not unfriendly to you or me but more
friendly to themselves,' who had bought the Hughes instrument

'to hold *in terrorem* over our heads.'[45] He was quickly proved right when, on March 16th, the American Company made an offer to lease the Morse lines on such niggardly terms that Morse and Kendall had no choice but to issue an ultimatum as to what terms they would accept,[46] and, when this was rejected, prepare for a long struggle.

Peter Cooper's second attempt at peace, made in March, 1857, proved even less fruitful. After a friendly meeting with Morse and Kendall, he arranged a conference of representatives of all important telegraph companies,[47] to be held in New York in June, the first real effort to bring order out of chaos in the telegraph field. Unfortunately it soon became evident that the American would join an association of telegraph companies only if they could, as Kendall wrote bitterly, 'dragoon' others into meeting 'their own terms,' that is, make them buy part of the Hughes patent. The conference broke up in fierce disagreement, Kendall asserting that he could get little satisfaction even out of the prospect of an Atlantic Cable if it was in the hands of men of such ruthless and 'grasping ambition.' Worse, however, was to follow. Hiram Sibley, who in 1856 had induced Ezra Cornell to join him in uniting the majority of Western companies in the formidable Western Union, now saw his opportunity to outsmart his great Eastern rivals, the Morse interests, by combining with the American Company against them. On August 10, 1857, a treaty was signed dividing up the country and sharing the Hughes patent among the 'Six Nations' : Western Union, the American, and four Western companies. 'Amos the Pious,' as Sibley called Kendall, had been doublecrossed.

'Kendall was shocked to learn of this amazing bit of perfidy.' And what of Peter Cooper? When Kendall wrote him for an explanation, he blandly answered that the American Company had heard that the Morse lines were demanding terms the American could not accept and the latter had therefore chosen more sympathetic allies. Though this was a pure evasion, not even the furious Kendall accused Cooper of taking part in the per-

· (239) ·

fidy; his mind had merely been poisoned by the insinuations of the unscrupulous Sibley. But Kendall and his partners did strike back, buying up competing telegraph lines in the West no less than in the East, supporting a competing Atlantic Cable project,[48] waging legal war on the American's new Philadelphia-to-New York line,[49] and finally, on March 10, 1858, memorializing Congress on the subject of monopolies.

Though Cooper told John D. Caton[50] that the American Company had a full answer to the 'ridiculous memorial presented to Congress by Amos Kendall and others,'[51] he was worried. Plainly Morse's and Kendall's property would have to be paid for, and the consolidation had better be made before the Morse patents ran out and wildcat companies sprang up everywhere. So he made a third and more vigorous effort at peace. On October 20, 1858, the 'Six Nations' added a seventh and became the North American Telegraph Association, of which Peter Cooper was one of the organizers and the first president. On March 28, 1859, Abram Hewitt replaced Cooper as president of the American Telegraph Company. Immediately negotiations were entered into with Kendall and Morse, and during the next year Cooper, Field, Sibley, and Norvin Green[52] all worked hard and continuously for consolidation.

Though negotiation was Cooper's particular forte, he did not find his part in effecting the union easy. None of the participants were given to sweet reasonableness, and Kendall was angered anew in 1858 by the American Company's extending its lines to Washington. Peter's letters show his growing annoyance with Ezra Cornell and Hiram Sibley no less than with Kendall for refusing to make any concessions. 'After a few days more of effort,' he told Sibley on June 17, 1859, 'I shall leave all telegraph matters to be managed [?] by parties who I trust will be more successful than I have been in throwing oil on the troubled sea of telegraph interests.'[53] Then in August, just when matters seemed finally settled, an entirely new bone of contention arose, involving another rising monopoly. The Associated Press, which through Daniel Craig had been for years working closely with the American Company, told the editor of the Philadelphia *Public Ledger,* a business associate of Kendall's, that his paper would be cut off from foreign news because of some editorial remarks he had made. Kendall's readily overheated blood boiled at seeing the telegraph become an instrument of fraud and oppression. Not until the principle of 'first come, first served' was made a stated policy of the North American Telegraph Association would he resume negotiations. This occurred on September 7th with the ready concurrence of both Hewitt and Peter Cooper, who, earlier in the year when a rival news agency had made similar accusations against the Associated Press and the American Company, had publicly expressed themselves in favor of the principle.[54]

The long struggle finally came to an end on October 12, 1859, in a momentous agreement which brought the Morse lines into the North American Telegraph Association. The American Company paid half of the cost of the whole consolidation, Western Union one-quarter, and these two companies became the chief powers in an organization which, with Peter Cooper at its head, controlled the majority of the telegraph lines of the country. The American Telegraph Company was completely reorganized with an authorized capital of $2,000,000. With 13,500 miles of wire and all the patents, best routes, franchises, and contracts with railroads, it was impregnable on the Atlantic coast, and through the North American Telegraph Association had access to the rest of the country. With Hewitt, Hunt, and Field as directors—Cooper resigned as director and sold his stock to his son and son-in-law on the formation of the new company—and Peter Cooper as president of the North American Telegraph Association, it seemed that the American Company could be kept from fighting with the rest of the industry, and the rest of the industry from bowing to Western Union.

Neither of these hopeful auguries were fulfilled. At the very beginning of the American Company's existence it nearly destroyed the North American Telegraph Association by trying, under the leadership of the self-willed Robert W. Russell, to enforce Kendall's law of 'first come, first served.' As a result of the furor that followed—Craig called the American's directors 'lottery swindlers, pettifoggers, illiterate cheats, rum sellers, drunken sots, and superannuated political knaves'—Hewitt and Field withdrew from the company they had helped form.[55] Though peace was restored in November, 1860, by Russell's resignation, the days of the American Company were numbered. Its failure to play along with Sibley on a transcontinental telegraph in 1861, and the Civil War, which broke its North-South lines and increased business on Western Union's East-West lines, gave the latter a stranglehold over the telegraph industry. For four more years a pretense of harmony was maintained, but on June 12, 1866, the American Company, threatened with the invasion of its territory by a new satellite of Western Union, accepted an offer of three shares of Western Union's shamelessly watered stock for one of its own,[56] and gave up the ghost. The last obstacle in the way of the new giant had been disposed of.

What Peter Cooper, the peacemaker, thought of the Frankenstein's monster he had indirectly helped to create he did not set down. For he had long ago 'retired from any active participation in telegraph affairs.' Even his presidency of the increasingly futile North American Telegraph Association had become merely titular when, on September 5, 1862, he handed it over to the rightful incumbent, Hiram Sibley. It is perhaps not without significance, however, that when Gardiner G. Hubbard made his premature attempt in 1867 to create a government-owned Postal Telegraph Company, he turned for help to Abram S. Hewitt.

Chapter 14

THE OPENING OF
COOPER UNION

THOUGH Peter had wanted no fuss to be made, there was nevertheless a small audience of workmen and curious by-standers on hand when, at 9:30 on Saturday morning, September 17th, 1853, Mr. Cooper and His Honor the Mayor laid the cornerstone of the Cooper Union. The basement had already been dug, but there was little else to suggest to the spectators either the substantial building that was to rise on these foundations or the thousands of boys and girls who would one day stream through its doors; and the rites that they witnessed had as much of the ludicrous as the prophetic about them. After burying copies of the Constitution, Washington's Farewell Address, the Bible in different languages, and various American coins and newspapers, Peter ceremoniously handed each of the workmen a bright American silver coin as a souvenir of their part in creating an institution that would give their children the education Peter had desired for himself. Various people then picked up trowels and began, each in his fashion and much to the amusement of the audience, to apply them to the cornerstone. 'His Honor,' reported the *Times*, 'used the trowel as delicately as he would lift a pea on his silver fork. Mr. Cooper, on the other hand, handled the implement and laid on the mortar with as bold and workmanlike a hand as though he had been brought up to the business; indeed, as a bystander observed, he took to the mortar like a brick.' Peter then made an earnest little speech thanking the mayor for laying the cornerstone, "where I trust it will rest forever with its contents on the foundation of eternal truth," the mayor responded with a few words about Cooper's liberality, and everyone went home.[1]

Yet the future, in cloudy and imperfect outline perhaps, already lay coiled in Peter Cooper's vision. It had begun to take shape as early as December, 1839, when Peter acquired the 16x22-foot lot at the northeast corner of Third Avenue and 7th Street from one Peter Palmer, who owed Cooper $6600 which it was 'not convenient for him to pay.' It had continued to grow through the dozen years during which he had been laboriously buying from different owners the other sixteen oddly shaped parcels into which the estate of Nicholas W. Stuyvesant had divided the block. And it had already taken specific form when, in July, 1852, he finally bought the last lot.[2]

In November, 1852, the *Times* was able to announce not only Cooper's appropriation of $300,000 for the enterprise and the tearing down of old buildings on the site, but many of the details then planned for the institution. The top would be an observatory 'with choice astronomical and microscopic apparatus'; the halls would be opened free for anniversaries, commencements, and the like; the laws for the government of the institution would be made by the students themselves, and 'expulsions will be made only by a majority vote of this whole body'; rooms would be set aside—this the *Times* considered a remarkable feature—for 'ladies' who might want to meet to study practical or natural science, and a sum of $500 was to be appropriated each year for the female who exhibited the greatest heroism or endured the greatest sacrifice for suffering humanity; the trustees were to be a judge of the United States Court, three judges of the Superior Court, the mayor, the oldest member of the Cooper family, the president of the Free Academy (the future College of the City of New York), the president of the Mechanics Society, and the editors of the city's principal dailies and weeklies. Two months later the *Times* supplied the public with a view of the elevation and plans, as given to them by F. A. Petersen, the architect. The building would be of stone and brick, with iron pillars supporting the stores on Third and Fourth Avenues; the third floor would be an 'Exhibition Room' with alcoves for statues; the fifth floor would be a lecture room and library; five rooms on the fifth floor on the Third Avenue side would be rented to artists; near one lecture room would be a room for physical experiments and instruments; there was to be a refectory on the Third Avenue side; a small engine would be used to supply a constant flow of pure air through the building, to be forced by a shaft ten feet in diameter from the basement to the roof.[3] The purposes and methods of the institution, too, were firmly if vaguely in Peter Cooper's mind in 1853.

Six long years were to pass between the laying of the cornerstone and the opening of the Cooper Union. The construction of the building had been delayed to allow both Harper & Brothers and the Assay Office to be erected. Then, though the beams were placed by the end of 1856, there were other delays, and the building was still in 'the course of erection on the block bounded by Astor Place, Third Avenue, Seventh Street, and Fourth Avenue' when on February 17, 1857, the Legislature passed Peter's application for a charter. On February 23rd Peter told Nahum Capen that, though he had 'hurried on the work on the building through all the cold weather by burning fires to prevent injury from frost,' he still couldn't 'with my best efforts' fix the time for completion.[4] The panic of 1857, which caused Peter to sell some of his stocks for the sake of his institution, again delayed matters, and it was May, 1858, before the doors of the great building with its million pounds of iron were opened.[5] It had cost not the $300,000 Peter had originally appropriated, but $630,000, and was to cost $30,000 more for equipment and teachers before it began instructing students. During 1858 a women's School of Design occupied the building, and the halls were opened to various groups. One of these, a committee of butchers, to whom Peter had offered the Great Hall free because of obligations he had felt for forty years, were so frightened by its size that Peter had to make their speaker go to the end of the hall and prove that he could be heard when talking in a moderate tone before they would use it.[6]

Still the institution was not functioning. Temporary market sheds on the south side of the building made the entrance filthy and deprived the Union of needed space; there were also legal difficulties about executing the deed of trust and amending the charter, which could not be straightened out until the Legislature met in January. Finally, on April 13, 1859, the Legislature passed the amended charter, permitting the trustees to apply, free of taxation, the revenues of all property held or to be held by them to the purposes of education. On April 29th Peter and his wife executed the deed of trust conveying the property. And on the evening of November 2, 1859,[7] the Cooper Union for the Advancement of Science and Art was formally inaugurated with a speech by Cooper and one by John W. Draper of New York University, whose theme, appropriately, was that belief in intelligence is the modern world's great contribution to civilization.

On November 7th classes started, and the Cooper Union took its place at the heart of what had come, in those six years, to be a great cultural center. At about 6th Street and Lafayette Place arose in 1854 the Astor Library, to which Astor had been induced in 1849 to leave $500,000. Across the street the Bible Society had in 1853 bought the property where Peter Cooper's grocery once stood. A few blocks away, on Irving Place, the Academy of Music went up in 1854; and on University Place in 1856 the New York Society Library. The Astor Place Opera House, scene of the Forrest-Macready riots in 1849, was purchased in 1850 for the new Mercantile Library. Of equal importance, Cooper Union stood at the head of the Bowery, which had already attained its unsavory reputation, offering a chance for regeneration to those who would take of its bounty.

In those six years many influences, including his own second thoughts, had been at work to modify and more sharply define Peter Cooper's views. These views had, of course, never been uniquely his own. In so far as Peter Cooper's ideas grew from his experience as a mechanic—and it is significant that he still liked to sign himself 'a mechanic of New York'—he had shared that experience with hosts of others. Moreover, he had drawn, as we have seen, on the educational ideas of his time and profited by the work of Rensselaer, Girard College, the French Polytechnic, and possibly also the Birkbeck Institute in London and the University of Pennsylvania, of which his friend Colwell was a benefactor. The efforts of the General Society of Mechanics, which educated boys and girls together and helped apprentices help themselves, were well known to Cooper, and, according to Hewitt, 'gave some direction' to his benefactions and taught him a lesson 'which he never forgot.' [8] The Lowell lectures, through the medium of Hewitt, had come to Peter's attention, helping him to decide to 'make provision for free lectures for the people.' [9] In the 'fifties two other institutions, Antioch College in 1853 and the Wagner Institute of Science in Philadelphia in 1855, attracted Peter's notice. Antioch, supported largely by Unitarians and dedicated by its first president, Horace Mann, to non-sectarian coeducation, asked Peter Cooper to be a trustee. Too busy to accept the offer, he nevertheless endorsed a loan to the college. Wagner, founded by William Wagner, a friend of Cooper's, aimed to teach both sexes and all religious sects the laws of nature and of God.[10] By 1859 the conception of a free education in science, art, and politics for the common man was no longer a novelty.

Peter Cooper solicited advice, too, from Hewitt, from his trusted legal adviser, John E. Parsons, whom Joseph Choate called one of the greatest legal minds he had ever known, and from various educators. As he told the Japanese charge d'affaires, who asked his advice on education in 1872, he had 'made myself but little aquainted' with the 'scholastic and scientific methods of the schools,' [11] and therefore needed help. He received it from such men as Francis Lieber, who in 1834 had planned the Girard College curriculum and was now professor of history and political science at Columbia; from Charles Matthews, a teacher of chemistry; from Alan MacWhorter of Yale; and from his friend Nahum Capen, postmaster of Boston in 1857 and a writer on education and democracy, who had contributed much to popular education since visiting European schools in 1835. Unfortunately much of the advice of these men was contradictory. Lieber, whose views Peter found to 'harmonize' so nearly with his own[12] that he wanted Lieber to set up at Cooper Union a 'department and professorship on the science of government,' emphasized advanced training in science, mechanical education in workshops, and instruction 'as to the political character of man, the nature of our institutions, and the mechanism of nations.' [13] Matthews, on the other hand, deplored any attempt to teach politics, since it would bring into Cooper Union the clamor of sects, and stressed practical science and mechanical pursuits.[14] MacWhorter liked neither Lieber's idea of a scientific school such as Dana had just organized at Yale—that was too specialized for Cooper's clientele—nor Matthews' emphasis on the practical: what was needed above all, he felt, were courses in the art of reasoning and of literature, conducted in regular classes by permanent teachers, to help raise New York's cultural level and end its reputation as a mere whirlpool of business, fashion, and iniquity.[15]

Even more confusing must have been much of the unsolicited advice that poured in on Peter. One anonymous correspondent in 1859 wanted to improve Cooper's 'magnificent and Godlike scheme' by the immediate addition of a whole host of things: a daily periodical, a printing press run by the same machinery as the ventilator (it must have been hard for Peter to resist this one), a reporter to comment on all books, maps, and inventions that came in, and an employment agency (an idea later cherished by Peter himself). A number of people wrote in asking for jobs or recommending others, including the great Louis Agassiz, who was deeply impressed by Peter's 'devotion to the public good.' Some wrote in merely to praise, as did an English friend of Cooper, Isaac Rawlins, who, despairing of his sect-ridden native country, wished he were not too old to come to 'your morning land to refresh myself among its clear skies, light hearts, buoyant spirits and strong commercial life.' Then there were the cranks, who wanted to convert this generous 'prince among merchants' into a Soldier of the Cross or some other image of their fanaticism. One curious and arrogant letter from the genealogist Jerome Bonaparte Holgate shows that even when Peter gave money he did not always earn praise. Holgate had worked twenty-five years on a philosophy of history and had come to Cooper in 1858 with a letter from Chancellor Ferris of the University of New York: 'After a careful examination of the matter in connexion with Professor Webster of the Free Academy you concluded to render a moderate assistance, so moderate that it retarded the completion of it some four years until the vigour and prime of my life was wasted in vain and fruitless efforts in removing annoyance and obstacles in the way of its completion.' Though America was unworthy of Holgate's efforts, he would still give Cooper Union the 'honour of first bringing before the world an analysis of history which for the first time reveals its laws.' [17] Peter must have been reminded of his brother, still languishing in Bloomingdale at his expense.

Knowing basically what he wanted—he could, as Hewitt discovered, be very stubborn even about details—Peter Cooper did not lose his head amid all this advice. But in the end he did take a great many of the suggestions of his friends. The amended charter of 1859 was written in Hewitt's hand and contained much of his thinking; and a good deal of what was in the amended charter itself was, at the advice of the trustees, modified in practice when the Union opened. Moreover, the educational experience of a whole generation found its way into Peter's new institution. It was neither a biological sport nor entirely Peter's own.

Yet there was nothing like Cooper Union in New York in 1859, nor is there really anything like it today. Adult education was non-existent except for lyceums, mechanics' institutes, the evening classes inaugurated in 1848 by Peter's Public School Society, and an occasional labor college, like the Albany Manual Labor University. Moreover, if Cooper's ideas were not original, they were part of the best and most advanced thinking of his time and were shared only by those at the forefront of intellectual development. The very willingness to donate so large a fortune to the public good while he was alive was itself almost unique. Astor and Girard gave money only after death, and other comparable gifts, like those of William Corcoran, George Peabody, and Matthew Vassar were made after Cooper Union was founded. Moreover, Cooper was, along with Horace Mann, one of the first in the nineteenth century to assert that wealth was a trust, a doctrine that he proclaimed loudly on numerous occasions.[18] Though private property was sacred 'so long as the rights of others are not thereby infringed,' he told the students of Cooper Union: "I cannot shut my eyes to the fact that the production of wealth is not the work of any one man and the acquisition of great fortunes is not possible without the cooperation of multitudes of men; and that therefore the individuals to whose lot these fortunes fall . . . should never lose sight of the fact that as they hold them by the will of society expressed in statute law, so they should administer them as trustees for the benefit of society as inculcated by the moral law." [19]

Cooper and his Union had more followers than antecedents. Peter, it will be remembered, knew both Matthew Vassar and Ezra Cornell, and influenced both of them in the uses to which they put their money in the 'sixties; Carnegie has admitted the inspiration of Cooper in his philanthropies; the engineer Edwin A. Stevens, a friend of Hewitt's, profited by the latter's advice and account of Cooper Union in setting up his Stevens Institute for Engineers in the 'sixties;[20] Drexel in Philadelphia, Pratt in Brooklyn, and Armour in Chicago got ideas from Cooper Union; above all the fabulously wealthy George Peabody, the American who went to England and made a fortune in the 'thirties, consulted both Hewitt and Copper when he was setting up his Peabody Institute.[21] 'Mr. Peabody, when in this country,' said Cooper, 'called at my house and inquired very particularly about my plans in relation to the Cooper Union, evidently having something in mind of what he might do with the immense wealth that he had accumulated, although he did not then tell me what his own plans were. . . . I gave him all the information I had at that time.'

Finally, Cooper Union was, in the deepest sense, very much Peter Cooper's. The influences that had formed him reached the world through his agency and through the medium of his personality. His had been the original dream, his were the basic ideas that went into the charter and were embodied in iron and mortar and classrooms and lecture halls. And his was the ever-present hand at the wheel. From the day the excavations began he watched over every line of the blueprints, and when the building started to go up he was in constant attendance, supervising the laying of every brick. To miss a few days at his institute on account of illness, as he had to do once in 1857, upset him greatly. Peter Cooper was the exact opposite of most rich men, who give money for an institution to be erected after they are dead. He conceived the idea when young, helped bring it to detailed realization, and then had the good fortune to live a quarter of a century to watch over it. During that quarter of a century he was seldom absent from it a day. Constantin Herzberg, who taught in the art department when it opened, remembers Peter at the Union until nine every evening in those early days, showing classrooms to visitors or seeing if anything was needed. No wonder that the Cooper Union not only reflected the specific ideas of its founder, but, even more important, was permeated with his influence. Cooper Union was in very literal truth Cooper's Union, and it would have been highly inappropriate had the Legislature not added his name 'against his express wish' that it be called simply the 'Union.' Even today the personality of the founder is very much a living presence to those who pace its halls. Often when students object to a rule or a method of procedure they will appeal to the words of Peter Cooper, who, they always feel, would have taken their side against authority. It is this that makes Cooper Union unique.

In Cooper's final, as in his earlier plans for Cooper Union, the combining of art and science was a basic concept. A 'proper union' of these two was, indeed, one of the three reasons[22] for the name of the institution. Cooper envisaged, on the one hand, study in the natural and social sciences (what he called the science of a republican form of government), and, on the other, attempts to inculcate a love of beauty and to give practice to the hand and the eye. He was ahead of his time in feeling that American education was too exclusively intellectual: men were taught to think, but not to work. They came out of the schools ready to be 'anything but workers in the world; so the idea of becoming a skilled artisan, a producer of something, is viewed with contempt.' [23] Yet in Cooper's thinking science actually took a far larger place than did art. He had little knowledge of or interest in the fine arts, and had it not already been in existence he might not have planned a School of Design. Moreover, for the purposes he had nearest to his heart, science was of far more importance than art.

The most obvious aim of Cooper Union, as set forth in

the original and amended charter, in a letter accompanying the deed of trust, and in several speeches Cooper wrote for the opening ceremonies, was to 'aid the efforts of youth to acquire useful knowledge, and to find and fill that place in the community where their capacity and talents can be usefully employed with the greatest advantage to themselves and the community in which they live.' [24] In brief, he wished to offer free to the laboring classes of both sexes the training in the mechanical arts and in the sciences that he had never had. Given the tools of a trade, they would be able to become self-reliant and successful persons with greater ease than had been possible for him. No one in America, with its unlimited opportunities, needed support, but only the chance to help himself. And that help Peter would give him.

Yet the last thing that Peter Cooper envisaged was a mere vocational school. Far transcending the practical aim was a wider social and cultural one; he wanted to make Cooper Union the gateway to a richer and better life for the community. In what exalted terms he pictured his institution is illustrated by one of his stories of the reason for the name 'Union.' Just after Peter had laid the cornerstone of his building an aged Bostonian named William Foster wrote him in praise of his intentions and expressed fear of the terrible destruction that civil war promised to the country, a destruction which would, because of the nature of the American people when aroused, be worse even than the Paris massacres Foster had witnessed. Peter immediately determined, he said, to put the 'single word Union on the most conspicuous front of this building looking to the south' and then invite the governors of all states and others to meet in New York and dedicate the building to a 'union of effort' to make a republican form of government a blessing to all. The invitation was considered impractical, however, by Cooper's friends and was abandoned, as was the further idea of having all the governors take a tour of the states together.

Cooper's deeper educational aims grew directly out of his religious views. This did not mean that Cooper intended to force his religious ideas on students or teachers. Nor did it mean that Cooper Union would cater only to believers in certain tenets. On the contrary he specifically provided in the deed of trust that 'neither the . . . Board of Trustees, nor any member thereof, shall in any way take into account any religious tenet or opinion of any professor or teacher . . . nor of any student applying for admission into said institution; . . . nor shall they permit any professor or teacher in said institution to make any discrimination among its students on account of their religious tenets or opinions.' [25] Cooper Union's strict adherence to this provision drew from Peter's old opponent, Bishop Hughes, words of the highest praise: 'I have seen all the great charities of the old world and in this, and I like this one the best. It is not sectarian, and its benefits are broader and deeper than all the rest.' [26] What was, however, implied was that Cooper's religious beliefs dictated his proposed educational program and provided the ends toward which he wished it to move. Peter was so well aware of this and so worried that his views might be questioned or misunderstood that he felt impelled to append the 'religious opinions that have taken an irresistible possession of my mind' to his speech at the laying of the cornerstone and to his letter accompanying the deed of trust. In the following decades he was to restate them in a dozen forms and to inject them into nearly everything that he wrote.

To summarize these ideas in a few paragraphs is to misrepresent them in several ways. Peter Cooper thought about his religion all his life, fragments of his cogitations appearing in the most unexpected places—among business notes and cures for rheumatism. As a consequence, his ideas and their expression have about them the strong flavor of his personality, and are imbued with a sincerity and a depth of feeling that are lost in condensation. His discourses gain, on the other hand, a coherence and exactness from summarizing that equally falsify them.

Peter Cooper never became a logician nor learned to say in a few precise words what could be strung out into endless vague platitudes.

Peter's basic belief was the liberal optimistic Unitarian doctrine that God was both all good and all-powerful. He had made the universe out of the elements of matter and—Peter was both pantheist and theist—infused it with His presence. This universe worked by inevitable and harmonious laws; and it had evolved according to these laws upward and onward through developments in the scale of being to consciousness. Man was the, · as yet, final product of God's power and love, and had been showered with all sorts of blessings. The universe was his to enjoy and subdue, a doctrine that justified the worker and the businessman. He had the intelligence to perceive God's laws, to understand that he was morally accountable to God, and to love God for His goodness, an idea that put Peter at variance both with the churches and their priestly mediators and with the puritans and their belief in man's incapacity to know God through his mind. And he had free will to make what he would of his own destiny. If he were wise he would use this free will to learn God's ways and thus become His partner in doing good to others. This was man's highest happiness, as Peter himself found. In building and watching over Cooper Union he felt he was doing God's work, and nothing gave him greater joy. As someone wrote truly, it was 'questionable if the Cooper Institute has benefited any of its pupils half so much as it has Peter Cooper himself.' [27]

What of evil, that perennial problem of all religions? Like all but the blindest fanatics, Peter was well aware that men were often vicious and even oftener weak. God, indeed, often seemed unjust, holding men accountable for their actions when they were apparently incapable of exercising the free will He had given them. Such considerations, stemming from modern doctrines of environmental determinism, led Peter to follow Jesus in putting charity before the justice that a sterner Hebraism would have demanded. When judging the behavior of students, he told the Cooper Union trustees, 'remember how frail we are, and how liable to err when we come to sit in judgment on the faults of others, and how much the circumstances of our birth, our education, and the society and country where we have been born and brought up, have had to do in forming us and making us what we are.' Indeed, he told an Episcopalian bishop who came to see him in 1874, a just God would give the poor slum boy the first chance at Heaven, since he had been deprived of the sight of God and turned by inevitable circumstance into a vagabond. Peter occasionally thought that perhaps he himself had had 'too good a time on earth' to deserve Heaven.

Though prevalent, evil to Peter was not, however, a basic part of God's universe, but a mere excrescence, a product of man's imperfect nature. There was nothing of a Hawthorne or a Melville in Cooper. God could, one supposes, have eliminated evil if he had wished to, but not without taking away man's freedom, his most precious heritage to an individualist like Peter. It was much better to do as God had done, make man free to commit errors but also to grow in intelligence and love until he had become God's partner in doing good. God gave him all the aid he required. He made it perfectly plain that the proper use of the garden of the world would yield benefits to man, its improper use unhappiness. Moreover, He gave the world Jesus as an example to follow, and He wrote His demands upon the face of the universe as well as in the Bible. If we would free ourselves from slavery to the 'creeds and systems of human device'—Catholic theology was only the worst of these—and study the example of Christ and the 'open field of nature where that which may be known of [God is] clearly seen, being understood by the things that are made,' the world would be saved. For, optimist and rationalist that he was, Peter could not believe that, knowing the good, men would choose evil. 'I believe that all men everywhere desire pleasure in preference to pain,' he told Lieber in good Benthamite style; only when they were 'led away and

· (256) ·

enticed' by their lusts and came to 'believe things good and pleasant and to be desired that in themselves are bad' would they embrace wrong.

Man's chief instrument in finding truth was science, the meaning of which Cooper extended to include the study of the laws that governed the moral as well as the material universe. He could thus talk about a science of a republican form of government, which was really a study of the principle of the Golden Rule embodied in American institutions, and of a science of immortality, which meant a study of God's ultimate purposes for man. 'The progressive steps that demonstrate the existence of a spiritual world are as natural as the steps that demonstrate planetary motion.' Once Peter watched at Ringwood the process whereby a caterpillar turned into a butterfly. This 'lesson' from nature gave him 'evidence of the immortality of man.' As the worm 'grovelling in the dirt' became a beautiful form, so would man doff his mortality and take on new life.[28]

How Cooper Union fitted into all this is obvious. Since men were both free and responsible and since to know the right was to do it, education was the obvious answer to the world's problems. Cooper Union would help men to help themselves, not so much in getting a living as in securing ultimate happiness. And it would do this by opening the gates of the natural and social sciences to them.

That Peter viewed these sciences chiefly in the light of the ideal rather than the mundane ends they served is evident from every pronouncement he made about his Union. He was moved to establish scientific courses, he told Lieber in 1855, because in a world in which 'there are no miracles to be wrought for our deliverance,' only by applying 'science to all the varied uses and purposes of life' could the causes that perpetuated misery in a world of abundance be fathomed and conquered. In the memorial to the Legislature he gave as his purpose in affording 'to the youth of our country the advantages of a scientific education,' his desire 'to aid the rising generation in becoming so

· (257) ·

thoroughly acquainted with the works of nature and the great mystery of their own being—that they may feel and understand those immutable laws that are designed in infinite wisdom and constantly operating for our good and so governing the destinies of worlds and men that it is our highest wisdom to live in strict conformity to these laws.' Similarly, the 'perpetual course of free lectures and instruction in the science and philosophy of a true republican government,' a science based 'on the golden rule that requires every individual, community, state and nation to do unto others as they would that others should do unto them . . . will stimulate industry and afford the best means possible to elevate our race by giving security and value to all the varied forms of labor.' Only if the scientific courses given at his Union achieved such high ends as these would Peter feel justified in his work and taste that everlasting joy of having become God's partner.[29]

Discovering the appropriate means for putting his aims into practice Cooper found to be a more complex problem than merely voicing his earnest desires. The final form of the deed of trust specified regular night instruction free to all who brought certificates 'of good moral character,' firstly, on the application of science to life, and secondly, on the science of a just and equitable form of government. To be sure that the second of these would not be neglected, Cooper said in a special note that the 'course of instruction on social and political science . . . shall have the preference over all the other objects of expenditure . . . and shall forever stand pre-eminent among them.' [30] But what form the instruction was to take remained doubtful in his mind. Neither the deed of trust nor the accompanying letter mentions classes in the social sciences. The only positive suggestions offered were public lectures and debates, student lectures to other students once a month on the problems of the city to teach them 'how to preside with propriety over a deliberative assembly,' and insistence that suggestions for the rules of the institution come from the students themselves. The physical sciences were to be imparted chiefly by lectures, demonstrations, and debates.

Peter had, indeed, far too much faith in the usefulness of simply showing students illustrations, lecturing to them, and letting them talk. His own experience had told him nothing of the value of regular instruction and a great deal about that of suggestion by visualization and by conversation. And he assumed that the artisan class, to which he wished to appeal, was too busy for extended and intensive courses. As a young man Cooper was, it will be remembered, fascinated by the exhibitions of living and stuffed animals, and by the dwarfs, giants, historical relics, waxworks, and mechanical devices at Savage's and Scudder's and Barnum's Museums. At the two latter he also attended the 'lecture rooms' devoted to 'moral melodrama' and enjoyed the 'cosmorama,' an exhibition of pictures of noteworthy scenery, foreign cities, and so on, looked at through round holes enhancing the effect of their illumination. In earlier days Cooper had also been to many lectures, this being the heyday of the lyceum movement, and his quick mind, unused to reading, had picked up much useful information there. Conversation and debate had likewise been profitable to him, so that he was convinced that if people could be brought together for interchange of ideas they would mutually profit.

All these influences weighed heavily in his plans for Cooper Union. One of his main objects was to set up a society called the 'Associates of the Cooper Union for the Advancement of Science and Art,' to consist of groups from the various sciences and professions—editors of the press were specifically to be included—who would use the facilities of the Union for lectures and discussions and who would encourage the sciences and the arts by awards for inventions and improvements. He also provided rooms where students and the practitioners of various handicrafts could meet and debate. Around the walls of the debating rooms were to be 'full-length likenesses of Washington, Franklin and Lafayette who, though dead, yet speak the language of truth and soberness.' The roof of the Union Cooper planned to enclose by a balustrade and to use for promenades or concerts on fine evenings. The Great Hall, which was built on the basement floor, he expected to be the scene of lectures and debates on all subjects and—much to the annoyance of many who did not share Cooper's liberal ideas—from all points of view. On the third floor was to be the reading room, literary exchange, art gallery, and the scientific collections, and on the fourth floor a cosmorama modeled after that in Scudder's Museum. Around the walls and in the alcoves of the third floor Cooper proposed to place books, maps, and paintings in glass cases; in the window spaces he planned to have scenes and exhibitions demonstrating 'the true philosophy of life.'

Over the museum and the scientific apparatus Cooper took particular pains. He bought a huge stuffed white whale for the centerpiece of the museum, which later found its way, fortunately, to the Museum of Natural History. And he planned, as he wrote to Lieber, to have a diorama so arranged that objects could be presented one piece at a time to an audience, until a ship or the whole human system had been built up before their eyes. 'I am now having prepared,' he added, 'a course of views to represent the contributions of matter from surrounding planets and systems that have resulted in the formation of our globe, with all the changes of its structure that have and are continually taking place.' A study of the changes in the 'material structure of our earth' and of all 'that has existed on its surface' or was 'treasured up in its bosom' would teach 'with an unmistakeable distinctness' how everything progressed in refinement and led to the development of intellectual life. Though he may have exaggerated their usefulness, Peter was amazingly farsighted in his employment of visual aids, the value of which we are just beginning fully to appreciate.

Peter's preoccupation with mechanical devices sprang as much from a simple interest in such matters as from a belief in their educational efficacy. In general, indeed, he planned the externals of his institution more intelligently than he did its educational program, which had to be much modified by others. When he urged that an employment agency be set up in the building, where people from all over the country could secure men and women of character, he was on solid ground.[31] And the general plan of his building no less than its details were sound and ahead of his time. His huge iron-girdered structure has weathered ninety New York winters and summers with remarkably little alteration. His idea for a large lecture hall in unused space below the street level where it was protected from street noises and where there could be no trampling downstairs in case of fire was a fine inspiration. The ventilation, which was achieved by a large fan run by a steam engine, was the wonder of later ventilating engineers. 'On one occasion during a scientific lecture, the experimental illustrations of which were on a large and imposing scale, the learned professor on the platform had the misfortune to crack an immense jar, in which he was exhibiting the brilliant combustion of phosphorus in oxygen gas. The white fumes of phosphorus acid floated out into the air, and began to diffuse themselves through the halls towards the ventilation outlets at the sides and rear. To one who knew the irritating nature of these fumes it seemed inevitable that the hall must be emptied of its crowded audience in a few minutes. Already coughing had begun on the front seats, when Mr. Hewitt, who was seated on the platform, quickly rose, and pulling a cord, reversed the currents of ventilation and opened a new outlet into the street, behind and above the platform. The curling clouds of vapour paused, wheeled, and retreated, and in another minute the air was perfectly pure. The lecturer had not even been interrupted. It was a beautiful and timely "experiment" not on the programme, and, to use the words of one who was present, "it was just the sort of thing to please Peter Cooper to the bottom of his soul." '[32]

One other innovation shows Cooper's amazing foresight. Though no really satisfactory elevator had yet been invented, he knew that elevators were coming, and left an oval space from top to bottom of the building. He expected, he says, to 'have either a garden or a museum of arts on the upper story and I knew that that could not be successful unless I could put machinery in there to carry people.' Elevators are now running in that space, though, since their builders were conventional men, they fill, except in front, only a square area in the shaft. Cooper was also careful to have his building amply furnished with water at all times, and so built his system of pipes and tanks that, at the ringing of a bell, water could be supplied to any part of the Union in less than a minute.

Peter had less trouble with the art side of his institute than he did with the science side. The School of Design, one of whose directors was Mrs. Hewitt, was already in existence and he had merely to take it over. The charming Henrietta Field helped Peter plan the new arrangements and agreed at Peter's 'personal solicitation' to supervise the work for a while.[33] Moreover, there were no complicated ends that Cooper envisaged the art school as serving; it was frankly a vocational school for young women. 'In order that females may share in the benefits of this institution,' wrote Peter in the memorial to the Legislature, 'the subscriber intends to set apart suitable rooms in the said building for an academy of design in which the art of engraving and design will constantly be taught with such further applications of science and art as are best calculated to widen the sphere of female employment.' He also clung to his 1853 plan of offering money—now $250—to the female student who merited it by 'efforts and sacrifices in the performance of duty to parents.' This was less for a reward than to 'encourage the exercise of heroic virtues that often shine in the midst of the greatest suffering and obscurity without so much as being noticed by the passing throng.' [34]

Cooper had had an interest in the plight of females since the days of his association with Joseph Curtis. No believer in the so-called rights of women, whose true place was in the home, he simply wished to prevent them from having, in the words of the second annual report of the Union, 'to resort for a livelihood to occupations which must be peculiarly revolting to the purity and sensitiveness which naturally characterize the feminine mind' or from being forced to marry bad husbands. 'This subject of unhappy marriages seemed,' wrote Susan Carter, who later directed the School of Design, 'to be a very prominent one in Mr. Cooper's mind. That women were often imposed upon, were ill-used and broken down, he had a lively conviction, and all his chivalry and sense of fatherly protection were enlisted to save them.' [35] Such an attitude itself was radical for his time and there was much shaking of heads, particularly when it was found that women were to be admitted to the regular night school as well as to the School of Design. But there was never any trouble. 'It gives me great pleasure to state,' wrote Hewitt in 1865, 'that we have seen no evil results whatever arising from the admission of young women to the same classes with young men at Cooper Union. On the contrary, we believe that both sexes are gainers by learning together. Of course there will be found evil-minded people everywhere, even in churches, but in six years we have not had a single case of scandal in Cooper Union and we should as soon think of excluding the young men as the young women.' [36] It is one of the greatest of Cooper Union's claims to fame that no one has ever been excluded from its walls because of sex, race, color, creed, or political opinion. Peter Cooper was a liberal without any of the qualifications fashionable in our sorry times.

Besides his plans for elementary instruction in art and science for artisans, Peter voiced one larger dream in his deed of trust.

In the not-too-distant future he hoped that Cooper Union would be, in the words of a letter written in 1858, a 'polytechnic school of the most thorough character and the highest order, based as nearly as possible upon the model of L'École Centrale at Paris.' The courses would, he assumed, begin where the scientific studies at the Free Academy terminated, and give a completely rounded scientific education. When he first planned his institution he had not thought of this as a distant dream. Naturally he could not carry the dream out himself, since he had had just enough money to get his building built and instruction started. But Peter had no pride of ownership. Indeed, the third meaning he gave to the convenient word 'Union' was that it signified a 'Union of public and private effort.' [37] Had they not confined themselves to apprentices, Cooper would have let the General Society of Mechanics administer his bounty. When he thought of creating a scientific school he immediately turned to Columbia University in the hope that 'with its large and growing revenues' it would take over the job. Unfortunately, Charles King, the president at the time, was an excessively cautious man, and the trustees and faculty were still wedded to the idea of a classical education for gentlemen. As MacWhorter wrote Cooper, the trustees had no practical knowledge of science, a discovery made to his annoyance by Professor Dana, the founder of the Yale Scientific School, when he accepted a lectureship at Columbia. So, none too politely—Hewitt referred to the 'peculiar circumstances' of their refusal—they turned Peter down.

He immediately made overtures to the Board of Education, which in those days controlled the Free Academy, and invited them to a conference on the suggestion made by 'many friends of that admirable institution' that they might supply the 'instruction required' for his school. To this suggestion 'I can have no possible objection,' he wrote, so long as the school 'is conducted in the thorough manner which I desire in order to produce engineers, architects and mechanics, worthy of the industrial development of our day and generation, and competent to grapple with the difficult practical problems presented by modern enterprise and progress.' He would supply rooms, and the board of control 'I have selected' would 'cheerfully' meet with a committee of the Board of Education to mature plans. It had been objected by some, Cooper added, that the public would be subjected to too much additional expense if this scheme were acted on. 'As I have no object or interest in making the offer, except to promote the public good, I trust that in your deliberations you will give due weight to this objection.' [38]

The objection was given due weight and carried the day. Peter was forced to postpone his plans and to carry on his school as best he could on his own. This he did by renting the first two stories of his building to pay the upkeep on the rest. He also gave up the complex idea, voiced in 1853, of having virtually every public body in the city sit on the Board of Trustees. The board became a close-knit organization of friends—Hewitt, Edward Cooper, Wilson G. Hunt, John E. Parsons, Daniel F. Tiemann, and himself. This group, which was characteristically charged by Peter never to mortgage the property or to go into debt for more than $5000 except in anticipation of rents, watched over Cooper Union without a change in their membership until Peter's death.

The possibility that some larger institution might take over Cooper Union as a scientific adjunct was, according to Hewitt, envisaged in the trust deed.[39] Actually the deed merely states that rooms in the Cooper Union building would be assigned to anyone who would establish a first-rate technological school in connection with a university or other qualified institution.[40] In 1868 the energetic Frederick A. P. Barnard, who had become president of Columbia, renewed overtures on the subject. Hewitt welcomed the opportunity—bearing, as he said, no personal grievance—and suggested an elaborate plan of amalgamation of the two institutions, which would have provided New York City in the 'sixties with a great university on the order of Cornell. But later Hewitt was forced to write sadly that Cooper Union could not be turned into the right kind of scientific school 'without such extensive alterations in the building as to make the idea impracticable if we have any regard to the comfort and probably the life of Mr. Cooper.' Peter had suddenly become very 'averse to alterations.' [41] So the plan was again dropped. Cooper Union, wrote Hewitt with some asperity in 1869, 'makes no pretense to be an institution for any but the working classes, hence it has no reputation and deserves none as a school of science.' In the twentieth century Cooper's great school was finally to have a full engineering program, though Columbia was not to administer it, despite overtures made once more by Hewitt in 1902 to President Butler.

When Cooper Union opened its doors in 1859 the polytechnic school was not the only unfulfilled expectation of its founder. Some of his plans were drastically altered by the good sense of his friends, some were unceremoniously dropped, either immediately or later on, some had to wait many years for realization. The museum, the cosmorama, the rooms for various trades to meet, and the roof garden disappeared at once. A large reading room replaced the museum, laboratories occupied the space of the cosmorama, discussion rooms became classrooms, and the roof was left unused. The art gallery existed for a time but was regretfully dissolved when Thomas J. Bryan gave his collection, which had been hung at Cooper Union, to the New York Historical Society. 'I gave up my plan' for an employment agency, Cooper wrote, because the trustees were worried that great throngs would loiter about and harm the place as a school for ladies. Through no one's fault the 'Associates' never did get organized. The second report of the trustees in 1861 voiced the hope that they soon would be and published the prospective rules in full; in 1864 a pamphlet was printed on the subject and scientists were urged to take the lead in setting up the organization; in 1865 Peter gave the American Geographical Society, of which he was one of the oldest members, rooms in the

Union as temporary headquarters. But that was all that ever came of the 'Associates,' despite Hewitt's efforts to get the Lyceum of Natural History and other scientific groups to meet at Cooper Union.

More serious than these losses was the inability for a time to find any means of fulfilling Cooper's dearest wish, instruction in the social sciences. Neither Hewitt nor Cooper wanted to imitate the current methods of indoctrinating students with the rights and duties of citizens through abstract, onesided, uninspiring texts on the 'science of government' and 'political philosophy.' Some attempts to give courses in political science under such men as Judge Benjamin Nott of Albany were made, but they were not very successful. Hewitt finally resorted, under the influence of the Lowell Institute, to the free popular lecture in the Great Hall as the solution of the problem. In 1863 twenty-one popular lectures were given, six on government, four on political economy, ten on the American revolution, and one—for some reason—on coral and coral islands.

Peter Cooper's program for the natural sciences was modified in the exact opposite direction. His suggestion for familiar lectures and debates was adopted for a time, but, in the words of the sixth annual report, 'the experience of the first year satisfied the Trustees that results of lasting value could only be attained by a thorough system of study, recitation and drill, beginning at the foundations of science and art, in the elementary principles of mathematics, and rising thence by slow and practical gradations to the applications of these principles to the higher walks of science and art.' As Hewitt wrote, 'we began with the idea of lectures to the working classes, without requiring recitations, but we soon discovered that we might amuse, but we could give no valuable teaching to the public in this way, and we abandoned the whole scheme, not as impracticable, but as practically of no value for the class for which Mr. Cooper founded the institution.' Today (1866) 'we attach but little consequence to popular lectures, and except upon the special department of

Social and Political Science, have preferred to expend the income of the Institution in regular and systematic instruction in the various departments of Science and Art, taking care to place at the foundation of the whole scheme a thorough mathematical training.' [42]

Peter Cooper often regretted the changes forced on him by circumstance or the good sense of his more expert friends. On one occasion, having climbed with a friend to the roof of the building, where he had once pictured happy throngs enjoying the view, he remarked sadly, "Sometimes I think my first plan was the best!" And who, viewing the use to which we have learned to put New York's roofs today, will deny that in this respect at least he was right? On the whole, however, even the stubborn Peter Cooper bowed to superior wisdom. Hewitt, with his Columbia education, obviously knew best about such matters, and Cooper left most of the administration of his institution to him and to the other trustees. It was Hewitt more than Peter Cooper who interviewed teachers, planned courses, and watched over discipline. Peter was happy to be the inspiration and guardian angel of the Cooper Union, supporting it with his money, firing it with his dreams, holding it together by his presence, and offering kindness and consolation to the students and an occasional bright idea to teachers, administrators, and superintendents.

Though there were minor features—the art gallery, soon to be abandoned, a debating society, and 'free readings' on Wednesday evenings in 'polite literature'—what Cooper Union offered mainly to the public during its early years was a night school of science and art, a School of Design for women, and a reading room.[43] Popular lectures on political science and a day school of science were to come later. The night school during the first year gave instruction to all-comers, regardless of previous education, in such varied subjects as chemistry, mechanical philosophy, mathematics, music, and architectural, freehand, and mechanical drawing, and offered 'certificates of proficiency' to those who took the final examination in June. The examinations were voluntary, as the trustees feared the 'public trial would deter many, especially those advanced in life, from joining the classes.' Beginning in October of the second year, 1860, a full three-year science course was offered,[44] and this was lengthened to five years almost immediately. Those pupils without the rudiments of knowledge were sent to the city night schools.

The Women's School of Design was a day school from the beginning, offering training in lead pencil and crayon drawings from casts and life, perspective and sketching from natural objects, painting in oil and water, and designing and drawing on wood, lithography, etching on stone, and painting on china. Starting under the painter T. Addison Richards, it was reorganized in 1865 by Dr. William Rimmer, well-known sculptor, painter, and physician, who disposed of incompetents and insisted that the ladies learn how to draw before they could paint.

The reading room was the only one of its kind in the city at the time. The other libraries—the Society Library, the American Institute, the Astor Library, the Mercantile Library—served a far more specialized clientele, and were not open at night. Only Cooper Union offered the general public a place to read from eight in the morning to ten at night, well-stocked with magazines and newspapers and books to draw workers from 'less desirable places of resort.' The hope of the trustees was that some day a free lending library could be opened in the Great Hall, but that was only a dream during the first five years, when the library had only four thousand of the twenty-five thousand volumes the trustees wanted.

The public was by no means unanimous in welcoming Cooper Union. Some objected to educating the masses at all and others to having all classes associate together. A considerable number were deeply suspicious of Cooper's intentions, especially when they saw the mercantile signs on the windows of the shops on the first two floors and read of the close-knit group of Peter's friends who would control the Union. The New York *Daily News* was especially vitriolic. It claimed that Cooper had executed the deed in favor not of a corporation but of the following:

'Peter Cooper (Himself)
Edw. Cooper (His son)
Abraham [sic] E. Hewitt (His son-in-law)
Daniel F. Tiemann (His step-son-in-law)
John E. Parsons (His attorney)
William G. Hunt (His business friend)

This is a capital arrangement. It keeps the concern in the family, and nobody has a right to complain.' Everyone has the right to do with his property as he wishes, 'though some ill-natured people, who pay heavy taxes, complain that the Cooper building is from some as yet unexplained cause, exempt from taxation, while other "people's" buildings are not. We have not ourselves been able to find out the least advantage to the Corporation or people of New York of this far-famed Cooper Institute. Will anybody tell us where it is?' [45] It was perhaps a reader of these lines whom Cooper overheard on a Bowery horsecar say to his neighbor: "There is Peter Cooper's building. . . . That man is a snake in the grass. See the stores on the ground floor. It is a commercial building, and he is trying to evade tax-payments by calling it an educational institution." Peter Cooper interrupted him, introduced himself, and said, "Alight, gentlemen . . . and come in with me. You have maligned me. Let me show you the building and explain it." When he had explained the reasons for the stores and described his aims, they were contrite, and one of them afterward offered a small gift.[46]

In general, however, the public welcomed his efforts and came quickly to appreciate them. As one lady said in later years, gazing at the portrait of Cooper, "Well, at any rate, *this* 'Peter' has not denied his Master." The artisans for whom the Union was intended responded with an avidity that was almost incredible. The scene on registration day was, according to Hewitt, 'beyond belief. . . . There was a mob assembled so large and eager that the efforts to register students almost resulted in a riot. It was incredible that there should be such a passion for learning among the toilers. Every class was filled in one night, and from that day there was never a vacancy in the Cooper Union classes.' About two thousand pupils were admitted to the various classes, though over six hundred soon dropped out.[47] Among those who remained in the night school—all but five per cent of whom were men—clerks, salesmen, bookkeepers, machinists, carpenters, and cabinetmakers predominated, their ages ranging from sixteen to fifty-nine. At the end of the year fewer than four hundred hardy souls braved the examinations, of whom two hundred seventy-five received certificates from Peter Cooper, with the admonition that "riches and competence are the legitimate fruit of knowledge, economy and labour." Five years later, though the enrollment had increased by only about ten per cent, the number of certificates given had more than doubled.

The reading room was patronized by all and sundry from the beginning. Three thousand people a week, of whom ten per cent were women, were using the facilities during the first year, and this figure jumped to forty-two hundred by 1863-4. More people entered its doors than entered those of all the other libraries of the city combined. Peter Cooper could well feel proud of his work.

Within the first year of its existence Cooper Union was twice given unexpected advertisement. The Prince of Wales, who was wined and dined until he was glad to retreat to the relative seclusion of the British Isles, was conducted by Peter Cooper through its halls. Far more important, a rising young politician from Illinois, Abraham Lincoln, decided to give Easterners a chance to look him over, and on February 27, 1860, delivered in the 'Great Underground Hall' of Cooper Union the speech that he himself believed made him President of the United States. He had been urged to come to New York by that old Jackson Democrat, William Cullen Bryant, who wanted a Republican candidate able to win the West and unite all groups in a way that Seward, the acknowledged Republican leader, could not. Bryant had been impressed by Lincoln's behavior in the debates with Douglas nearly two years before, and now decided it was time to get a personal impression of him. Most New Yorkers agreed with him. Despite the inclement weather they crowded into Cooper Union to view the gaunt giant from the West of whom they had heard so much. Bryant presided, David Dudley Field led the speaker to the platform, and Peter Cooper looked on from the audience at one of the most distinguished gatherings ever to assemble in New York.

The first impression was what some of Lincoln's friends had feared. Dressed in new clothes, the work of an unskilled tailor, with his large feet, his clumsy hands, of which at the outset he was very conscious, his long head capped by a shock of hair not thoroughly brushed out, he reminded one a little of a rock that no summer green could soften, as well as a little of a scarecrow. He was not used to talking in large halls, and his voice was at first high and harsh and hard to understand. But as he warmed to his speech his voice became low and gentle and clear, and his gestures less labored and uncouth; the titters and cries of "Louder!" that had at first greeted him subsided into respectful attention. Lincoln gave his audience none of the ornate oratory that they had been used to from Clay and Webster. In closely reasoned phrases, showing a deep knowledge of constitutional history, he developed the text: Does anything in the federal constitution forbid the federal government from controlling slavery in the federal territories? There were no rhetorical fireworks, no anecdotes, no witticisms, only the restrained language, the fairness and sympathy, and the compact reasoning of the statesman. The Republicans were not radicals, he said, they would yield to the South if they could, and they intended to leave it alone; but they could not call slavery right, they could not yield to threats of secession, and they would not return slaves or allow the extension of slavery into the territories.[48]

The audience streamed out into the night, many of them determined that this man should be President and many others sure that he would be despite anything they might do. Cooper Union had been, almost at its outset, the scene of a great piece of popular education. Firmly established already as one of New York's great institutions, it was to go on year after year turning out hundreds of men and women equipped by knowledge and understanding to preserve the America Lincoln was so soon to give his life to save.

PART THREE

The Young Are Never Old

(1859-1883)

Chapter 15

THE CIVIL WAR

WHEN Cooper Union opened its doors Peter Cooper was within a year of the traditional limits assigned to the life of man. And had he then been called to that immortality toward which he looked with such confidence, he could have gone with a sense of work well done. He had made a fortune, he had played a major part in at least two great public enterprises, and he had won the esteem and love of generations to come by the creation of Cooper Union. His life was long entered on what he considered its last phase, in which, having made a fortune, he was to carry out his philanthropic projects. He was entitled to spend the few years that perhaps remained to him in the quiet retirement of the family circle, from which he might emerge occasionally to make suggestions about his Union or to lend his influence to some worthy project.

The thunder of impending civil war, whose premonitory rumblings had already affected his plans for the Union, forestalled for the moment, however, any thought of withdrawal from public affairs. Shortly after Lincoln's election and South Carolina's secession in the fall of 1860, Peter went to Washington as one of the representatives of the Chamber of Commerce (of which he had become a member in 1859), on a delegation headed by A. A. Low to find out what President Buchanan intended to do. The delegation got little satisfaction out of the President, who was late for the appointment, professed ignorance of anything except what appeared in the 'penny newspapers,' and said he was powerless to act. Only Senator Seward, so soon to play a prominent part in Lincoln's cabinet, would listen to them, and they returned home in disgust. But Peter would not give up hope for peace. Until the war broke out he bombarded both Lincoln and Senator John Sherman with letters of suggestion and encouragement, and on December 18, 1860, supported John J. Crittenden's proposal to reestablish the line of the Missouri Compromise.

Like so many Jacksonian Democrats, Peter Cooper had, as we have seen, been placed in a quandary by the prospect of war and had avoided taking a public position as long as he could. Coercion even to free the slaves was against his deepest instincts, so that he had no sympathy with the Abolitionist extremists. Moreover, he was traditionally a friend to the South, from which had come many of the great Jacksonian leaders of the past, and hostile to those industrialists—they were far fewer than the 'economic interpretation' of the Civil War has led us to believe —who were willing to encourage a war that would put down Southern planters. On the other hand, he could not tolerate, any more than Jackson could when he was President, the destruction of the Union that would result from granting the right of secession or the victory of slavery that submission to Southern demands implied. With the pro-slavery wing of his party, represented by Tammany Hall and Fernando Wood with his backing of anti-Negro immigrants, he had even less sympathy than he had with the Abolitionists.

All that seemed solid to Peter Cooper in these trying days was the Constitution, that sacred embodiment of the moral law on which both sides tried so hard to base their arguments, and he strove for compromise on grounds of a strict adherence to its provisions. Having in 1788 reluctantly permitted slavery to become part of the Constitution as the price of union, we ought not now give the South legal justification for secession—a right all Americans granted if the government was tyrannical—by denying them their due under the Constitution. Even if it was necessary to return slaves to their masters, to guarantee non-interference by the North in Southern affairs, to resurrect the Missouri Compromise, such action should be taken, he told Senator Sherman in February, 1861, to assure the South that the Republicans would 'secure them every right and privilege due in equity or legally. . . . Would it not be a great stroke of policy,' he added naively, 'for the republican members to rise above all parties and platforms and rely on the growth and strength of the North and offer to secure to the South the right to take their slave property into any of the territory now owned by the United States?' If slavery was an evil, as it undoubtedly was, the best means to end it was not force but, in the words of a letter written to Lincoln on March 20, 1861, only 'kind forbearance,' that 'most beautiful feature of Christianity.' After all, Peter told the President in somewhat the tone of a father lecturing an adolescent, 'the almost omnipotent power that the circumstances of birth, education and those interests that surround us are constantly exerting to form the differing opinions that prevail in the different sections of our widespread country' made Southern views inevitable.[1] They were not necessarily all evil, either, Peter added with a tolerance that went beyond his usual vein, and 'it becomes us all to gather' wisdom, of which no one man has a monopoly, wherever we can.

With the firing on Fort Sumter, Peter's conflicts were instantly resolved. As he told Nahum Capen in May, the North's honest efforts 'to maintain peace and friendship were met by a relentless war, waged for the destruction of the Constitution and the dissolution of the Union.' The South, not the North, had broken the bond of the Constitution, and men of good will were at last relieved from all obligation to uphold 'an institution so at war with natural justice and all the dearest rights of a common humanity.' So Peter rushed to join John A. Dix and other loyal Democrats in a great demonstration of pro-war sentiment held on April 20th in Union Square.

Speaking from the chief of the six platforms erected for the occasion, he called on everyone to unite in putting down an enemy "not only determined on our destruction as a Nation, but to build on our ruins a Government devoted with all its power to maintain, extend, and perpetuate . . . an institution that enables thousands to sell their own children into hopeless bondage. Shall it succeed? You say, No! and I unite with you in your decision. . . . Let us . . . unite to sustain the Government by every means in our power, to arm and equip, in the shortest possible time, an army of the best men that can be found in the country." If this appeal seemed obvious and perhaps unnecessary it must be remembered that the North was not united and that the rulers of New York City in particular were little short of traitors to their country. Fernando Wood went so far in the fall of 1861 as to charge the national administration with prolonging the war 'while there was a dollar to be stolen from the National Treasury or a drop of Southern blood to be shed.' [2]

In the ensuing years Peter Cooper did everything that his seventy years permitted to help the war effort. He was the first man to appear at the door of the Sub-Treasury to buy a war bond on the morning the first loan was issued, and was an early member of the Union League Club, formed in 1863 to support the war. He paid for a dozen or more substitutes to serve in the army, going down, as a friend said, 'whenever he had nothing else to do' and signing up for one;[3] and he showered the government with military, economic, and spiritual advice. Even his business correspondence with purchasers of glue, usually so free of the personal or general, contains talk of how to save the Union.[4] Nothing was too small or too great not to be worth a letter to the President or to a member of the cabinet: he would one day write to introduce a sympathetic London editor, John Adams Knight; the next to recommend a builder of 'invulnerable ships of war' and better cannon, Clinton Roosevelt; a third

to urge an increase in the number of rapid-shooting guns, a
dozen of which 'properly managed and supplied with ammunition would have killed more men and horses in the Battle at
Bull Run than were killed with all the men and by all the guns
used on that occasion'; and a fourth to propose the establishment of a chain of submarine telegraphic communications along
the coast.[5] Above all, he wrote about financing, a subject that
had always been of prime interest to him and which was soon to
become almost the central concern of his life.

Although the country was in excellent condition in 1861,
the Treasury was empty. Even before the war started Peter
wrote in alarm to Senator John Sherman, 'You may not realize
the extent of the difficulty that will be found in negotiating the
loans that will be required to carry on the government.' The
'principal moneyed institutions' fear that unless the two border
states adhere to the Union, government securities will be so de-
preciated 'as to put it out of the power of those who desire to
sustain the Government to do so.' [6] Chase, the Secretary of the
Treasury, a lawyer and former governor of Ohio with little
knowledge of finance, was soon in a quandary. Of the three possible ways of financing the war—the issuance of paper currency,
taxes, and borrowing—he preferred the two latter, but, as
Cooper predicted, loans were hard to negotiate and unpopular,
since they put the government at the mercy of banks, and the
government was afraid—as it always is in America—to tax too
heavily. During the whole course of the war only $667,163,247
was raised by a five-to-ten-per-cent income tax and other taxes,
as against $2,621,916,786 by loans and Treasury notes. So when,
at the end of 1861, an empty Treasury and fifty millions of un-
paid bills forced some action on Chase, he had no real choice
but to issue paper currency.

Cooper gives his friend Silas M. Stilwell, who was close to
Chase in Washington at the time, credit for what then occurred.
According to Cooper, Stilwell tried to argue Chase into issuing
Treasury notes, failed, and went home. When he got there he

received a telegram asking him to come back and devise a plan. Actually it was Congress that forced Chase's hand, the House passing on February 25, 1862, an act authorizing the issue of $150,000,000 of Treasury notes, the first of $413,000,000 of such notes to be issued, and making them legal tender for internal and external debt. They also issued $500,000,000 of so-called '5-20 bonds' (payable in twenty years and redeemable in gold in five) at six per cent, to be sold for coin and the new Treasury notes, which were to be made convertible into these bonds.

Peter Cooper was enthusiastically in favor of this scheme. On January 13, 1862, he had sent a petition through Chase[7] to the House and Senate favoring a government issue of money, which, he was proud to hear from Stilwell, the latter had seen in Chase's hands. On February 24th he wrote to Senator Sherman that he highly approved the House plan since it provided the country with a 'uniform circulating medium . . . adapted to the business wants of the nation' and saved the country from reliance 'on the tender mercies of Banks and brokers. . . . These local Banks . . . offer the greatest facilities for the artful and the designing to take advantage of those who are so unwise as [to] place themselves in their power;' they are a power to be feared and boast that they control the government. Peter had gotten over none of his antipathy to banks. Moreover, he was still a hard-money man. He hoped, he said, that the government would not miss the opportunity 'not only to coin gold and silver but to so regulate the value of all that shall be allowed to pass with the character of money that all shall have a uniform value throughout the country and be convertible into specie with the least possible loss and inconvenience to all who hold it—I believe that no one can be more opposed to an unrestrained paper circulation than myself.'[8] The Treasury notes, with their legal-tender clause and their convertibility privilege, seemed to him as sound as gold. And perhaps they would have been had the Senate not taken away their legal-tender status on import duties, had not their quantity been left unspecified, and, worst of all, had not Chase, in order to sell five-per-cent government bonds, later taken away the conversion privilege into the six-per-cent bonds. As a result of these changes, to all of which Peter was violently opposed, currency dropped from $98 in gold in 1862 to $39 in 1864.

Peter was not as opposed in 1862 to the idea of national banks as he was to state and local banks. Like so many who opposed the latter and shied away from irredeemable paper currency, he supported Elbridge Gerry Spaulding's National Banking Act in 1863. Although he was, a few years later, the bitterest enemy of the national banks, Peter acted in 1863 as commissioner to receive subscriptions for a national bank of the City of New York. He did so, he claimed afterward, only to save the nation and at the personal solicitation of Chase, who came to New York to persuade him; he was not, he added, long connected with the institution.[9] When, ten years later, he was asked to be a director of a granger's mortgage bank on the plea that it united capital and labor, he wrote, 'Nothing that you could offer would induce me to accept the responsibility of consenting to become a director in the bank you propose.' [10]

Along with his attempts to aid the war effort, Peter continued to work for an equitable and merciful peace. Though the South was morally in the wrong, it was still necessary to find some way of reuniting the nation, for, as he told Lincoln, 'it has been well said by Doctor Channing that an old phlegmatic race might be divided with less peril than a neighborhood of all grasping Communities that would meet everywhere in the markets of the world as rivals where a struggle to supplant each other would soon be deemed the perfection of policy.' The problem was how to show the South that the North used force only because and to the extent that it was necessary to free the people of that region from designing men. The issue was complicated by the fact that, as Peter told William Foster, the South was deeply guilty. Having formerly apologized for slavery, it now defended it, and that corrupted the best of men. 'A fatherly correction must follow—one that will affect them not willingly but of necessity for their profit.' Moreover, as early as the fall of 1861, a year before the first Emancipation Proclamation, he was convinced that slavery must go: 'I find that every day's reflection confirms me more and more in the belief that slavery is our national sin, and as "there is no peace to the wicked," so I fear there is no well grounded hope for peace or rest for our nation until we are willing as a people to both labor and suffer to secure to posterity their right to life, liberty and the pursuit of happiness.' [11]

Peter fought out his problem during 1861 in a long series of letters to his friend Capen. Capen planned a pamphlet on the subject of peace and urged Cooper to permit his letter to Capen to form part of the pamphlet. But Peter was reluctant to do so as he was too much in doubt as to a solution, and didn't want to recommend a plan that could not be carried out. When Capen's pamphlet, the *Indissoluble Nature of the American Union,*[12] appeared in December, 1861, recommending a mild compromise condemning both sudden abolition and secession, it was addressed to Cooper, who supplied a few soothing but inconsequential remarks. Peter could not, however, long be silent. In January, 1862, he wrote an open letter to Lincoln setting forth his views, and followed this up during the next two years with two more letters to Lincoln, one to Governor Seymour, and one to John Crittenden, the author of the earlier compromise suggestion.[13]

Cooper tried to hold, as one newspaper remarked about his 1862 letter, to the compromises of the Constitution 'even to the ungrateful duty of delivering up fugitive slaves.' In 1863 in his letter to Crittenden he recommended a plan to purchase the slaves from the South as a final gesture to show the North's good intentions and to win over the border states. The plan, he contended, would be of benefit to the South, which would now have its own laborers plus 'as many more from the North as they would like to employ.' [14] As he told Gladstone twenty years later, in recommending to the British prime minister that he

· (284) ·

solve the Irish problem in a similar manner by purchasing the land and selling it to the tenants, the whole cost of the 4,000,000 slaves would have been not more than two to four billion dollars as against the eight billion that the war cost, not to mention the loss of life and property and the hatred engendered.[15] As late as 1864 Peter appealed to Lincoln to ask the South 'to stop the effusion of blood by a return to the paternal care of your government,' and to assure Southerners that the North carried on the war in the 'most reluctant self-defense.'

Yet Peter was inevitably drifting toward sterner views. In his first letter to Lincoln he had advocated rendering 'contraband of war the slaves and property of all persons found in arms against the laws and government of the country.' A year later he had come reluctantly to the conclusion that the terrible 'necessity' he wished to avoid in 1861, 'organizing and arming the blacks of the country,' was no longer postponable. The slaves who cultivated Southern fields had to be overcome as well as Southern armies, and the best way to do this was to offer them freedom and a soldier's bounty for fighting in the Union Army.[16] In May, 1863, Cooper joined Bryant and Greeley in a memorial to put General Frémont at the head of an army of Negroes, a request that Frémont wisely refused.[17]

Such opinions were gradually driving Cooper out of the Democratic party. Though he later said he had not 'acted with the Democrats since the arbitrary exercise of power, displayed at a political meeting over which I was presiding' some time in the 'fifties,[18] he still was numbered in 1864 among the so-called 'War Democrats.' This was, however, the end. Horatio Seymour, the leading Anti-War Democrat, had become governor of New York in 1862, and had immediately proceeded to disgrace the party in Peter's eyes by his sabotage of the Lincoln administration, his virtual instigation through his speeches of the terrible draft riots in the summer of 1863,[19] and his desire to make peace by returning the slaves to their masters. In September, 1863, Cooper addressed a public letter to Seymour, urging him in the strongest terms to work on his Democratic friends, who, by sympathizing with the South, endangered the Union.[20] By 1864 it was evident from the platform on which General McClellan, the Democratic candidate, was forced to stand that the party was determined to be the party of appeasement. Peter and his War Democrat friends backed Lincoln for a second term and became Republicans, or Unionists, as the broadened Republican party was then called.

Their contribution to the Republican cause was no mean one. Most of us have forgotten how bad Lincoln's chances for reelection seemed during much of 1864. The country was sighing for peace, and the Chicago platform of the Democrats, proclaiming the war a failure, was deeply appealing in its call for an armistice and a convention of states to negotiate a peace. On the other hand, Lincoln had dissatisfied the radicals by his veto of their severe reconstruction bill in July, and, though they eventually gave up the attempt sponsored by Chase, Greeley, David Dudley Field, and others to replace him by Frémont, they were not wholeheartedly behind him. Because of General Sheridan's September victory over General Early at Winchester, Republican chances improved enough so that Thurlow Weed stopped telling Lincoln that his election was an impossibility. But the situation was still serious and a compromise peace still a possibility when a rally of War Democrats was called to meet at Cooper Union to support Lincoln and continuation of the war.

Thomas Hughes has given Cooper the entire credit for this rally. According to Hughes, a representative from a group of staunch Boston Unionists, sent to New York to arouse the friends of Union there, went straight to Cooper as one who 'in an ugly squall, never said, "Go, boy, and reef that topsail," but always "Come, boys, let us do it." ' He asked Peter for letters of introduction. "There's no time for letters or palavers," Peter answered, "just get into my buggy." It was standing in the street as usual, the horse tied to a lamppost, and away they went into the center of the business quarter of New York at noon, the old gentleman piloting with characteristic recklessness, which would have brought anyone to grief who was not known to every streetcar conductor, omnibus driver, and drayman. 'From door to door we drove,' reports the New Englander, 'through the crowded streets, stirring up one timid friend, holding back the next who wanted some other method, insisting with all against delay, or doubt, or change of plans, till in half the time anyone else would have taken Peter Cooper, with his big Union at his nod, had arranged for the great meeting.' [21]

The meeting, held on November 1st just a week before the election, was certainly one of the most important events of the campaign. In response, according to the *Herald,* to a 'trumpet call' all the leading Jacksonian or War Democrats were present, and when 'Major General Dix, Francis B. Cutting, Peter Cooper and other well known staunch supporters of the Democratic party in the days of its pristine glory made their appearance on the platform,' they were greeted with an enthusiasm that must have done much to decide the waverers in the dense throng.[22] The hostile *World,*[23] which accused Cooper of having been opposed in 1862 to a restoration of the Union, paid the meeting the tribute of violent denunciation and abuse in advance and proclaimed it a frost when it occurred. General Dix, said the *World,* was a mere timeserving spy and the other so-called Democrats were ciphers.[24]

Not many months after Lincoln's election, the Union, which the *World* professed 'no reasonable expectation' of seeing 're-stored within the ensuing four years' or perhaps ever again,[25] was reestablished. Almost immediately Peter Cooper went before his countrymen to plead for the disabled veterans of the war, making it clear that he at least did not think the duty of Americans was over when the last gun had been fired. 'I trust,' he said, 'that the Government will not hesitate to tax my property and the property of every other man to an amount sufficient to provide for the comfort of our disabled soldiers and the families dependent on them for support.' [26] In 1866 he supported the Christian Alliance, devoted to helping widows and orphans of volunteers,[27] and also the Southern Relief Association, organized to care for the destitute there. Nor did Peter immediately desist from his new habit of advising the government, and showered President Johnson, as he had his predecessor, with schoolmarmish letters about charity and understanding gained from studying the causes of behavior.

He had now, however, gone the whole distance toward Republicanism, showing himself far more a supporter of radical efforts to keep the South in bondage than of the attempts of the moderates like Weed and Seward and Dix to temper justice with mercy. In 1866 Cooper told Johnson that, despite brave words about traitors and treason, he was much too lenient with the South, which must, as Congress had ordained, accept Northern occupation until it had done justice to the Negro, purged itself of its old leaders, and given guarantees for the future.[28] For eight years Cooper continued to wave the bloody shirt. In 1868 he wrote Capen: 'I have no hesitation in saying that every man who loves his country and desires to secure for it peace and prosperity in the future should vote and use every honorable influence to secure the election of General Grant and Schuyler Colfax in preference to electing Horatio Seymour and General Blair. . . . Those who were the strongest advocates for secession and were leaders in the late rebellion are now doing all they can to secure their election.' [29] In characteristic fashion he wrote Seymour to the same effect. He was sorry, he told the latter, to see men calling themselves Democrats uniting with the leaders of the rebellion to build up a 'white man's government' for the purpose of disenfranchising 4,000,000 blacks.

In 1872, again brushing aside all other issues, he advocated in a public address keeping the Republican machine in power because the contest over slavery 'is not yet over'; the country was still in danger from those who 'once levied war against it with bullets, and who now seek to overthrow it with ballots.'[30] To John A. Dix, running for governor of New York on the Republican ticket in 1872, he was even more explicit. It would be worse than folly to place 'the government in the hands of a party made up of all the disloyal, the disappointed and dissatisfied men of our country. . . . I am entirely at a loss,' he concluded, 'to account for the infatuation that has induced my esteemed friend Horace Greeley to allow himself to be the candidate of a party so at war with all that he has written and said in denunciation of these men and the principles that control them.'[31] Cooper had apparently become an orthodox supporter of big-business Republicanism.

Chapter 16

FATHER COOPER

WITH the return of peace in 1865 the time had evidently come for Peter finally to seek retirement. To the public in general he had already become a benign father-image. His fringe of beard had turned white, the hair streaming down his back was iron-gray, the set of his jaw had softened, and his blue eyes peered from behind his four-lensed spectacles with more benevolence than fire. The slight stoop of his figure was accentuated by the plain old black coat, soft black felt hat, and old-fashioned stock that he still habitually wore, which made him look like a well-to-do farmer or retired tradesman. The journalists of the day seized on this image, accentuated the more saintly aspects of the personality it embodied, and proceeded to worship that personality in the high-flown periods characteristic of the age. In 1855 Beach had been content to remark, with some restraint, 'no man more fills the public eye at the present day by constant and untiring efforts for the public welfare';[1] in 1881 the *Herald* cried, 'Heaven can do a long time without him, for heaven is peopled with the good; but New York has only one Peter Cooper.'[2] This transformation of attitude began in the middle 'sixties.

The New York *Observer* set the new tone in 1865. On looking at Peter Cooper, said the *Observer,* one got no impression of

a 'man of force, accomplishment and purpose.' It was his be-
nignity and simplicity that struck one, as he hitched his self-
driven 'one horse chaise, very much the worse for wear and age,'
to a post, put the blanket 'carefully in, and making all right and
snug,' entered his Union. It was a beautiful sight, the writer
went on, to 'see him come into the great lecture room, crowded
with eager multitudes. . . . He speaks slowly and with a feeble
voice, but his presence commands such profound silence and
attention, that he is heard over the large hall. He moves like a
father among his children.'[3] In the same year *Frank Leslie's
Chimney Corner*,[4] though it mentioned Cooper's bold, massive
features, evidences of originality and decision, also laid chief
emphasis on his patriarchal look and goodnatured simplicity.
The 'one horse, four-wheeled, covered vehicle . . . generally
well coated with mud' was there too in the *Chimney Corner* account, with Peter sitting in the 'middle of the single seat . . .
bolt upright, looking straight ahead through his spectacles.'

To the public this oft-mentioned vehicle, familiar sign of
Peter's presence, soon became the most beloved emblem of the
man. To his admirers his refusal to use it at night—"I use my
horse during daytime, I let the horse rest evenings"—was a symbolic example of his benevolence. Its appearance by day produced an effect that seems astonishing, and we ought perhaps
make some discount for rhetorical exaggeration. According to
one account, whenever his carriage was sighted traffic stopped
until he had passed, the coachmen of the rich no less than hack
drivers and draymen giving way to him. (Peter's notorious
recklessness as a driver may have played some part in this defer-
ence.)[5] Men leaped to open his coach at the door and hats came
off as he appeared in the streets.[6] Peter had become before the
end of his life a revered figure even among the city's worst elements. He could go anywhere in perfect safety 'because the very
roughs had become his guardians, and would have fallen into
ranks about him in any danger, and held their lives in pawn for
his safety.' His presence lit up careworn faces, who looked at him

as if to say, "It cannot be so hard a world as we thought it was, since Peter Cooper stays in it to give it his benediction." [7]

The Saint Peter of the popular imagination was a very respectable saint and one of the town's most dignified citizens. Even his situation in New York seemed to symbolize his new status. By 1870 the 23rd Street district had ceased to be an outlying part of town and had become the fashion center of a New York that was being built up solidly to the edges of Central Park. In 1860 Washington Square was still sacrosanct, Delmonico's was at 14th Street, and the Astor House, the great hotel, was still at Broadway and Vesey Street. But in 1859 Amos R. Eno, amid jeers from the knowing, built his huge Fifth Avenue Hotel at 23rd Street and Fifth Avenue on the site of a roadhouse cottage, and within a few years it had become the leading hotel in America. The hotel itself and the 'charmed circle' of houses within a few blocks of it contained most of New York's leading citizens, from Commodore Vanderbilt, Russell Sage, and Chauncey Depew to Tilden, Thurlow Weed, Roscoe Conkling, and James G. Blaine. The Hoffman House, Democratic headquarters, stood nearly up against the Republican Fifth Avenue Hotel; Booth's Theatre was at 23rd and Sixth Avenue and the Madison Square Theatre at 24th Street and Fifth Avenue. Peter Cooper's house at 22nd Street and Lexington Avenue was now but one among many stately homes of moneyed New Yorkers, and Cooper was at home in all of them. In the New York of fast stages, brownstones, choking brimstone matches, 'segars' and segar store Indians, wax flowers under round glass, stereoscopic views and tintypes, horsehair furniture, hoop skirts and bustles, Peter Cooper was a leading citizen. It was he, without a second thought, who was appointed to do the honors to the Prince of Wales in 1860. The success of the Atlantic Cable and the part Cooper played in the Civil War added to his stature and his respectability.

The trouble with this popular view was that it was but a partial and distorted image of the man. His contemporaries were

hopelessly deceived as to the amount of energy, vision, and rebellion that still lurked behind Peter's benevolent pink face
fringed with its silky hair. He had no more intention in 1865
of retiring than he had had in 1830. Even to playing the role expected of him—attending to his family, gracing public functions, dispensing alms in wider and wider circles, and supervising his Union—he devoted himself with an assiduousness that
would have taxed the strength of many younger men. And this
was not enough for him. Living on far beyond the normal span
of human life into the garish post-Civil-War world, he was by no
means content to exist merely as a symbol of the past quietly
putting the finishing touches to his life. It is no exaggeration
to say that the last decade and a half of Peter Cooper's life was
the busiest and richest of his whole career. And the least conventional. Freed from ordinary business cares and from providing
for his family, he could throw himself into new and untried
business ventures with an abandon formerly denied him. Having achieved the status of respectable pillar of society, he no
longer needed to act the part. Peter Cooper did not like the po-
liticos and bankers and industrialists of America's Gilded Age,
and he rebelled against them with all the fire and energy of a
young man. Almost the last of the Jacksonian liberals, he joined
a new generation of liberals in the first of the many assaults on
the entrenched power of modern industrial capitalism. His admirers, who continued to see him as a kindly, respectable old
gentleman, passed such behavior off as mere eccentricity. But
they misjudged Peter. His Greenbackism grew as naturally
from the central core of his being as did his inventiveness, his
business activity, and his philanthropy. To many of those who
mourned his passing it was this Peter Cooper they mourned, the
crusty individualist whose democratic instincts and courage inevitably precipitated him into post-Civil-War radicalism.

Peter Cooper never traveled during his whole life farther than a few hundred miles from New York, except for his Newfoundland trip and one later tour through the South. Though he had once wanted to go to Europe, he was now satisfied to stay home; spending money abroad instead of in America where it could benefit one's fellow citizens had become, he felt, 'our national sin.' [8] So he remained, except for summers at Ringwood or sometimes Newport, or trips to Washington or Albany or Boston, in New York at his spacious home on 22nd Street. In 1869 his wife died in the 56th year of their married life, taking from the old man 'my nearest and best earthly friend and the guiding star of my life.' She fell asleep, he told Capen, with no struggle, 'as in the arms of infinite wisdom and with as much calm confidence as I have ever seen her go to sleep in the days of perfect health.' [9] For months Peter lived a sort of half-life; but he never whimpered or complained, and was soon completely himself again. His children were still with him, and his grandchildren were becoming a large and noisy reminder of continuing life.

Amelia and Edward were completely devoted to their father and watched over him with elaborate care; while Edward and Abram took most of the ordinary worries of life off his hands so that he could devote himself to his pet projects. Only once did any of them give him occasion for serious concern. In 1878 Edward was elected mayor of New York by a coalition of anti-Tammany, pro-Tilden Democrats and Republicans, and very quickly showed that he was too kindly and indecisive a man for the job. Within a few months he had both alienated the independent voter by appearing to be a mere Tilden henchman and been outmaneuvered by a combination of Republicans and Tammany Democrats. The press, reflecting the disillusionment with a reform mayor that so often overtakes New Yorkers, was vituperative and scornful. One magazine, *Puck*, made a direct appeal to Peter Cooper. Asserting that Mayor Cooper disgusted the public, angered the press, and pleased no one, *Puck* called on the old man to chastise his son with the palm of his hand. They liked, they said, Peter's institute and glue and words 'from the recesses of his air-cushions; but as to raising sons—especially political sons—we do think that Peter has, so to speak, petered out. . . . Let him ride into the lists with his bounding air-cushion, let him boldly tackle his obstreperous progeny.' [10] To all this Peter answered not a word, and by the time his son left office in 1880 most of the press had reversed its views to the extent of feeling that Edward had done his best under trying circumstances.

Peter's grandchildren—with the birth in 1871 of Erskine Hewitt, Amelia's and Abram's sixth child, there were eight—must have been a sore trial to their grandfather. Running sleds down the front steps through the front door and dropping large snowballs on passersby from the roof of the stable were the least of their activities. Young Peter Cooper Hewitt, aided by the only slightly less ingenious Edward Ringwood, made a horse fiddle (a box over which a plank rubbed with rosin was drawn) ; tied silk threads to the lamppost and parlor window to knock off the hats of pedestrians; drove a spike with a quarter soldered to the top into the ground and watched pedestrians vainly try to pick up the money; filled chocolates meant for Hewitt's guests with wood; hoisted the Gramercy Park benches to the top of the flagpole and then tied the flagpole ropes to the top branch of a tree, which they had sawed almost through; and put gunpowder and giant firecrackers under the house of the park watchman. These exploits, a natural reaction to the respectability and orderliness of their father's house, were not always appreciated by the neighbors, despite the exalted position of the Cooper-Hewitt family, and there was often an angry policeman at the door. He very seldom caught the boys, who had sawed the bottom bars in the Gramercy Park fence as a means of escape and would hide in the space below the floor of the stable. Both the Hewitts and Peter Cooper accepted this behavior with remarkable equanimity. Hewitt would bail the boys out of jail when they did occasionally get caught, and Amelia cheerfully paid the damages for broken windows and disconnected door-bell wires, often in advance of any request, as she always assumed her sons were responsible for what happened in the neighborhood.

Peter adored his grandchildren and had a good word for each of them, from Amy ('an excellent girl of humble disposition') and Sarah ('full of life and gaiety') to Peter Cooper, later the inventor of the mercury-vapor lamp, and Edward Ringwood ('one of the nicest boys'). The old man came out and worked with his grandsons in the workshop he had built for them above the stable, and hired a professional mechanic to teach them, insisting, however, that they learn to do things for themselves. He also built a gymnasium for them in the stable. Though he occasionally preached to them on the evils of destroying the property of others or of misusing tools, a passion with Peter, he was a far more indulgent grandfather, as is usually the case, than he had been a father. In return the children loved the old man and were amused by his eccentricities. His winter shoes of rabbit fur, the new air-cushion made by his friend Mr. Goodyear, his oldfashioned razor, his practice of soaking new shoes for two months in linseed oil, his parsimonious use of old envelopes for autographs, his habit, which he thought healthful, of rocking across his walking stick placed under his rocker, his going to sleep in church, like Sir Roger de Coverley, with his head against the column behind his pew—all came under their observant eyes, to be recalled years later. Occasionally they played tricks on him. Once small Peter Cooper and Sally, taking advantage of his softheartedness, dressed as beggars and got two dollars out of him by pouring out a sorrowful tale. When they later confessed to the imposture, he showed pleased though perhaps feigned surprise and refused to accept the return of the money.[11]

During the last dozen or more years of his life Peter's daily existence fell into a fairly fixed routine. Up early, he breakfasted in his room or with his grandchildren and by 9:30 was at Cooper Union, where he passed the morning. In the afternoon he spent some time at his Burling Slip office, but was home by three for a rest before callers began to arrive. Often in the evening he returned to the Union. This routine involved far more activity than one might imagine, and it was frequently interrupted. The Lexington Avenue house was usually alive with guests; and old and young, including the suitors of the Hewitt girls, wanted to 'go across the hall' and chat with Peter. "I remember," said Edward Shepard, "how gladly and graciously he used to hold with both hands the hands of one young and very unimportant friend of his, and I was but one of a host." [12] Important visitors, too, were always dropping in. According to Edward Hewitt, Bell brought him the telephone he had invented; Edison came to see him and explained the phonograph to him; Christopher Latham Sholes tried to interest him in the first imperfect typewriter. Bryant called and once defended Italian as against modern Greek in Cooper's parlor by reciting a passage from Dante with such rapture as to become completely oblivious to his surroundings.

Peter's home was virtually the headquarters of visiting Englishmen, whom, whether they liked it or not, Peter carted off to his Union, to public schools, or to various of his charities, all the while hymning the glories of the city he so much loved. Richard Cobden was one of his visitors, and it is amusing to find the old high-tariff advocate claiming that he saw eye-to-eye with the great free-trader on the mutual benefit to be derived from an equitable interchange of commodities between England and America.[13] Tom Hughes's letters describe an astounding breakfast he had at Cooper's in 1870, though it is doubtful if the abstemious Peter, who, according to Hewitt, lived mostly on crackers and milk for the last twenty years of his life, partook of much of it. It began with a 'huge slice of melon and glass of iced water following with grapes, pears, and peaches as we liked;

then a cup of coffee to wash down broiled chicken, soft crab, sweet potatoes and chops; then a form of hominy and cream, to conclude with a saucer full of peaches and cream.' [14]

Peter was forced, as a leading citizen, to take part in much strangely assorted public entertainment, from dinners in honor of the Cable to receptions for the Mexican and Chinese ambassadors, protest meetings against Napoleon III's threatened interference in Mexican affairs, and a gala welcome for the representative of the one country which had been wholly on the North's side during the Civil War—Russia. And Peter himself was much entertained and honored in later years. In 1879 he received the Bessemer medal for his efforts in behalf of the iron trade, and was deeply touched, though he couldn't go to England to receive it.[15] On his eighty-eighth birthday, in the same year, he was given an LL.D. by the University of the State of New York, in the presence of the presidents of all the New York colleges and the faculty and regents of the university, who came in a body with the chancellor at their head. Peter, who was himself on all occasions, 'surprised the company by repeating a long and appropriate quotation from Pope, without the omission of a word.' [16] (Edward Hewitt confirms this statement. He and his sister, Nellie, sat behind a screen with the text in their hands.) Five years previously he had been honored at a reception at Delmonico's given by Sorosis, a women's organization, for his efforts in behalf of the higher education of women; and at another and larger reception at the Arcadian Club, a club of newspapermen, painters, singers, and actors. On this latter occasion, attended by the presidents of Cornell, Princeton, and Columbia as well as by scientists, judges, and such literary lights as E. C. Stedman, Bret Harte, and Bryant, the reporters were most moved by the 'mingling of the white hairs of beard and head' and the 'flushed and moved faces' of Cooper and Bryant as the two octogenarians clasped hands.[17]

Cooper was honored in other less conventional ways. According to Edward Ringwood Hewitt, who accompanied him to

Washington in 1876, when Peter entered the House of Representatives Blaine spied him, stopped a speech he was making, and said he saw in the gallery "the most distinguished and best-beloved citizen of the United States." Given the privileges of the floor by unanimous consent, Peter was escorted to a seat next to the Speaker's desk, the ten-year-old Edward trailing behind with the omnipresent cushion.[18] In 1881, on the assassination of Garfield, Cooper was asked to speak for five minutes or write something 'because . . . apart from the Mayor or Chief Magistrate for the time being you are preeminently the "First Citizen" of New York.' [19]

Public efforts in behalf of the downtrodden were also occupying more and more of Peter's attention in the 'sixties and 'seventies. The most important of these—he was, of course, on the boards of many institutions such as the S.P.C.A. and the Home for Old Men and Aged Couples—were his work for the Indian and the immigrant. The immigrant had concerned Peter since his days on the Common Council, and he therefore welcomed the opportunity, offered by the opening-up of western lands after the Civil War, to aid the western movement. In the late 'sixties his Emigrant Protective Society, supported by such men as Frederick Ohmstead in the *Times,* offered the new arrivals railroad fare to get them out of town; he also gave his support to an English company, the American Emigrant Company, 'one of the most useful and benevolent undertakings of the age,' which gave immigrants information that protected them from cheats and helped them to go cheaply in groups to new lands. In 1870, along with friends like Marshall Roberts and William E. Dodge, whose connections respectively with the Southern Trans-Continental Railway and the Texas Central Railroad made them interested parties, he signed and distributed under his signature a circular for a more elaborate plan of emigration. Colonies were to be set up on a business basis through a National Emigration Bureau in New York, which would operate depots

· (299) ·

to employ transient labor while it was waiting and to collect a land-buying fund to be held on interest in a bank. The organization, which was precluded from pecuniary interest, would, Peter said, distribute labor and settle the country without harming private interests.[20]

The Indian problem was a knottier one. Exploited and robbed, brought to Washington and induced to sign treaties that sold their birthright for a mess of pottage, their tribal customs destroyed with the loss of their land, the Indians had been turned from the peaceful tribes that Peter knew in his youth into desperate fighters determined on victory or extinction. As the transcontinental railways spread west in the 'sixties, pushing Indians out of the territories assigned to them by Monroe in 1817 and provoking renewed violence, the situation became acute. While many Westerners, who bore the full brunt of Indian attacks, called for wars of extinction, philanthropic Easterners began to awaken to the need of a very different policy. Among the most prominent of these was Peter Cooper. Egged on by friends who sent him long screeds on the plight of the red men, he formed, with Howard Crosby, chancellor of New York University, Professor B. M. Martin of that institution, and the Reverend J. M. Ferris, secretary of the Board of Missions of the Reformed Church, the New York Indian Peace Commission. His view, as expressed at a meeting called in 1868 to advocate the claims of the 'poor persecuted remnant of suffering Indians . . . driven from their ancient homes by every form of cruelty and deception that the arts of civilization could invent,' was that only when Indians were 'regarded and provided for as human beings,' when 'every contract made with them' was 'carried out to the very letter,' and when they had been encouraged by peaceful means 'to adopt our laws and become citizens with the right to represent their wants and their grievances in the government of our country,' would tranquillity be restored. The method was not simply to assimilate them into the population, since that would mean, as others pointed out, dispossession, exploitation, crime, and vagabondage, but to bring them to citizenship through educating them on suitable reservations.

Cooper and his friends were remarkably effective. A joint committee of Congress had in 1867 revealed abuses in the administration of Indian Affairs, and a peace commission of army officers had asserted in the same year that Indian wars were due to our unjust treatment of the Indian.[21] Backed by these reports and an aroused public sentiment, the New York Indian Commission sponsored a bill in Congress setting up large, easily subdivided reservations, from which traders and speculators were to be excluded and on which Indians could learn to be self-supporting, rising from stock-raising through agriculture to mechanics and civil education, the 'order of nature, and the law of all human development.' Though proper reservations were not immediately forthcoming, in 1869, as a result of the commission's efforts, ten commissioners to act with the Secretary of the Interior were appointed to manage Indian Affairs, and the Grant peace policy was inaugurated.

The future looked hopeful. In 1871 Peter Cooper had the pleasure of presiding over a public reception given at Cooper Union to a deputation of Cheyenne, Arapahoe, and Wichita chiefs (who had come east to confer with Grant), at which Little Raven and Buffalo Good told of Indian injuries.[22] The most famous of Indian chiefs, the Sioux Red Cloud, who had fought bravely against Major James Powell in 1867 and had been won over to friendship with the whites by William Blackmore the following year, also spoke at Cooper Union in full Indian costume. For Peter he signed little two-inch-high pictures giving the full history of the Sioux nation, and sent him an Indian buffalo robe of beautifully tanned leather, which ended up as a laprobe for Peter's gig.

Unfortunately the bright hopes of solving the Indian problem soon evaporated. Corruption crept into the administration of Indian Affairs, and when Congress sustained the 'ring' of Indian contractors against the commission, the latter resigned.

From 1879 to 1913 reservations were cut to one-third their former size, rather than enlarged, and the Indian, exploited all along the way by grafters in the West and politicians in the East, was hurried into citizenship at a fabulous cost in money and suffering. Red Cloud, symbol of peace, saw his tribe moved callously from place to place until it was completely impoverished. In 1888 old John Beeson wrote to Hewitt that he was coming east about a new Indian Bill and hoped that Hewitt, now mayor of the city, would make a speech for him 'as Peter Cooper used to do at my meetings.' Tired and discouraged, Beeson would at eighty-five still be able to carry on the good fight he and Cooper had waged for nearly forty years if Peter Cooper and other old friends 'who have gone above, were now in earth life.' [23]

It was the little deeds of charity, however, not the big public acts that took most of Peter's time. His distant relations, who seemed almost universally incompetent, were alone a heavy burden. Without straining the reader's patience it is difficult to give any idea of the way in which Peter was badgered by nephews, nieces, grandnephews, grandnieces, and a host of others with even thinner ties of blood. They wrote to him from upper New York State, from California, from Maryland, from Nebraska, from Kansas, from Virginia, from Illinois, from Indiana, from Minnesota, from Texas, from Tennessee, asking for a hundred dollars here, a loan to get them started in business there, a few dollars to help stock a farm, the chance of a job, and so on. Some had improvident husbands, some had unfaithful wives, all were living on the ragged edge of destitution. To all of them Peter responded with help, and usually found himself supporting them for life. One niece, who merely asked Peter for 'something to do' in 1860 to end her 'galling' feeling of dependence, was still begging Amelia for money in 1905, and others leaned on him for periods nearly as long. Year after year they wrote to Peter, telling him they were sorry they couldn't

pay him back as the crops had failed, they were sick, they had
lost their jobs, they had been robbed, their husbands beat them
. . . one sometimes wonders, scanning their querulous or proud
or despairing letters, how Peter's faith in America's limitless opportunities survived.

If charity began at home, it was never confined there. Peter
loved his fellowmen, and that meant all of them, the rich and
the poor, brain workers and laborers, and the competent and
the incompetent, whom the impatient Hewitt could never
abide. He particularly loved to talk to men with ideas, and to
help such men start a magazine, open a church or a school,
market an invention, or begin a new business. Once when
Cooper was in Philadelphia a storekeeper rushed out and drew
him into the store. Peter had, years before, started the man in
business, and he was now so grateful that he would not let
Peter out until he had selected a complete set of dishes—in, as
his grandson observed, the worst possible taste.[24]

In theory Peter did not believe in doling out charity, except
to such helpless people as the children in lodging houses and
industrial schools, for whose clothing and entertainment he gave
$10,000 on his golden wedding in 1863. But he never abided
by his theory. When his grandson asked him why he did not
practice what he preached, he said, very simply, that he could
not help himself. The truth was that Peter really enjoyed giving
away money. Susan Carter said that she stopped telling Peter
about poor students in her School of Design because he would
slip a bill into her hand before she had finished talking; nothing
refreshed his spirits more than to hear of some girl whom his
benevolence had helped. His home and office were accessible to
anyone, and his pocketbook more so. The result may be imagined. When someone was in trouble and prayed to God for help,
God usually thought of Peter Cooper, and the petitioner immediately turned to him. His neighbor in Burling Slip says he
was harried by applicants for aid, whom the clerks had to keep
out of his office; but they surrounded Peter's carriage 'and every

one received money from him.' Beggars besieged his house. The situation reached a climax in the depression winters after 1873 when, according to the *Tribune,* Peter Cooper sat at his desk every day from three to six-thirty and handed out 'newly-coined half dollars' and dollar bills to every applicant, the piles being 'replenished every hour by the servant in attendance.' His rule was to give everyone fifty cents, and if the case seemed urgent to double the amount and request a written history authenticated by a clergyman. As early as two-thirty there were crowds in front of the house, and Peter often handed out two hundred dollars a day, and one week fifteen hundred dollars. He never asked these people if they were worthy, actually favoring atheists because they had no church to turn to.[25]

Inevitably Peter's gifts were not always well directed. In 1864 he drew down on himself the ire of Walter Barrett for joining Wilson G. Hunt and A. A. Low in starting a fund for the relief of indigent merchants, by establishing a fire-insurance company with a capital of $200,000, all profits over seven per cent to go into the fund. 'What ought to be asked of a Divine Being,' wrote Barrett, 'for a city whose leading capitalists are so rotten with avarice that they want seven per cent for a Divine charity . . . when they can't get six in regular business.' [26] Usually, when Peter made a mistake, it was in the other direction. On one occasion an angry nephew begged him to stop giving money to the nephew's wife, an 'artful woman who has made my married life a continuous sacrifice—thwarting all my plans and bringing upon me everywhere a load of debt and embarrassment.' Cooper's papers list a number of investments in inventions, for most of which he paid considerable sums: the Gullman sewing machine ($10,000, settled for $5500); the Mumford machine ($5000); a universal feed machine ($5500); three-quarters of the Feber machine ($6000); the Freeman electric light ($500); and a 'crystallized Egg Stock' patent, in which Peter sank over $20,000 (this last, one assumes, refers to a plan for desiccating eggs and glue on which Peter took out a patent in 1875). Most if not all were worthless. On one, however—a patent for a hinged bar to hold window shutters in place, in which Peter had invested $1000—, his grandson collected $2800 a year for several years.

Hughes gives a diverting example of Peter's persistence in supporting a worthless project. When he was nearly ninety a plausible inventor came to him with the patterns of a patent turbine waterwheel and pump, which he wanted Cooper to finance. Peter not only financed it but had it erected at Ringwood. After the bright brass wheel and pump had been erected, P. R. George, the Cornish manager at Ringwood, took one look at it and turned to Peter Cooper: "That wheel could never do the work." To prove his assertion he gripped the shaft in his hands and stopped the whole machine. Peter's jaw fell, as he sat in his garden chair watching, and he at once intervened between the outraged inventor and the strong-wristed Cornishman. But he sent the inventor back to New York with additional funds to make further experiments. On his return the inventor was injured by the fall of part of the building where the wheel was stored, and Peter, getting up in the middle of the night, nursed the injured man and paid his doctor's bill. When a second test proved unsuccessful, Peter once again sent him to New York, from where he never returned. Peter was left with a useless piece of junk and a hole in his pocket where $10,000 had been.[27]

The ingratitude of some of the recipients of his kindness must have hurt Peter most. There is a good deal of truth in the comment that if you want a man to hate you put him under obligations to you, and there were many who could not bear the burden of Cooper's favors. One half-crazed man, the editor of a collection of Peter's sayings, took a reporter along with him to watch him whip Cooper, and ended by breaking a window.[28] Another man, whom Peter had helped and who had then cheated Cooper, threw snowballs at his house; when the coachman ducked him in the snow, Peter said it was too bad, the man was enjoying himself so.[29] Peter was fortunately dead when one niece traded on his name, appealing to his daughter on the grounds that people in her small town were saying with lifted eyebrow, 'could it be I was a niece of Peter Cooper?'

Hewitt, a proud and touchy individual, was deeply perturbed by seeing Peter made a fool of, and took an almost venomous delight in refusing appeals that reached him before they did Peter. When one woman asked for $250 on the ground that such a sum was a mere drop in the bucket to Peter, Hewitt gave her $50 and refused to turn over her letter to Cooper. "How can you possibly have any knowledge of his affairs," he told her, "which would warrant such a statement?" After Peter's death he refused to continue aid to a Mrs. O'Malley. Because Peter had helped her was no grounds for continuing the help: 'He was in the habit of giving to the just and unjust alike, and he rarely knew the merits of any case which he relieved,' a remark that ought to have silenced any but the most hardened beggar.[30]

Peter, so careful of the last penny in a business deal, had, on the other hand, no great fear of making ludicrous mistakes when it came to charity. Once in a while he thought it was necessary to teach someone a lesson, as he did two well-to-do bank clerks who got money out of him just to prove they could play on his sympathies. Allowing the report to circulate that he knew of the cheat but not the names, he took out a warrant against 'parties unknown' for getting money on false pretenses and placed the matter in a detective's hands. The two men fled and wrote cowering letters of apology, which, after keeping them in suspense for a time, Peter accepted with the penalty only of a fatherly lecture.[31] Very occasionally he denied a request. 'Had I been in your place,' he told one nephew who planned to buy a farm beyond his means, 'I would have found something to do—I would have bought and sold matches or popcorn or any other honest means of keeping out of debt.' Only once, to the author's knowledge, did he exhibit any bitterness. 'My experience in loaning money,' he admonished one pleader, crossing out the words 'to relatives,' 'has been very unfortunate.'

Usually Peter took the prospect of being dunned philosophically. When the committee of the Arcadian Club called on him to invite him to dinner he immediately brought ten dollars out of his pocket and asserted that that was the best he could do. "Why Mr. Cooper," said the spokesman for the group, "I didn't come here to get money." When this was finally conveyed to Peter, he jammed the bill back into his pants and a look of astonishment came over his face. "Don't want any money! Well! They all do! I'm to come to a reception? Certainly! Certainly! Beg a thousand pardons! I'll be there! Good day! Good day!" [32] Peter's general attitude was that it was better to be deceived by many than to deny one person in need. He had plenty of money, he enjoyed giving, and he was superior to anything the public might say of him. Nor is there any suggestion that contact with the cheaters and time servers who swarmed around him embittered him in the slightest. Fortunately he was dead when one of the enterprising businessmen of his day, anticipating our ingenious advertisers by half a century or more, used his name to sell porous plasters: Peter Cooper, read the advertisement, loved his fellowmen, but one could be useful on a business basis too; even education was less pressing than healing diseases.[33] But he would probably not have minded. Once, when he was observing how differently people in an art class at the Union painted a model, Peter Cooper exclaimed that this should teach us charity by showing how the same person could be different 'according to the way he is looked at by various people.' His faith in human nature, which suffered severe trials during his last years in the political arena as well as in his charitable work, remained firm to the end.

Chapter 17

CANALS AND ELEVATED RAILROADS

At THE end of the Civil War Peter retired from business. He had long had only a nominal connection with the iron company, and he now turned the glue factory over to his children and his brother. His domestic telegraph interests had been liquidated before the war, and with the success of the cable his worries on that score were over. He could well afford to leave the major tasks of postwar industry to the capitalists of a new generation: in June, 1864, when the Civil War income-tax law was in operation, he paid a $5341.40 tax on an income of $106,-879;[1] and he wrote in the *Reminiscences* that he left his family nearly as well off as though he had never built Cooper Union '. . . and I still feel sometimes as though I am somewhat in debt to the world.'[2]

Yet Peter could never quite leave business alone. According to his grandson a man came over from Brooklyn every morning during the 'seventies to tell him how much the glue factory sales had been the previous day. And to the end of his life he was always ready, despite his many other interests, to finance a new venture. Edward Hewitt tells of Cooper's listening to a meeting at his house arranged by Clarence King for the purpose of combining telephone patents, which could be bought up for $400,-000. At first Peter said merely that the idea sounded good and

· (308) ·

he only wished he were younger; then, at 9 o'clock, standing at the door to say good-night, he suddenly said he would put up half the money. The telephone business ought to be a good one (as Edward Hewitt quotes him), "because everyone wants to talk more than anything else." The others decided, though, that the expenses of litigation were too great, so that they lost the opportunity to acquire the telephone. Peter did, however, have some hand in financing the first attempts at a Pacific Cable, and was one of the pioneers in organizing a company to build a canal across the Isthmus of Panama.

This latter effort occurred in 1868.[3] The American government first became interested in plans for an Atlantic and Pacific canal between Central and South America in 1826, when Henry Clay ordered a survey of a route through Nicaragua; and in 1837 Horatio Allen got a number of leading citizens to prepare a plan for a Nicaragua Canal to be presented to Congress. The next thirty years were filled with wild and abortive schemes to build canals in half a dozen places, from Nicaragua (where Cornelius Vanderbilt in 1849 opened a route by steamboat and coach) to various routes across the Isthmus of Panama, which the United States spanned by a railroad in 1855. Most of them were vitiated before they started by disagreements as to the most feasible path and by squabbles between France, Britain, and America, each of which exerted more effort in gaining favorable treaties with Central and South American countries than in building a canal. By the late 'sixties, however, with the Suez Canal nearing completion, a Panama or Nicaragua Canal began suddenly to seem a real possibility. In 1868 Secretary of State Seward started to negotiate a treaty between the United States and Colombia looking toward the construction of a canal across the Isthmus of Darien, and by September had progressed far enough so that it seemed desirable to consult some 'enlightened capitalists' about the idea. Whom should he turn to but Peter Cooper?

Seward realized that what he was doing was somewhat improper, since negotiations between countries were usually, as he told Peter, 'conducted in mutual confidence.' So wouldn't Peter simply invite the others to meet Seward? These others, among whom were William Evarts, William H. Vanderbilt, and Marshall O. Roberts, had by a fortunate coincidence incorporated themselves as the Isthmus Canal Company the day before Seward's letter was sent to Peter, and were quite ready to meet Seward. So, too, was General Acosta, the former president of Colombia and now the Colombian minister to the United States. Shortly after the meeting, which took place at Peter's house, the existence of the new company was divulged to the public. Immediately Peter, who was president, was swamped with advice and encouragement. An English and a French engineer offered their services; a member of the French legation and an American in Peru urged him to use their surveys of the Isthmus; a man named Eastern sent him a long screed proving by elaborate calculations that there was just one place to dig a canal; an ex-senator wanted to be in on the scheme; and a man named Friese hoped the canal would follow a 'republican plan' and not, like the Suez, an 'imperial' one. Fortunately, perhaps, for Peter, both the Senate and the Colombian government repudiated the treaty in April and the company went out of business.

Cooper did not, however, drop the idea. Not long afterward he made a speech showing how the government could build a sea-level canal without cost to itself or the people by creating postal savings banks and using the investments of the public to construct the canal. He also added a plan for cutting through rock by sand blasters, and then using the chunks of rock removed by the blasters for the sides of the canal.[4] The government paid no attention to Peter. Though an Interoceanic Canal Commission, appointed by Grant in 1869, made surveys of all seven possible routes, no attempts to build a Panama Canal were made by the Americans until the final successful effort under Theodore Roosevelt in the twentieth century. All American efforts in the 'seventies were concentrated on a Nicaragua Canal, and when negotiations with Nicaragua collapsed in 1876, the United States dropped out of the picture and allowed the French under Ferdinand de Lesseps, who had built the Suez Canal, to try their abortive scheme of a sea-level route at Panama.

Much more than for such eminently respectable and highly sponsored projects, Peter still had a yearning in his old age for the small individual venture, the fly-by-night invention or the new business that he could personally exploit. There was nothing he liked better than to be asked, as he was in 1875, to speak before the Master Mechanics' Association, where he thoroughly enjoyed himself pointing out that the safety valve of a steam engine ought, as he discovered 'by accident' when looking at their model engine, to be lowered, not raised, if the water in the boiler was low, since if the safety valve was raised the water forced up the sides of the hot dry iron would generate too much steam and cause an explosion.[5] As B. M. Johnson, who wanted Cooper to set him up in a machine shop in 1873, said truly, 'in all probability while your life and health remain to you it will be your pleasure to be at all times having something done in machinery.' No wonder Peter liked to finance the inventions of others. No wonder, too, that when he was over eighty he once more brought out his two favorite schemes of half a century before, the endless chain and the rotary engine, and made strenuous efforts to gain public acceptance for them.

It was talk of elevated railways for New York that inspired Peter's new endless-chain idea. He had been interested in elevated railways as early as the 'fifties, when he had helped finance a scheme of Randall, the engineer who had laid out the streets of Manhattan, for an elevated railway which could be boarded without stopping the trains and to which passengers could be conveyed by elevators. A model was exhibited at Castle Garden, and a larger one, constructed to carry passengers around the Crystal Palace, was lost when the Palace burned down in 1858.[6] In 1869, two years after the first one-track experimental elevated had been built from the Battery through Greenwich Street and Ninth Avenue to 30th Street, he recommended to John Jacob Astor, Robert Lenox, Wilson G. Hunt, and others Melville C. Smith's plan for an arcade railway in Broadway, with the street raised to the second stories of the houses.[7] Then, in January, 1872, in a letter to William P. Ogden of Westchester, he outlined his own fantastic scheme.

If an elevated railway was to be built on Third Avenue, Peter told Ogden, the best means of locomotion was stationary power at the ends of the line, which would draw an endless wire rope to which would be attached an endless row of eight-wheeled cars. This method was the safest, it would eliminate sparks, noise, smoke, and dust and not frighten horses, and would cost half of any other method proposed. To prove his faith Peter was willing to take $100,000 of the stock if his idea were put into execution. The roadway, Peter added, could best be placed on each side of Third Avenue, or possibly, as he wrote in one letter, right through the second stories of the houses. 'The cars can be supported by strong iron posts planted on each sidewalk of the street so that the weight of the cars will be directly over the posts making it convenient for all to make business places of their second stories, and at the same time make a shelter from storms for the front of their stores, by extending a glass or wooden sidewalk from their houses on a level with the line of the cars. The doors of the cars would be all on the side towards the houses, so that persons can get in and out at any place on the line during the stopping of the cars at their appointed places.' [8]

Receiving no response, Peter repeated his proposal in 1873 and again in 1874 to both Ogden and H. G. Eastman, adding the suggestion that freight cars could be inserted at intervals, that the wires might be greased to prevent noise, and that stopping every five blocks would be enough to insure egress for everyone anywhere. When the letter to Eastman appeared in the *Herald*, that newspaper was finally constrained to notice his efforts. Peter was, they said, New York's 'kindly star. . . .

Though not so bright a body as Venus, the study of his motions is almost as interesting as that of the lovely eve star. . . . When dry, practical questions are trying other men's patience, the genial face of Cooper rises above our horizon and with oracular wisdom solves the difficult problems for his puzzled fellow citizens. . . . Mere practical people suggested railway tracks, solidly built, so as to last for ages. Mr. Cooper suddenly appears with a drum and a wire to pull us out of the mire of perplexity. Mr. Cooper will fight out rapid transit on this wire line and drum if it takes all the session.' [9] The rest of the world agreed with the *Herald*. Plans for the hideous structures that until recently marred four of New York's avenues, and that were a noisesome and filthy menace when little steam engines, spitting grease and sparks, chugged over them, went steadily ahead.

Peter did not fight the plans, which were sponsored by his friend Cyrus Field. Field united competing companies in the spring of 1877 and by August, 1878, had laid a Sixth Avenue road to Central Park and a Third Avenue one to 42nd Street. Peter even took $5000 worth of stock, predicted success for the company, and scouted rumors that the road would hurt commerce.[10] But he refused to be a director of Field's company; he deplored the reduction of the value of his property along the line of the 'El'—his own property lost half its value, he said, and $2600 houses were renting for $1600—, and he still believed his scheme better, particularly after he had seen the new El in operation.

In 1879, therefore, he once more presented it to the public; and this time, on May 14, 1879, he applied for and was granted a patent on his idea. Though his plan was essentially the same, he had made some changes, and, characteristically, had thought of many new details. Presumably he would now use the already existing tracks, and, to reduce noise going over rail joints, suggested filling the rail groove with gutta-percha and enveloping the chairs with India rubber so they would clamp the rail firmly. To stop the noise of the flange rubbing on the side he recommended the use of an inclined wheel or of sand. Trains were no longer to be endless, but were to come in sets, with occasional freight cars in between. This of course necessitated having stations exactly equidistant, and in order to make stopping easier Peter suggested that the rails be slightly raised at the stations. His plan, Peter insisted, would restore property values and save wear and tear on the rails, since his trains and track could be lighter. Since the whole system was on a dead level— ups and downs balanced out—less power would be needed. A telegraph signal could start the trains.[11] According to Peter, the engineers of the Elevated had been interested in his scheme but had already contracted for iron and locomotives. The projectors, however, he had not been able to win, despite much effort on his part. Nor did he now. Peter was forced to carry his beloved endless chain with him to the other world.

The resurrection of the rotary engine came as a byproduct of a business venture into which the indefatigable Peter threw himself in the 'seventies: an attempt to operate steamboats profitably on the Erie Canal. Less ambitious or important, perhaps, than many other efforts of his—none of his biographers so much as mentions it—this project, which won Peter's active interest and participation as had no business venture for years, is of great biographic interest, revealing a side of Peter's nature that the public had assumed was long buried.

Peter was still, it turned out, the man who had started a glue business on a shoestring and built himself out of odds and ends a locomotive that would run. He could, he showed, be just as combative and competitive and unwilling to concede defeat at eighty as he had been at thirty, and just as able to engross himself in the details of a piece of machinery or to haggle over a few dollars. The circumstances, though, had unfortunately changed. Unable to be on the job all the time, he was taken advantage of as he would not have been in the past by men who knew he was wealthy and expected to make a good thing of it.

And he had chosen a losing game. Either out of regard for the public welfare or a sentimental attachment to the Erie Canal and the idea of a rotary engine, he tried to do what his native shrewdness would once have told him was impossible. The story of the canal adventure is a story of continual frustration, ending, despite all Peter's persistence, in total defeat.

The Erie Canal, on which so much of New York's prosperity had depended, had by 1862 been greatly enlarged at a cost of $33,000,000, tolls and freight rates had been drastically lowered, and the canal was doing a thriving business: in 1868, the best year in its history, it carried $305,301,920 of freight, and in 1872, the top tonnage year, 6,673,570 tons. But ominous clouds were gathering. The 'Canal Ring' was taking a terrible toll in graft on repairs and improvements, and the railroads were rapidly stealing the lion's share of freight business, a condition that would obviously grow worse with the consolidation of the New York Central and Hudson River Railroads. It did not augur well that whereas in 1850 the canals had carried 81.1% of freight traffic in New York, in 1873 they carried only 35% of it.

In 1869 the aroused businessmen of the Chamber of Commerce and the New York Produce Exchange met to consider ways of prosecuting corrupt officials and protecting the trade of the canal. The meeting was held in the rooms of the Citizens' Association, of which Peter Cooper was president, and Peter himself made a speech deploring the high tolls and freight rates. Peter also contributed a letter to the New York State Canal Convention, which met at Rochester on January 20, 1870, to consider tolls and contracts. Though the depredations of corrupt officials were not effectively checked until Tilden's campaign against the Ring in 1875, which nearly made Tilden President of the United States, some improvement followed these efforts: a Canal Commission was appointed to supervise the affairs of the canal, tolls were reduced another fifty per cent, and plans were laid to stimulate increased use of the canal.

To effect this last purpose greater speed, not greater cheapness, was recognized to be the prime need; it was already possible to bring a bushel of wheat, that cost 42.6 cents a bushel to transport from Chicago by rail, for 23 cents by canal, and yet canal traffic was falling. And speed could be achieved only through some means of locomotion other than the plodding horses which towed the barges from Lake Erie to the Hudson. The success of the locomotive and of the oceangoing liner naturally turned men's thoughts to steam.[12]

The first recorded use of steam on the Erie Canal was in 1858, when the *Charles Wack,* carrying a three-quarters cargo and towing a full cargo boat, made the trip from Buffalo to Troy in seven days and returned with half-freight and no tow in four days and sixteen hours, averaging three and one-half miles an hour. The enthusiasm created by this exploit stimulated a host of further efforts in the early 'sixties, but despite great expenditure of money and skill all were failures. The problem of using power economically in the narrow confines of a canal on boats offering as heavy resistance as did canalboats had proved insuperable, and was to continue to offer a virtually insurmountable challenge to all subsequent attempts. Nevertheless, in 1871 the canal commissioners, to encourage efforts, offered a $100,000 bounty to anyone who would successfully place a steam canalboat (tug- or bank-towing was excluded) on the Erie Canal. The conditions of the competition were strict: a single boat carrying two hundred tons must average three miles an hour on three round trips on the canal. In 1871 only one boat, the *A.H.H. Dawson,* competed; and in 1872, though there were twelve boats, only three made the round trips. The competition was therefore extended through 1873, with a great public trial provided for from Syracuse to Utica in October of that year.

Peter Cooper made it clear in the 'seventies and even as late as the 'eighties that he still believed his endless-chain idea of 1820 was the real solution for the Erie and other American canals, particularly in the ice-free South. 'If I was a younger man,' he said in 1873, 'I should want no better chance of fortune than a grant that would allow me to place a chain on both sides of the Erie Canal, with the privilege of charging one half the amount that is now being expended in towing the boats.' Boats would not have to pass over each other's towline; horses would not need to be changed; two men could handle the boats, as, with nothing to do but steer, one could sleep; costs would be reduced over fifty per cent.

He couldn't, however, resist the challenge offered by the state's bounty. As early as December, 1870, he had told the guests at a public dinner at Delmonico's that he was sure that transportation could be doubled and the 'price of freight . . . reduced by the introduction of steam for towing the boats, without any injury to the banks of the canal.' [13] In February, 1871, he asserted publicly that the problem of steam on the canals had been solved.[14] So, after spending a good deal of money helping others to place their inventions on the canal, he determined in 1872 to compete himself. He bought two stern-paddlewheel canalboats, the *Port Byron* and the *Montana,* as well as a yacht, the *Signet,* hired a man named W. R. L. Ward to run the boats under an agreement by which Ward got half the profits and the state award after expenses were paid, and contracted with William Taylor & Sons on February 14th to build him an engine, a boiler, and a wheel for $3700, to be delivered April 1, 1872.

The experiences of the first year were not reassuring. Though none of the boats was thoroughly tested in 1872, and the *Port Byron* was one of three boats to complete the required trips, she made the worst time of the three, averaging 2.685 miles per hour as against 2.727 for David P. Dobbins' *William Newman* and 3.29 for William Baxter's *William Baxter.* The *Montana* 'performed very unsatisfactorily' and did not compete again.[15] Peter in the meantime had had the first of many characteristic fights with the builders of his engines. The engine Taylor was building was not finished until July 3rd, two months beyond the date due, and since it was, according to Peter, made of inferior materials, he refused to accept it. In rebuttal Taylor & Sons accused Peter of constant interference—Cooper's spokesman admitted that the old man was in constant attendance, 'advising what to do, and how to do it'—and alterations of plans. Determined at first to use his 'Cooper engine,' a rotary engine, he had then, Taylor said, ordered a crank engine, 'actuated as we believe by a fear that his own engine would not prove a success'; before either engine was finished Cooper had twice changed his mind about which engine he wanted built. Once more, as in the days of the *Tom Thumb,* Peter had trouble deciding between success and his rotary engine.

What happened in 1872 was but a prelude to the headaches of 1873. Early in the year Peter bought another boat, the *A. S. Webster,* whose screw, as Peter wished, was in a cavity in the bow, but which was found to run better backward. On this boat he determined to make a real test of his compound rotary engine, and on February 8, 1873, made an agreement with Ball & Jewell of Greenpoint to build him such an engine in accordance with plans furnished by Frederick Ortlieb Constructing Engineers, to be delivered May 1st for $5500.00. To show his confidence in the rotary engine he had B. M. Johnson build him another on a plan of Johnson's for the *Signet.*

The comedy of disappointments that followed can only be touched on briefly here. The engine of the *A. S. Webster* cost far more and took far longer to construct than Cooper had anticipated, and its shaft broke at a crucial moment, causing Peter, as he wrote bitterly in September to Ball & Jewell, to lose 'all chance of competing for the State prize besides the mortification of defeat.' [16] Though Peter paid Ball & Jewell a good deal more than their contract called for, they were not satisfied, and for four months nagged the old man—in vain—to pay their debts.[17] Johnson built Peter an even less satisfactory engine, insulted Peter behind his back while working for him,[18] and demanded payment despite the 'thousands of dollars' that Peter had lent him in 'my efforts to befriend you' and that Johnson had, according to Peter, squandered. Johnson's demand, which the exasperated Peter considered as 'gross an insult as you can well offer,' was peremptorily refused, Peter vowing that if it were made again he would 'print and send to the public a full statement of the facts.'

The builders were, it must be admitted, in a difficult position in dealing with the tough and fiery old man. No one seemed able to make a really satisfactory rotary engine, or, as one builder said, 'machinery of any kind that will stand the wear and tear of canal navigation under the present unfavorable circumstances.' Moreover, Peter tended to hover over those who worked for him, and to assume stubbornly that he knew all the answers. When he wrote, 'I have made too much iron and have had too [much] to do with machinery not to know that a five inch shaft of good iron could not be broken by any power generated with the application of it to a screw turning in the water,' that was, as far as Peter was concerned, final. But those who made contracts with Peter did so willingly. He was far more generous than most men would have been in advancing money over and above his contract, and he showed great patience with bungling subordinates. The canal project was a business proposition, not a charity, and Peter rightly fought—not always successfully—against the tendency of those with whom he dealt to assume he was the pot of gold at the end of the rainbow.

The final blow in 1873 was the failure of Peter's other entry, the *Port Byron,* to win any of the prize money. The race, witnessed by Peter, occurred on October 15th,[19] and though none of the five competing boats—the *Baxter, Newman, Port Byron, Central City,* and *Pope*—really qualified, the commissioners decided in February, 1874, to say that Baxter and Dobbins had complied with the law and to award the former $35,000 if he put seven boats similar to the *Baxter* on the canal, and the latter $15,000 for three boats similar to the *Newman.* Peter was as angry as a ballplayer on whom the umpire has called a third strike. 'I was at the famous race,' he wrote publicly, 'which convinced me that there was not in that famous trial a single boat that could fulfill the requirements of the law or earn her own living.' If an award was to have been made all five boats should have shared equally. The *Port Byron,* indeed, deserved a handicap, because when she started the current was stronger and there were more boats to meet. It would have been better, however, to have given no awards, to modify the law to meet the conditions of the canal, and to continue the law in force through 1874. 'As to myself,' Peter concluded with a fine show of disinterestedness, 'I have long since retired from mere money making and you are sufficiently well acquainted with me to know that it was only to benefit my native state and city and if possible cheapen the necessities of life that I entered into this contest.' All Peter forgot was his love of a good fight.

He was not yet ready to give up that fight either. 'I still think,' he wrote, 'that steam can be profitably introduced upon the canal. With this view I have engaged the services of an engineer of experience in all manner of craft to entirely remodel my boats and their motive power from plans and improvements suggested by my trip through the Erie Canal and I have reason to hope that the result will promote the general welfare.' Peter's housecleaning was thorough. He forced Ward, whose $300 of monthly expenses and constant usurpations of authority irked him excessively, to resign, and hired in his place Hugh MacKay, inventor of a method of towing by steam, who proved for a time the most satisfactory co-worker Peter had. And he reluctantly gave up the idea of using any of his old boats in the competition, though he later changed his mind about the *A. S. Webster* when it came back into his hands after he had sold it.[20] In their place he purchased a new horse canalboat, the *Peter Cooper,* which he converted early in 1874 into a sternwheel steamer on a plan submitted by McKay. This time Peter's contract, made on February 6th with the New York Safety Steam Power Company, called, be it noted, for a vertical not a rotary engine, to be delivered March 15th for $2100. Cooper's thought was to have McKay run the *Cooper* and have it tow the reconverted *Port Byron,* the law having now been amended so as to include towing under the terms of the renewed subsidy.

For a moment—on May 6, 1874, when Dobbins offered to pay $7000 for the *Peter Cooper*—Peter's resolution to carry on wavered, and he urged Dobbins to buy all his boats. But the deal fell through, Dobbins selling out to Baxter and urging Peter to do the same, and Peter returned with renewed doggedness to his original plans. The *A. S. Webster,* now commanded by D. F. Littell, was put on the run from New York to Troy in June, despite Dobbins' warning that she would never succeed as a steamer. The *Peter Cooper,* under the captaincy of McKay, ran between New York and Buffalo from June to late November, towing first the *Port Byron* and then a new barge, the *Edith.*

The year 1874 finally put an end to Peter's faith in the *Webster* and her rotary engine. Even on the first trip she sprang so many leaks and had such boiler trouble that Littell dared sleep but eight hours in four days. Then in July the engine, whose smooth performance had so exhilarated Littell in June that he wished Peter could be along to enjoy the ride,[21] broke down because of wear in the cylinders and trouble with the packing in the pistons. The *Webster* lay idle all through August, while bills poured in and the men fought for their pay. The final ironic touch was supplied by McKay, who, 'knowing the faith you have in them,' asked Peter at the end of August if he was interested in a new, guaranteed 'improved rotary engine' for the boat.[22] Peter was not. On September 5th he journeyed to Fishkill for the manifest purpose of selling the *Webster.*

The *Peter Cooper,* which Peter asserted in May would 'be the best boat in all her appointments that has ever been upon the canal,' was less of a disappointment. On nearly every trip McKay reported enthusiastically on her speed and on her reception by upstate editors, canal commissioners, and others, who called her the 'only steam canal boat afloat.' At the end of the year McKay published a little pamphlet report on the *Peter Cooper* and *Edith*, claiming that his success showed what could be done, and that he was willing to prove Peter's clear right to the $100,000 state award by running a whole season under official observation.[23] But the *Cooper* had not really been a success either. She had not made money. Nor did she 'appear,' according to a later official report, 'to have accomplished anything in the way of improvement.' [24] Despite McKay's glowing reports, Peter had been ready to sell the boat as early as August. Only his captain's enthusiasm, which the old man was never able to resist, kept the experiment alive into 1875. McKay assured Peter that the losses of 1874 could be explained by a combination of high charges for tolls and the like, and low freight rates caused by the suicidal and therefore inevitably temporary competition of the railroads. Peter gave him one more chance.[25]

1875 was the end. No talk of how the *Cooper* had done better towing two barges than the Baxter boat had towing one, or of how big welcoming crowds at Syracuse and elsewhere called the *Cooper* the 'Boss Steam Canal Boat,' could impress Peter any longer or make him willing in August to pay $1500 for a new boiler. For several years the *Cooper,* rebuilt at Greenpoint, carried shingles from Baltimore to North Carolina, until she was finally sold in 1879. McKay, who continued to captain her on the Baltimore run, 'had many difficulties to contend with,' as he told Peter sadly when the old man, exasperated at having constantly to bail him out of trouble, at one point gave the Old Dominion Steamship Line a power of attorney to seize the boat. The last word from McKay, who wished 'to end as I began, thinking of you as my best friend,' was a plea in 1881 for $1450, which he claimed Peter had promised him when the boat was sold.

Peter need not have felt personally chagrined over his failure. Though by 1875 steam had come to the canals to stay, neither steam nor anything else could save the Erie Canal from the railroads. Everything was suggested or tried: single boats and boats towing or pushing one, two, or three barges; boats with engines in front, boats with paddlewheels, imitations of fishes' tails and ducks' feet; engines along the bank, a track on the bottom of the canal with floating locomotives, a cable on the bottom for steam-towing. This last, the Belgian system, was tried as early as 1871, was given approval by a meeting of the Boat Owners Association held February 7, 1877, at Cooper Union, at which Peter Cooper gave words of counsel, and was extensively experimented with in the late 'seventies. It too, however, proved a disappointment, as the cable interfered with other boats, and was abandoned in 1880. By 1882 it was generally admitted that steam, like horsepower, had failed to pay for itself. In the 'eighties and 'nineties, though tolls were abolished, conditions continued steadily to deteriorate until by 1908 tonnage had dropped to 2,602,035 as against the 6,673,370 of 1872. The once all-important waterway was carrying but four per cent of total freight. The canal era was over, and nothing Peter Cooper or anyone else could do would bring it back.

a New Jersey farm through the building with the same eager enthusiasm as he did the Prince of Wales, the Empress of Brazil, Count de Lesseps, or Arthur Stanley, the great liberal dean of Westminster.

Peter almost always attended the Saturday evening lectures. Arriving late, accompanied by Edward Hewitt carrying the omnipresent rubber cushion, he was greeted with a round of applause as he took his seat in the old armchair used by Lincoln. The poor lecturer, who could not see him enter, was often badly upset. Peter was also, of course, invariably present at all important functions, beaming with cheerfulness. Practically every year at commencement Peter made a speech on one of his favorite subjects—how he happened to found the Union, the importance of science, the need for love and faith—, his papers being literally crammed with notes and jottings for these speeches, of which he sometimes made three or four copies in his own handwriting. It is hard to believe, reading his words, that these addresses were not a trial to the listener. Peter had little sense of humor, he was deeply wrapped up in his role of spiritual adviser, and his general theories had become stereotyped long years before. Those who heard him, though, have denied that this was so; the look on his face and the light in his eye gave life and meaning to the most banal platitudes. Besides, Peter always made his appearances more impressive by emphasizing what might each time be true: that this was one of the last times he would ever meet his friends. It was hard not to be moved when he concluded a speech—a good dozen years before his death—by calling it "a kind of last will and testament of the garnered experience of an old friend, whose days are almost numbered, and who asks only to be remembered as 'one who loved his fellow men.' " Peter Cooper had become father personified, and it mattered little what he said.

His radiant presence, indeed, and the aura that surrounded him became more and more his important contribution to the institution. One of Cooper Union's prize pupils, the Serbian-born inventor Michael Pupin, who had found a spiritual refuge in the Union when things looked blackest, has testified to Cooper's effect on young men of genius. Pupin had been looking at Christian Schussele's painting, 'Men of Progress,' on the wall: 'One day, while reading in the Cooper Union Library, I saw quite near me an old gentleman standing and carefully scrutinizing what was going on. I imagined, at first, that he had stepped out of that painting. . . . The ambidextrous youth behind the library desk told me afterward that the old gentleman was Peter Cooper, the founder of Cooper Union. . . . He looked as I imagined the Patriarch of Karlovci must have looked. He was a striking resemblance to St. Sava, the Educator, as he is represented on an ikon in our church in Idvor. . . . His personality as revealed by his appearance inspired me with awe, and I read everything I could lay my hands on concerning his life; then I read about the lives of the other great men who were associated with Peter Cooper in that historical painting.' [3]

Hundreds of people came to Cooper Union receptions in May just to look at him and shake his hand, and mechanics and workers brought their children to be presented to 'Uncle Peter,' who stood for hours to receive them. A tactful worker once said, "When I saw you a year ago, Mr. Cooper, I thought it was the last time you would be here. I am glad to see you alive now." Peter, undisturbed, replied, "It can't be for a very great while now." Yet there he was each year 'with his smiling face and interested look, and his soft white hair waving over his shoulders, amid flowers, lights, and the cheerful music,' his presence brooding 'like a benediction over the swaying and singing crowd.' [4]

If even at the beginning Cooper Union had been too great an undertaking for Peter Cooper to supervise himself, how much more was this true in the ensuing years. Yearly receipts and expenditures in the year Peter died were about $50,000, as against about $30,000 in 1861; the number of teachers had risen from sixteen to thirty-six; the number of readers in the reading room from around 250,000 to 475,988; the number of students admitted from 2000 to 3200; and the certificates given from 275 to 955. The art school was so crowded in 1883 that students had to wait fully a year to gain admission. Though relatively few finished the complete science course—ten graduated in 1882, the top figure—ninety-eight degrees were given between 1864 and 1883.[5]

The trustees had as their constant goal an art school that would give the principles of art no less than the practice, and a school of technology offering a broad scientific education. They were hampered, however, by the lack of preparedness of the students to whom they catered for advanced theoretical work, a point that 'cannot,' Hewitt said, 'be too strongly insisted on.'[6] Perforce Cooper Union remained utilitarian in aim, its night schools confining themselves to giving specific elementary training in science and art (supplemented in 1871 by a course in English literature under J. C. Zachos), its day school for women catering to 'artisans' and not to 'artists.' Within these limits Cooper Union was, as Hewitt said, a 'wonderful success.'[7]

This was especially true of the day school for women, in whose occupational opportunities Peter was so vitally interested. A *Times* reporter who attended the art classes in 1872 was impressed by the faces (nine-tenths of which were 'more than good looking') flushed with the excitement that 'comprehension of the beautiful never fails to give,' and the 'bright-colored dresses' standing 'out in warm relief around the colorless plaster and against the darkened walls.'[8] By 1882 the 275 girls in these classes were, according to Hewitt, earning over $40,000 a year. Much of this had been earned in the new photography, color photography, and wood-engraving classes that had been added to the school by the mid-'seventies. Other courses, outside the art school proper, had also been opened by the trustees, who welcomed new sources of possible income for women. The telegraphy class, started in the fall of 1868 under the auspices of Western Union, had over three hundred graduates by 1876. Then in the early 'eighties came instruction in that marvelous new invention, the typewriter, whose existence Peter Cooper had recognized in 1879 by installing a typist at Burling Slip—putting her, according to the story, in a separate room with glass walls.

The night school also prospered, and soon began, as Peter had hoped it would, to attract talented boys to the Union. A young apprentice named Augustus St. Gaudens, whose father made shoes for the Cooper family, spent all his evenings from the time he was thirteen at the Union, and there received his first artistic training. 'The feeling of profound gratitude' never left him. St. Gaudens' statue of Peter Cooper, which now stands in front of the Union, was a labor of love, and its completion was almost endlessly postponed because the sculptor made twenty-seven sketches of the figure with various compositions of hat, coat, and cane before he was satisfied.[9] Michael Pupin got his first ideas of the phenomenon of heat and learned English at Cooper Union; his adeptness in the mechanical drawing classes at the Union won him a job as assistant shipping clerk in a cracker factory. More ordinary boys and girls also had reason to be grateful; at least one young clerk found the debating society at the Union the road to Congress. The chief beneficiary, however, was the public. As the *Herald* said truly in 1880, if New York was way ahead of Philadelphia in manufacturing, the credit should go in large part to Cooper Union, which educated labor to the high standards of skill necessary in the modern world.[10] The *Times* prediction, made in 1872, that soon America would no longer be dependent on Europe for skilled artisans, was rapidly being fulfilled.

For those who wished a broader cultural education, the reading room, still the best in the city, offered wide opportunities, its four thousand books having increased by 1875 to eighteen thousand. The library also provided the greatest headache for the trustees. As Pupin testified, many people, 'sad-looking victims of the economic crisis,' came there to keep warm more

· (329) ·

than to read. Others, as the music teacher complained, were mere 'loafers and idlers who swarm about, staring at the pictures *and* at the women (young and old) who pass up and down stairs.' [11] Some were thieves, whose depredations even the 'veteran of the police, who was chosen by Mr. Cooper from a number of picked men,' could not always stop. They 'drew books from the library only to steal them,' and mutilated and sold the plates of illustrated books to the print shops. They 'stole even the Bibles that were scattered over the tables by the Bible Society; they mutilated the newspaper files, and actually cut off the rods that held the newspapers in place and sold them as old brass.' [12] Nothing was more characteristic of Peter Cooper than his reluctance in the face of these depredations to allow restrictions. He was sorry, he said, for those who needed money so badly.

The Saturday evening free lectures provided, all through this period, virtually the only cultural instruction offered by the Union and the only means whereby Peter Cooper's desire to teach the social sciences was carried out. Recognized as a regular feature of the institution in 1868, they soon became a great success, drawing some fifteen hundred people weekly into the great auditorium. Getting the proper speakers to talk in the proper way on proper subjects was a task requiring endless time and experiment. The audience, 'not much recruited from the general public,' was made up 'to a great extent of thoughtful working people,' who were 'eager for facts but restive under purely literary lectures, or morally didactic ones' and would not listen to anyone on any subject for more than an hour and a half.[13] 'If you entertain, interest and stimulate them,' one lecturer on China was told, 'so that they think of the Chinese with greater tolerance, and are led to read and study more about them, it is as much as a single popular lecture can be expected to accomplish.' Most speakers, even after being coached, proved unsatisfactory, especially the college professors on whom Hewitt at first largely depended.[14] When he was very fortunate he managed to secure such speakers as the great John Tyndall, who gave his 'lectures on Light' at the Union in 1872, and enthralled large audiences with his experimental machines, his electric light, and his screen to show prismatic hues. Usually, since he could pay at the most fifty dollars and preferred paying only traveling expenses, Hewitt had to be satisfied with lesser talent, which had to be carefully scouted. 'The course is not a medium for experiments.'

Theoretically, to fulfill Peter's orders, the lectures should all have been on the social sciences, and consequently Hewitt got as many speakers through the American Social Science Association as possible. But since the audience tended to be the same each year, lectures couldn't be repeated, and appealing subjects were not endless. Besides, 'Speakers on social science who are not "cranks" are *so* rare!' Moreover, many subjects in this field were too controversial for Hewitt's liking, including women's rights, 'living issues in economy,' like the silver question in 1877, that 'come too near party politics,' and 'partisan' discussions of the labor question. Indeed, the lecture program was not intended to promote partisanship on any subject or 'to be used as a medium for the denunciation of any class of citizens. We want speakers who inform, not inflame, the minds of their audience.' [15]

As a consequence of all these things, Cooper Union lecture courses ranged in subject matter from accounts of round-the-world journeys to instructions in cooking and discussions of temperance, in which Peter Cooper had always been much interested. The nineteen lectures in 1875-6, for example, included talks on explorations in Africa and Iceland, on psychology, on music, on optics, on royal and domestic life in Siam, on the Greek Temple and the atomic theory, on the territorial history of the United States, and on the geological record of man.

On other than Saturday evenings the Great Hall was rented to outsiders, and became New York's favorite meetingplace. If there were restrictions placed on Cooper Union lecturers, there were none on what might go on at other times. In 1874 Hewitt freely permitted workers to meet at the Union to protest against police brutality so long as they paid the usual $250 and gave a bond in case of breakage. Peter Cooper allowed the notorious Victoria Woodhull, advocate of woman's suffrage and free love, to use the Cooper Union platform, and when he was criticized for doing so, answered by letting her come again.[16] He himself, according to one account, led the great atheist Robert Ingersoll to the platform after there had been threats of violence should he appear.[17]

With the educational and business details of the Union, Peter concerned himself relatively little. These he left to Hewitt, who spent most of his evenings watching over the curriculum, staff, and investments; to J. C. Zachos, curator of the library, professor of English, and the compiler of Cooper's campaign biography; to Rossiter W. Raymond, a mining engineer, who was at once a business lieutenant of Hewitt's, director of the Cooper Union lectures, and Peter Cooper's personal adviser, traveling companion, and later biographer; to Susan Carter, who in 1872 became head of the School of Design; and to the other trustees of the Union.

Yet Peter was anything but a mere spiritual presence hovering over his Union. He guided overall policy, keeping the Union true to his faith in tolerance and freedom and to the balance of ideal and material ends that he sought. He personally initiated improvements large and small, from fire extinguishers, about which he took special pains, to the addition of new floors. Nothing escaped his eagle eye, whether it was the need for new plaster casts or the work of the plumbers. When additions to the building were made in his ninetieth year, he watched every brick being put in place as assiduously as he had in 1859; when a fire started from escaping gas he managed to be there to help put it out. He always insisted he was ready to die when just one more plan he had in mind was completed. Nothing made him happier in the last year of his life than seeing thirty girls at work over their typewriters, the fulfillment of his latest dream. He never ceased to regret that such ideas as a plan for a thrift shop or an employment agency could not be carried out.

Peter's financial aid was, of course, his basic contribution. Very rarely does any institution have all the money it needs, but Cooper Union, both during Peter's life and for many years thereafter, was so seriously short of funds that the day-to-day work was often threatened and necessary improvements had to be put off from year to year. Peter was compelled, he wrote in 1880, 'to see hundreds go away with tears in their eyes for want of room and means to provide teachers for them.' Teaching salaries were so low that many good men were 'constrained to terminate their connection' with the Union.[18]

The trouble was that when Cooper founded his institution he donated the building but gave no endowment, counting on rents and outside help to keep the school going. But the public was slow to respond to what they considered a family affair, and though there were occasional small gifts—a total of about $3000 was given in the first ten years—Hewitt asserted that J. P. Morgan's $10,000 donation to the Art Library in 1892 was 'the first considerable gift that the Cooper Union has received outside of Mr. Cooper's family.' [19] Despite the need of an endowment Hewitt refused, until after Peter's death, when the 'institution can no longer be said to be a personal one in any sense,' to appeal for funds. The Union was thus dependent on rents. It never had the use, therefore, of its first two floors until the turn of the century, or of the Great Hall most evenings of the week. Even so, rents proved woefully inadequate, particularly after the coming of the El to Third Avenue depressed values. Peter quixotically demanded $100,000 of El stock at a large discount as compensation,[20] but all the Union got was some $500 out of Cyrus Field for moving classrooms to the Fourth Avenue side of the building.[21] The largest income the Union received, the $10,000 a year from the American Bank Note Company, which took the top floor in 1868, proved a mixed blessing since the vibration of the presses eventually necessitated major repairs to the building.

Under the circumstances Peter did the best he could. For a time the initial cost precluded any great new outlays, but he met the annual deficits each year, which came to between five and ten per cent of expenditures—$18,600 during the first ten years. Then in 1871, on his eightieth birthday, he gave $100,-000,[22] plus permission to draw on him for $50,000 more. The interest on at least half this gift was to be used for a lending library for the use of workers and mechanics. In characteristic fashion Peter was very specific about details of construction, insisting that the 'great weight of the library' was to be on the Third Avenue side, and that 'no brick should be removed that can in any way lessen the strength of the building.' [23]

Finally, when he was nearly ninety, Peter contributed another $100,000 for major additions to his building. These consisted of two partial stories on the south side, called the Southeast and Southwest Pavilions, with a dome containing a room and a lighted clock, whose six-foot face would be visible as far as the eye could reach down the Bowery. A new hydraulic elevator was to be put in to the top. At the same time Peter had 7th Street undermined and arched over from Third to Fourth Avenue for a large extra room, and had an additional excavation made under Fourth Avenue to hold barrels of petroleum and the building's boilers. Never able to resist fostering some public improvement, he had 7th Street paved over after the excavation with blocks of cement and gravel mixed in such proportions as to make what he considered the last word in roadways, and planned to do the same thing on one side of Third Avenue as a more perfect test.

These improvements aroused all Peter's boyish enthusiasm, not a technical detail of the construction either of the roadway[24] or of the new additions to the building escaping him. This could be very trying to the contractors, since the old man insisted on everything being perfect where his building was involved. If things did not suit him, his usual mildness deserted him. In 1874 a man named Carl Bocking had built a machine for lighting the Institute with gas, and when he failed to produce the machine and the fifty or sixty burners for which Peter had paid, Peter wrote him a letter that Bocking considered the most insulting he had ever received. After Peter had had the gas analyzed and found it to be unsafe, he felt even less friendly toward Bocking. 'I shall expect you,' he told him, to take the fluid 'out of the building before night or I shall have it poured in the street.'

Similarly—though with considerably less justification— Peter denounced J. D. West & Company for overcharging him when, in 1880, they installed their 'Patent Square Lightning Rod' from the new dome of his building to the ground. Haggling like a storekeeper, the old man insisted that West had used more wire than the contract called for,[25] and that, even if he hadn't, Peter was entitled to a reduction, since he wasn't a man of immense wealth, like Moses Taylor, but a philanthropist trying to make every dollar count in educating youth. West, who had gotten Peter's approval for all alterations and had been looking 'for praise instead of censure,' was understandably shocked. 'Such a charge coming from such a source' rankled more the more he thought about it. 'We are well aware,' he told Peter, 'of our insignificance in comparison with you—we are unable to build such a monument to our fame as you have done —would that it were otherwise, yet our character is as dear to us as yours to you and we boldly assert that you had no grounds for the above assertion.' Moreover, West couldn't see why he should contribute to Peter's monument, from which he would 'get not credit or glory.' Cooper Union was a fine thing, 'but we are troubled with smaller matters in a smaller field—and need all we can earn for our families.'[26] Peter appears for once to have been silenced.

When Peter started to construct his extra stories he did so, he told a *Herald* reporter, primarily to fulfill his old dream of a museum of science and art, which, like so many of his dreams, he had never abandoned. The underground room he planned as a workshop for artisans and the new rooms at the top as the home of an organization called the 'Inventor's Institute.' In the underground room he saw in his mind's eye 'wheels and cogs and pulleys and belts, long racks of tools, and busy young fellows at work educating their fingers to use files and rasps and turning lathes. It was a pretty picture, and I resolved to put it into execution.' [27] He never did, however.

With the Inventor's Institute he had better luck, though not exactly in the way he had planned. Encouragement to inventors through his Union was an idea cherished by Peter for many years, and at one point he planned to allow a room in the building to be used to make and sell the patent sewing machines in which he was interested. When in the 'sixties a man named C. A. Lamont proposed founding an institute on Broadway to secure patents for people and to exhibit and sell their inventions, Peter immediately lent him $20,000 to help establish the business and later to get out a magazine, the *Industrial News*. Though one Z. C. Robbins accused Lamont of swindling him out of $5000 on an Arizona gold-mining claim and an egg-crystallizing patent—evidently the egg-desiccating plan Peter had also invested in—Peter continued to have faith in Lamont, and decided to install him in the Union under his own supervision. This would be of benefit to Lamont's institute, which would gain advertisement, and to Cooper Union, which would have models of machinery at work for the boys to study. Having induced a man named David A. Burr, whom he evidently trusted, to join the Institute as his representative, Peter informed the press that the addition to Cooper Union was being made primarily to house a museum of new devices and machinery similar to the Kensington Museum in London. There was just one hitch. The trustees refused to sanction this use of the new rooms, Hewitt brutally informing Burr that as Cooper 'has gotten you into this matter he must see you through with it.' A compromise was finally reached whereby the new rooms were turned into class-rooms for the Art School, and the Inventor's Institute was installed on the ground floor. In 1884 the Institute was self-supporting and paying rent to Cooper Union. A modicum of Peter's original vision of a vast museum of the useful arts had, for a few years, come into being.

Peter Cooper had thus given, before he died, upward of $900,-000 to Cooper Union, a large sum for a man worth, even when he was wealthiest, not over $2,000,000. At his death he willed another $100,000 to the Union and then added a further $100,-000 to be paid out of his residuary estate at his special request. Unfortunately, in 1884 the foundations of Cooper Union were suddenly found to be weak, and it took two years and cost $315,-000 to rebuild them. Cooper's children made good the $300,000, so that Peter's original endowment remained intact.[28] If this money proved pitifully inadequate to carry on the Union much less to expand it in the twentieth century, that was hardly Peter's fault. Fortunately, public response, though slow, eventually materialized. In the late 'nineties the estate of Peter's brother William suddenly contributed $340,000 to the Union, and shortly thereafter John Halstead left it $250,000 and H. H. Rogers another $250,000. On top of this, in 1902 Andrew Carnegie gave $600,000 on the condition that it be matched by an equal amount from Peter's children, which was obtained by their breaking a trust intended to be paid at their deaths. Cooper Union started the year 1903 with an endowment of approximately $2,000,000, and for the first time the whole great building could be devoted to the purposes for which Peter had originally intended it.

Today Cooper Union still stands foursquare facing the Bowery, a living reminder that only that which was 'most mortal' of Peter Cooper is gone. As in the days when the founder was alive, his Union offers free practical help and hope for happiness and a better life to thousands of every creed and color among the citizens of the city and country he so much loved. An art school and a school of applied science continue to be the basic divisions of the institution, thus preserving the union of art and science 'in their application to the varied and useful purposes of life' that the founder so much cherished. The forum still fulfills Peter's desire for popular instruction in the science of a republican form of government. The reading room and library yet offer refuge and enlightenment to New Yorkers from every walk of life. Cooper Union remains the embodiment of Peter Cooper's dream.

As he would have wished, however, it has grown and changed in order the more effectively to fulfill those dreams in a modern setting. Its meager resources have expanded into a $12,000,000 endowment and plant, which now includes a second building, the Hewitt Memorial Building, across Cooper Square, and a thousand-acre Engineering Camp on the Ringwood property in New Jersey. The art school has become a well-equipped professional school with a library and a museum, the Museum for the Arts of Decoration, begun by two of Peter's granddaughters. The school of science has developed, as Peter so long hoped it would, into a highly accredited school of engineering, granting professional degrees from both its day and evening classes. Although Cooper Union last year accommodated 1740 students— 269 in the day and 468 in the evening art session, 421 in the day and 582 in the evening engineering session—there are usually six applications for each place (to be won by competitive examination) in the school. The once-tiny library now contains 125,000 volumes and subscribes to five hundred periodicals and five hundred series of government publications. The forums, occurring three times a week, embrace philosophy, politics, art, science, and all the varied intellectual activities of modern man.

This broadening of the scope of education evidenced in the forums has extended to other activities, and is perhaps the proudest achievement of Cooper Union in recent years. Both the art and engineering curricula contain a full sequence of humanistic social studies preparing the students for citizenship and a richer life no less than for a career. Peter Cooper's hope of combining the cultural and the practical, nearly lost under the impact of late-nineteenth-century utilitarianism, has been notably revived. Under the able leadership of Dr. Edwin S. Burdell, whose scientific humanism aims to reach beyond art and science to a concern for the society that made the student and to which he must contribute, Cooper Union moves confidently into the future. Peter Cooper can feel well satisfied that the warm breath of his life and vision still radiates down the canyons where live eight millions of human beings.

The 'Cooper Union idea' took such a great hold of Peter Cooper that he was not satisfied to confine it to New York, and a half-dozen years before his death he made a somewhat abortive attempt to extend it to the South. Like George Peabody, Peter had long felt it to be but common justice that Northerners should help rehabilitate the once-prosperous states of the Confederacy. In what better way could he give this help than by establishing a trade school for women in that area, similar to his Union?

By a happy coincidence a man named Thomas Bomar, who owned a piece of property in Limestone Springs near Spartanburg, South Carolina, conceived much the same idea in 1877. His property had once housed a prosperous school of 150 girls, founded in 1845 by Dr. Thomas Curtis and carried on by the latter's son, William, until the Curtises lent $70,000 to the rebels and lost their school.[29] Bomar had bought the property for a song and tried to reestablish the school, but had not succeeded. Somehow or other he heard of Peter Cooper, and immediately decided that an industrial school like Cooper Union was just what the South and his particular property needed. His eight hundred acres, high in the mountains, healthful, well supplied with good water and dotted with large fruit trees, was a perfect location for such a school. There were several large buildings, which might accommodate a resort hotel as well as a school. And there were limestone deposits on the surface which, with the proper modern machinery, could be made to pay for the school. In case Peter had any doubts, Bomar supplied him with letters praising the property and suggesting that the state would surely be willing to take it over as a 'manual labor school.' As a trump card he added a note from the pastor of the Baptist Church of Spartanburg saying that an industrial school was practicable, possible, and desirable: 'But alas! alas! the money, the money where is that to come from? . . . Oh that some noble, good hearted brother or friend in the north who has large means and large heart—would see it as we do and help us in this our hour of need.' [30]

Peter Cooper was obviously their man. A report from Theodore Bourne, whom Peter evidently trusted, confirmed him in his intention. According to Bourne, few places were more eligible 'for the purpose for which you design it.' The building was basically sound and could be used as part-hotel and part-institute, or an institute could be built nearby for $3000. If Peter purchased the property, values would immediately rise, a settlement would spring up, and village lots could be sold to rich Charleston and Atlanta people. Peter might call his institute the Bedell Cooper Union of South Carolina, and the state would undoubtedly form a new county and call it Cooper County. Charles Petty, who shared an interest in the property with Bomar and was a member of the state legislature, wrote that he could get the property and the endowment free of taxation.[31]

Peter moved quickly though cautiously. On December 7, 1877, two weeks after Bourne's letter, he deposited $12,000 to Bomar's account in the Seventh Ward National Bank, payable when Bomar executed a bond and mortgage on his property.

Later he increased the loan to $17,000, with the privilege of purchasing within a year for $26,000. Though he was convinced that he had discovered a new Arcadia, Peter was determined to find out if the place could support itself before he made a final decision. With his Cooper Union experience behind him, he had developed a dislike for ventures that, as he put it, had to be supported by begging. Besides, an industrial school such as he planned must be self-sufficient if it was to teach others to be so. Thinking, too, that it ought to be sponsored by the state, Peter sent a memorandum to Governor Hampton on January 12, 1878, asking under what conditions South Carolina would accept the buildings and one hundred acres to maintain a 'Manual Labor Institution or a School of Science and Arts applied to the useful and necessary purposes of life, for young women similar to the branches and pursuit now taught in the Cooper Union of New York.' [32]

For a time everything seemed to go well. On February 20, 1878, Bomar wrote that his experimental school, called the Limestone Springs Female High School, would be in operation in two weeks and that the very idea of its establishment had increased property values fifty per cent. The Limestone Springs Lime Works had also been set up, and though rain, bad roads, and the scarcity of labor had slowed up the work, kilns were being built. In characteristic fashion Cooper aided Bomar by sending him various technical papers on the cultivation of jute, tea plants, and other possible sources of income, and a glue to be dissolved in water and spread on grains or seeds before planting. Various people wrote to Peter telling him that education and sources of employment other than labor in the fields, which paid only twenty-five to thirty cents a day, were just what the South needed to dispel ignorance and immorality. Though the establishment of factories was the great hope, the girls in Peter's school could in the meantime learn embroidery and other home industry, and improved methods of agriculture. Bomar claimed that he would give his 'very existence, even life, to have the honors that you are already reaping in regard to the establishment of the "Free Institute" here. Prayers are ascending, not only from the pulpits, but from the hearthstones all over the South.' [33] On May 7th Peter chartered a 'Pullman Hotel Car' and, accompanied by his daughter, his daughter-in-law, one of his granddaughters, and Raymond, made a two-thousand-mile tour of the South, stopping, of course, at Limestone Springs. He returned more enthusiastic than ever, telling Bomar that he regarded the South as 'by nature the most highly favored part of these United States.' He now avowed himself ready to make a 'permanent arrangement to secure the successful accomplishment of an educational institution on the excellent plan that you have offered to the public,' and hoped that trustees would soon be appointed, headed by the governor.

The glowing prospects were, however, deceptive. Though the lime quarries were eventually leased, the kilns were never built, Bomar's school did badly from the first, and the state quickly lost any interest it may have had. By October, 1878, Peter, who in the course of the year had had to increase his loan to $24,500, was already contemplating disposing of the place as a sanitarium for white invalids and a farm school for Negroes. Though he hung on stubbornly for another year, he finally had to admit defeat. When, at the end of 1879, the Spartanburg Baptist Association agreed to operate the school, he reluctantly turned over his bonds and mortgages to them for cancelation. Bomar, who continued to write of the 'éclat given to the place through its connection with Mr. Cooper' and the 'great fabric' that would eventually 'arise to forever bless' Peter as a 'benefactor to mankind,' went bankrupt and dropped out of the picture.

Peter dropped out too. In the fall of 1881 the Baptist group opened their school, which they named the Cooper-Limestone Institute in his honor, but there is no evidence that it long remained or ever was the sort of institution Peter contemplated. In 1890 it appealed to Hewitt for money, and received the following characteristic reply: 'It would have been better for Mr.

Cooper if he had not devoted any of his very moderate estate to other purposes than the execution of his plans for the Cooper Institute in this city. He was undoubtedly misled originally in regard to the investment in your state but to the extent that your institution has profited by it, his heirs have no regrets, but they cannot add to the contribution which he made.' [34] Today the school is a women's college charging tuition and giving a regular academic course. The only memory of Peter Cooper in Limestone Springs (now called Gaffney) is his portrait in the administration building of Limestone College and his name attached to one of the dormitories; and it is probable that few of the young ladies who attend the college know why the building is so named. New York City, not South Carolina, was to contain Peter's monument.

Chapter 19

BEARDING THE TIGER

JUST as he expected to retire from business after the Civil War, so Peter undoubtedly planned to stay out of the politics of the postwar period. He had done what he could in the 'forties and 'fifties for his city's government, and he had reluctantly played his role in national politics during the war. Now others must take over. Yet even before the war ended he had sallied forth once more to engage the dragon of municipal corruption, and this was but the prelude to greater events which were nearly to crowd Cooper Union off the stage of his life. The trouble with Peter Cooper was that he could never stand a stench in the nostrils emanating from what ought to have been God's world. When the all-too-familiar smell reached him, he simply had to gird on his rusty armor and do battle, however persistently the calendar and the mirror told him he ought to be playing on the floor with his grandchildren.

Even people less sensitive than Peter Cooper began to notice by the middle 'sixties that the air around City Hall seemed somewhat more tainted than usual. In 1863 William Tweed had become head of Tammany Hall, and had immediately formed his notorious 'Ring,' composed principally of the astute and retiring Peter B. Sweeny, 'Slippery Dick' Connolly, the financier, and the three judges, John H. McCunn, Albert Cardozo, and George G. Barnard. Together these gentlemen, with help from the complacent John C. Hoffman, who became mayor in 1865, quickly gained a stranglehold on the city. It had been hoped that depredations by city officials had been checked by the charter of 1857, which had given the state the power to levy taxes and to appoint the commissions that administered the city. But it was an organization set up by the reformers to decide on the budget and to appoint sheriffs, coroners, and jurors, the bipartisan Board of Supervisors for New York County, that was at first Tweed's chief instrumentality of corruption. Tweed, who was president of this board four times, always managed to gain a majority of votes by the simple expedient of bribing one member of the opposing party, and was thus able to take a percentage on all bills audited. He was also deputy street commissioner, with the result that though $500,000 was paid for street-cleaning the streets were not cleaned. In the late 'sixties the Ring was taking a 65% to 85% cut on city contracts, while the tax levy rose from $11.99 to $25.11 between 1860 and 1870, assessments from ten to twenty-three million, and the city debt from nineteen to seventy-three million.[1]

Peter Cooper and his friends had the distinction of becoming alarmed about this situation long before it had developed its worst features or before most of the citizenry were anything but mildly aware of it. Peter himself had as early as 1860 offered a room in Cooper Union rent-free if the citizens would appoint a member from each ward and a paid lawyer and clerk to act as a Committee of Safety. Nothing came of this. But three years later, on December 12, 1863, a group of aroused citizens convened and formed an organization called the Citizens' Association, with headquarters at 813 Broadway.[2] On January 25, 1864, Peter Cooper and fourteen other men, including August Belmont, Hamilton Fish, and William E. Dodge were appointed a committee to arouse the public to the danger of the current state of affairs.

They immediately issued a long circular explaining in detail to the citizens how the Ring was impoverishing them. The city's franchises were being given away, her wharves were falling to pieces, her streets were filthy and badly paved, her sanitary code and her tenement house laws were not enforced, her judiciary was suspect, and her schools were run by incompetent and corrupt officials. The Citizens' Association had been formed, they said, to secure charter changes and to give information to the public to help them elect honest men to office. For the next six or seven years, a longer time than any previous reform organization had functioned effectively, this group, with Peter Cooper as the president and guiding spirit, fought tenaciously against the mounting catastrophe around them. As the catastrophe developed, others grew fainthearted, but Peter never did, and toward the end he virtually *was* the Citizens' Association.

During the early years, when the association struggled single-handed against Tammany, its work covered virtually every detail of municipal government, from the city's expenses for stationery and printing—city advertisements helped silence adverse press comment—to the nature of the Common Council's powers. In the first two or three years alone it sent out two million pamphlets and called some three hundred public meetings, besides conducting lawsuits, making investigations, and sending representatives to Albany to press for legislation. The association protested to a grand jury the $4,350,000 already spent by 1868 on a courthouse intended to cost $1,000,000 (it was eventually to cost $8,000,000 and to be the top scandal of the era), the cost of street-cleaning, the failure to give city contracts to the lowest bidder, and other matters. In 1868 Peter Cooper appealed personally to Reuben E. Fenton, the Republican governor who had succeeded Seymour in 1866, and to William Wheeler, in charge of changing the New York State constitution, to push through needed reforms. In the same year he did his best to keep John C. Hoffman from becoming governor, believing—quite rightly as it turned out—that his election 'would prove to be the Greatest Calamity that has ever befallen our City State and nation with the exception of the rebellion through which we have passed.' In 1868 or early 1869, in probably his most effective communication to the public, Peter appealed to the workers, as he had to Fenton, to elect good men to office, to give them the responsibility of appointments of heads of departments and bureaus, and to force them to secure underlings from those shown qualified in examinations—a Civil Service System—, these underlings to be given security and pensions for good behavior. 'We may as well employ the blacksmith to repair our watch,' he told the workers, 'as to employ unprincipled men and then expect them to legislate wisely and well.' The 'struggle to obtain wealth without labor,' he added, has caused men to enslave their fellowmen and to pierce 'themselves and their whole country through with many sorrows.'

It would be pleasant to report that the efforts of Peter Cooper and his associates met with immediate and widespread response and were followed by a prompt cleaning of the Augean stables. They did have some successes. By bringing charges against Francis I. A. Boole, the city inspector, they prevented his nomination for mayor in 1865, though they lost their case in court. They got the tax levy somewhat reduced, they had street-cleaning taken from the city inspector, they took a small step toward honest elections by having registration end two days before election and securing non-local inspectors, and in 1865 they helped inaugurate the city's first paid fire department against the united opposition of the volunteer companies. Above all, in 1866, with cholera threatening the city, they finally engineered a Metropolitan Health Bill creating a city Board of Health. They were probably proudest of their feat in getting Sweeny, the city chamberlain, not to pocket the $100,000 interest on public money held in banks in 1867, though he was stealing more than that every month. Yet, despite their earnest efforts, they made very little real impression on city affairs, and most of the books on the period fail to mention their work at all. As Peter said in 1871, quoting Pope, 'all hear, few heed, none understand.' Indeed, at the very moment when they were issuing their most optimistic summary of their work, at the end of 1868, Tweed had just succeeded in his aim of gaining control of the chief offices in both city and state. He became state senator, Hoffman was swept into the governorship by strongarm gangs and by 41,112 aliens newly naturalized for the purpose, dapper A. Oakley Hall, Tweed's candidate, became mayor, and Tweed-owned judges succeeded to all judgeships below the Court of Appeals. The Tweed Ring of history, whose thefts have been estimated at between $100,000,000 and $200,000,000, really dates from 1869.

The failure of the Citizens' Association was inevitable. They had pitted themselves against new and powerful evils in American life, which it would be unduly optimistic to say we have yet learned to control. On the one hand were the great new corporations, which were willing to pay any sum to secure their ends. Not the least of Tweed's power came from his association with Gould and Fisk, by whose aid he made over half a million dollars in Erie stock in four months. On the other were the great hordes of immigrants, untrained in democratic ways, whose votes could be purchased for a song—a problem that, as Arthur Schlesinger, Jr., says, made even the stoutest Jacksonian Democrats question their beliefs. It is to Peter Cooper's credit that his experiences in city affairs never made him waver in his ultimate faith in democracy. Along with all this was an apathy on the part of ordinary citizens which only the really colossal frauds of 1870 and 1871 could shatter. A few respectable citizens sending out chaste appeals and detailed comments on complex municipal affairs were unlikely to stir even a faint response.

Despite their professed optimism Peter Cooper and his colleagues were not unaware of the nature of the situation that faced them. As they said sadly in 1866, 77,475 voters out of 128,-975 were foreign-born, and most of them could not even read the exposés of the association. Moreover the association knew, as Peter wrote, that 'so long as capitalists are obliged to seek legislative aid to legalize legitimate undertakings just so long will it be almost impossible to keep the fountains of legislation pure.' Yet this very statement, implying as it does that the evil arose from the political rather than from the business world, suggests the limitations inherent in the viewpoint of a group composed, as was the Citizens' Association, of businessmen.

Peter himself was deeply concerned over the plight of the ordinary worker, whose savings Tammany was also stealing and whose livelihood was constantly menaced, as Peter said, by the gaping holes in the streets that destroyed his cart and horse. But even for Peter the threat to business assets was the prime issue; the 'contest,' as he wrote to Fenton, was 'between property and those who desire to possess it unlawfully, between that portion of the community which has raised by honest industry our city to be the metropolis of America, and the parasites who fasten on its prosperity to stop and destroy it. Year by year, citizens of New York are driven by the high taxation to leave the island and carry their industry and accumulated property into neighboring states.' As property owners, the members of the Citizens' Association were prone to put saving against public improvement, and it is not chance that they favored abolishing the College of the City of New York (Peter Cooper was not on the committee that proposed this) and opposed a public appropriation for 'such places of luxurious amusement' as the proposed Metropolitan Museum. It was against the principles of good government, they said, to do 'anything for the people which they can do as well for themselves.' They therefore proposed selling the public markets to individuals, bringing revenue to the city, and keeping the government out of business. For the great masses of the people, hungry for help, the Citizens' Association offered very little to inspire enthusiasm.

They were also somewhat more naive than they needed to be. Their experience with Richard O'Gorman, whom they supported for corporation counsel as a reformer and who then cost the city in less than two years almost $500,000 in judgments, salting away $152,974.32 himself, ought to have served as a warning. Unfortunately it didn't, and in 1870 and 1871 we are forced to witness the sad spectacle of Peter Cooper helping Tweed secure just the charter for the city that Tweed wanted, then giving him moral backing in the years when Tweed committed his greatest thefts. According to Tilden, Cooper had no illusions that Tweed was a good man, but merely thought that it was better to deal with him than with a new gang of ruffians.[3] The trouble with this theory is that it suggests a cynical willingness to compromise that was foreign to Cooper's nature. The truth seems to be, as Peter's unpublished correspondence no less than his public statements show, that he was completely taken in by Tweed. As were others. 'The most remarkable feature of the affair,' wrote a historian of New York City, 'is the success with which the conspirators hoodwinked even those citizens who were really opposed to them . . . a remarkable influence seems to have blinded the eyes of the reputable element in the city.'[4] In 1871 Tweed was moving in fashionable circles, and there was even some talk of raising a statue to him. In the fall of 1870, just before the election, he managed to get such respectable citizens as Moses Taylor and Marshall O. Roberts to give Comptroller Connolly's books a clean bill of health, some said by a threat to raise the assessments on their real estate.

Peter himself was not wholly without excuse. There were some grounds for believing, as Tilden says Cooper did, that a man with as much money as Tweed had would no longer be ambitious of wealth and would be on the side of the taxpayers. Peter could not imagine a man insatiable of wealth and power. Moreover, Tweed's professions of turning over a new leaf were very convincing. Needing moral support to get his charter through, he opened negotiations early in 1870 for what appeared to be complete capitulation to the Citizens' Association. Tired of fighting the association he would, he told its secretary, Nathaniel Sands, agree to any program that would satisfy Peter

Cooper and his colleagues. If the association would get the Legislature to pass the necessary laws, he and his friends would give a 'solemn promise to do all in their power to bring about a good government for our city.' [5]

Finally, Tweed's charter embodied sound principles for which the association had been fighting for years. It gave the government of the city back to the city, abolishing the Board of Supervisors and uniting city and county. And it increased enormously the power of the mayor, who received the right once belonging to the Common Council and then to the state to appoint all heads of departments and most city officers for four- to eight-year terms.[6] As Peter rightly said: 'This is the true Democratic doctrine—make elections as frequent as you please, make constitutions and laws as stringent as you like, but when you want anything done, when you come to choose an executive officer, clothe him with the whole power of the state to do what is necessary, and then hold him to strict and frequent account for his discharge of the trust.' This was the doctrine of the Jacksonians, who had, as have most liberal movements, exalted the executive as against the legislative branch of the government. The charter also created a Board of Public Works, uniting the street and Croton water commissions, a needed Department of Docks, and a Board of Audit, composed of the mayor, comptroller, and commissioner of public works. Peter was pleased with everything about the charter except its failure to provide for the 'removal of the heads of departments for incompetency, or dishonesty' ('but not for a difference in opinion in relation to national or State politics') without the consent of six judges of the Court of Common Pleas. It is not remarkable, therefore, that he should have strongly urged its passage in the Senate and counted its enactment into law as one of the association's proudest achievements.

Peter might, however, have paused to wonder how the charter happened to pass the Senate by the overwhelming vote of thirty to two, when not long before it had been almost unanimously disapproved. Passage of the charter which Peter had piously urged on the Senate had cost Tweed a good million in bribes. But it was worth the cost. At last Tweed no longer needed, in order to control the affairs of the city, to bribe half the Legislature in Albany or the Board of Aldermen. A Board of Audit, made up of Mayor Hall, Comptroller Connolly, and himself as head of the Board of Public Works, did all the city auditing. And his appointees were in every public office for at least four years. A charter that in the hands of honest men was an effective municipal instrument and whose main provisions were reenacted a dozen years after Tweed's downfall was, in the hands of the Ring, a noose around the city's neck.

Peter Cooper was unperturbed by portents of disaster. As he told the Citizens' Association just before the charter passed, he had confidence in Tweed and Mayor Hall. And he continued to have until the end. It is pathetic to see the old man writing to Tweed or to Hall or to Connolly as to good friends, in the full expectation that they would heed his protests and make the reforms he suggested. Would they appoint Andrew Green a park commissioner? Would they make Calvin L. Hulberd collector of the Port of New York? Would Tweed please stop tearing up the plaster pavement on 8th Street and take care of the worn stone on other streets? Occasionally Peter would grow impatient. In January, 1871, he upbraided Sweeny for not pushing economies fast enough; the work on the courthouse, he wrote, still continued, no debt-limitation law had been passed, the city was still paying fraudulent claims, there were still needless openings of streets; without reductions in expenditures the benefits of the charter would be illusory.

But Tweed threw enough sops to Peter to keep him content. He had Hall veto a bill requiring reflectors on all lamps, which would have cost the city $15 a lamp, he appointed some good men to the Boards of Docks, Public Works, and Education, and he made Nathaniel Sands head of the Tax Commission. When Peter protested against a bill of Tweed's to permit unlimited

expenditure for additional water for the city, Governor Hoffman put a five-million-dollar limitation into the bill; when
Peter again protested, Tweed assured him he had no intention
of spending the whole amount, and then wired him he had
reduced the limit to $1,000,000. As the evidence of broken
promises increased, Tweed accepted the men suggested by the
association to investigate charges against various officeholders,
and Peter was confident that these men would 'put . . . an end
to all further improper use of the public money.'

Tweed was amply repaid for any concessions he made to
Peter by the latter's unswerving support. In February, 1871,
Cooper assured a reporter for the *Star* that there was nothing
illicit in the contemplated sale of the public markets: "Mr.
Tweed and Mayor Hall have been too sincere in their reforms
for me to doubt them now." [7] In the same month he did his
best to get the Chamber of Commerce to support Tammany.
In March, Sands, with the rumored backing of Cooper, Taylor,
Field, Fish, and Gould, tried to buy or silence the *Times,* the
only opposition newspaper.[8] And in May the Citizens' Association, insisting that on the whole Tammany had improved local
government, endorsed the Tweed ticket in the aldermanic elections.

Cooper's behavior, particularly his praise of Tweed before
the Chamber of Commerce, drew down upon him a vitriolic
attack in the New York *Times.*[9] From anyone else this praise of
Tweed would, they said, have been impudence; in Peter's case
it was 'weakness and credulity.' Fortunately, the chamber refused to endorse Tweed, and the 'nice little game which Peter
Cooper undertook to oblige his dear friends of the Ring, was
effectually spoiled.' But failure 'does not render it less contempt-
ible, or abate the disgust which Mr. Cooper's active participation in it must excite among decent people.' Had Peter been
proved right about Tweed, the *Times*'s attacks would have
made little difference. But in July, 1871, the *Times*—along with
Thomas Nast and his *Harper's* cartoons the chief thorn in

Tweed's side—published the county accounts given them by the dissident Democratic Sheriff James O'Brien, which showed Ring thefts of at least $6,000,000. In September, Cooper's friend William F. Havemeyer, Tilden, and others formed the Committee of Seventy to fight Tweed, and when the Ring tried to sacrifice Connolly to the popular outcry and he appealed to Tilden, the latter secured a complete exposure of the Ring's system by installing Andrew H. Green in Connolly's place. In the fall elections, despite Tweed's famous taunt, "What are you going to do about it?," the reformers swept into office. Though Tweed was reelected to the State Senate, he did not dare take his seat, and had to resign as commissioner of public works and as grand sachem of Tammany. Eventually he went to jail, where he died in 1878. The three Tammany judges were removed (Cardozo was allowed to resign), Sweeny fled to Canada, and Connolly to Europe. The Ring was broken.

So, for all practical purposes, was the Citizens' Association. When the *Times*'s revelation first broke, the association summoned a public meeting, but called it off in the interests of harmony when the *Times* questioned the motives of the summoners. Then a worse blow fell. It was discovered in October that Nathaniel Sands, who had been paid $10,000 a year for eight years by the association, had turned traitor. The association had been very pleased and not a whit suspicious when Connolly had asked him to head the Tax Commission, nor had they begrudged him the added $10,000 or the $5000 each that his sons were to get. Then disenchantment came with a rush. Peter suddenly discovered that for two years Sands had been 'carrying on a negotiation with a member of the ring entirely unbeknown to anyone of our association by which he has taken $75,000 additional from the taxpayers of the City.' This $75,000 was for helping to negotiate an illicit $15,000,000 city loan for the Ring. Since Sands had been, under Cooper, the active leader of the association, this meant that all of them, as they now came to realize, had been the unwilling tools of Tweed.

If Peter was in any way crushed by the Tweed and Sands revelations, he never showed it. He acted promptly when, on October 23rd, he heard 'with inexpressible sorrow' of Sands's defection. 'It was about ten o'clock at night when I was shown a contract between Mr. Sands and Mr. Connolly—at nine o'clock the next morning I met him at the office. And in the presence of Mr. Henery I asked him if it was true that he had received the $75,000. He acknowledged that he had received it and attempted to justify himself in having taken the money.— We contended that his conduct was a violation of the trust reposed in him and a positive violation of law. We demanded and received his resignation on the spot.' For the rest, Cooper had no apology to make. The association had, he wrote, achieved important ends: the charter was in itself good; though Tweed had broken his promises, he had accomplished some fine things; the association had done all they could to keep him to his word; and finally, if Cooper's idea of a dozen years before had been acted on—the Committee of Safety idea—the city would have escaped the disgrace and loss to which it had been subjected. Peter suggested reviving this latter idea and having it sponsored jointly by the association, the Committee of Seventy, and a new Committee of Sixteen that had been formed.

Nor did Peter cease working actively for good government; unlike lesser men, he was not concerned if in the course of labors for the good he occasionally made a fool of himself. But after he resigned in 1871 as president of the Citizens' Association[10] (with a lengthy speech reciting all he had done by way of public service for half a century) he made only one contribution to municipal affairs that needs special mention here.[11] In 1872 the Republicans swept the country and the state and, as a result of the work of the Committee of Seventy, the city too. Immediately they became as partisan as their opponents had been, bending all their efforts toward modifying the Tweed charter to preserve their majority in the Board of Aldermen. Peter, deeply disturbed, wrote immediately to Senator Benedict and Governor Dix in Albany and finally to Grant in Washington,[12] warning that a Republican ring was as fatal to good government as a Democratic one. Its machinations would alienate the independent Democrats, who had overthrown Tammany, and, by helping an unregenerate Democratic machine to return to triumphant power, 'inflict loss and injury on the city such as no one can now calculate.' The statesmanlike gesture—and also the correct principle—was to clothe Mayor William H. Havemeyer, elected by ninety-nine per cent of the good people, with responsibility and power, and thus free the city from state and national politics.

Peter's predictions were borne out in 1874 by Democratic victories in both city and state, and we are still striving fitfully for the non-partisanship at which he aimed. It is understandable, however, that with the mayor's depredations fresh in mind, no one in 1872 listened to the representative of the discredited Citizens' Association. The new charter of 1873 gave the Board of Aldermen veto power over the mayor's appointments, a provision from which Edward Cooper was to suffer when he became mayor in 1878, and vested all legislative power in a single-chamber Common Council. The Citizens' Association, seeing 'no reasonable hope of success at the present time,' finally went out of business in 1874, leaving the facts on file for the time when presenting them would 'produce the necessary redress.' Peter's disillusionment with the Grant administration on this question did not push him out of the Republican party. But when other issues arose to influence him, it made departure easier.

Chapter 20

PETER COOPER FOR PRESIDENT

PETER COOPER was driven out of the Republican party by the financial policies of the government during and after the great panic of 1873. The problem that reached its climax in those years arose out of the creation, during the Civil War, of hundreds of millions of dollars of Treasury notes, or greenbacks. Almost all the Republicans of importance, backed by the bankers and the big industrialists, wanted to redeem these notes and resume specie payments, the only question being whether contraction of greenbacks should accompany resumption. To the business community in general it seemed essential to restore the credit of the government abroad by placing American currency once more on a gold basis; the bondholders naturally wanted resumption and the payments of bonds in gold; and the bankers were anxious to get rid of bills of credit issued by the government, the desirability and the legality of which had been questioned since the days of the Constitution. After several half-abortive efforts to secure their ends—there was some funding of short-term debt and contraction of greenbacks—the deflationists won a great permanent victory in 1869 when Grant decided that the Civil War bonds, which had been issued in greenbacks and had once been inter-convertible with greenbacks, were meant to be paid in gold.[1]

Then, on April 22, 1874, they won an even greater success. The stringency of credit and money at the time of the 1873 panic, which many blamed on the government's contraction policy, had stimulated Congress to pass a bill to increase greenbacks permanently to $400,000,000. Grant vetoed this bill. Finally, in the teeth of inflationist opposition, a Resumption Act was pushed through Congress ordering resumption of specie payments on January 1, 1879. The fat was in the fire.

These dry-as-dust issues hardly seem the food to nourish revolution. Nor is it probable that Peter Cooper thought they were when, in 1869, he sent a modest petition to Congress opposing greenback contraction and advocating a plan of his own for an adequate currency. He was so lukewarm about the whole question that he did not pursue the matter further until December, 1873,[2] when he was moved to write Grant that, had his plan been adopted, 'I think you will agree' there would have been no panic. Though now fully committed to Greenbackism, he could still, on March 4, 1874, sit complacently on the platform at a meeting expressly called to prevent passage of the bill to print more greenbacks.[3] Even when, in 1875, he suddenly began a vigorous campaign in favor of his scheme, it is doubtful if he knew how deep or how far to the left his proposals were to carry him. Peter was merely pursuing thoughts he had had for nearly forty years, and, though he had added a twist to them that to many appeared to be a complete about-face, there seemed to him nothing more radical in advocating such views than in opposing municipal corruption or a steam elevated railway. His writings on the subject in 1875 are, indeed, both measured in tone and moderate in content.

The inspiration for Peter's new twist was a drygoods merchant named Edward Kellogg, who, disgusted at being unable to pay his debts in the panic of 1837 though he had plenty of assets, sat down and wrote two books on money, the first of which appeared in 1843 and the second, *Labor and Other Capital,* in 1849. Unnoticed at the time, they were reprinted in 1861 and won a wide hearing. Like Cooper, Kellogg started with the premise that property, the product of labor, was sacred. But few actual workers reaped their just deserts because of fluctuations in the value of the gold on which money was based, and the high and changing interest rates, which put people at the mercy of capitalists. Kellogg's solution was the creation of a paper currency to be issued by the government against interest-paying mortgages secured by double the amount of landed estate and fundable into long-term bonds. Under this plan the government controlled interest rates and thus kept them down, and this in turn—since the value of money, according to Kellogg, was dependent on the interest it could earn—meant a stable as well as an ample currency.[4]

Peter Cooper did not, in 1875, subscribe to Kellogg's mortgage scheme. The money he required was already outstanding in the form of greenbacks, and he suggested merely that greenbacks be made permanent legal tender for all debts, taxes, and duties. Peter was not an inflationist. Greenbacks should not be increased or decreased except as the population increased or decreased, and should be redeemable by being interconvertible with government bonds bearing a low rate of interest. As he insisted in answering his critics in the *Evening Post,* who spoke in 1875 of his 'New Departure,' [5] 'I am as much opposed to an irredeemable currency, and an inflated and irresponsible paper money as I ever was.' But 'I should be sorry to be among those who learn nothing from the past. . . . "Hard money," or what is equivalent to it, a paper currency at all times redeemable in gold and silver, can no longer be relied on to answer the wants of this country.' Gold was itself a commodity, which fluctuated with the demand; and it could be drawn off by foreigners (of whom Peter was growing more and more suspicious), causing a panic in any country on a gold standard. Government-issued greenbacks provided both a more elastic and a stabler currency. Moreover, the attempt to contract them, which was causing untold misery by depriving people of needed funds, was unjust;

greenbacks had been 'worked out and paid for by the people in the labor, material, and service which they had rendered to the Government during our struggle for the nation's life.' To redeem them by issuing bonds payable in gold was to tax the people to pay bankers and foreign bondholders, many of whom already held bonds which they had bought with a fifty-cent dollar.

That Cooper thought his ideas on the currency moderate and even orthodox is indicated by his coupling them with his ultra-respectable views on the tariff. During the war tariffs had been raised by successive bills until by 1864 the average rate was 47.7% on dutiable goods, as against a previous 18.8%. When the war was over even industrialists who had previously taken little part in the controversy joined to prevent reduction in these admittedly high rates. By 1870 high tariffs had become an unshakable part of the creed of the very men who, with occasional exceptions like Henry C. Carey, Peter's chief mentor on the tariff issue, were most opposed to any scheme for a managed currency.[6]

Peter's tariff views had not changed since the 'forties, but they had grown more extreme and had become for him a much more central article of faith. From 1866, when he began contributing to the *Iron Age*[7] and became president of the American Industrial League (an organization to 'educate' people about tariffs), until the last year of his life, when he sent a long letter of advice to President Arthur's tariff commission, Peter wrote continuously and vehemently in favor of high duties on foreign goods.[8] For to Peter, whose kindly views of human nature stopped at the Atlantic Ocean, foreigners had become the villains in a war that would continue 'as long as men do not love their neighbors as they do themselves.'[9] His *The Dangers of a War of Commerce*[10] contains a long and bitter account of England's free-trade policy, which, he claimed, had been more destructive of life and property than 'all the wars of conquest that have taken place in the civilized world during the period of time.' From

India to America, it had been England's policy to break up native manufacture and force English goods on her colonies even at the cost of making her own children work fifteen to seventeen hours a day at starvation wages to undersell competitors.[11] The only way America could avoid India's lot was to use her tariff to dry up imports, stop the drain on gold, and thus permit payment of foreign debts. Increased native production would keep home prices and profits down, supply employment and high wages to labor, and provide a market for farm products. Only a few importers and foreigners would find no place in this happy scheme of things.

If these views were orthodox Republicanism, so was Peter's reaction to the efforts of labor unions to gain higher wages and shorter hours by strikes. If those now striking, he wrote on one occasion, knew the struggles employers were compelled to make 'in order to be sure to be able to pay their men and leave something on their balance sheet to compensate them for their labor and the risks that all employers are compelled to meet . . . they will rather pity their employers than throw unnecessary difficulties in their way.' To Jason S. Schultz he wrote in 1874: 'I would most gladly if I could show fellow working[men] their great mistake in their organized efforts to force their employers to pay as much for a poor workman as for a good workman. . . . All the . . . restraints and the taxes they levy on their different orders to maintain strikes have done as much to break up the regular business of the country and drive commerce from our city as any one thing with which I am acquainted.'

The attempt to secure an eight-hour day particularly annoyed him, as he told John Reid in 1866, when the latter, counting on Peter's sympathy with labor, asked him to speak at a mass meeting on the subject. 'For myself I have given in labour and attention to business more than twelve hours a day through a large portion of a long life. . . . I have done this in the firm belief that it was my right and the right of every other man to work as many hours each day as I or they may think.' 'I should have regarded it as a terrible hardship,' he wrote later, 'if I had found myself compelled to contribute out of my small earnings of twelve shillings per day to maintain strikes that would have prevented me from getting into a business that has given me a house and home. . . . Instead of striking and combining to compel employers to pay them higher wages they [workingmen] should combine their capital and labour to carry on the different mechanical and agricultural employments on their own account and take the entire profits to themselves following the example of thousands of the working men of Germany who are now doing this with great advantage to themselves and their country.' Peter was, in other words, an advocate of producers' cooperatives, which were very fashionable in England when Cooper wrote this in 1866, and which some workers' organizations in America had begun to sponsor. Such cooperatives, Peter believed, would win the ready sympathy and help of businessmen.

Peter Cooper remained in 1875 an opponent of governmental or any other form of paternalism. Though a believer in temperance, he refused to advocate prohibition, 'as he had but little faith in the efficacy of law to accomplish what the moral nature could not do.' The government had the task of protecting the country against foreigners, which made a protective tariff as much its business as the creation of an army in wartime. It also established the rules of the game by passing general laws and regulations. Since money was a standard of value needed by all in the game, it was the function of government, not of private individuals, to create and control it. Peter saw nothing inconsistent with his other beliefs in his currency views.

He was perhaps right. But consistency is not always the most appreciated of virtues. However much his business associates might accept his other views, they could not go along with his ideas on the currency. He might have discovered this as early as 1869, when the usually friendly *Herald,* in answer to a letter of Cooper's on the currency, told the 'old women of the Citizens'

Association' and Peter Cooper in particular to stop talking about finance, of which they knew nothing.[12] He might have been warned when his old friend Wilson G. Hunt, alarmed by the greenback craze, 'turned his assets into gold and locked the proceeds in a safe deposit company';[13] or when all his friends— Field, Hunt, A. A. Low, Marshall Roberts, Moses Taylor, and others—signed a petition on April 15, 1874, to have Grant veto the bill expanding the currency.[14] In the ensuing years he certainly discovered it, since every respectable newspaper and even his son and son-in-law opposed him.[15] As he said gaily in 1878, 'Now these two boys of mine . . . are smart, able and very intelligent in everything but this money question. But whenever this question comes up they talk like boys ten years old.' [16] When Peter fought the Ring in the early days he may have been in a minority, but he had the respectable on his side. On the currency issue he soon found himself considered a traitor to his class.

Peter also soon learned, or thought he learned, why the business world was so opposed to his views. There were a great many who disagreed with him on rational grounds. Although the modern world is still experimenting with managed currencies similar to the one Peter advocated, and we no longer are as sure of the exclusive virtues of the gold standard as we once were, there are perfectly valid reasons for believing that Peter's scheme would have led to disastrous political manipulation and possibly to a runaway inflation; there are even better reasons for thinking that no manipulation of the currency can cure the economic ills of society. But a great many who opposed Peter— most of them, Peter thought—did so for quite other reasons. They did not, as did Peter, really believe in the world of small private businessmen, farmers, and artisans which had been Peter's dream for America since the days of Jackson. They did not want to see the government acting as an umpire securing freedom and opportunity for all alike. To the generation of industrialists and bankers and railway builders that grew up after the Civil War, America was a paradise for them to exploit. Though they might talk of individualism, what they really meant was a system that left them at liberty to control others through giant corporations. The government was there to protect them by setting up a tariff, by keeping down labor unions, and by establishing a currency and a banking system that gave them control of the financial machinery and protected the bondholders. As Thaddeus Stevens said bitterly of the agreement to pay bonds in gold, it was 'speculation in favor of the large bondholders, the millionaires, who took advantage of our folly in granting them coin payment of interest.' Peter Cooper failed to see that the protective tariff and the suppression of unions—he still seemed to believe that the individual could bargain on an equal basis with the employer—were part of the pattern. But he did understand the implications of Republican financial schemes.

Finally, Peter quickly discovered why this seemingly unexplosive issue of the currency aroused such passion among his acquaintances; as in the days of Jackson, it had become the focus of general discontent. If Peter had lost by his currency views the favor of the respectable, he soon found he had plenty of support among dissatisfied workers, farmers, and even small businessmen. The thought that bankers and merchants were taking their currency away and strangling them through control of credit and the creation of a crushing bonded indebtedness could, in the 'seventies, unite all the less-favored groups in America as no other issue. Increase in the number of greenbacks, Kellogg's mortgage loan scheme, payment of the national debt in legal tender notes, and abolition of the national banks became the battlecries of the time.

Though as early as 1868 George H. Pendleton's mild Greenbackism (nicknamed the 'Ohio rag baby') had a wide enough appeal to farmers to be made a plank in the platform on which Seymour ran for the Presidency,[17] and though echoes of Greenback slogans could still be heard in the great Populist movement of the 'nineties, it was in the half-dozen years after the crisis of 1873 that Greenbackism attained its greatest heights as an independent, countrywide political movement. The first national Greenback political party was formed, under the inspiration of the Indian Farmer's party, at Indianapolis in November, 1874. Scarcely two years later the party was ready to throw its hat into the Presidential ring. On May 17, 1876, Greenbackers from eighteen states met in Indianapolis under the leadership of Moses W. Field, a Detroit merchant and Republican congressman, and nominated the first Greenback candidate for President of the United States.

Peter Cooper's reaction to the reception of his currency views was immediate and characteristic; far from retreating, he threw himself wholeheartedly into a venture in which he had previously been only mildly interested. In 1869, though the National Labor Congress in Philadelphia had presented him with a resolution thanking him for his currency views, calling him 'the representative working man of this great nation,' and asking him to their conference in 1870, he had not been stirred to join them. In 1872 he had supported Grant without qualification, and continued to do so through 1874. But when the administration failed to heed his many warnings in 1875 he was ready for action. The country had a suicidal $271,000,000 of imports, he wrote in 1875, and $34,000,000 of interest to pay on a debt of over $2,000,000,000; property had shrunk to half its value; many were unemployed, while the rich were getting richer; and prices were down, not because of overproduction but because of under-consumption by a people without enough credit or currency. In January, 1876, Cooper presided over a mass meeting of workers held at Cooper Union to end unemployment, and passionately urged them to use their efforts, not in striking, but in spreading the gospel that Greenbackism would end the depression.[18] On March 31st he journeyed to New Haven to warn a huge audience in the Music Hall that the money power was destroying them. The New Haven *Union,* in commenting on the event, said that hundreds were turned away and were unable to see the 'grand old man' who, in his eighty-sixth year, had come seventy-five miles to tell them the truth. Then suddenly, on May 18th, Peter found himself unanimously nominated for President of the United States by the Greenback convention at Indianapolis.

The motives of those who conferred this honor on Peter were not above suspicion. Western Greenbackers, more inflationist in their views than Peter, were for David Davis of Illinois, and if they accepted Cooper it was, as 'Brick' Pomeroy's *Democrat* later implied, in large part because of a 'promise of financial assistance to the party' from him. This was supposedly given by the secretary of the convention, Wallace Groom, editor of the New York *Mercantile Journal* and Peter's personal representative at the convention,[19] though there is no suggestion that he offered the assistance in return for political favors. Since few imagined that a man eighty-five years old would make the best showing in a campaign, the charge has probably some truth, and Peter did in fact contribute more in money than he did in campaigning. Even so, he disappointed many dunning Greenbackers. 'Mr. Cooper was expected,' wrote a Knights of Labor opponent two years later, 'to "come down" with a lot of money but he didn't "come down." It was found that he was more intent upon circulating documents than giving away his money.' [20] Poor Peter, like so many rich men who wanted to do good, was often haunted by his wealth. Yet his nomination was also a tribute to the love and respect borne him by the ordinary people of America, who, the politicians realized, would be more likely to trust him despite his wealth than they would anyone else. The *Herald,* hardly sympathetic to the Greenbackers, gave the politicians due credit: nominating Cooper 'shows an elevation of tone not often seen in our politics. It brings back the days when we had a Livingston and a Rufus King in public life.' 21

Peter himself seems to have been taken aback by the nomination, though his choice in February by the state Greenback convention must have given him some warning. At first he peremptorily refused, and told a *Herald* reporter that his refusal was likely to be final.22 Then, both flattered and moved by the seriousness of the situation, he agreed to stand if the two major parties failed to include a Greenback plank in their platforms. He was obviously confused. When a reporter suggested to him, probably as a bait, that he might be the "great unknown," he replied with disarming frankness, "Yes, I see, I see. God knows I love my country and would cheerfully lay down my life for her in this dark hour of her need." It was perhaps his duty to run. A few weeks later he was even more worried. "With a split at St. Louis [where the Democratic convention was being held] and the election of President thrown into the House of Representatives, I regard my possible selection as President of the United States with positive alarm. . . . And yet I am ready for the sacrifice. . . . God knows I pray against it . . . but if it must be Cooper, Cooper is prepared." 23 Only a man who really didn't want to be President could have been so naively and unjustifiably worried that he might be. He certainly did everything he could, short of refusing, to avoid the position. He called at Tilden's house and told him he'd vote for him if he'd endorse Greenbackism; then he prayed for ex-Governor Allen of Ohio, indorsed by the Westerners, to be nominated by the Democrats; then he tried to get Allen nominated as Greenback candidate.

To no avail. Tilden was nominated by the Democrats, who, though they urged repeal of the resumption law, did so because they felt it hindered resumption. Hayes and the Republicans were, as Cooper wrote, hopelessly hard-money advocates. Allen refused all Greenback offers. So Peter decided that as an honorable man he had to stay in the field, though "if I were elected I believe the duties of the office would kill me before the term had half expired." [24] On July 25th he gave his reasons to the rival candidates: 'I have . . . consented, with great reluctance, to go before the people—not for the strife of office, not for the petty triumphs of a successful candidate, but for the vindication of a great principle that underlies all true Republican or Democratic Institutions—namely, that the interest and happiness of the whole people are superior to the demands or interests of any one class'—the bondholders and foreign investors. The platform he stood on was in exact accordance with his principles; it urged repeal of the Resumption Act, favored United States notes convertible into United States bonds with not over 3.65% interest, attacked the sale of gold bonds abroad, and generally asked for government surveillance of business. His running mate, chosen when Newton Booth of California declined, was Congressman Samuel F. Cary of Ohio, spokesman for the Cincinnati trade unions, who had been one of the first Western labor men to take up Kellogg's doctrines and help organize the Greenback party.

It would be idle to pretend that the Greenbackers put on one of the great third-party campaigns or that they made any very significant contribution to one of the most famous Presidential struggles in American history. Moses Field, who conducted the campaign, did little to organize it or give it vigor. Moreover, if, as the *Herald* complained, the Cooper candidacy 'has been the standing jest of the campaign and a topic of infinite merriment to the small wits of the party press on both sides,' there was some justification for the attitude. The kindly, earnest, naive old gentleman with his air-cushion, his four-lensed glasses, and his silver locks falling over his shoulders was hard to think of as either a militant savior or a menace. He knew little about politics, he was too old to trek across the country to further his cause, and he was as usual taken advantage of by all and sundry, from politicians to poll watchers, a whole army of whom came after him for a promised $5. Even the ballots and posters he ordered distributed either fell into the hands of Democratic thugs or were sold to them, as Peter claimed, by his lieutenant, Wallace Groom.[25] In the end, though for a moment the Greenbackers frightened the *Herald*,[26] Peter won only 82,640 votes out of some 8,000,000 cast, and less than 1500 in New York.

Yet, as always with Peter Cooper, there is another side to the story. If he could not campaign as he might have at thirty, the indomitable old gentleman did all that was humanly possible, and there was something stirring as well as humorous and pathetic in watching him drag himself from convention to convention and meeting to meeting, everywhere earnestly exhorting his hearers in quiet fatherly terms to save their country before it was too late. The press, always hostile, Peter claimed, to minorities, may have scoffed, but thousands of ordinary people came out to listen and shake his hand. There was a huge mass meeting at Cooper Union on August 30th, where he was greeted with deafening cheers, as even the *Herald* admitted; and there was another on October 20th, attended mostly by young trade unionists, who wildly applauded 'the friend of the working man, the protector of the poor and distressed.' The votes Peter received were no gauge of his strength, as is generally true of third-party candidates, and certainly not of his influence. In the sordid jamboree of post-Civil-War politics Peter Cooper stood like a shining symbol of the better world that America had once promised to be. A voice calling across the chasm of forty years from the days of Jackson, he reminded a blind generation that the American dream could not long survive thralldom to the monopolists and moneychangers. People listened and they did not forget. The old philanthropist, whose millions and his many years left undimmed his vision of an America of equality and opportunity, was starting, not finishing something. Within two years Greenback votes had swelled to 1,000,000, and later other leaders, with perhaps better ideas than the Greenbackers, were to take up the burden of liberalism.

Peter Cooper was a not insignificant link between the days of Jackson and those of Wilson and Roosevelt.

In 1877 the depression, dissatisfaction with the contested election results, bloody strikes, and the difficulties caused by the Resumption Act brought more and more laborers and farmers around to Greenback views, and on February 22, 1878, at Toledo, Western Greenbackers united with Eastern labor reformers to form the National or Greenback Labor party. The platform of this party, like that of the Independent party, accorded with Peter's views, though it added a demand for an income tax and the resumption of silver coinage, stopped in 1873, which he had not previously sponsored but which he now approved. The day of the Greenbackers seemed at hand and Peter threw himself with renewed ardor into an attempt to get the new party's platform accepted by laborites and farmers in New York. Though he never admitted it officially, Peter was generally considered to be the chief if not sole financial support of the leading Greenback newspaper in New York, the *Advocate,* a large weekly quarto distributed for twenty-five cents and having a circulation in 1878 running into the hundreds of thousands. At the end of July Peter sent its business manager, Walter H. Shupe,[27] to the Syracuse convention of the National party as head of a delegation pledged to support the Toledo platform.

Once again Peter's foray into politics proved disillusioning. As the Greenbackers grew in strength they began, as new parties will, to split into hostile factions. A large group of Greenbackers led by Brick Pomeroy were real inflationists; they violently opposed the interconvertibility feature of the Greenback proposals, preferring absolute fiat money, and demanded immediate payment of all outstanding gold bonds in greenbacks, a form of direct repudiation that Peter Cooper would never sanction. A second group, made up of members of the new and as yet semi-secret labor organization, the Knights of Labor, were as opposed as were the inflationists to the Toledo convention. To make matters worse in New York, upstate was opposed to the city. The result was chaos. New York City sent to the Syracuse convention, besides Shupe's delegation, two other competing groups. The leaders of the convention, averring that the city was a den of iniquity anyway, threw them all out and proceeded to write a platform favoring absolute money and a repudiation of debt, doctrines that captured the National party before the fall elections. Shupe indignantly announced that the Syracuse convention had been stampeded by a 'secret organization,' and appealed to Peter Cooper. Peter, 'a deep shade of sadness, caused by the scenes which had occurred the day before at Syracuse . . . delineated on his philanthropic face,' called 'pathetically' for peace and for paying off the bondholders to 'be done with them once for all.' [28]

But he couldn't even bring peace to the city delegations, though he did unite the two Greenback wings. At a meeting on August 16th, characterized by the *Tribune* as one of the most 'turbulent political assemblages' ever gathered in the city, the labor group, headed by James Connolly and George Blair, accused its two opponents of being mere hirelings of John Sherman and anti-Tammany Democrats. Any attempt at amalgamation was given up.[29] Peter's final disillusionment came in December. In August Shupe had hired as editor of the *Advocate* B. S. Heath, who had once written for Pomeroy's *Democrat* and whose *Pekin Legal Tender* had been an influential Illinois Greenback paper. Peter himself welcomed Heath to the *Advocate,* taking him by the hand and telling him that he was offering him a 'wider field for your vigorous pen,' which he so much admired.[30] But within a few months the *Advocate* was dying, and Heath had resigned in disgust, claiming that Shupe was swindling Cooper and the Greenbackers by selling out to the Tilden Democrats.[31]

Even that experience did not end stubborn Peter's mixing in Greenback affairs, though he allowed Zachos to announce on April 5, 1880, that he had 'entirely withdrawn from all active participation in politics, and "especially all local politics." ' In March, 1880, he tried to get David Davis to run for President on a Greenback ticket, telling him that he could 'be elected by the largest majority any President has received since the government was founded.' When the Greenbackers, assembled in turbulent convention in St. Louis, finally nominated General James B. Weaver of Ohio, Peter wrote to him twice urging on him the advisability of fusion with the Democrats, a proposal that had almost caused Brick Pomeroy to walk out of the convention and destroy the party.

Peter's final significant political gesture (he was still sponsoring Greenback meetings and contributing to Greenback papers in 1883)[32] was an offer, made to B. S. Heath in May, 1881, to give $100 to each of ten speakers and $50 to support a Greenback paper in every state in the union if the party would choose the chairman and follow the program that Peter outlined. The money, needless to say, was accepted. But by then nothing could save the party. Its great success in 1878 when, despite dissension, it had elected fourteen congressmen, won a third of Maine's electorate, and polled a million votes nationally, had been the high point of the movement. The lifting of the depression and the success of resumption in 1879 lost the Greenbackers all but some 300,000 votes in the 1880 election, and by 1882 most of their supporters had gone over to the Democrats. Though there was a Greenback Presidential candidate in 1884—there was still one in 1948—the movement as an important political force was at an end.

The decline of the movement could not seriously discourage Peter. Though he worked actively for the party, he was at heart less the politician than the propagandist of principles, and no temporary defeat could prevent the ultimate triumph of those principles. In Peter's long career there is nothing more remarkable than the tenacity with which he held to this latest-born of his faiths, or the energy and thought and passion that he devoted to promulgating it. During the last seven years of his life he wrote and spoke literally hundreds of thousands of words in behalf of his currency views, the volume of words swelling rather than diminishing as he approached and passed ninety. The year of his death he collected some of his writings in a long book, *Ideas for a Science of Good Government*. He addressed his friends—businessmen, bankers, editors, congressmen, Presidents—and when they didn't listen the first time, he addressed them a second and third time. He said that he had sent out 2,000,000 documents.[33]

It is useless to pretend that one would want to read more than one or two of these appeals, or that any one of them was a masterpiece of English prose. As a matter of fact Peter never learned to write coherently, as his many painstaking handwritten rough drafts indicate, and he quite frankly allowed Zachos to edit and polish his work for him. Yet it is remarkable how much learning, logic, and plain sense went into Peter's effusions. Peter studied carefully the history of his country,[34] the works of the Founding Fathers, government reports, and the statements of legislators and executives from Franklin, Madison, Calhoun, and Webster on down, and all the recent works on economic and political theory. A few weeks before he died he was reading J. B. Dixwell's *Promises of Free Trade* and Henry George's *Progress and Poverty*, the latter of which not only did not frighten him but seemed a powerful plea for reform and the opening of a new era of commonsense political economy, far superior to that of Adam Smith, Malthus, and Mill. In tone Peter's writing was usually calm and measured, but it could rise into real eloquence when he was deeply moved. Though always very positive in his views, Peter was ever courteous to an opponent, and severely reprimanded A. A. Hardenberg, a hard-money congressman, for not distinguishing between abuse and an honest difference of opinion. Peter had no reason to feel ashamed of either the manner or the matter of his contributions to his country's economic and political thought.

The most astonishing thing about these contributions is the way in which they reveal how Peter's mind grew in his last years. Peter was eighty-four years old when he began seriously to ponder the Greenback issue, an age when most men, if they have survived at all, have long ceased to have any new ideas. Yet his economic views in 1875, far from being an end product of his thinking, were but a rough beginning for a truly amazing development in a man of his age. Not only was he constantly evolving new details and perfecting his scheme, but the somewhat narrow idea of a new currency had before his death expanded into a whole view of the nature of post-Civil-War economic society and a deep insight into the way to handle it. And the older Peter got the more radical did his views become, the more passionately and intensely did he espouse them.

Though the core of Peter's interest remained his managed currency, he was almost bound to progress beyond this mere piece of machinery the moment he threw in his lot with farmers and workingmen. There could be no legal-tender government money so long as the banks opposed it, and Peter became, within a short time after 1875, an irreconcilable opponent of the recharter of the national banks when their charters expired in 1883. No Marxian socialist could have been more scathing in his denunciation of the moneyed powers than this wealthy businessman who never forgot what he had learned in the days of Jackson. He became one of those who have been accused of believing that bankers sit around 'eating bonbons, and drinking wine, and passing resolutions' hostile to the public interest. Peter was acquainted with many bankers, and knew just what they were doing.

No scheme ever before devised, he told Congress, was more sure 'to fertilize the rich man's fields by the sweat of the poor man's brawn than our present system of organized National Banks.' 'The dealers in money,' he wrote less than a year before his death, 'have always, since the days of Moses, been the dangerous class, so dangerous that Christ found it necessary to upset the money changers and with small cords he drove them out of the Temple dedicated to public worship.' [35] They were willing to bribe and threaten and use every art and intrigue to gain their ends. These ends were the slavery of the American people, achieved by converting greenbacks into a huge national debt and controlling the volume of currency, which allowed them to expand or contract credit and raise and lower prices at will. Not satisfied with a fair profit, they were even trying to get higher interest rates and were litigating for exemption from local taxes to add to the double interest they already received on their bank notes.[36] Banks should be limited to their true function of lending money on their own capital at fixed rates of interest.

As he looked deeper Peter discovered, as he had not in the past, that bankers were not the only culprits. Industrialists, whom Peter once had extolled so highly, were now also selfish, hiring labor 'for the smallest consideration for which it can be obtained.' Owners of transportation were worse. "Why," Peter asked Senator Beck angrily, "should Messrs. Gould, Vanderbilt, Sage, Miller, Huntington, Croker . . . and a few hundred bankers in New York be permitted to accumulate their hundreds of millions of dollars, by simply controlling the money and transportation, that should belong to the whole people?" "Monopolies of all kinds must be at the expense of the people and the happiness of the whole nation," he announced angrily to the convention of the National party in Boston in 1879. "Misgovernment and the faults of the ruling class have always proved in history the trouble and sorrow of nations. . . . There is fast forming in this country an aristocracy of wealth—the worst form of aristocracy, that can curse the prosperity of any country. For such an aristocracy has no country. . . . Monopolizing corporations, whether in the shape of banks or railroads, have no soul."

Legislators and politicians were, unfortunately, no counterweight to this grasping aristocracy. 'The Government,' he told President Hayes, seemed to administer the finances of the country 'as if there were but one interest in the nation to be promoted, and that the profit of those who desired to fund their money with the *greatest security,* and to make money scarce and of high rate of interest.' There were in office too many 'professed politicians, who are seeking for the spoils of office and the attractions of power—men who are ready to lend themselves to all special and partial acts of legislation, if they can only advance their own individual interests.' Such 'ignorant and corrupt legislators' had chartered the banks; they had also given 'away immense tracts of land to heartless corporations, thus creating land monopolies, like those that now curse the British Isles.' 'I consider the persistent class legislation of Congress since the war,' he told Representative Hardenberg, 'a worse despotism than that of Great Britain before the Revolution.' Peter did not, however, make the mistake of putting the blame primarily on the politicians, as he had in discussing municipal affairs, but placed it squarely where it belonged. If the 'Republican party was thoroughly under the influence and control of banking institutions,' and if 'incorporated capital . . . now controls nearly every legislative body in the land,' it was because of the selfish ruthlessness of businessmen. Not content merely to corrupt others they had themselves worked their way into legislative halls; in defiance of the express intention of the Founding Fathers, Congress contained, in 1881, a hundred and twenty bankers, fourteen merchants, ninety-nine lawyers, thirteen manufacturers, and seven doctors, as against four mechanics and not a single farmer or laborer.

In coming to these alarming conclusions Peter had to give up some of his most cherished beliefs. The capitalists of the

Gilded Age had finally dispelled Peter's faith in the beneficent results to society of simply leaving people alone. Men might be initially good—though even that he occasionally seemed to doubt, quoting with approval Franklin's remark that they were 'proud spirited little animals, not fit to be trusted with power' —but environment had so corrupted some of them that no education could hope to effect reform. It was 'literally impossible,' he wrote, 'for men whose business it is to deal in money to avoid legislating in favor of their own interests as a class.' And this meant that the poor, the ordinary man did not have the opportunity to which he was entitled and which American society had once offered him. It is ironical that Peter should have come to these conclusions at just about the time that the doctrine of the sanctity of property and the equating of godliness and riches were becoming a self-conscious philosophy in the hands of the ministers and college presidents and Horatio Algers of the Gilded Age.[37] If there was ever any justification for such beliefs, that time had long passed, and Peter Cooper must have smiled bitterly to see the robber barons appropriating a sanction of which they had made a mockery.

What could be done? Perhaps only a revolution would save America, and Peter did not shrink from this conclusion. "There may at some future day be a whirlwind precipitated upon the moneyed men of this country," he told an astonished group of bankers assembled in convention in 1882. For "what a man soweth, that must he also reap somewhere, somehow and at some time, by the operation of laws so wise and so good, that they will never require to be altered, amended or revoked." When a government abuses and usurps power it is the duty of the people "to throw off such government and to provide new guards for their future security." The right of revolution was guaranteed by the Declaration of Independence, which said that government was founded to secure life, liberty, equality, and the pursuit of happiness, and that if it became destructive of these ends the people could alter or abolish it. Peter went so far as to praise the leaders of the Knights of Labor, who told their brothers not to strike but to use their wages to buy guns and ammunition and three months' provisions—they could then "like honest working men demand and obtain and maintain their inalienable constitutional rights."

Peter still had faith, however, that the American people would 'vindicate their rights and secure their own welfare,' and, without resort to arms, take over their government and make it an instrument for justice to all. What did this involve? Here again Peter showed how far he had traveled in the few short years since he first began promoting his currency doctrines. From being, along with most industrialists, a believer in the least possible government he became very nearly an advocate of the social service state. This was an easy transition for younger humanitarians like Henry George, but for an old Jacksonian, with a Jacksonian's traditional fear of too much government, it was very painful. The entering wedges were the tariff and the currency, the latter of which Benton and other Jacksonians had always believed the government should control.[38] From this Peter went on to interest rates. Having been put on a committee of the Chamber of Commerce to repeal the usury laws, he soon found that, like his friend Capen, he violently opposed such repeal.[39] 'Money is so unlike every other article,' he wrote, 'that I believe a man has neither a legal or a moral right to take all that he can get under all the circumstances that may arise'; moreover, it was too easy to create an artificial scarcity and run up exorbitant interest rates. The government, therefore, must control interest rates. Gradually Peter's views expanded to include other things, until by 1882 he was ready to become a vice-president of the Anti-Monopoly League, whose basic doctrine was that 'corporations, the creation of the state, should be controlled by the state.'

For the most part Peter's view remained the old Jacksonian one that the government should act as umpire and equalizer, preventing injustice but rarely initiating positive services. 'In

every civilized country,' Peter stated in summary of his position on one occasion, 'the law requires as an indispensable pre-
requisite that parties should stand on equal ground in order to
make a valid contract. The grand object of all law is to prevent
the strong from oppressing the weak by taking an undue advantage of his necessities. Even the woman who consents to her
own dishonor can recover heavy damages from her seducer.
. . . When money is loaned by one individual man to another
their moral character has to stand before the community. In
our country a large part of the loans is made through banks
which have no souls. No single individual is responsible for it
as a legal being.' At other times, however, he went further, emphasizing what he called the paternalistic role of the state. The
government must use its powers 'as a father is bound to use
the powers that God has given him to provide for the wants, the
weakness and inexperience of his children that are dependent
on his care.' A government that neglected its duty was like a
'father who would bring children into the world and then leave
them to be devoured by wolves.' This implied not only the negative role of making impartial laws but the positive function
of securing 'advantages for a whole people collectively, which
they could not secure for themselves, as individuals.'

In the many specific measures he advocated, Peter drew no
fine distinction between the two, recommending, if the situation
called for it, tasks for the government to perform that ran directly counter to the traditional role assigned to the state in
America. On currency matters alone he soon went far beyond
his original ideas. By 1879 he was recommending a modification
of Kellogg's land plan, apparently suggested by a man named
Shelden Baker. The people were to get their money back by
receiving loans from the counties on mortgages at three per
cent up to one-half the value of the land; the counties in turn
were to borrow from the states at two per cent, and the states
from the federal government at one per cent. Peter also urged in
1881 that the government establish postal savings banks to re-

ceive deposits of the people at two and one-half per cent interest, a measure in which he placed great faith. The national debt, which Peter was never willing to repudiate, could thus be paid; if Treasury notes were legal tender the banks could use the deposits to buy gold and silver.[40] After the debt had been paid, the savings banks could perform the true function of banks, lending money to 'responsible persons, who would use it to commence some profitable business, allowing them to keep up the interest and pay the principal at their convenience, when it will be reloaned to some enterprising mechanic or working man.' This had been Peter Cooper's practice in the old days.

Turning from the currency, Peter had a whole host of progressive recommendations. High on the list was a civil service for government employees, to be run by a Civil Service Commission, an idea shared by many others at the time and soon to come into being. Citing, as he was fond of doing, the example of the Chinese government, which trained its aristocracy for government office and gave them strict examinations, he said: 'There is nothing that will save our country from a premature decay and eventual ruin but such a civil service as that which has preserved China as a nation for more than five thousand years and now forms the great strength of England as a nation.' Peter also wanted the government to set up industrial schools to do for people in general what he was doing for New Yorkers. Even more radical were his proposals that the government establish a program of public improvements on a large scale to give employment, and that the state, not private individuals, build the Northern and Southern Pacific Railroads. Finally, he strongly urged that the unoccupied land in the West be given to the people. Had Peter lived long enough he would certainly have applauded Franklin Roosevelt, though he might have thought him too conservative.

CONCLUSION

EVEN Peter Cooper could not live forever. During all the last years he maintained his good health, being freer, as he said, from aches and pains on his ninety-first birthday than when he had been a boy carrying a grocer's basket about the streets. If his eyes were dimmed, he never felt old, he told the guests at the Arcadian Club, because his faith remained ever fresh: "My experience of life has not dimmed my hopes for humanity; . . . My sun is not setting in clouds and darkness, but is going down cheerfully in a clear firmament lighted by the glory of God." Even on his ninety-second birthday he was in excellent health, though not, Peter told a *Herald* reporter, as robust as he was accustomed to be.[1]

But he was being reminded more and more of death. His old friend William E. Dodge died on Peter's ninety-second birthday, almost causing the celebration to be given up. 'Of the twenty-two gentlemen who came to Mr. Cooper's ninetieth anniversary dinner, eleven have already died,' Hewitt wrote at the time. Peter, like many old men, was thinking more and more of the past, and it was in the spring of 1882 that he dictated his autobiography to Ella Fawcett, a girl educated in the Cooper Union stenography classes. "It is very curious," he told James Parton about this time, "but somehow, though I have none of the pains and troubles that old men talk about, I have not the same luxury of life—the same relish in the mere act of living—

· (381) ·

that I had then. Age is like babyhood come back again in a certain way. Even the memories of baby-life come back—the tricks, the pranks, the boyish dreams; and things that I did not remember at forty or fifty years old I recollect vividly now. But a boy of ninety and a boy of nine are very different things, nonetheless. I never felt better in my life except for twinges occasioned by my nitrogen experiment. But still I hear a voice calling to me, as my mother often did when I was a boy, 'Peter, Peter, it is about bed-time,' and I have an old man's presentiment that I shall be taken soon." [2]

Late in March, 1883, he caught cold at a Board of Trade dinner when he was kept waiting too long in an insufficiently heated anteroom. But it seemed trifling, and on Thursday, March 29th, he showed the businessmen of the Twilight Club through Cooper Union. On Saturday morning he came to the Union at eleven and paid a visit to the Inventor's Institute. Zachos, however, found him looking weak, and his daughter, to no avail, urged him not to go for his usual walk. On Sunday a cough developed, which forced him to stay in bed the next day. By Tuesday he had pneumonia and the end was plainly in sight. Whispering farewell in turn to each of those who surrounded his bedside and giving his last instructions about the Union, which haunted even his dying breath, he went peacefully to sleep at three-thirty on Wednesday morning. When the nine-o'clock edition of the papers appeared on the streets, 'one after another the flags stole half way up the mast on the public buildings' and a whole city went into mourning.

And so our chronicle has come full circle to that astonishing tribute of bowed heads and sorrowing hearts that accompanied Peter Cooper to the grave. Each for his own special reasons and some just because they sensed vaguely that one of their great citizens had died, New Yorkers came out to view the coffin and follow the funeral procession as it wound its way down Fourth Avenue and Broadway to the ferry, past the new County Court House, 'against the iniquity of which Peter Cooper raised his virile voice,' past the 'nigger graveyard' of his youth. Even businessmen, pouring out of Wall Street offices, turned for a moment to walk beside the procession to the foot of Broadway, where 'amid the whistling of the ferry-boats and the rattling of the elevated trains . . . a transfer of the hearse and its attendant guards was made, and a final farewell to the city he loved so well shut out the past.' [3] His own generation knew his worth, whether they simply loved him as a man or applauded him for making money or were aware of his contributions as inventor, philanthropist, and defender of democracy. And for a moment they raised him into an idol, a hero of a city without heroes.

But even as the ferry pulled out of the slip oblivion took up its appointed task. Symbolically, only four carriages entered the darkening Greenwood cemetery under the bare and dripping trees of early April. There was no ceremony or service as the coffin was laid in the vault. Then 'the carriages rolled away, the people scattered and only the leafless trees stood about, with the moisture made by the morning rain dropping like tears upon the place beneath where lay all that was most mortal of Peter Cooper, the friend of the working man.'

It is sixty-five years since that day. Generations who knew not Peter Cooper have come and gone, and a New York which he would find barely recognizable has risen in the intervening decades. The last traces of a world in which an aspiring mechanic could make a fortune simply by personal shrewdness, prudence, and hard work are nearly obliterated; the doctrine of a benevolent moral law working through human destiny seems but a mockery of current reality. To the majority of harried New Yorkers, Peter Cooper is but a name on the facade of a large building, and to many who know of him he is merely a quaint old gentleman from a vanished era. Symbol of the early nineteenth century merging with and enriching the post-Civil-War decades, he belongs so evidently to the past that it is hard to imagine that he also belongs to the present.

Yet Peter Cooper does belong to the present. An American

to have been the main stumbling blocks, and there were obvious scholarly defects in the book that she may also have noted. Only fifty copies were printed, and, except for a few given to Hughes, they were stored in the basement of the Hewitt home. Today they are in the possession of Cooper Union, though several have been distributed to other libraries.

Until Hewitt died in 1903 there always remained the promise of a satisfactory biography, but it never materialized. Rossiter W. Raymond, for many years director of the Cooper Union Forum and the author of several chapters of Hughes's book, published in 1901 a brief account of Cooper's life (*Peter Cooper*), and that remained for over fifty years after Cooper's death the only published biography of the founder of Cooper Union. In 1935 Professor Allan Nevins finally made some amends to Peter Cooper for the long neglect from which he had suffered. His biography of Abram S. Hewitt, *Abram S. Hewitt: With Some Account of Peter Cooper*, contains the story of Cooper's life, and is certainly the best thing in print on the subject. But since Professor Nevins devoted most of his time and attention to Hewitt, his account of Cooper is unavoidably inadequate. One further work, which has been invaluable to me, is C. Sumner Spalding's *Peter Cooper: A Critical Bibliography of his Life and Works*, published in 1941.

The primary manuscript sources of Cooper material are two autobiographies, an eleven-page fragment written in Cooper's own hand about 1866, and the lengthy account dictated in 1882. The latter, referred to in the text as the *Reminiscences*, once existed in a typescript seen by both Hughes and Raymond. Though I have not been able to find this typescript, the original stenographic notes turned up recently at Cooper Union, and these I have had newly transcribed. Evidently Peter Cooper or someone else doctored the original notes, since the old typescript—that is, the portions quoted by Hughes—differs considerably from the new one. Where both versions exist I have followed the account that appeared to me best to represent Cooper's intention.

Also basic are the Cooper and Hewitt papers at Cooper Union, the Cooper-Hewitt collection at the Library of Congress, and the Cooper and Hewitt letterbooks, of which the originals are in the New York Historical Society Library and typed and edited selections at Cooper Union. These vast collections, though invaluable, are somewhat disappointing to a biographer in search of personalia. Both the letterbooks and the Library of Congress collection are composed in large part of business letters, orders, receipts, and so forth, pertaining to the Trenton Iron Company and the glue business. The Cooper Union material, though of a less routine nature, has few personal letters. Peter Cooper rarely left home and his children were about him most of the time. When he did write, he found it 'extremely difficult' to speak of 'matters personal to myself.' Even the *Reminiscences* run to anecdote and factual account more than to a record of impressions or of the details of Cooper's inner life.

Personal friends, who might have supplemented the record, are all dead. Fortunately, one of Peter's grandchildren, Edward Ringwood Hewitt, is still alive, and he has been kind enough to give me his memories of his grandfather's last years. For the rest I have had to rely—except for occasional letters picked up in sundry places and mention of Cooper in other manuscript collections—on printed materials: on the files of the New York newspapers during Peter's lifetime, on contemporary magazine articles, on early biographies of Cooper, and on books and articles on various aspects of American life. Zachos' *Opinions of Peter Cooper* contains a report of conversations with Cooper, and Nevins' *Abram S. Hewitt* has excerpts from an apparently lost manuscript account of the Cooper family written by Peter's granddaughter, Eleanor Hewitt. Contemporary accounts are particularly rich for Cooper's later years, and the chief danger for a biographer is to think of Peter Cooper as always having been a kindly old man pottering about New York's familiar streets. The more important of my specific sources, too numerous to list here, have been given due recognition in the footnotes.

Notes

INTRODUCTION

[1] Hughes, Thomas: *Life of Peter Cooper*, London, 1886, p. 8.
[2] He would have admired Peter Cooper more had he been more like Dr. Arnold of Rugby, and he made a notable effort to get his portrait of the old industrialist to resemble the prophetic schoolmaster.
[3] Unidentified clipping in Hewitt papers.
[4] *Frank Leslie's Sunday Magazine*, vol. 13, p. 650.
[5] The *Nation*, vol. 36, p. 312.

Chapter *1*

HUDSON VALLEY DUTCH AND ENGLISH

[1] Many of the important facts in this section have been derived from Miss Grace Wilmarth's invaluable genealogical history of the family of Obadiah Cooper, privately printed in 1946 under the title *Obadiah Cooper (Tailor at Albany 1713-1742) His Wife, Cornelia (Gardenier) Cooper, and their Descendants.*
[2] Hughes: *op. cit.*, p. 12.
[3] As late as 1878 Peter was asked to reimburse one L. C. Keith for having begun and kept a new suit alive. Keith, the husband of a descendant of Peter Cooper's aunt, Mary Cooper Thorne, whose relatives had retrieved a portion of the property, now decided that it was useless to continue, God having apparently decided against his having the land, and that Peter had better turn over the papers to the State of New York. According to his grandson, Peter threw the papers in the fire because, he said, he had done nothing to improve the land and others, who had, should not have this suit hanging over their heads. (Cooper papers: letter, Aug. 24, 1878.)
[4] *Op. cit.*, vol. 16, p. 23.
[5] See for this period Nettels, Curtis P.: *The Roots of American Civilization*, New York, 1939; Smith, James H.: *History of Dutchess County New York*, Syracuse, 1882.
[6] Only a very persistent genealogist would dare follow the fortunes of the Cooper family into the second and third generations. Six of the seven sons of Obadiah of Albany had sons named Obadiah, and it became necessary to distinguish them by middle initials. Other names also keep cropping up persistently in each generation—John, Hannah, Mary, Jacob or James, Cornelia—until the

identity of any one them becomes a difficult matter to establish. When cousins married, the situation could become a hopeless tangle. Obadiah Cooper, Peter's grandfather, had, for example, a son named Obadiah. He also had a daughter Mary, who took as her second husband Obadiah Cooper, the son of John Cooper, the oldest son of Obadiah of Albany.

For those who are interested I here append the record of Peter Cooper's paternal uncles and aunts, as gleaned from the family Bible and Miss Wilmarth's book:

Children of Maria Fonda

(1) Cornelia, married John Wright Clark of Fishkill in 1764.
(2) Pieter, 1746-1748.

Children of Esther Terboss

(1) Obadiah O., merchant of Fishkill. Born 1750, married Dinah Van Wyck (1755-1783) in 1772 and Elizabeth Brush in 1793.
(2) Catherine, married John Dubois and then Casperus Romeyn.
(3) Mary, born 1752, married Benjamin Thorne in 1769 and Obadiah Cooper in 1803.
(4) Jacobus or James, born 1753, died about 1811. Married in 1777 Jane Campbell (the sister of Peter Cooper's mother).
(5) John, Peter's father, born 1755.
(6) Annatje or Hannah, born 1763. Married Stephen Smith.
(7 & 8) Isaac and Abraham, twins, born 1767. Abraham died in 1775.

Both of James Cooper's children and all seven of Obadiah O. Cooper's children died in infancy, the records of their births and deaths, meticulously recorded in the family Bible, supplying a sad commentary on the uncertainty of life in the eighteenth century.

[7] Cooper, Peter: *Reminiscences*, pp. 16-17; Cooper papers. (Since the references to the Cooper papers are of no great use to the reader, I have usually omitted them unless I am quoting a dated letter. Unfootnoted quotations in the text are usually from the Cooper papers.)

[8] *Reminiscences*, pp. 156-157.

[9] *Reminiscences*, p. 18; Bancroft, George: *History of the United States of America*, New York, 1884, vol. 5, pp. 24 ff.

[10] *Reminiscences*, p. 19; Bancroft: *op. cit.*, vol. 5, p. 186.

[11] Roberts, James A.: *New York in the Revolution as Colony and State*, Albany, 1898, p. 135. A Dinah Van Wyck married his brother Obadiah; he therefore may have been serving under a relation.

[12] John Campbell also had a son Thomas, a boy at the time of the Revolution, whom Cooper mentions several times in his *Reminiscences* but whom Hughes for some reason refers to as Samuel. A Thomas Campbell, either the brother or the son, is listed in the New York directory for 1786 as a potter. A Thomas Campbell, presumably the brother, was married in 1765 to Jemima Oakley, the sister of John's wife, and John signed the marriage certificate.

[13] In 1777 John Cooper's brother James married a Jane Campbell. According to Miss Wilmarth she was Margaret Campbell's sister. But since Sarah and John Campbell were only married in November 1761, Jane Campbell, if she was their daughter, could have been only fifteen in 1777 even had she been Margaret's twin.

[14] See Nevins, Allan: *Abram S. Hewitt*, New York, 1935, p. 47.

[15] Cooper papers.

[16] Cooper-Hewitt papers in the Library of Congress: letter, Jan. 12, 1846 (from T. L. and A. T. Smith).

[17] *Annals of the General Society of Mechanics and Tradesmen.* The Society was founded in 1785 and Campbell became a member the following year.

[18] *Reminiscences,* p. 179.

[19] Made of logs fifteen feet high, it had slits through which to observe and shoot at the Indians, since the logs, though placed as close together as possible, were never cut entirely straight.

[20] John's brother, Hugh Campbell, was buried in the Brick Church and was therefore evidently a Presbyterian, but John and his wife were buried in the Moravian Church yard in John Street.

[21] Cooper papers.

[22] Zachos, Prof. J. C.: *The Political and Financial Opinions of Peter Cooper,* New York, 1877, p. 2.

[23] *Every Saturday,* New Series, vol. 2, p. 402.

[24] Wilmarth: *Obadiah Cooper.*

[25] Bryce, Lloyd S.: 'The Example of a Great Life,' *North American Review,* vol. 152, pp. 410-422.

[26] Cooper papers.

[27] For this and the following paragraph see especially Pomerantz, Sidney I.: *New York, An American City 1783-1803,* New York, 1938.

[28] Smith, Arthur: *John Jacob Astor, Landlord of New York,* New York, 1929, p. 48.

[29] The words of one of Cooper's great-granddaughters quoted in Nevins' *Abram S. Hewitt,* p. 48.

[30] Wilmarth: *Obadiah Cooper.*

[31] Cooper papers.

[32] Peter Cooper—and everyone who has written about him—says he was the fifth of nine children. It is curious that he should have made such a mistake. If one omits his stepbrother, he was the fifth child, but then only of eight. If one includes Martha's child he was the sixth of nine.

Chapter 2

A ROLLING STONE

[1] *The Reception of Peter Cooper by the Arcadian Club on his Eighty-fourth Birthday, February 12, 1874.*

[2] Bryce: 'The Example of a Great Life,' *North American Review,* vol. 152, pp. 410 ff.

[3] Zachos: *op. cit.,* p. 1.

[4] As an illustration of how impossible it is to point out the sequence of John Cooper's moves, take the following, the first from Cooper's memories in 1866, the other from what he told Zachos in 1876. In 1866 Cooper wrote that when he was twelve or thirteen, that is about 1802, his father built a brewery in Peekskill and a year later another in Newburgh, where he stayed for two or three years. 'He then again removed to Brooklyn and went back into hats and keeping cows for the sale of milk,' in which occupations Cooper assisted him until he was seven-

teen. In 1876 Cooper says that after the brewery episode in Peekskill his father moved to Catskill, where he made bricks and hats, and that he then moved to Brooklyn. The Newburgh episode here follows the Brooklyn one, and it was at brewing in Newburgh that Cooper was kept employed until he was seventeen.

[5] Mrs. Van Cortlandt had been Joanna Livingstone. The Van Cortlandts had retired to their estate in 1795, where she died in 1808, her husband in 1814.

[6] Hughes: *op. cit.*, p. 40. If they did not catch them the first time, the process had to be repeated.

[7] *Frank Leslie's Popular Monthly*, vol. 16, p. 23.

[8] Cooper papers.

[9] Hughes: *op. cit.*, p. 45.

[10] Hughes: *op. cit.*, p. 47.

[11] Bryce in the *North American Review*, vol. 152, pp. 410 ff.

[12] *Reminiscences*, p. 79.

[13] New York *Herald*, Feb. 12, 1879.

[14] *Reminiscences*, p. 105.

[15] *Reminiscences*, pp. 160, 162.

[16] *Reminiscences*, pp. 56-57.

[17] For example, he tells of one of his father's apprentices who ran through a large fortune after coming of age and was in danger of being sold at public auction to anyone who would pay the debt. The man walked sixty miles to get the advice of John Cooper, who suggested that he apply to a rich uncle for relief. He took the advice and was saved. Just why he didn't remember the rich uncle himself and save himself a long hike is somewhat of a mystery. (*Reminiscences*, p. 161.)

Another favorite of Cooper's was the story of the bankrupt who took advantage of the new bankruptcy act and, going to the country and turning religious, began to pry into his neighbors' morals. When on one occasion he taxed a holy but slightly cynical patriarch with his sins the latter retorted that he was well aware how strict an account his Heavenly Father kept of his sins. If the bad outnumbered the good, 'I suppose I will have to take the benefit of the act.'

[18] *The Science of religion, as explained by Peter Cooper to the bishop* [1874].

[19] *Reminiscences*, p. 6.

[20] It is possible that modern psychiatry might find some evidence of Cooper's ambivalent attitude toward religion in the excessive number of accidents that befell him. Revolting against a harsh God, he felt guilty, and attempted subconsciously to punish himself. The trouble with such a theory is that it is out of key with everything else we know about Peter Cooper, who was anything but a guilt-haunted person.

[21] *Reminiscences*, p. 80.

[22] From an eleven-page fragment of autobiography, written in 1866.

[23] Lester, Charles Edward: *Life and Character of Peter Cooper*, New York, 1883, p. 11.

[24] 1866 autobiography.

[25] Hughes: *op. cit.*, p. 50.

[26] One day in 1868 when his associates got into a heated argument over whether a method of producing steel blooms directly from phosphorized ore really produced steel, he broke in impatiently: "Very well, Gentlemen . . . what matter whether it be steel or not. We see that it does what steel does; the rest is of no moment at all, it seems to me." (*Mining Record*, vol. 13, p. 260.)

[27] He also, according to the account he gave his grandson, Edward Ringwood Hewitt, bought a big black cigar, which made him deathly ill.

Chapter 3

COACHMAKER'S APPRENTICE

[1] Hughes: *op. cit.*, p. 51.

[2] The turn that Broadway takes at 10th Street and the failure of 11th Street to run through from what is now Fourth Avenue to Broadway were due to the protests of old Hendrik Brevoort, who refused to let his property be invaded.

[3] Though Burr got his company chartered in 1799 as a water company, it was an open secret that he was really interested in starting a bank and secured that privilege in his charter.

[4] Valentine, D. T.: *Manual of the Corporation of the City of New York* for 1857, p. 422.

[5] Wilson, James Grant (editor): *The Memorial History of the City of New York*, New York, 1893, vol. 3, p. 303.

[6] Cooper, Margaret Adelia: *Some Old Letters and Bits of History*, New York, 1901, p. 12.

[7] Brown, Henry Collins: *Valentine's Manual of Old New York*, 1924, p. 225.

[8] Valentine: *Manual* for 1868, p. 828.

[9] Myers, Gustavus: *The History of Tammany Hall*, New York, 1917 [1901], pp. 23-24.

[10] According to several sources, Peter's original idea when he came to New York was to go into business for himself as a brewer, but he was unable to raise the capital to build the superior brewery that he had in mind. See Laura C. Holloway: *Famous American Fortunes*, Philadelphia, 1885; *Annual Reports of the Chamber of Commerce*, vol. 26, p. 2. The trouble with this story, besides Cooper's failure ever to mention it, is that Peter Cooper had far too strong views about borrowing money to start out in life in this way. He apparently hated brewing anyway.

[11] According to Valentine's *Manual* for 1857, Ross at Broadway and Fair Street was a more important firm.

[12] See Houghton, George W. W.: *The Coaches of Colonial New York*, New York, 1890.

[13] Hughes: *op. cit.*, p. 60.

[14] *Harper's Weekly*, in an article on Cooper in 1874, insisted that he did go into the coach business in 1815 and that one could see his sign, 'Peter Cooper, Coach and Wagon Maker,' in one of the cheaper streets. Later this shop supposedly went to the sheriff. All this is pure fiction, the source of which is a mystery. (*Harper's Weekly*, vol. 18, p. 173.)

[15] Cooper papers: undated letter.

[16] Emmet came to America after the failure of his famous brother Robert's uprising in 1803. In 1812 he was made attorney-general of New York.

[17] Hughes: *op. cit.*, p. 56.

[18] As Cooper's biographers tell this story, there is something radically wrong with it. Cooper is supposed to have been present at the dinner, which reputedly

took place when he was a leading citizen. But Fulton died when Peter was still an unknown mechanic in Hempstead in 1815. Moreover, the *Chancellor Livingston*, the boat whose launching the dinner was celebrating, was planned but not built during Fulton's lifetime.

Chapter 4

A TASTE OF INDEPENDENCE

[1] Peter refers to this visit any number of times, but never mentions the name of his brother. In favor of its being James is the fact that he was the only full brother of Peter who was old enough to have established himself independently. Nevertheless, my own feeling is that the brother was Thomas. Though only eighteen at the time, Thomas was living in or near New York in 1813 and did live in Hempstead later in life. He married a Hempstead girl, Mary Lester, in 1818. James spent most of his life in or near Baltimore.

[2] There was a small steam ferry—just one—that ran to Brooklyn. One could also hire handsomely painted rowboats with fancy names.

[3] See Margaret Cooper: *Some Old Letters.*

[4] Workers on the state road in 1812 received 46¢ a day. The usual laborer's wage after 1820 was 75¢ to $1.25 a day.

[5] Cooper papers. The previous legal history of the patent is amusing and instructive. Mollenoux took out his patent in April, 1811, and, reserving the New York rights for himself, sold the New England and Maine rights to Seth Hart. He found, however, that two Danbury men, Eleazer Sprague and Hiram Wildman, were competing with him on a patent taken out by Sprague on May 9, 1810. Fortunately for Mollenoux his patent was better, and in August, 1811, he induced Sprague and Wildman to stop making and selling their machine and to make and sell Mollenoux' for one-third of the profits in both New York and New England. The eight old machines possessed by Sprague and Wildman might, however, be sold so long as Mollenoux and Hart received two-thirds of the profits. Until December, 1811, Sprague was privileged to sell his machines for full profit outside New York, New England, and Maine. The profits for all new inventions were to be shared between the four; if there were improvements the two-thirds rule applied.

[6] John L. Cadwalader, in asking Hamilton Fish to give Hughes some of his memories of Cooper, says that Hughes was short on facts for Cooper's life between the ages of twenty-one and twenty-five. There is, however, in Cooper's papers and elsewhere a good deal of information that was evidently not available to Hughes or subsequent writers. (Hamilton Fish papers in the Library of Congress: letter, Oct. 27, 1885.)

[7] Nevins: *Abram S. Hewitt*, p. 57.

[8] *Reminiscences*, p. 27.

[9] See Flick, Alexander C.: *History of the State of New York*, New York, 1937, vol. 5, p. 17.

[10] *Letter from Peter Cooper to Horatio Seymour*, New York, Aug. 13, 1868.

[11] 1866 autobiography. Peter usually gives the amount as $500, 'as near as I remember.' In one version it is $600 (*Reminiscences*, p. 113).

[12] Hughes: *op. cit.*, p. 61; *Reminiscences*, p. 114; clipping, Jan. 22, 1863, in Cooper papers.

[13] 1866 autobiography.

[14] 1866 autobiography.

[15] See Cooper papers: letters, Oct. 3 & Nov. 30, 1813.

[16] 1866 autobiography.

[17] Cooper papers: letters, April 2 & June 14, 1814.

[18] Cooper papers: letters, March 16, June 14, & Aug. 6, 1814.

[19] Cooper papers: letter, May 4, 1815; 1866 autobiography.

[20] *Register of Marriages*, St. George's Episcopal Church.

[21] Cooper papers: letter, Jan. 7, 1814.

[22] His direct ancestors were Robert, married Blanche [?] in 1647; David, born 1648, married Anne Pawlett in 1679; Richard, 1692-1762, married Phoebe [?]; and Sylvanus, died 1773, married Sarah Cromwell on March 19, 1750. Genealogy of the Bedell family in the Queens Borough Public Library.

[23] Her parents were Benjamin Raynor and Mary Lester, the daughter of a British officer.

[24] Sarah's brothers and sisters, with several of whom Peter later had relations of one sort or another, were Manzies Raynor, 1803-1886; Mary, married Benjamin Clowes in 1804; Stephen, died 1847, married Elizabeth Baker; Phoebe, born 1786, married James Hall; Margaret, married Increase Baker in 1812; Benjamin, born 1789, married another Sarah Bedell; Silvanus, married Eliza Mosher; and Rebecca, born 1796, married Peter's brother William in 1818.

[25] *Peter Cooper: A Tribute in Commemoration of the Hundredth Anniversary of his Birth*, 1891.

[26] *Reminiscences*, p. 133.

[27] *Reminiscences*, p. 50. Once in the 'seventies, when a lecturer talked on storms at Cooper Union, Peter jumped up in the audience and told of the waterspouts. (Raymond, Rossiter W.: *Peter Cooper*, Boston, 1901, p. 93.)

[28] Hughes: *op. cit.*, p. 62.

[29] Copy of patent; Hughes: *op. cit.*, p. 63; New York *Herald*, Feb. 21, 1879.

[30] Cooper papers: letter, March 19, 1815. There are a number of letters from this girl to Sarah in Newburgh from 1813 to 1815. They contain, besides much gossip, a log and romantic narrative of a trip through the New Jersey and Pennsylvania mountains (which remainded her of Ann Radcliffe's description of the Pyrenees) to Chester and Bethlehem. They also contain comments on the war and a description of the fireworks celebrating the peace in February, 1815. She knew Peter and mentions several times having seen him. John Cooper still owned property in Brooklyn, the rent of which Thomas Cooper was trying to collect. On one occasion in 1813 Peter expressed to Sarah's friend disapproval of his mother's intended visit to Brooklyn until those rents were paid.

[31] Cooper papers: letter, June 18, 1815.

[32] Hughes: *op. cit.*, p. 63.

[33] New York *Herald*, Feb. 21, 1879.

[34] Cooper papers: letter, Feb. 26, 1883.

Chapter 5

GROCER AND INVENTOR

[1] Flick: *History of the State of New York,* vol. 5, p. 349.
[2] Cooper papers: letters, April 4, 1815, April 21 & Sept. 27, 1816, March 26 & April 7, 1817.
[3] Two other Bedells, Stephen and Silvanus—the names of two of Benjamin's brothers—are also listed as grocers in the directory for 1815-16, one as Benjamin's partner at 61 Elizabeth Street. In 1826 Peter bought groceries from Silvanus Bedell.
[4] *Longworth's American Almanac, New York Register and City Directory,* 1818-1819. It is possible, as has been suggested, that there was an earlier store farther downtown on the Bowery at Rivington Street.
[5] The directory lists the firm at the old address for three years, though Peter in one place says he moved in the course of the second year.
[6] This is the best solution I can suggest of a tangled little puzzle. Peter's repeated statement that he went into business for himself cannot be doubted. But the directory of 1821, the only one to list Peter Cooper separately at the corner of Stuyvesant Street and the Bowery, also lists the firm of Bedell and Cooper and Benjamin Bedell as an individual at the same address. The 1822 and subsequent directories, through 1828, list only Benjamin Bedell at the address and do not list Peter at all.

By calling the new address 8th Street and Fourth Avenue, Nevins makes it sound as if Peter moved farther than he did. Stuyvesant Street in those days ran to Fourth Avenue, then called the Bowery, up to 14th Street. 8th Street received its name only in 1828.
[7] Stokes, I. N. Phelps: *The Iconography of Manhattan Island,* New York, 1926, vol. 5, Feb. 19, 1821. See also Nevins, Allan: *Hamilton Fish,* New York, 1936; Harlow, Alvin F.: *Old Bowery Days,* New York, 1931; Martyn, Carlos: *William E. Dodge,* New York, 1890; Haswell, Charles H.: *Reminiscences of an Octogenarian of the City of New York,* New York, 1896.
[8] Hamilton Fish papers in the Library of Congress: letters, June 18, 1884 & Dec. 19, 1885.
[9] Cooper papers.
[10] *Reminiscences,* p. 63.
[11] *Reminiscences,* p. 154.
[12] *Index of Conveyances Recorded in the Office of the Register of the City and County of New York,* vol. 140, p. 357.
[13] Miss Eleanor C. Hewitt's ms. family history, quoted in Nevins' *Abram S. Hewitt,* p. 58.
[14] *Reminiscences,* p. 137.
[15] *Reminiscences,* pp. 65-70; Cooper papers; Hughes: *op. cit.,* p. 68; New York *Herald,* Feb. 21, 1879.
[16] *Minutes of the Common Council of the City of New York, 1784-1813,* New York, 1917 (June 26, 1820). In several accounts Peter erroneously gives the date for this experiment as 1823.

[17] New York *Herald*, Feb. 21, 1879; *Reminiscences*, p. 69.

[18] Hughes: *op. cit.*, p. 69.

[19] In one place he calls the loss two-fifths (see Hughes: *op. cit.*, p. 90). Zachos quotes him as saying the gain was as five to eight (*op. cit.*, p. 16).

[20] *Railroad Gazette*, vol. 15, April 13, 1883, 'Peter Cooper and the First Locomotive,' reprint of address made to Master Mechanics' Association, May 12, 1875.

[21] Peter never learned to make his engine durable or tight. His grandson later tried vainly to get him to see the value of piston rings.

[22] Zachos: *op. cit.*, p. 16.

[23] Vreeland may also have needed the money. He owed back taxes in 1822 on a lot in the Eighth Ward (New York *Evening Post*, May 24, 1822).

[24] 1866 autobiography. Professor Nevins gives the date as 1827. But by 1827 Peter was already a highly successful businessman.

[25] Zachos: *op. cit.*, p. 4.

Chapter 6

A SMALL PRIVATE BUSINESS

[1] This land belonged to Effingham Schieffelin, alderman in 1828 of what was then the Twelfth Ward. In 1825 Peter rented some of this land for seventy-five dollars a year; in 1827 he added another of Schieffelin's meadow lots to the property he leased.

[2] In what is now Madison Square.

[3] Cooper papers.

[4] It is possible, of course, that Peter did not pay cash and merely liked to remember the key transaction of his life in that way. Despite his feeling about debts, he was not averse to contracting ordinary business obligations. In 1826, for example, he handed Captain William Whitlock sixty shares of fire insurance stock as collateral for the payment of a note for $1355.

[5] *Minutes of the Common Council*, October 29, 1821.

[6] Unlike the other streets named, Madison Avenue was not part of the 1807 plan.

[7] *Reminiscences*, p. 181. Cooper says in another place that he lived where Dr. Spring's Brick Church was later built. This was, however, just north of the Thompson farm at 37th Street and Fifth Avenue.

[8] Smith: *John Jacob Astor*, p. 266.

[9] *Index of Conveyances*, book 202, p. 287; book 290; book 338, p. 355; book 418, p. 349; book 525, p. 520. Cooper says erroneously that he originally purchased four lots and then later five more. The southernmost of the lots he sold to his brother William in 1841, but repurchased it in 1849.

[10] Renamed Fourth Avenue from 4th to 14th Streets about 1850, when the Bowery's reputation had become unsavory.

[11] Hewitt letterbooks, April 7, 1897.

[12] Haswell: *Reminiscences*, p. 111; *cf.* also Jenkins, Stephen: *The Old Boston Post Road*, New York, 1913, p. 99; White, Bouck: *The Book of Daniel Drew*, New York, 1938, p. 67.

[13] His accountbooks show that in the year he bought the land he paid out over $350 for wood, clay, bricks, planks, shingles, and stone.

[14] *Reminiscences*, pp. 53, 181; *Dictionary of American Biography*.

[15] Jenkins: *The Old Boston Post Road*, pp. 106-107; White: *The Book of Daniel Drew*, p. 61.

[16] Stokes: *Iconography*, vol. 5, Dec. 27, 1831.

[17] Some of the statements about his children in the *Reminiscences* do not square with the facts found among Cooper's papers. Cooper says in the *Reminiscences* that Peter William was three when he died, but his dates are given as December 20, 1822, to March 16, 1824. Sarah Amanda's operation was supposed to have taken place on 28th Street, but she died two years before Cooper bought that property. Benjamin Bedell, Cooper's second child, is referred to as Edward Augustus in the *Reminiscences*.

[18] Hughes: *op. cit.*, pp. 74-76; *Journal of Commerce*, Jan. 28, 1856. Hughes for some reason places Cooper's offer in 1861, during the Civil War.

[19] Hughes: *op. cit.*, pp. 77-79.

[20] Edward R. Hewitt writes: 'The glue factory accounts were always kept in two divisions, one the operating expenses at the factory, and the other the sales and collections at the New York office. The New York office never knew what was going on at the factory except what the factory manager chose to tell them.' At the end of the year the factory manager took the 'office accounts and the factory accounts to his room' and made up the balance sheets. 'This usually took him about a week to do and no one knew what had been made for the year until he was through.'

[21] Stiles, Henry R.: *The Civil, Political, Professional and Ecclesiastical History . . . of Brooklyn, N. Y.*, New York, 1884, vol. 2, p. 758.

[22] When the factory was moved to Bushwick its earnings jumped, according to Edward Hewitt, to over $100,000 a year, a figure that tripled in the succeeding forty years.

[23] Judson, Isabella Field: *Cyrus W. Field*, New York, 1896, p. 42.

[24] Cooper papers: speech to students of Cooper Union in 1871.

[25] *History of the Great American Fortunes*, Chicago, 1908-10.

[26] New York *Evening Post*, April 4, 1883; Clipping from the *National View* in the Cooper papers.

[27] Cooper-Hewitt papers in the Library of Congress: letters, Oct. 16, 1852, & July 14, 1853.

[28] Lester: *Life and Character of Peter Cooper*, p. 19.

[29] New York *Herald*, April 7, 1883.

[30] *Reminiscences*, p. 46.

[31] Cooper-Hewitt papers in the Library of Congress: letter, Feb. 17, 1847 (from Edward Cooper).

[32] *An Address to the graduates and students assembled in the hall of Cooper Union, on the occasion of the Commencement exercises, May 31, 1877.*

[33] Martyn: *William E. Dodge*, p. 78. In his *Reminiscences* Peter tells a characteristic story from his own knowledge of the rise from rags to riches. One day, passing up Chesapeake Bay on a steamboat, he was accosted by a stranger who identified himself as a boy named Harris whom Cooper had played with in Newburgh. He was now—this was in the 'thirties—the possessor of one of Baltimore's handsomest stores. He had, he told Peter, come to Baltimore with only seventy-five cents and a jackknife. 'Not seeing any better opportunity, he deter-

mined to go into the woods and with his jackknife he cut such limbs and little trees as would make nice canes and finished them up as well as he could and took them under his arm and went from house to house selling canes.' He thus accumulated a small sum and hired a shop in which he made canes, and this was gradually expanded into the great store of today. (*Reminiscences*, pp. 204-205.)

[34] The sources of the material on economic history are chiefly Clark: *History of Manufactures*, vol. 1; and Hacker, Louis M.: *The Triumph of American Capitalism*, New York, 1940.

[35] *Reminiscences*, p. 150.

[36] *Reminiscences*, p. 151; Clark, Victor S.: *History of Manufactures in the United States*, New York, 1929, vol. 1. p. 379. See also Dewey, Davis Rich: *Financial History of the United States*, London, 1922.

[37] *Reminiscences*, p. 123.

[38] One great capitalist of a later era, Andrew Carnegie, adopted the same principle. Hating speculative trading and Wall Street promoters, he was able to invest money in hard times when others did not have it.

[39] Fox, Dixon Ryan: *The Decline of Aristocracy in the Politics of New York*, New York, 1919, p. 303.

[40] Stokes: *Iconography*, vol. 5, May 10, 1825.

[41] Hardie, James: *The Description of the City of New York*, New York, 1827.

[42] See Valentine's *Manual of Old New York* for 1825; Stokes: *Iconography*, vol. 5; Hardie: *The Description of New York*; Wilson: *The Memorial History of New York*, vol. 3; and Lossing, Benson J.: *History of New York City*, New York, [1884].

[43] Parton, James: *Captains of Industry*, Boston, 1888, p. 318.

[44] Carter, Susan N.: 'Recollections of Peter Cooper,' *Century Illustrated Monthly Magazine*, vol. 27 (vol. 5, new series), p. 219.

[45] Powell, Rufus W.: *Glue Statistics*, Brooklyn, 1893, pp. 14-15.

[46] See United States Department of Agriculture: *Department Bulletin No. 1500*, June, 1929, 'The Gluing of Wood,' p. 5; United States Tariff Commission: 'Glues, Gelatins & Related Products,' Report No. 135, Second Series, p. 13.

[47] According to his grandson, Peter was the first to use sulphuric acid to neutralize the residual lime.

[48] Hewitt papers: letter, Dec. 13, 1869.

Chapter 7

THE TOM THUMB

[1] *Reminiscences*, p. 91.

[2] Latrobe, John H. B.: *The Baltimore and Ohio Railroad; Personal Recollections*, a lecture delivered before the Maryland Institute, March 23, 1868, Baltimore, p. 2. Latrobe's account is invaluable, and has been used extensively in what follows. Hungerford, Edward: *The Story of the Baltimore & Ohio Railroad, 1827-1927*, New York, 1928; and W. S. Wright: 'The Romance of American Railroads,' in *Railroad Man's Magazine*, vols. 18 & 19 (1912), are also valuable.

[3] One of Cooper's associates, Columbus O'Donnell, told Peter that the name

Canton was given the property by his father, the former owner, in honor of his Chinese bride, who had received her weight in gold as a marriage dower.

[4] Cooper, followed by his biographers, says erroneously that the Canton Company was not formed until later, when Peter sold his holdings.

[5] Hughes: *op. cit.*, p. 95.

[6] Clippings in Cooper papers.

[7] New York *Evening Post*, April 22 & July 22, 1829.

[8] He refers to it sometimes as a shop and occasionally as a rolling mill. He may, however, have had a machine shop besides the foundry, as he certainly did have a carpenter shop, built for him in 1831 at a cost of $1296.

[9] The aged statesman sailed June 28, 1830, but remained in Russia less than a month.

[10] This Jerome was the son of Napoleon's brother, Jerome, King of Westphalia, who in 1803 had married Elizabeth Patterson, daughter of the Baltimore merchant William Patterson, whom Peter quoted as having such high hopes for the B. & O. Napoleon had made his brother dissolve the marriage and his wife had returned to Baltimore with her son, Jerome. Though on good terms with his father, the young man spent most of his life in Baltimore. He also had a son, Jerome, born in 1832.

[11] New York *Herald*, April 28, 1878.

[12] *Reminiscences*, pp. 30-31.

[13] New York *Herald*, Feb. 12, 1879.

[14] The rails were of wood faced with iron spiked to the wood. If a spike came loose one of the flat rail strips would come loose and curl up like a snake's head, offering great danger to passing trains.

[15] 'A horse was placed in a car, and made to walk on an endless apron or belt, and to communicate motion to the wheels. . . . The machine worked, after a fashion, well enough; but on one occasion, when drawing a car filled with editors and representatives of the press, it ran into a cow, and the passengers being tilted out and rolled down an embankment, were naturally unanimous in condemning the contrivance. . . . Following the horse-power car came the "meteor." This was a sailing vehicle, the invention of Mr. Evan Thomas. . . . It required a good gale to drive it, and would only ride when the wind was what sailors call abaft, or on the quarter. Head winds were fatal to it, and Mr. Thomas was afraid to trust a strong side wind lest the meteor might upset. So it rarely made its appearance unless a nor'wester was blowing, when it would be dragged out to the farther end of the Mount Clare embankment, and come back, literally, with flying colors.' Brown, William H.: *The History of the First Locomotives in America*, New York, 1871, pp. 123-4.

[16] In one place Peter says that the horsecars didn't pay and the road stopped. The horsecar excursions paid very well indeed, and the road was never actually abandoned.

[17] *Railroad Gazette*, vol. 15, p. 225, 'Peter Cooper and the First Locomotive.'

[18] John H. B. Latrobe, Raymond, and Nevins all use the 1829 date.

[19] Cooper's memory is not always trustworthy about such matters. He says that his problem was to get his engine around Point of Rocks on the Potomac, a place not reached by the railroad for some years.

[20] According to Edward Hewitt, the boiler of the *Tom Thumb* later figured in a patent suit, and Peter was admitted to be the inventor of the vertical boiler.

[21] Latrobe: *The Baltimore and Ohio Railroad*, p. 7.

[22] *Ibid.*

[23] *Railroad Gazette,* vol. 15, p. 225.

[24] Hughes: *op. cit.,* p. 98. The *Reminiscences* place the episode of the pipes before the trouble about the wheels. My selection of the order given in Cooper's account in the *Railroad Gazette* is purely arbitrary.

[25] Latrobe: *The Baltimore and Ohio Railroad,* p. 7.

[26] *Railroad Gazette,* vol. 15, p. 225.

[27] Hughes: *op. cit.,* p. 98.

[28] The figures were as follows: 1st mile in 6 minutes and 50 seconds; 2/5; 3/6; 4/4:30; 5/5:25; 6/6; 7/5:30; 8/6; 9/5:45; 10/7; 11/7:30; 12/7:30; and 13/6:30, giving a total of 1 hour and 19½ minutes for the 13 miles.

[29] *Niles Weekly Register,* Sept. 4, 1830, p. 17.

[30] Latrobe: *op. cit.,* pp. 7-8.

[31] Hughes: *op. cit.,* p. 102.

[32] Hughes: *op. cit.,* p. 108, quoting a contemporary source.

[33] Hughes: *op. cit.,* p. 106; Cooper papers: draft of a lecture by Peter Cooper before the Canton Institute, Feb. 12, 1880.

[34] Nevins: *Abram S. Hewitt,* p. 200.

[35] This shop passed through a succession of hands. Edwin A. Abbott had it from 1835 to 1839, Charles W. Bentley in 1839 and 1840, two men named Benit and Rose in 1841, Harrison, the agent of the Canton Company, in 1842—and usually the rent was behind. Cooper was constantly asking various people—Henry Fitz, Horace Abbott, and his brother James, who lived in Baltimore—to collect it for him. Then in 1843 Fitz accused Harrison of profiteering at Peter's expense. Harrison, whom Peter had given permission to rent out the shop, had leased it to two young men at a very low rental so he could charge them for the use of the machinery. This machinery had been mortgaged to the Canton Company, and Harrison bought it in for $875, though Fitz had secured a lessee of the shop who would buy the machinery from Cooper for $850. To top it all, Harrison refused to pay the back rent as he had agreed, and tried vainly to make the new lessees pay it.

[36] Fitz was to receive $5000 only if his Canton deal went through; though the deed did not go through, he had received Binney and Monroe's bond for $5000, which he had realized on with some loss, fifteen shares of Canton stock worth $44, and ten shares worth $54. True, Fitz had made efforts to befriend Cooper, and Cooper was grateful; but while Fitz was doing Peter's Boston business Peter was in Baltimore and Washington attending to Fitz's.

[37] Cooper papers: letter, April 29, 1848.

[38] Cooper papers: letter, June 22, 1848.

Chapter 8

THE EDUCATION OF PETER COOPER

[1] *The Reception of Peter Cooper by the Arcadian Club.*

[2] *Bulletin of the American Geographical Society,* vol. 15, p. 349, 'In Memoriam, Peter Cooper.'

[3] In most states the last restrictions on the suffrage had been wiped away in

the 'twenties. In New York, for example, the issue was decided in 1822, when, despite the protests of conservatives like Chancellor Kent, most property qualifications for voting were dropped.

[4] *Reminiscences*, p. 54.

[5] See Schlesinger, Arthur M., Jr.: *The Age of Jackson*, Boston, 1945.

[6] A certain John March thought Cooper was so fervently a Van Burenite as to be willing to assail March's character 'for certain expressions I in a moment of excitement uttered to you' about Van Buren. (Cooper papers: letter, Jan. 23, 1841.)

[7] *Reminiscences*, p. 153.

[8] The Locofoco, or Equal Rights, party were the radical democrats in New York. They got their name from being forced on one occasion, when their opponents turned off the gas, to use the new locofoco matches to illuminate their meeting hall.

[9] See Curti, Merle: *The Social Ideas of American Educators*, New York, 1935, p. 15.

[10] See Gabriel, Ralph Henry: *The Course of American Democratic Thought*, New York, 1940.

[11] See Cooper's letter to Cornelius M. Lawrence in 1846, asking the latter to restore Curtis to the Customs. (Ms. in the New York Public Library: letter, March 17, 1846.)

[12] Sedgwick, Catherine Maria: *Memoir of Joseph Curtis*, New York, 1858, p. 182.

[13] *Reminiscences*, p. 63.

[14] *Reminiscences*, pp. 58-62.

[15] There was one romantic story about Ann Curtis' work on Blackwell's Island that Cooper particularly loved to tell. Among the inmates was a beautiful and unfortunate lady who had eloped with a young man and been brought to New York. When the young man deserted her, she had made the mistake of asking the wrong policeman for lodgings and had ended up in a house of ill fame, which was raided almost immediately on her arrival. Miss Curtis brought her to the Women's Home and then found a place for her in Massachusetts where she could learn to braid straw for ladies' hats. At the end of two or three years she had the good fortune to be discovered by a wealthy uncle, who dressed her up in the fashion of the day and took her to Saratoga. There her beauty won the hand of a rich New Yorker. She had the good sense to confess her past to him after he was too far gone in love to be cooled off by the information, and ended by living in great style in New York. Years later she drove up to see her benefactors, who were much gratified at what they had achieved.

[16] See Chadwick, John White: *William Ellery Channing*, Boston, 1903.

[17] Dewey, Mary E.: *Autobiography and Letters of Orville Dewey*, Boston, 1884, p. 89; New York *Herald*, May 14, 1839. Pews sold for from $300 to $1200 in the body of the church, and for as low as $125 in the gallery.

[18] *National Journal*, March 26, 1881, report of a speech of Cooper's delivered at the Forsyth Street Methodist Church.

Chapter 9

CITIZEN OF NEW YORK

[1] New York *World*, Feb. 11, 1879.

[2] Hardie: *Description of the City of New York*, p. 154.

[3] *Minutes of the Common Council*, March 3, 1831; New York *Evening Post*, March 4, 1831. He may have agreed with the committee that the people, not the Common Council, should decide this issue.

[4] *A Brief Investigation of the Causes which created the late Controversy on the Election of Mayor.* By a Democratic Member of the Common Council, p. 19; Myers: *The History of Tammany Hall*, p. 81.

[5] New York *World*, Feb. 11, 1879.

[6] *Reminiscences*, p. 104; *Minutes of the Common Council*, 1830.

[7] New York *World*, Feb. 11, 1879.

[8] Wilson: *Memorial History of New York*, vol. 3, p. 396.

[9] *Minutes of the Common Council*, loc. cit.

[10] Cooper papers: oath before Effingham Schieffelin, alderman of the Twelfth Ward.

[11] Hughes: *op. cit.*, p. 112.

[12] New York City Fire and Water Committee: *Report of the Committee relative to introducing into the City of New York a supply of pure and wholesome water*, p. 6.

[13] Peter's biographers have given the impression that he was the chairman of this commission and thus the leading spirit in the whole Croton project.

[14] King, Charles: *A Memoir of the Construction, Cost and Capacity of the Croton Aqueduct*, New York, 1843, is the source of much of this discussion.

[15] *Proceedings, the Board of Aldermen of the City of New York*, May 18, 1840.

[16] 'Document 8 of the Board of Aldermen,' in *Documents of the Board of Aldermen of the City of New York*, vol. 7, p. 69.

[17] *Proceedings of the Board of Aldermen*, July 27 & Nov. 16, 1840; 'Document 59,' in *Documents of the Board of Aldermen*, vol. 7, p. 701.

[18] 'Document 83,' *Documents of the Board of Aldermen*, vol. 7, p. 821.

[19] Hughes: *op. cit.*, p. 116.

[20] 'Document 83,' *Documents of the Board of Aldermen*, vol. 7, p. 821.

[21] Cooper papers: letters, May 16, May 18, & June 2, 1841.

[22] *Ibid.*, July 25, 1842.

[23] Nevins, Allan (editor): *The Diary of Philip Hone, 1828-1851*, New York, 1927, vol. 1, p. 609.

[24] *Reminiscences*, pp. 3-4.

[25] New York *Herald*, Dec. 17, 1840.

[26] 'Document 28,' *Documents of the Board of Aldermen*, vol. 7, p. 375.

[27] New York *Herald*, Feb. 16, 1841.

[28] At first the city refused, as it so often did, to honor the Legislature's decision, and passed its own ordinance setting up three separate forces: the watch, the municipal police, and the police proper, each to be appointed by a different person. Mayor Harper appointed the first two hundred, called 'Harper's Police,' in 1844, but then the ordinance was repealed.

[29] *Petition of Peter Cooper in Relation to the Prevention and Extinguishing of Fire*, 1854.

[30] New York *World*, Feb. 11, 1879.

[31] New York *Evening Post*, April 8, 11, 12, & 16, 1840. New York *Herald*, April 14, 1840.

[32] The chief sources used in this section are the *Minutes of the Public School Society* in the New York Historical Society library; Bourne, William Oland: *History of the Public School Society of the City of New York*, New York, 1873; Brann, Rev. Henry A.: *Most Reverend John Hughes, First Archbishop of New York*, New York, 1892; Bancroft, Frederic: *The Life of William H. Seward*, 1900.

[33] Dodge, David Stuart: *Memorials of William E. Dodge*, New York, 1887, p. 57.

[34] Catholic historians could be as self-righteous as Protestant ones. Bishop Hughes's biographer says that the bishop was unpopular only with the 'dishonest, the untruthful, and the bigoted.' Hughes's later praise of Cooper Union shows that he did not consider Cooper, at least, one of the bigoted.

[35] Of the Catholic position on the Bible the Society finally cried in desperation: 'They charge us with teaching infidelity and a religion adverse to Christianity, and yet condemn us for using, unless accompanied by their own explanation, that which is the foundation of the Christian religion.'

[36] New York *Herald*, Sept. 22, 1840.

[37] Unless the city authorities, who were under the thumb of the Public School Society, applied for such control.

[38] New York *Herald*, March 17 & 23, 1842.

[39] Cooper papers: letter, April 4, 1842 (Cooper to Varian).

[40] Judd, Orrin: *Maclay Memorial Sketching the Lineage and Obsequies of Hon. William B. Maclay*, p. 54.

[41] Brann: *John Hughes*, p. 85.

[42] In 1851 the Public School Society paid grammar school principals $1000 a year, first assistants $750, second $450, third $250, and fourth $200. Primary school principals were paid $350 a year, second assistants $125.

Chapter 10

A MAN'S CASTLE

[1] Eleanor Hewitt in Nevins' *Abram S. Hewitt*, p. 146.

[2] *Ibid*, p. 144.

[3] *Industrial News*, vol. 4, p. 57.

[4] Cooper papers: letter, Jan. 1, 1854 (Cooper to Schofield).

[5] Edward Hewitt tells a charming story of his great-uncle, who in later life was a great yachtsman. Debarred at eighty from racing in the Narragansett race because he had promised his wife that he wouldn't—there is also a suggestion that he broke the regulations by having too long a boom—he was nevertheless on hand for the start of the race. Turning to his captain, he told him that he was forbidden to race, but why didn't they just run up to Newport and watch the boats come in?

[6] Cooper papers: letter, Feb. 27, 1841.

[7] New York *Evening Post*, May 2, 1828.

[8] Nevins: *Abram S. Hewitt*, p. 76.

[9] Ms. 'Journal of a Pedestrian Tour to the White Mountains.'

[10] Charles and John Hewitt papers: letter, Sept. 26, 1859.

[11] New York *Herald*, April 19, 1882.

[12] *Reminiscences*, p. 181.

[13] Lossing: *History of New York City*, p. 402.

[14] Harlow, Alvin F.: *The Road of the Century; The Story of the New York Central*, New York, 1947, p. 126. See also Stokes: *Iconography*, and Collins, F. A.: *The Romance of Park Avenue*, New York, 1930.

[15] In 1842 the Common Council ordered that no steam trains were to go below 32nd Street, and some time thereafter the transfer point was shifted to the 32nd Street station, at first a roundhouse and repair shop.

[16] Nevins: *Abram S. Hewitt*, p. 61.

[17] See Pine, John B.: *The Story of Gramercy Park, 1831-1921*, New York, 1921.

[18] Clipping in the Cooper papers from the *Mail and Express*, April 4, 1883.

[19] Charles and John Hewitt papers: letter, January, 1863.

[20] *The New Yorker*, Oct. 29, 1938, 'A Reporter at Large,' by Geoffrey T. Hellman.

Chapter 11

ENTREPRENEUR

[1] *Reminiscences*, p. 166.

[2] [Beach, Moses Yale]: *The Wealth and Biography of the Wealthy Citizens of the City of New York*, New York, 1845, & New York, 1855. Astor in the 1845 edition was put down at $25,000,000, and his son at $5,000,000. Fifteen other men were listed as worth over $1,000,000.

[3] Nevins: *Abram S. Hewitt*, p. 605.

[4] *Reminiscences*, p. 123.

[5] Cooper papers: letter, May 12, 1835.

[6] *Journal of the Franklin Institute of the State of Pennsylvania*, February, 1836.

[7] [*A Letter from Peter Cooper to the members of the Congress of the United States,*] 1882; E. R. Hewitt: *Those Were the Days*, pp. 42-43.

[8] See Mott, Jordan L.: *Report to the Inventors of the United States by a Member of the Executive Committee*, April, 1854.

[9] Very occasionally Peter was opposed to some improvement. Thus in the 'fifties he signed a memorial against the use of Jones' Wood at 86th Street and the East River as a park, on the basis that it was too far on the side of the town and that the riverfront should be preserved for commerce. This seems today a narrow and wrong-headed viewpoint, but in 1856 the $5,000,000 to purchase Central Park seemed sufficient expenditure for a time. (Ohmsted, Frederick Law, Jr., and Kimball, Theodora (editors): *Frederick Law Ohmsted, Landscape Architect*, New York, 1922, p. 29.

[10] New York *Times*, Feb. 9, 1855.

[11] New York *Herald*, July 12, 1870.

[12] Or discovered by anyone else.

[13] New York *Evening Post*, March 21, 1845.

[14] Cooper-Hewitt papers in the Library of Congress: letter, Aug. 27, 1855 (from Ira B. Davis).

[15] A scrapbook in the Cooper papers contains a speech delivered October 15, 1852.

[16] See Lynch, Denis T.: *'Boss' Tweed.*

[17] New York *Times,* June 6, 1853.

[18] *Ibid,* Nov. 3, 1854.

[19] See MacLeod, Donald: *Biography of Honorable Fernando Wood,* New York, 1856. This biography was part of Wood's campaign to make himself appear to be a reformer.

[20] Cooper-Hewitt papers in the Library of Congress: letter, Jan. 28, 1856.

[21] New York *Herald,* April 20, 1858.

[22] He was occasionally found on curious committees, such as one, of which he was chairman, to proffer mediation in the Crimean War in 1854. See printed circular in the New York Historical Society Library.

[23] Cooper papers: letter, July 5, 1856; letter signed by Peter Cooper and others, Sept. 25, 1856, in the Edwin D. Morgan Collection in the New York State Library.

[24] In July, 1841, he had been a vice-president of a meeting in the park opposing a national bank law. (New York *Herald,* July 16, 1841.)

[25] The letter was published in the *Herald* on July 21st.

[26] Cooper-Hewitt papers in the Library of Congress: letter, July 11, 1846 (Colwell to Cooper).

[27] *Q.v.* (Chap. VIII). Cooper never published these remarks.

[28] New York *Times,* Feb. 9, 1855; Cooper papers: letters, Aug. 31 & October 17, 1859 (to Capen).

[29] *Index of Conveyances* (for Brooklyn) book 76, p. 273; book 96, p. 120; book 128, p. 393.

[30] Though the factory was built in 1838, it is possible Cooper did not move in until 1840, as Edward Cooper said. But Stiles in his history of Brooklyn is certainly wrong in giving the date as 1845, as is Professor Nevins, who implies it was 1848.

[31] Cooper papers: letter, June 22, 1848 (Cooper to George Dodge).

[32] Nevins: *op. cit.,* p. 145.

[33] Hewitt papers: letter, Jan. 24, 1861 (Cooper-Hewitt to Osgood Field).

[34] Hewitt papers: letter, Dec. 13, 1869.

[35] *Index of Conveyances,* book 441, p. 37.

[36] There was already in existence a third patent, that of Royal E. House, and weak House lines had already been opened from Washington to New York and from there to Boston and Buffalo.

[37] See Thompson, Robert Luther: *Wiring a Continent,* Princeton, 1947.

[38] New York *Herald,* June 24 & Aug. 7, 1840.

[39] Cooper papers: letters, Dec. 25, 1841, Feb. 1, 1842, & Aug., 1842; New York *Herald,* March 26, 1842. Nevertheless, the Erie stockholders in November put up his name again as a director, wanting the strongest names they could find in New York (New York *Herald,* Nov. 18, 1842).

[40] See Holbrook, Stewart H.: *The Story of American Railroads,* New York, 1947; Harlow: *The Road of the Century;* Hungerford, Edward: *Men of Erie,* New York, 1946.

Chapter *12*

NEW JERSEY IRONMASTER

[1] Background material for this chapter comes chiefly from Clark: *History of Manufactures*, and Swank, James M.: *History of the Manufacture of Iron in All Ages*, Philadelphia, 1892.

[2] Thomas invented his hot-blast method in 1829 and perfected it in 1836. In 1839 he was brought to Pennsylvania, where he built a completely successful furnace for the Lehigh Crane Iron Co. Geissenhainer, a Lutheran clergyman, worked with his experimental furnace in New York as early as December, 1830, took out a patent in December, 1833, for the manufacture of iron and steel with anthracite, and, before his death early in 1838, had made pig iron successfully by his process in Schuylkill County, Pennsylvania.

[3] Schuyler, Hamilton: *The Roeblings: A Century of Engineers, Bridge Builders and Industrialists*, Princeton, 1931, p. 59.

[4] Cooper papers. Of these, $19,253.86 was for merchandise. Though this is called a balance sheet, it includes no figures for cash or fixed assets, and lists liabilities of $55,080.02—$23,465.16 owed to Thomas Cooper & Co., $29,053.10 to Peter Cooper.

[5] Clark: *History of Manufactures*, p. 518.

[6] New York *Herald*, Oct. 28, 1840.

[7] Peter gives this early date in a letter to C. E. Detmold in 1843.

[8] P. 161.

[9] See Cooper papers and *Journal of the Franklin Institute*.

[10] Cooper papers: letter, March 31, 1840.

[11] A German civil engineer, he became a Maryland iron manufacturer in 1845, and in 1852 was supervisory architect on the Crystal Palace.

[12] Hewitt to a reporter of the New York *Sun*, Jan. 19, 1903, quoted in Nevins' *Abram S. Hewitt*, p. 83.

[13] Cooper-Hewitt papers in the Library of Congress: letter, Dec. 24, 1845 (Charles Hewitt to Peter Cooper). The New York *Herald* reported the opening of the ironworks on October 27th.

[14] Hewitt papers: letter, Dec. 22, 1884 (to Miller, Peckham & Dix).

[15] *Transactions of the American Institute of Mining Engineers*, vol. 34, p. 186.

[16] The firsthand sources of material on the iron business are the annual reports of the company and the Cooper-Hewitt letterbooks in the Hewitt papers.

[17] Hewitt papers: letter, April 17, 1846. In 1846 and 1847 the new Hudson River Railroad, the New York & Harlem, the Rutland & Burlington, the Vermont Central, the Michigan Central, the Utica & Schenectady, and the Syracuse & Utica all bought rails at from $71.50 (Syracuse & Utica) to $80 a ton (Vermont Central, for 10,000 tons) or more. (Nevins: *Abram S. Hewitt*, pp. 86-89; Cooper papers, letters, March 28, 1846, & Oct. 14, 1846.)

[18] Part of a tract belonging to the Penn family and the scene of iron-manufacturing from long before the Revolution, these mines had supplied the Continental Army with much of the cast and wrought iron that it used. Idle and aban-

doned by 1840, the mines were still capable of turning out a fine, tough iron, a mixture of red hematite and blue magnetite. Under Hewitt's management they turned out three thousand tons a month between 1851 and 1853, and supplied virtually all the ore needed by the Trenton mills during these years.

[19] He applied for a patent on an endless chain for railroads in September, 1853, and took out a caveat on the subject in March, 1854. What he claimed as new was a combination of known principles, by which a railroad could be constructed without ordinary grading expense and be free from snow and ice. Power or gravity could be used. (Ms. in New York Public Library.)

[20] Swank: *History of Iron*, p. 435.

[21] At first it seemed as if Peter Cooper had done a good stroke of business in 1847 by inducing the rising young wire-rope maker, John A. Roebling, to set up his shop in Trenton, as for a while Roebling bought his bridge wire from the Trenton Iron Company. But he was soon drawing his own wire as a competitor, and eventually stopped buying even the rods from which the wire was drawn in Trenton. For once Peter Cooper's shrewdness outsmarted itself. (Schuyler: *The Roeblings*, p. 74.)

[22] *Reminiscences*, p. 118; Hewitt papers: letter, Nov. 9, 1898.

[23] Hewitt papers: letter, Jan. 31, 1856.

[24] John Wilson: 'Special Report on the New York Industrial Exhibition,' *British Parliamentary Reports, 1854*, vol. XXXVI, 42, 43, quoted in Nevins' *Abram S. Hewitt*, p. 119.

[25] Of this, $323,510.72 represented rolling and puddling mills, $41,051.69 the wire mill, and $71,000 the entire stock of the Trenton Water Power Co.

[26] Hewitt gives the following details of dividends: March, 1848, 20%; August, 1850, 18%; January, 1852, 12%; February 1853, 6%; March, 1854, 25%; September, 1854, 5%; June, 1856, 8½%. A payment for 1855 is evidently not recorded.

[27] Professor Nevins says that in 1853 he was worth $175,000 in his own right and stood firmly on his feet, but as I read the facts that $175,000 was merely a hope. He was, if the Iron Company were sold, to have all over $500,000 that it might realize. $300,000 had just been offered for one-half, and Hewitt was entitled to the other half plus property worth about $75,000, less $200,000 he owed Peter Cooper. In other words he owned an equity of $175,000 in property the value of which when and if he actually sold it is never given.

[28] Hewitt papers: letter, Oct. 9, 1901.

[29] *Ibid.*, March 23, 1858.

[30] *Ibid.*, April 25, 1854.

[31] *Ibid.*, June 12, 1857.

[32] Cooper papers: letter, Nov. 13, 1849 (to Edward Cooper).

[33] Hewitt papers: letters, April 25, 1854, & March 23, 1858.

[34] Hendrick, Burton J.: *The Life of Andrew Carnegie*, New York, 1932, vol. 2, p. 275.

[35] Nevins: *Abram S. Hewitt*, p. 262, quoting Nicholas Murray Butler's memory of Hewitt's remarks at a dinner to Carnegie in 1900.

[36] Cooper, Peter: *Ideas for a Science of Good Government*, New York, 1883, p. 333.

[37] Peter Cooper was very wary about getting mixed up in the politics that accompanied the laying of street railways. In advising Nahum Capen about laying down tracks in Boston in 1856, he asked that his letter not be published, 'as I

am so largely interested in the manufacture of iron.' (Cooper papers: letter, May 5, 1856.)

[88] Trenton Iron Company, annual report, Aug. 15, 1867.

[89] Charles and John Hewitt papers: letter, Dec. 14, 1867. In 1868 Hewitt offered Jay Gould the Trenton works for $500,000, but Gould had other plans.

[40] As early as 1856 he had experimented unsuccessfully with the then-new Bessemer process at Phillipsburg, and it is understandable that he failed to see its possibilities since none of his American contemporaries did either. But what shall we say about the following statement made in 1867 about Bessemer steel in Europe?: 'It is quite evident that the business is overdone. The inventor and public have, for once, profited at the expense of the manufacturer.' (Swank: *History of the Manufacture of Iron,* p. 407.)

Chapter 13

WIRING OCEANS AND CONTINENTS

[1] Cooper ms. in the library of the American Historical Society.

[2] *National Geographic Magazine,* vol. 7, p. 108 (1896), letter from Hewitt.

[3] The chief sources used for the story of the cable, besides Cooper's own writings, are Field, Henry M.: *The Story of the Atlantic Telegraph,* New York, 1892; Harlow, Alvin F.: *Old Wires and New Waves,* New York, 1936; and MacDonald, Philip B.: *A Saga of the Seas,* New York, 1937.

[4] Field: *The Story of the Atlantic Telegraph,* p. 36.

[5] *Ibid.,* p. 37.

[6] Judson: *Cyrus W. Field,* p. 61.

[7] Hewitt papers: letter, Aug. 12, 1858.

[8] Hewitt papers: letter, Feb. 14, 1896 (to General A. W. Greely).

[9] Judson: *Cyrus W. Field,* p. 61.

[10] His friend Taylor got him a price of $400,000 from the government for his ship, the *Illinois,* worth according to army estimates about a half of that amount; the *Union,* which he sold to the government for $100,000, was said to have sunk almost at once. Roberts was also accused of making himself a fortune out of naval contracts in the Mexican war by getting himself made naval agent in charge of these contracts.

[11] As an investor in Cuban sugar plantations, president of the City Bank, and purchaser for $5 a share of the Delaware & Lackawanna Railroad, worth $240 a share in seven years, he built up a fortune estimated at $40,000,000.

[12] There are two apparent contradictions in Peter's account. He says at one point they were forty miles from shore when the cable was cut, or halfway over. Since the cable was paid out at a mile and a half an hour, according to him, it is hard to see how twenty-four much less forty miles could be laid by afternoon of even the long Newfoundland summer day.

[13] He had had $39,000 worth of bonds.

[14] Cooper's account books in Cooper papers; New York *Herald,* Dec. 20, 1872.

[15] In 1865 Peter owned only three shares, but he had sold two shares in 1857 and had sent some more to be sold there in 1858.

[16] Hewitt papers: letters, Feb. 9, 17, 18, March 4, & April 20, 23, 27, 1857; Cooper-Hewitt papers in the Library of Congress: letters, Feb. 4 & Feb. 10.

[17] Cooper papers: letter, July 7, 1857 (to Field).

[18] Cooper papers: letter, Aug. 31, 1857.

[19] Hewitt papers: letter, Oct. 6, 1857.

[20] Hewitt papers: letter, March 31, 1858 (Peter Cooper to Hewitt).

[21] Cooper-Hewitt papers in the Library of Congress: letter, Aug. 3, 1858 (George Peabody to Cooper).

[22] McClenachan, C. T.: *Detailed Report of the Proceedings Had in Commemoration of the Successful Laying of the Atlantic Cable,* By Order of the Common Council of the City of New York, New York, 1859, pp. 25, 37, 87, 137.

[23] Cooper papers: letter, Aug. 31, 1858.

[24] Cooper papers: letter, Sept. 3, 1858. 'Towards evening cirrus clouds gathered around, and at sunset a heavy cumulus cloud lay around the horizon to the N.W. and S.W. . . . Suddenly an aurora of great brilliancy burst forth a little east of north and immediately another, of similar brightness and beauty burst out upon the cloud a little east of south. From the horizon up to about 10°, it had the appearance of a great fire upon the Earth, which reflected from the clouds in a bright reddish light so strong as to cast visible shadows which crossed each other, in that extremely dark night.'

[25] Harlow: *Old Wires and New Waves,* p. 237.

[26] Zachos: *op. cit.,* p. 11.

[27] Zachos: *op. cit.,* p. 12. Peter has his dates somewhat mixed. In his account he makes it appear that another cable-laying was attempted soon after the 1858 disaster, and that then 'some two years' elapsed before the events above described, which Peter says led to the laying of the final successful cable. Actually, there was no effort to lay a cable between 1858 and 1865. The one to which Cooper's Quaker friend contributed was not the successful one, but the 1865 cable, the laying of which Cooper had placed much earlier. It was this 1865 cable that, as Cooper noted, was later fished up out of the ocean and made to work.

[28] Johnson papers in the Library of Congress: letter, May 19, 1865.

[29] Cooper says that the workmen let the cable lie in the vats provided for it before it was put on shipboard without covering it with water. (Zachos: *op. cit.,* p. 13.)

[30] Zachos: *op. cit.,* p. 12.

[31] Cooper papers: report on resigning as president of the Citizen's Association.

[32] See Cooper-Hewitt papers in the Library of Congress: letter, Jan. 17, 1868 (Sandberg to Hewitt); Jan. 4, 1868 (Anglo-American to Hewitt) .

[33] Field brought about a preliminary agreement on March 10, 1868, about which he wrote Peter jubilantly, 'Glory to God on high: Peace on earth and good will to men.' Hewitt, it would appear, had plans of his own, which Field's willingness to reduce rates spoiled. See Cooper-Hewitt papers in the Library of Congress: letter from Field; Hewitt papers: letter, Aug. 3, 1869.

[34] Judson: *Cyrus W. Field,* p. 262.

[35] Cooper papers: letter, March 7, 1868.

[36] See Hewitt papers: letters, May 18 & June 23, 1867 (Hewitt to Edward Cooper).

[37] The rate for the first five months had been £100.

[38] They used only five per cent of the facilities.

[39] Cooper papers: letter, Dec. 10, 1868.

[40] New York *Herald*, March 20, 1869.

[41] Hewitt papers: letters, July 1 & July 22, 1869.

[42] The original 1865 cable was defunct by 1873, the 1866 one by 1877.

[43] The Maine Telegraph Company, the New Brunswick Electric Telegraph Company, and the House-operated Boston & New York Printing Telegraph Company, which Daniel H. Craig had bought for the Associated Press.

[44] Mabee, Carleton: *The American Leonardo, A Life of Samuel F. B. Morse*, New York, 1943, p. 328.

[45] Thompson: *Wiring a Continent*, p. 305.

[46] The ultimatum came from the Magnetic Telegraph Company, Morse's original line from New York to Philadelphia.

[47] Including Kendall for Magnetic, Cooper and others for American, John D. Caton for the Illinois & Mississippi, John Butterfield for the New York & Buffalo, and Hiram Sibley for Western Union. (Cooper papers.)

[48] Tal Shaffner's. It was at this time that Morse got off the board of the Atlantic Telegraph Company.

[49] This last caused Hewitt to complain bitterly against those trying to stop the men who were 'in fact' the Atlantic Cable projectors from getting to Washington. This is 'no petty affair affecting a single local interest,' he wrote Robert E. Stockton. (Hewitt papers: letter, Dec. 1, 1857.)

[50] Of the Illinois & Mississippi Telegraph Company.

[51] Caton papers: letter, April 19, 1858 (Peter Cooper to Caton).

[52] Of the New Orleans & Ohio Telegraph Company.

[53] Cooper papers.

[54] The news agency, run by two men named Johnson and Zabriski, accused the American Company of refusing to transmit other than Associated Press foreign news over its wires from Sackville on the Nova Scotia border to New York. They not only stirred up the public against an Atlantic Cable in the hands of the monopolists of the American Company, but struck back by gaining for themselves a six-hour preference on the Halifax to Sackville lines of the Nova Scotia Telegraph Company. Hewitt, president of the American Company, immediately denied that he had made the first move, and made it clear that when the Nova Scotia lines rescinded the preference given to Johnson and Zabriski the American Company would reciprocate in kind. Peter Cooper, who said he had assured Johnson that there would be no discrimination, stated emphatically that he 'did not think the American Company would be made a party to so great a public wrong.' See Hewitt papers: letter, June 30, 1859; Cooper-Hewitt papers in the Library of Congress.

[55] *Remarks of Robert W. Russell . . . in reply to the statements of Messrs. Abram S. Hewitt, Cyrus W. Field, Henry J. Raymond, etc., June 29, 1860*.

[56] In 1864 Western Union had $22,000,000 of stock on 44,000 miles of lines as against $2,000,000 of American Company stock on 23,000 miles.

Chapter 14

THE OPENING OF COOPER UNION

[1] New York *Times*, Sept. 19, 1853.

[2] *Index of Conveyances:* book 401, p. 574; book 610, p. 363.

³ New York *Times*, Nov. 27, 1852; Jan. 21, 1853.

⁴ Cooper papers: letter, Feb. 23, 1857.

⁵ New York *Times*, May 6, 1858.

⁶ DeVoe, Thomas F.: *The Market Book*, New York, 1862, vol. 1, p. 555.

⁷ New York *Herald*, Nov. 3, 1859; New York *Tribune*, Nov. 3, 1859.

⁸ 'Speech of Honorable Abram S. Hewitt' in *General Society of Mechanics and Tradesman, New York Centennial Celebration*, New York, 1885, pp. 20-22.

⁹ Hewitt papers: letter, April 30, 1898.

¹⁰ See *In Memoriam: William Wagner*, Memorial Address by Richard B. Westbrook, March 7, 1885; *The Life of Horace Mann*, by his wife, Boston, 1865; Cooper papers: letters, Sept., 1854, May 29 & June 4, 1860.

¹¹ New York *Times*, March 30, 1872.

¹² Lieber was the author of *Political Ethics* (1838) and *Civil Liberty and Self-Government* (1853). See Harley, Lewis R.: *Francis Lieber*, New York, 1899.

¹³ Cooper papers: no. 234, March 1, 1855.

¹⁴ Cooper papers: letter, Feb. 10, 1853.

¹⁵ Cooper papers: letter, March 11, 1858.

¹⁶ Cooper papers: letter, Dec., 1859.

¹⁷ Cooper papers: letter, Nov. 9, 1863.

¹⁸ It is rather surprising to find Hewitt of all people crediting Carnegie with being the first to compel 'wealth to recognize its duties, not merely as a matter of moral obligation, but of decent self-respect on the part of men who control large fortunes.' Hendrich: *The Life of Andrew Carnegie*, vol. 2, p. 19.

¹⁹ Cooper papers: address to students in 1871.

²⁰ Nevins, Allan (editor): *Selected Writings of Abram S. Hewitt*, New York, 1937, p. 14.

²¹ By 1869 Peabody had expended $9,000,000 on various public institutions, the largest sum given away by anyone up to that time. See Martin, Edgar W.: *The Standard of Living in 1860*, Chicago, 1942, p. 292.

²² *Vide infra* for the other two.

²³ Cooper papers: clipping from *Mercury*, April 8, 1883.

²⁴ 'Letter from Mr. Cooper, Accompanying the Trust-Deed,' in *Charter* etc., pp. 26, 27.

²⁵ Cooper papers: clipping from *The People*, December, 1902.

²⁶ *Charter*, pp. 24-25.

²⁷ *Every Saturday*, vol. 2, p. 402.

²⁸ *Reminiscences*, p. 92. The *Reminiscences* are full of vague and ambiguous lessons Peter learned from nature—from vegetation growing at the bottom of the canal near his mill to a great leaf that he found at Port aux Basques when they were waiting for the cable.

²⁹ *The Charter, Trust Deed and By-Laws of the Cooper Union for the Advancement of Science and Art, with the Letter of Peter Cooper Accompanying the Trust Deed*, New York, 1881, contains Cooper's later plans. The 1857 memorial to the Legislature and earlier material are in manuscript among Cooper's papers.

³⁰ *Charter*, p. 20.

³¹ There was to be a man and boy in charge. On the wall were to be boxes provided with clasps for the deposit of student qualifications and references.

³² Hughes: *op. cit.*, p. 169.

³³ See Rachel Field's *All This and Heaven Too*, New York, 1938; Hewitt papers, letter, Nov. 19, 1860.

³⁴ *Charter*, p. 27.

[35] *Century Illustrated Magazine,* vol. 27, pp. 218 ff., 'Recollections of Peter Cooper,' by Susan N. Carter.

[36] Hewitt papers: letter, Oct. 27, 1865 (to George H. Brown).

[37] Hewitt papers: letter, Oct. 5, 1858.

[38] Hewitt papers: letter, Oct. 5, 1858 (Cooper to the Board of Education).

[39] Hewitt papers: letter, Oct. 23, 1902 (to Nicholas Murray Butler). 'In drawing up these papers,' wrote Hewitt, 'I foresaw, not merely the possibility, but the necessity of such a union, in which the independent existence of the Cooper Union would be preserved.' The deed, according to Hewitt, provided that fees might be charged in a technological school.

[40] *Charter,* p. 21.

[41] Hewitt papers: letter, Dec. 18, 1869.

[42] Hewitt papers: letter, June 26, 1866.

[43] *The Cooper Union Annual Reports* are the source of most of the following.

[44] The course in the first year consisted of algebra and geometry, including conic sections, and trigonometry. In the second year there were chemistry and physics, descriptive geometry, mechanical, architectural, or freehand drawing. The third-year curriculum included analytical mechanics and mechanical philosophy, and the continuation of some of the second-year subjects.

[45] Undated clipping in the Cooper papers.

[46] Nevins: *Abram S. Hewitt,* p. 182.

[47] Of the 1366 who stayed, 866 were in the night school, 380 in the vocal music school, and 120 in the School of Design. Of those in the night school, 164 were in B. S. Hendricks' mathematics classes, 105 in Len Reuben's mechanical philosophy class, 280 in John C. Draper's chemistry class, 111 in John F. Miller's architectural drawing class, 104 in Richard S. Smith's mechanical drawing class and 102 in his freehand class. The music class was given by Dr. Charles Guilmette and had 225 men and 155 women in it.

[48] *Outlook,* vol. 130, p. 220, "The Speech that Won the East for Lincoln,' by George Haven Putnam; Nicolay, John C. & Hay, John: *Abraham Lincoln; A History,* 1890, vol. 2, pp. 211 ff.

Chapter 15

THE CIVIL WAR

[1] Lincoln shared Peter's tolerant view of slaveholders as victims of circumstances.

[2] Myers: *The History of Tammany Hall,* p. 196.

[3] He at one time petitioned Congress to permit individuals to provide for men wholesale in this way.

[4] Cooper-Hewitt papers in the Library of Congress: letters, May 3 & Nov. 27, 1861.

[5] Lincoln papers in the Library of Congress: letters, Dec. 16, 1861; April 2, 1861. Chase papers in the Library of Congress, letter, March 10, 1862. In April, 1862, he had to write Stanton regretfully of the failure of one of these cables built without enough strength to withstand being raised by anchors. (Stanton papers: letter, April 24, 1862.)

[6] Cooper papers: letter, Feb. 4, 1861.

[7] Chase papers in the Library of Congress: letter, Jan. 13, 1862.

[8] Cooper papers: letter, Feb. 24, 1862.

[9] New York *Herald*, Feb. 12, 1879; newspaper clipping in the Cooper papers, Oct. 21, 1863.

[10] Cooper papers: letters, Sept. 15 & 21, 1874.

[11] Cooper papers: letter, Dec. 5, 1861.

[12] *The Indissoluble Nature of the American Union considered in connection with the assumed right of secession: A letter to Hon. Peter Cooper, New York,* Boston, 1862.

[13] The second letter to Lincoln was printed in 1863 by the Loyal Publication Society under the title *A Letter from Peter Cooper To His Excellency, Abraham Lincoln*. The Seymour letter was also published by the Society in the same year under the title *The Death of Slavery*.

[14] Cooper papers: letter, Aug. 10, 1863.

[15] Cooper papers: letter, Dec. 18, 1880.

[16] Letter to Lincoln, 1863.

[17] Nicolay & Hay: *Abraham Lincoln*, vol. 6, p. 456.

[18] Cooper papers: letter, March 16, 1880 (to David Davis, People's Candidate for President).

[19] A week before the draft riots Seymour appeared at the Academy of Music and, comparing Lincoln to Charles I for refusing, in tyrannical fashion, to compromise with the South, warned of mob tyranny equaling Lincoln's. The answer was a demonstration protesting the draft, which began with a raid on a colored orphan asylum, and which cost 1200 lives and $2,000,000 in property damage before it was stopped after four days by troops shooting to kill. Thirteen men were killed near Peter's house at Third Avenue and 21st Street.

[20] *The Death of Slavery.*

[21] Hughes: *op. cit.*, p. 188.

[22] New York *Herald*, Nov. 2, 1864.

[23] The *World* was in those days the sort of paper that would print an unsigned letter supposedly by a member of the Republican inner circle saying that unfortunately it would be necessary to wipe out every white man in the South, but that the resulting freedom and equality would be worth the sacrifice. (New York *World*, Oct. 26, 1864.)

[24] New York *World*, Oct. 24, 26 & Nov. 2. 1864.

[25] New York *World*, Nov. 10, 1864.

[26] Cooper papers: speech, 1865.

[27] Elihu B. Washbourne papers in the Library of Congress: letter, Dec. 13, 1866.

[28] *Reconstruction*, Peter Cooper to President Johnson [1866].

[29] Cooper papers: letter, Sept. 10, 1868.

[30] *Peter Cooper's Address [to his] Fellow-citizens*, Oct. 22, 1872.

[31] Cooper papers: letter, Aug. 23, 1872.

Chapter 16

FATHER COOPER

[1] [Beach]: *The Wealth and Biography etc.*, 1855 edition, p. 21.

[2] New York *Herald*, Feb. 26, 1881.

[3] New York *Observer*, vol. 43 (1865), p. 117.

[4] Vol. 1, p. 106.

[5] Ironically, his only accident occurred when he was standing still. Another vehicle hooked his wheel and turned his chaise over. *Reminiscences*, p. 42.

[6] Susan Carter in the *Century Illustrated Monthly Magazine*, vol. 27, pp. 218 ff.

[7] Funeral sermon by Dr. Robert Collyer in New York *Herald*, April 6, 1883.

[8] New York *Herald*, Feb. 12, 1879.

[9] Cooper papers: letter, Dec. 29, 1869.

[10] *Puck*, May 28, 1879. See also files of New York *Herald* for this period.

[11] See Hewitt, Edward R.: *Those Were the Days*, pp. 3-10.

[12] Address, March 8, 1904, at Cooper Union.

[13] *Reminiscences*, p. 207.

[14] Unpublished letter, Hughes to his wife, Sept. 9, 1870.

[15] He asked Isaac Lowthian Bell to receive it for him. (*Iron and Steel Institute Journal*, no. 1, p. 26.)

[16] *Frank Leslie's Illustrated Newspaper*, vol. 47, p. 463; New York *Herald*, Feb. 12, 1879.

[17] *The Reception of Peter Cooper by the Arcadian Club.*

[18] Hewitt: *Those Were the Days*, p. 59.

[19] Cooper papers: letter, Sept. 24, 1881.

[20] *A Circular in Regard to Emigration and the Distribution of Labor throughout the United States and Territories*, New York, 1870.

[21] The sources for the following paragraphs are the Cooper papers; an anonymous pamphlet of the period called a *Thorough Digest of the Indian Question*; Dodge (editor): *Memorials of William E. Dodge*; Walker, Francis A.: *The Indian Question*, Boston, 1874; and Moorehead, Warren K.: *The American Indian in the United States*, Andover, 1914.

[22] Dodge: *Memorials of William E. Dodge*, p. 175; Hewitt: *Those Were the Days*, p. 15.

[23] Hewitt papers: letters, June 16 & 28, 1888.

[24] Hewitt: *Those Were the Days*, p. 61.

[25] *The Magazine of American Art*, vol. 9, reprinting an article in the *Tribune*.

[26] Barrett, Walter: *The Old Merchants of New York City*, New York, 1870, vol. 5, p. 283.

[27] Hughes: *op. cit.*, p. 236.

[28] *Truth*, Nov. 16, 1880.

[29] Hewitt: *Those Were the Days*, p. 62.

[30] Hewitt papers: letters, Feb. 18, 1880, & Jan. 12, 1884.

[31] New York *Evening Post*, April 4, 1883.

[32] *The Journalist*, Dec. 20, 1902.

[33] New York *Times*, April 6, 1883.

Chapter 17

CANALS AND ELEVATED RAILROADS

[1] Hewitt's income in the same year, after deductions of $600 for each of his children, was $30,508 and Mrs. Hewitt's $7421.

[2] *Reminiscences*, p. 185.

³ See Johnson, Willis Fletcher: *Four Centuries of the Panama Canal*, New York, 1907.

⁴ *Reminiscences*, p. 108.

⁵ *Railroad Gazette*, vol. 15, p. 225.

⁶ *Reminiscences*, p. 112.

⁷ *World Reformer*, vol. 1, no. 1 (Jan., 1870). Tweed was mixed up in this venture in his usual unsavory way.

⁸ *Reminiscences*, p. 112.

⁹ New York *Herald*, Feb. 8 & March 12, 1874.

¹⁰ New York *Herald*, May 22, 1877. Later on Peter helped bring about friendly feeling among Field's employees at a reception Field gave at his house for his workers after a strike, by telling the employees the story of his life for an hour. The workers all thought, Field's biographer says, that the *RSVP* at the bottom of the invitation meant 'Reduced Salaries Very Probable!' (Judson: *Cyrus W. Field*, p. 299.)

¹¹ New York *Herald*, April 21 & July 7, 1879.

¹² The chief secondary sources I have used in this section are Whitford, Noble E.: *History of the Canal System of the State of New York*; Boynton, H.: *History of Steam on the Erie Canal*, New York, 1873; Hepburn, A. Barton: *Artificial Waterways of the World*, New York, 1914; *Annual Report of the State Engineer and Surveyor* for the year 1891, Albany, 1892; and the columns of the New York *Herald* for the period.

¹³ Cooper: *Ideas for a Science of Good Government*, p. 358.

¹⁴ New York *Times*, Feb. 3, 1871.

¹⁵ See *Annual Report of the State Engineer* for 1891.

¹⁶ Cooper papers: letter, Sept. 30, 1873.

¹⁷ Cooper papers: letter, Jan. 31, 1874. For those interested in the details, the main fights were about the shaft and the boiler. Peter had already paid $2000 more than his contract called for when the shaft broke early in September. The Fishkill Company, which had made the engine, insisted that they were not responsible, that the materials from the West Point Foundry were of the best iron 'fagoted in one piece,' and that the shaft broke because it was too small. Peter, on the other hand, asserted that it failed because a good piece of iron was joined to a bad with the 'mere appearance of a weld,' but agreed to advance another $500 anyway to keep the Fishkill Company from being 'sold out.' When in October the Fishkill Company continued to insist on payment for the new shaft, Peter decided to pay half the bill 'instead of looking to you for a larger part of the injury I have sustained.' When they still insisted, he repeated all his grievances, said the $2000 already paid had been virtually a gift, and offered to sell the engine back to the Fishkill Company for 'two-thirds the amount that was paid for it.' Peter finally paid $200 in December, after Ortlieb had assured him that the Fishkill Company was not responsible, and the latter had refused to try to collect from the West Point Foundry.

The boiler, for which Cooper paid $2000, cost, Ball & Jewell insisted, $3344. Claiming Ortlieb had approved it and that they were only getting costs out of it, they asked Peter for $1300 to pay Continental Motors and prevent them 'from being sold to pay for this Boiler. . . . We are both new beginners in business and have no stock in trade except what we have in our business.' From August to January they continued to write Peter until finally he offered them the engine Johnson had made in payment. When this was refused, Peter wrote the letter quoted in the text, and, though they were still importuning him a month later, saying 'we are sorely puzzled to know what to do in this matter,' there is no record of his paying them further.

[18] According to a sworn statement of a Captain William Baker, 'Johnson flew into a great passion because Mr. Cooper had asked him if he had lost any time and with many oaths he said, "The damned old devil asked me if I had not lost some time during the week." I asked him then, "Has he paid you for the whole week?" to which he replied, "Damn him! If he had not paid me for full time, I would not have worked another stroke on the Boat, and I would have fixed the Engine so that neither he nor anyone else could work it."' Cooper papers, June 1, 1874.

[19] New York *Herald*, Oct. 16, 1873.

[20] Peter also tried unsuccessfully to dispose of his yacht, the *Signet*. All he had to show for his efforts in the end was an imperiled friendship, a not uncommon occurrence when Peter offered to lend someone money. On May 20, 1874, J. Frank Wright, the owner of a grammar school at 60 Chrystie Street and a great admirer of Peter Cooper as an educator, offered to trade Peter ten lots that he owned at Uniontown, New Jersey, worth $6000, for the *Signet,* and also asked Peter to lend him $5000 at 7% on an island near Syracuse said to be worth $25,-000, to relieve him of a 10% mortgage. Though Cooper took a verbal option on the lots, he decided against taking them; instead he offered Wright an $11,000 mortgage on the Syracuse land covering both the debt and the *Signet,* but added that four persons, including Hewitt, had advised him not to as the land was worth no more than $5000. Wright was suddenly furious. His Syracuse land was worth more, despite what others said; he had no intention of mortgaging his property for a boat; and Cooper *had* agreed verbally to take the New Jersey property, Wright having even gone so far as to engage a captain and a crew for the boat. 'I am only a poor school teacher and you are a millionaire, but my word is good for all I say: I never yet had a note go to protest and I never made a square bargain and then backed out. I would not do the last thing for all the wealth of Peter Cooper.' In his usual calm manner Peter explained that he had no occasion to be relieved of a contract he had never made, and assured Wright that he would be sorry he had 'abused a friend who was trying to help you . . . whilst I will have the satisfaction of knowing that I intended to do you a kindness and that I have done more than I had ever offered to do in any of the conversations that I have had with you.' Wright cooled off, and though he still believed Peter verbally bound, asserted he would not offer him a 'wanton insult for all the property and all the money we have talked about thrice told.' Peter renewed his offer of a loan, but Wright finally decided he couldn't afford a boat.

[21] Cooper papers: letter, June 2, 1874.

[22] *Ibid:* letter, Aug. 30, 1874.

[23] McKay, Hugh: *Steam on the Canals; Report made to Hon. Peter Cooper,* New York, 1875. From August 6th to November 22nd he had made three trips down and two trips up, carrying 1818 tons in eighty-three days of running time at a cost of $2,282.87. His costs, he claimed, were $1.25 a ton as against $1.67 for the *Baxter* and $2.02 for horse boats.

[24] *Annual Report of the State Engineer* for 1891.

[25] He insisted only that McKay install a new patent wheel made by a man named Patterson. Though McKay protested, saying this was an admission of defeat that would please the Baxter crowd and disappoint the people of Utica,

Rochester, and Buffalo, who wanted the *Cooper* to come up the canal under the same conditions as in 1874, he acquiesced.

Chapter 18

COOPER AND HIS UNION

[1] Lloyd Bryce: 'The Example of a Great Life,' in *North American Review,* vol. 152, pp. 410 ff; Susan Carter: 'Recollections of Peter Cooper,' in the *Century Illustrated Monthly Magazine,* vol. 27, pp. 218 ff.

[2] Joseph Mitchell: 'The Old House at Home,' in *The New Yorker,* vol. 16, p. 21. For years after his death the chair was draped in black.

[3] Pupin, Michael: *From Immigrant to Inventor,* New York, 1923, p. 77.

[4] Susan Carter in the *Century Illustrated Monthly Magazine,* vol. 27, pp. 218 ff.

[5] *Annual Reports of the Cooper Union.*

[6] They got no help in solving their problem from the experience of European schools, a number of which Hewitt visited in 1866. The London Working Men's College, though commendable, belied its name; the School of Arts and Trades in Paris was for the few; the schools of the Brothers of Christian Doctrine in France were mere trade schools.

[7] *Annual Report of the Cooper Union,* 1867-1868; Hewitt papers: letter, June 26, 1866.

[8] New York *Times,* Oct. 31, 1872.

[9] Saint-Gaudens, Homer (editor): *The Reminiscences of Augustus Saint Gaudens,* New York, 1913, vol. 1, p. 45; vol. 2, p. 108. When it was finished he complained that his collaborator, Stanford White, had made the pedestal and architectural background too delicate for the heavy figure of the man.

[10] New York *Herald,* April 15, 1883.

[11] Hewitt papers: letter, Dec. 14, 1868.

[12] New York *Herald,* Feb. 12, 1881.

[13] Hewitt encouraged a five-minute intermission to allow those to leave who lived in lodging houses that closed or who came by horsecar from far away.

[14] Rossiter W. Raymond felt that Columbia, Princeton, Stevens, and Yale together couldn't turn out more than eight good speakers. 'At Columbia, there are Chandler and Newberry; at Stevens, Thurston and Morton; at Princeton, Brackwell and Young; and at Yale, Silliman and perhaps Frank Walker.' Hewitt papers: letter, Nov. 7, 1877.

[15] Hewitt papers: letter, Aug. 7, 1878 (Rossiter W. Raymond to Justus H. Schwab).

[16] The *Herald's* account of her appearance at the Union in 1873 is too good to be omitted. The place was filled, said the reporter. 'In the audience was a large element of women of an indefinable status, not exactly of the leisure nor of the working class. On the platform were a good many old stagers, who may be found at any time at a free love or spiritualistic seance. A few young girls, with prematurely old and knowing faces, were mixed in among the older dames.' Miss Woodhull wore a black skirt, a black braided jacket fitting tight around the waist with collar turned up about her neck, and a small crimson tie. Her hair, parted near the middle, fell 'in a careless cut over her ears and down the turned up collar of

her jacket.' Though her voice occasionally broke up like the 'notes of a dilapidated flute,' in the main she was heard. Her audience, freed from inhibition by the absence of policemen, cried "Go in, old gal!", "Wet your whistle, old woman," all through the performance. Though there was enough blasphemy to 'gratify the many corrupt and hoary headed old sinners who came to listen,' on the whole Miss Woodhull disappointed the 'vast congregation of prurient minds' who came to hear 'naughty words on naughty subjects.' Refusing to cater to the 'peculiar tastes of the young store clerks and the old lecherous vagabonds' who attended, she confined herself to a dry discussion of politics. She taunted the audience for accepting tyranny, she denounced woman's dependence on men and the failure of the law to protect her when she was married, and predicted bloody revolution. (The New York *Herald*, Oct. 18, 1873.)

[17] Harlow, Alvin F.: *Old Bowery Days*, New York, 1931, p. 532.

[18] Zachos received $1500 a year as curator when he was appointed, which he raised to $2000 by adding extra literary duties around the library. Most teachers received $2.50 a night for teaching, and the whole salary paid to twenty-two night-school instructors in 1868 was only $4800.

[19] Hewitt papers: letter, Feb. 17, 1892.

[20] New York *Herald*, April 21, 1879.

[21] Hewitt papers: letter, Nov. 8, 1878 (Hewitt to Field).

[22] He had considered such a gift in 1868, but it never materialized because it was contingent on Columbia's taking over the Union.

[23] Unfortunately, the $100,000 was given in Township of Pompton, New Jersey, bonds, which defaulted on interest and principal when the bonds became due in 1880. A settlement had to be made, involving a $25,000 loss and the payments of the principal at the rate of $5000 a year.

[24] The stone would, he wrote in the *Reminiscences*, be of uniform thickness and hardness, and could be laid in herringbone squares, which would prevent rutting by wagons going over them. The only foundation necessary was a smooth, hard bed of earth or gravel, though broken stone might be used. The roadway could be 'almost on a dead level, causing no sliding of the carriages as they pass, and avoiding the disposition of horses to slide by being put on an angulation.' (*Reminiscences*, pp. 201-202.)

[25] Peter especially objected to the wires along the 'very costly ornamental fence' on the roof, which he accused West of putting in merely as a 'show card to promote your own interest.' His building, Cooper asserted proudly, was one great lightning rod anyway, with its twenty-eight iron columns, its twenty miles of steam pipes connecting with boilers twenty feet under the street, and its ten miles of gas pipes.

[26] Cooper papers: letter, July 2, 1880.

[27] *Mercury*, April 8, 1883.

[28] *Annual Report*, May 28, 1887; Hewitt papers: letters, May 29, 1885, & June 4, 1883; [Beller, William E.]: *Peter Cooper; a Tribute in Commemoration of the Hundredth Anniversary of his Birth*, [1891], p. 34.

[29] Originally the house was a meetingplace of politicians, and, according to Bomar, Calhoun and others had plotted secession there.

[30] Cooper papers: letter, Nov. 15, 1877.

[31] Cooper papers: letters, Nov. 23 & 25, 1877.

[32] Cooper papers: letter, Jan. 12, 1878.

[33] Cooper papers: letter, April 18, 1878.

[34] Hewitt papers: letter, Oct. 30, 1890 (Hewitt to Rev. I. W. Wingo).

Chapter 19

BEARDING THE TIGER

[1] The chief secondary sources used in this section are Wilson: *The Memorial History of the City of New York;* Lynch: *'Boss' Tweed;* Myers: *The History of Tammany Hall;* Harlow: *Old Bowery Days;* Alexander, De Alva Stanwood: *A Political History of the State of New York,* New York, 1909; Foord, John: *The Life and Public Services of Andrew Haswell Green,* New York, 1913.

[2] *The Citizens' Association of New York: Publications 1864-1874* is the source of much of this section. Cooper's private papers, however, contain much unprinted material.

[3] Foord: *The Life and Public Services of Andrew Haswell Green,* p. 87; Lynch: *'Boss' Tweed,* pp. 324-5.

[4] Wilson: *The Memorial History of the City of New York,* vol. 3, p. 550.

[5] Cooper papers: a statement of Cooper's reasons for resigning from the Citizens' Association.

[6] The comptroller and corporation counsel, still by the charter to be elected, were made appointive a year later.

[7] New York *Star,* Feb. 3, 1871.

[8] Lynch: *'Boss' Tweed,* p. 354.

[9] New York *Times,* Feb. 3, 1871.

[10] He called himself president once in 1874 when writing to the *Herald* (New York *Herald,* Feb. 12, 1874). Actually John A. Weeks was president then, though Peter was still on the executive committee.

[11] As late as 1877 his name appears among those who waited on the 'reformed' Tammany mayor to urge him to run the government on 'business principles.'

[12] The letter to Benedict is dated February 17, 1873, the one to Dix, March 15, 1873, and the one to Grant, March 26, 1873.

Chapter 20

PETER COOPER FOR PRESIDENT

[1] Modern research, according to Chester Destler (*American Radicalism, 1865-1901,* New London, 1946), suggests that legally the bonds could have been paid in greenbacks. European bankers and even August Belmont did not think before 1869 that the government was obligated to pay the principal in gold.

[2] Mr. Spalding in his *Peter Cooper Bibliography* dates Cooper's Union League speech on the currency 1867, probably because that is the date given in Cooper's *Ideas on the Science of Good Government.* But the speech, apparently never delivered, seems to belong to 1876. It refers in almost the same words as a speech of that date to the shrinkage of values in the past three years. There was no such shrinkage between 1864 and 1867, though there was a recession in 1866. Moreover, Professor White of Cornell is mentioned in the speech, and Cornell was opened only in 1868.

[3] *Proceedings at the Mass Meeting of Citizens in the Cooper Institute, New York, March 24, 1874 on National Finances.*

[4] See Kellogg, Edward: *A New Monetary System*, Philadelphia, 1875. Kellogg believed that so long as you kept interest low you could expand the currency indefinitely without causing inflation.

[5] *Peter Cooper's 'New Departure'; An answer by him to certain criticisms on his 'Letter on the Currency'* [1875].

[6] See Taussig, F. W.: *Tariff History of the United States*, New York, 1914 [1892].

[7] John Williams of the *Iron Age* asked him on August 2, 1866, to contribute articles to 'enlighten the public mind and influence the public sentiment' as one of a number of gentlemen of the 'highest literary and moral standing.'

[8] For a full list of his writings on the subject see Spalding's *Peter Cooper: A Critical Bibliography of His Life and Works.*

[9] Theoretically he still believed that if all nations were equal free trade might work.

[10] The full title is *The Dangers of a War of Commerce and the Necessity of a Tariff and of an Unfluctuating Currency to National Prosperity.*

[11] Peter quoted liberally from Macaulay, Fox, Burke, Peel, and others. He also cited England's behavior in Ireland, Portugal, the West Indies, and China, where she forced the sale of opium at a cost of 500,000 deaths.

[12] New York *Herald*, Feb. 3, 1869.

[13] Conant, Charles A.: *The Progress of the Empire State*, New York, 1913, vol. 1, p. 329.

[14] Judson: *Cyrus W. Field*, p. 292.

[15] Hugh McCulloch, Secretary of the Treasury in the 'sixties, sat next to Peter at a dinner for Bayard Taylor, and was regaled with his currency views. 'How such an opinion,' he wrote later, 'could be entertained by such a man was to me incomprehensible.' (*Men and Measures of Half a Century*, New York, 1888, p. 415.)

[16] New York *World*, Nov. 6, 1878. In 1890 Hewitt told Seth Low that Cooper, in his desire to benefit the masses, 'often advocated doctrines which you and I regard as fatal to the welfare of society.'

[17] Discussion of the early Greenback movement may be found in Destler: *American Radicalism 1865-1901;* Haynes, Fred. E.: *Third Party Movements Since the Civil War*, Iowa City, 1916; Commons, John R. (and others): *History of Labour in the United States*, New York, 1921. Before the spread of Pendleton's ideas, farmers had been attracted by Greenbackism in the form of the extremist ideas of Henry Clay Dean, which the Cincinnati *Enquirer* sponsored in 1867 to wrest control of the Democratic party from August Belmont and Eastern capital. Labor's interest in Greenbackism also went back to 1866 or 1867, when an economic depression made producers' cooperatives (such as Peter believed in) and political agitation for Kellogg's schemes seem more attractive than efforts to raise wages. But with the return of prosperity in 1869, labor lost interest in Greenbackism, and leadership of the movement passed to Western farmers. Nevertheless, Wendell Phillips led a National Labor Reform party to the polls in 1870 on a Greenback platform; in 1872 David Davis was nominated for President on a soft-money platform, though he refused to stand; and the Labor Congress of 1873 had a Greenback plank in its platform. In the later history of the movement labor played an important if subsidiary role.

[18] *Report of the Immense Mass Meeting of Workingmen at Cooper Institute,
January 10, 1876.*

[19] Commons: *History of Labor in the United States,* vol. 2, pp. 170-171.

[20] New York *Tribune,* Aug. 20, 1878.

[21] New York *Herald,* June 6, 1876.

[22] New York *Herald,* May 19, 1876.

[23] New York *Herald,* May 20 & June 12, 1876. When the reporter averred that
$50,000 a year wasn't much of a sacrifice, Peter answered, "I shouldn't touch the
money. I should give it away or turn it over to the Cooper Union perhaps."

[24] New York *Herald,* June 29, 1876.

[25] Peter was unusually bitter about Groom, whom he publicly accused of failing to do what he had promised. Groom claimed Cooper had destroyed his reputation, and, despite Edward Cooper's attempts to mollify him, sued Peter for
libel in 1878. The newspapers enjoyed themselves thoroughly at the trial, where
Peter appeared with his usual air-cushion and insisted, despite his lawyer's best
efforts to 'keep the old gentleman down to the questions,' on going over 'the
greater part of his lifetime.' The *World* couldn't resist the following: 'Peter
Cooper paid for poking political papers before persons in all places, and if the
political papers Peter Cooper paid for poking before persons in all places were
not poked before people in every place, where were the political papers that
Peter Cooper paid for poking before persons in all places poked.' (May 24, 1878.)
Peter claimed in court that he had put all his confidence in Groom, 'thinking
him a Christian,' and that Groom had failed to distribute any but 600 of 15,000
documents and 75,000 ballots despite the $5000 paid for tickets and polling
booths. The jury, influenced perhaps by testimony that Groom had said he'd
turn over Cooper's & Cary's facilities to the Democrats for $600 or perhaps merely
by Cooper's position, refused to render Groom a verdict, and a second jury the
following January dismissed the case. Yet, though Cooper said he would write
the same accusing letter again, he would seem to have been unfair to Groom.
Eben Moody Boynton, a Greenbacker in whom Peter had confidence, told the
latter that what happened was not Groom's fault, and said the Brooklyn press
and legal experts agreed Peter was liable. Peter, wrote Boynton, was 'incapable
of intentionally wronging Mr. Groom,' and yet had 'done him great and almost
irreparable injury.' He ought to forgive: 'You are not infallible—to err is human.' But Peter did not forgive. This betrayal was one too many for him, and he
had to have a scapegoat. (Cooper papers: letter, Jan. 21, 1879; New York *World,*
May 23, 24, & 25, 1878; New York *Herald,* May 23, 24, & 26, 1878, and Jan. 22 &
23, 1879.)

[26] With the election so even, three to five thousand Cooper votes in New York
might, the *Herald* opined, give Hayes New York and with it the election. Or, if
Cooper won one state, say Indiana, where his chances were best, it was probable
no one would get a majority. As it happened, Cooper did contribute to defeating
Tilden, though not, despite his 17,000 votes in Indiana, as the *Herald* anticipated. The Greenbackers elected five senators to the Illinois legislature, and they
helped put David Davis into the Senate early in 1877. Thus Davis, a supporter
of Tilden, had an excuse for not sitting on the electoral commission that decided
the disputed election. Abram Hewitt, who was Tilden's campaign manager, certainly thought that lost Tilden the election. (See Nevins: *Abram S. Hewitt,* pp.
366-7.)

[27] Shupe had been a lawyer and president of People's College at Havana, New

York. Once worth $120,000, according to his claim, he lost it speculating. He was, he said, paid $20 a week by the *Advocate*. (New York *Tribune*, July 29, 1878.)

[28] New York *Tribune*, Aug. 3, 1878; New York *Herald*, July 24 & July 25, 1878.

[29] New York *Tribune*, Aug. 17, 1878. 'If Mr. Cooper,' said the *Tribune*, 'is the order-loving citizen he has always been thought to be, he will seriously consider whether he can afford to encourage any further a political movement in which this riot-plotting secret league [The Knights of Labor] has and must ever have the controlling power.' (New York *Tribune*, Aug. 3, 1878.)

[30] See Heath, B. S.: *Labor and Finance Revolution*, together with a Biography of the Author [by Louisa M. Heath], Chicago, 1891.

[31] Cooper papers: letter, Dec. 11, 1878. Cooper must have been of two minds about Shupe's action, since his son was running for mayor as a Tilden Democrat.

[32] Cooper papers: letters, May 9, 1879, & Feb. 27, 1883.

[33] For a nearly complete list of his published writings on the subject see Spalding: *Peter Cooper: A Critical Bibliography of His Life and Works*.

[34] Peter was particularly fond of citing in his defense the popularity of legal-tender notes before the Revolution, and the fact that the British government stopped them because they made the colonists prosperous. He claimed, indeed, that suppression of bills of credit was more a cause of the Revolution than the Stamp or Tea Acts.

[35] *An Open Letter to the Hon. President and Gentlemen of the Tariff Commission* [1883].

[36] As Peter showed, bankers were permitted to issue notes up to ninety per cent of government bonds deposited by them in the Treasury, and thus received interest both on the bonds and on the loans made to people with the bank notes; the American people, in the meantime, were being taxed to pay interest on the bonds, while the banks held the people's property as security on their loans.

[37] Carnegie at least was ruthlessly frank in admitting that not virtue but superior energy, determined by the blind law of fitness, governed success. Yet he too glorified the rich man in a way that Peter Cooper had never done and was certainly not doing in the 'seventies.

[38] Even this was too much for Hewitt, who said that if the government issued currency it would imperil individual rights, destroy freedom, and pave the way for 'centralized despotism.' (Hewitt papers: letter, May 9, 1881.)

[39] *Annual Reports of the Chamber of Commerce*, vol. 9, 1867, p. 69.

[40] Even without savings banks, Peter had said earlier, the debt could be paid off if the government money was legal tender. People would pay coin for it, which could be used to pay the debt.

CONCLUSION

[1] New York *Herald*, Feb. 13, 1883.

[2] Parton: *Captains of Industry*, pp. 329-30.

[3] New York *Herald*, April 8, 1883.

INDEX

Abbott, Horace, 117, 118, 119, 201, 202.
Abbott Iron Works, 117-118.
Abolitionists, 154, 278.
Abram S. Hewitt, Nevins, 175, 208.
Academy of Music, 246.
Acosta, Gen., 310.
Adger, Thomas (barge), 224-226.
Advocate, 370, 371.
Agamemnon (ship), 229, 230.
Agassiz, Louis, 249.
Albany, N. Y., 3, 5, 7, 57, 71, 80, 105, 116, 145, 148, 160, 161, 162, 184, 189, 197, 294, 346, 352, 356.
Albany Manual Labor University, 250.
Albany Regency, 126.
Aldermen, Board of, 352, 356.
Aldrich, E. F., 185.
Alexandria, Egypt, 233.
All Souls' Church, 135-136.
All This and Heaven Too, Field, 180.
Allaire, James P., 201.
Allen, Gov., 367.
Allen, Horatio, 108, 116, 198, 199, 203-204, 309.
Allen, Samuel Clesson, 126.
Allen, Stephen, 145.
Allen Street, 195.
Alms House, 38.
American Atlantic Cable Telegraph Company, 236-237.
American Bank Note Company, 333-334.
American Bible House, 58.
American Geographical Society, 266-267.
American Emigrant Company, 299.
American Industrial League, 360.
American Institute, 269.
American Museum, 17, 40, 89.
American Revolution, 5, 8, 9-14, 15, 38, 45, 88, 209.
American Social Science Association, 331.
American System, 125.
American Telegraph Company, 238-242.
Andoun, Lewis, 120.
Andover mines, 209, 210, 216.
Anglo-American Telegraph Company, 227, 234, 235-237.
Anti-Catholicism, 156-163.
Anti-Monopoly League, 378.
Antioch College, 247.
Arabia (ship), 232.
Arabian (locomotive), 116.
Arcadian Club, 298, 307, 381.
Arcularius, Gen. Henry, 138.
Armour, 251.
Art Library (Cooper Union), 333.
Arthur, Chester Alan, 360.
Aspinwalls, 67.
Assay Office, 211, 245.
Associated Press, 235, 240-241.
Associates of the Cooper Union for the Advancement of Science and Art, 259, 266-267.
Astor, Henry, 17, 91.
Astor, John Jacob, 17, 18, 61, 89, 250, 312.
Astor, William B., 71, 213.
Astor House, 292.
Astor Library, 246, 269.

Astor Place, 58, 89, 220, 245.
Astor Place Opera House, 246.
Astors, 67, 100.
Atlantic (locomotive), 116.
Atlantic Cable, 122, 166, 218ff., 239, 240, 292, 298.
Atlantic Telegraph Company, 227, 230, 231, 234, 235-236.
Audit, Board of, 351, 352.
Avenue A, 195.

Bailey, Col., 9.
Bailey, Gen. Theodorus, 35.
Bain, 197.
Baker, Capt. John, 5.
Baker, Shelden, 379.
Ball & Jewell, 318.
Baltimore, Md., 65, 66, 80, 86, 99ff., 168, 195, 196, 200, 201, 206, 322.
Baltimore & Ohio Railroad, 101, 108ff., 199.
Bank of New York, 17.
Bank of Newfoundland, 227.
Banker's Magazine, 193.
Baptist Church (Spartanburg, S. C.), 340.
Barnard, Frederick A. P., 265.
Barnard, George G., 345.
Barnard, Henry, 130.
Barnum's Hotel (Baltimore), 104.
Barnum's Museum, 40, 259.
Barrett, Mr., 57.
Barrett, Walter, 304.
Battery, 17, 26, 35, 231, 312.
Baxter, William, 317, 319, 321, 322.
Baxter, William (canalboat), 317, 319.
Bay of Bulls, Newfoundland, 230.
Beach, 183.
Beck, Sen., 375.
Bedell, Benjamin (brother-in-law of Peter), 57-58.
Bedell, Benjamin (father-in-law of Peter), 52.
Bedell, Mary Raynor, 52.
Bedell and Cooper, 58.
Beecher, Catherine, 130.
Beeson, John, 302.
Bell, Alexander Hamilton, 297.
Bellevue, 61, 62, 73, 141.
Bellows, Dr., 52, 135-136.
Benedict, Sen., 356.
Benton, Thomas Hart, 125, 126, 127, 378.
Bessemer, 216, 217.
Best Friend (locomotive), 116.
Beverwyck (Albany), N. Y., 5.
Bible Society, 246.
Bigelow, John, 180.
Binney, Amos, 117.
Birkbeck Institute, 247.
Blackmore, William, 301.
Blackwell's Island, 134, 141.
Blaine, James G., 292, 299.
Blair, Gen., 288.
Blair, George, 371.
Bloomingdale Asylum, 171, 249.
Bloomingdale Road, 38, 71, 73.
Board of Supervisors for New York County, 345.
Board of Trade, 382.
Boat Owners Association, 323.

Bocking, Carl, 335.
Bogart, Mr., 36.
Bomar, Thomas, 339-342.
Bonaparte, Jerome, 104.
Bond Street, 35, 179.
Boole, Francis I. A., 347.
Booth, Newton, 368.
Booth's Theatre, 292.
Boston, Mass., 35, 36, 71, 80, 92, 197, 205, 208, 236, 286, 294, 375.
Boston Post Road, 173.
Bourne, Theodore, 340.
Bowery, 35, 38, 58, 91, 99, 178, 195, 246-247, 270, 334, 337.
Bowery Hill, 58, 179.
Bowery Savings Bank, 138.
Bowery Village, 58.
Bowling Green, 17.
Brandy Moody Point, 26, 61.
Brassey, Thomas, 233.
Brazil, Empress of, 326.
Brest, 236.
Brett, John W., 221, 223, 227.
Brett, Robert, 8.
Brevoort's Garden, 58.
Brick Church, 224.
Bright, Charles T., 227, 228, 229.
Brinkerhoff, Col. Abraham, 10.
British (*see* Great Britain)
Broad Street, 18, 59.
Broadway, 11, 14, 17, 25, 34, 35, 36, 38, 58, 59, 71, 89, 135, 173, 292, 312, 336, 382, 383.
Brodhead, Richard, 228.
Bronx River, 145.
Brooklyn, N. Y., 22, 26, 60, 76, 79-80, 194, 195, 251, 308.
Brooklyn Heights, N. Y., 43.
Brougham, Lord, 56.
Brown, Benjamin M., 138.
Brown, William H., 109-110.
Bryan, Thomas I., 266.
Bryant, Sarah L. (barge), 223, 224.
Bryant, William Cullen, 128, 136, 181, 190, 272, 285, 297, 298.
Bryce, Edith Cooper, 325.
Bryce, Lloyd, 27, 324.
Bryson, David, 138.
Buchanan, James, 277-278.
Bucks County, Pa., 216.
Buck's Horn Tavern, 73.
Buffalo, N. Y., 88, 197, 316, 321.
Buffalo Good, Chief, 301.
Bulerd, Richard, 59.
Bull Run, 281.
Bull's Head Tavern, 36, 73.
Bull's Head Village, 73.
Burdell, Dr. Edwin S., 339.
Burgoyne, Gen., 10.
Burling Slip, 196, 297, 303, 329.
Burr, Aaron, 5, 17, 26, 35.
Burr, David A., 336.
Burtis and Woodward, 38-39, 40, 44.
Bushnell, David, 77.
Bushwick, 173, 194.
Butler, Benjamin, 126, 127.
Butler, Nicholas Murray, 266.

Calais, France, 219.
Calhoun, John, 373.
Calvinism, 6.
Camden & Amboy Canal Company, 63.
Camden & Amboy Railroad, 199, 205, 207, 208.
Campbell, John, 11-14, 16, 128.
Campbell, Sarah Oakley, 11.

Campbell, Thomas, 11.
Canada, 218ff.
Canal Commission, 315ff.
Canal Street, 25, 35, 173.
Canton Company, 102, 117-121, 168.
Canton Iron Works, 117.
Cape Breton, N. S., 218.
Cape Breton Island, Can., 219.
Cape North, Can., 219.
Cape Race, 232.
Cape Ray, Can., 219, 223, 224.
Capen, Nahum, 190, 191-192, 229, 245, 248, 279, 284, 294, 378.
Capitol (Washington, D. C.), 211.
Cardozo, Albert, 344-345, 354.
Carey, Henry C., 126, 360.
Carnegie, Andrew, 33, 84, 215, 250-251, 337.
Carroll, Charles, 101, 114.
Carter, Susan, 93, 263, 303, 324, 332.
Cary, Samuel F., 368.
Castle Garden, 219, 311.
Catherine Ferry, 62.
Catherine Slip, 43.
Catholics, 156-163, 256.
Caton, John D., 240.
Catskill, N. Y., 22.
Cebra, John Yates, 138.
Cedar Street, 35, 89.
Central America, 309-311.
Central City (canal boat), 319.
Central Park, 149, 151, 292, 313.
Centre Street, 25.
Chambers Street, 25, 34, 36, 38, 173, 177.
Channing, Dr., 283.
Channing, William Ellery, 135.
Charleston Railroad, 203.
Charlestown, Mass., 158.
Chase, Salmon P., 281-283, 286.
Chatham Square, 73.
Chatham Street, 25, 36, 89.
Cherry Street, 18, 201.
Cheves, Langdon, 86.
Chicago, 195, 251, 286, 316.
China, 380.
Chinese War, 232.
Choate, Joseph, 181, 247.
Christian Alliance, 288.
Cincinnati, Ohio, 368.
Citizens' Association, 315, 345ff., 362-363.
City Hall, 17, 25, 35, 37, 150, 231, 344.
City Hotel, 17, 27, 35.
Civil Service Commission, 380.
Civil War, 125, 190, 192, 193, 194, 196, 215, 222, 242, 253, 277ff., 292, 298, 299, 308, 344, 357, 360, 364.
Clarendon, Lord, 227.
Clarendon Hotel, 218-219, 222.
Clay, Henry, 77, 125, 186, 272, 309.
Cline, Anthony, 168.
Clinton, De Witt, 37, 62, 88, 155.
Clinton, George, 10.
Clinton, Sir Henry, 10.
Clinton County, N. Y., 48.
Clowes, Benjamin, 60.
Clowes, Mary Bedell, 60.
Cobbett, William, 86-87, 128.
Cobden, Richard, 297.
Coe, William S., 138.
Coenties Slip, 18.
Coleman, 37.
Colfax, Schuyler, 288.
Collect (Pond), 25, 36, 37.
College of Physicians and Surgeons, 17, 135.
College of the City of New York, 244, 349.
Colonnade Row, 89.

Colombia, 309, 310.
Columbia County, N. Y., 46.
Columbia University, 173, 174, 248, 264, 265-266, 298.
Colwell, Stephen, 147, 148, 192, 247.
Commission of Indian Affairs, 301.
Committee of Seventy, 354, 355.
Committee of Sixteen, 355.
Common Council, 58-59, 62, 99, 122-123, 127, 138ff., 186, 187, 188, 189, 231, 299, 346, 351, 356.
Common Pleas, Court of, 351.
Congress, 10, 176, 185, 186, 228, 229, 236-237, 240, 282, 288, 299, 301 309, 310, 329, 358, 367, 374.
Conkling, Roscoe, 292.
Connecticut, 28, 55.
Connolly, "Slippery Dick", 344, 350, 352, 354, 355.
Connolly, James, 371.
Constable's, Arnold, 173.
Cooper, Annatje (Hannah), 4.
Cooper, Benjamin Bedell, 53, 60.
Cooper, Cornelia, 7.
Cooper, Cornelia Gardenier (Mrs. Obadiah), 3, 5.
Cooper, Cornelia Redmond (Mrs. Edward), 182.
Cooper, Edith (Mrs. Lloyd Bryce), 325.
Cooper, Edward (brother to Peter), 22, 79, 169-172, 249.
Cooper, Edward (son of Peter), 76, 172-175, 181-182, 190, 194, 195, 197, 205-207, 213, 214, 215, 265, 270, 294-295, 356.
Cooper, Hester Bos (Esther Terboss) (Mrs. Obadiah), 7.
Cooper, James, 19, 43, 55, 168.
Cooper, John (brother to Peter), 11, 19, 22, 168.
Cooper, John (father of Peter), 7, 9-11, 14-19, 20, 21-22, 23, 28, 29-30, 31, 45, 47-48, 51.
Cooper, John Campbell, 53, 60.
Cooper, Margaret Campbell (Mrs. John), 11, 14-15, 24, 45.
Cooper, Maria (Mary), 4.
Cooper, Maria Cropsey, 169.
Cooper, Maria Fonda (Mrs. Obadiah), 7.
Cooper, Martha, 19, 60-61, 168.
Cooper, Martha Pinfold (Mrs. John), 11, 19.
Cooper, Obadiah, 3-5, 6, 7, 8-9.
Cooper, Peter, (canalboat), 320, 321-322.
Cooper, Peter William, 60, 75, 76.
Cooper, Pieter, 7.
Cooper, Pieter (stepbrother of John), 20.
Cooper, Sarah, 19, 55, 60-61, 168.
Cooper, Sarah Amanda, 60, 75-76.
Cooper, Sarah Amelia (*see* Hewitt, Sarah Amelia Cooper)
Cooper, Sarah Bedell (Mrs. Peter), 50-54, 59-60, 94, 165, 262, 294.
Cooper, Thomas, 4.
Cooper, Thomas (son of John) 19.
Cooper, Thomas (second son of that name of John), 22, 43, 168, 184, 200, 202, 203.
Cooper, William, 22, 80, 168, 195, 337.
Cooper & Hewitt, 206, 213-214, 216.
Cooper-Limestone Institute, 342.
Cooper Park, 194.
Cooper Square, 58, 338.
Cooper Union, 6, 40, 47, 58, 109, 122, 130, 131, 155, 157, 161, 163, 166 168, 174, 183, 191, 209, 211, 213, 215, 220, 243ff., 291, 297, 301, 308, 323, 324ff., 344, 345, 365, 369, 381, 382.
Corcoran, William, 250.

Cornell, Ezra, 239, 240, 250.
Cornell, Robert C., 159.
Cornell University, 265, 298.
Cortlandt Street, 36, 40.
County Court House, 382-383.
Court of Appeals, 348.
Coutant, Gilbert, 102.
Craig, Daniel, 241, 242.
Crittenden, John J., 278, 284.
Croker, 375.
Cropsey, James, 171.
Crosby, Howard, 300.
Croton, N. Y., 23.
Croton Aqueduct, 145-151, 154, 155.
Croton Aqueduct Department, 146, 147-148, 351.
Cruger, Nicholas, 71.
Cruger Mansion, 72.
Crummarsie-Vly, 180.
Crystal Palace, 231, 311.
Cummings, Amos, 92.
Cunard, 232.
Curse of Paper Money and Banking, The, Cobbett, 86-87.
Curtis, Ann, 134.
Curtis, Joseph, 132-134, 184, 263.
Curtis, Dr. Thomas, 339.
Curtis, William, 339.
Cutler, Pliny, 117.
Cutting, Francis B., 287.
Cuyper, Claes Janson, 4.

Daily News, 270.
Daly, Chief Justice Charles P., 124.
Dana, Charles, 248, 264.
Dangers of a War of Commerce, Cooper, 360.
Darien Isthmus, 309.
Davies, Alderman, 149.
Davis, David, 366, 372.
Davis, Phineas, 116.
Dawson, A. H. H. (canalboat), 316.
Delafield, Dr., 75-76.
Delafield, Mr., 198.
Delaware & Hudson Canal, 100.
Delaware & Hudson Railroad, 100.
Delaware River, 204, 205.
de Lesseps, Count Ferdinand, 311, 326.
Delmonico's, 292, 298, 317.
Demilt Milk Dispensary, 184.
Democrat, 366, 371.
Democrats, 84, 124ff., 134, 138ff., 186ff., 277ff., 293, 348, 363, 364, 378.
Dennis, Aaron, 48-49, 57.
Depew, Chauncey, 292.
d'Erlanger, Baron Emile, 236.
Detmold, Christian E., 203-204.
Dewey, Dr. Orville, 135.
DeWitt Clinton (locomotive), 116.
Dillex, I., 231.
Dix, John A., 127, 279, 287, 288, 289, 356.
Dixwell, J. B., 373.
Dobbins, David P., 317, 319, 321.
Docks, Department of, 351, 352.
Dodge, George, 119, 120, 196.
Dodge, William E., 80, 84, 119, 190, 199, 233, 299, 381.
Donghoregan Manor, Md., 114.
Douglas, Stephen, 228, 272.
Dover, England, 219.
Drake, John, 57.
Draper, John W., 246.
Drew, Daniel, 73, 91.
Drexel, 251.
Dryden, 136.
Duane, James, 179.

Duane Street, 11, 13, 14, 22.
DuBois, Jr., Matthew, 8.
Dubuque & Pacific Railroad, 199.
Dubuque & Sioux Railroad, 199.
du Faur, William Von Faber, 203.
Durham Iron Works, 216.
Dutch Church (Fishkill), 4.
Dutchess County, N.Y. (*see also* specific place), 4, 7, 10, 46.
Duxbury, Mass., 236.

Early, Gen., 286.
East Broadway, 179.
East River, 40-41, 61-62.
East Wareham, Mass., 167.
Eastern, Mr., 310.
Eastern Post Road, 71, 73.
Eastman, H. G., 312.
Easton, Pa., 210.
Eckford, Henry, 100.
Ecole Polytechnique, 131, 247.
Edison, Thomas, 297.
Edith (barge), 321, 322.
Education, Board of, 162, 163, 264-265, 352.
Edward VII, 165.
8th Street, 73, 100, 352.
18th Street, 180.
Eleventh Avenue, 195.
Ellicott's Mills, Md., 107-108, 110, 113-114.
Emancipation Proclamation, 284.
Embargo Act of 1807, 36.
Emerson, Ralph Waldo, 130-131, 136.
Emigh, Nicholas, 4.
Emigrant Protective Society, 299.
Emmet, Thomas Addis, 40.
England (*see* Great Britain)
English and Mix, 92.
English Channel, 223.
Enneke's, 5.
Eno, Amos R., 292.
Episcopal Church (Hempstead), 53.
Episcopalians, 135.
Erie Canal, 61-64, 88, 101, 184-185, 314ff.
Erie Railroad, 197, 198, 216.
Erskine, Robert, 209.
Essay on Man, Pope, 136.
Essex County, N.Y., 48.
Europa (ship), 232.
Europe, 173, 174, 176, 194, 218ff., 294.
Evarts, William, 181, 310.
Evening Post, 37, 88-89, 128, 359.

Face Fall, 5.
Faraday, 227.
Fawcett, Ella, 381.
Federal Hall, 17, 40.
Federalism, 124.
Fenton, Reuben, E., 346, 347, 349.
Ferrero, 173.
Ferris, Chancellor, 249.
Ferris, Rev. J. M., 300.
Ferry Street, 96.
Field, Cyrus, 81, 84, 180, 181, 218, 219-221, 222, 223, 224, 226-230, 232-233, 235, 236, 238, 240, 241, 242, 313, 333, 353, 363.
Field, David Dudley, 180, 222, 231, 272, 286.
Field, Henrietta, 180, 262.
Field, Henry, 180, 220.
Field, Matthew D., 219, 223.
Field, Moses W., 365, 368.
Field, Osgood, 195.
Field, Rachel, 180.
Fifth Avenue, 70, 71, 89, 179, 180, 292.
Fifth Avenue Hotel, 292.
Finley, Ebenezer Z., 102.

Fish, Hamilton, 59, 62.
Fishkill, N. Y., 3, 4, 7-9, 10, 11, 12, 15, 16, 321.
Fishkill Creek, N. Y., 23.
Fisk, Jim, 180, 348, 353.
Fitz, Henry, 118, 119-121, 201.
Five Points, 37.
Flodder, Jansen (Jacob Janse Gardenier), 5.
Fonda, Jellis, 7.
Fly Market, 43.
Forrest-Macready riots, 246.
Fort Constitution, N. Y., 10.
Fort George, N. Y., 17.
Fort McHenry, Md., 101.
Fort Montgomery, N. Y., 10.
Fort Orange, N. Y., 3.
Fort Sumter, 279.
42nd Street, 70, 145, 149, 173, 177, 313.
46th Street, 195.
48th Street, 195.
Foster, William, 253, 283.
14th Street, 73, 89, 122, 178, 292.
Fourth Avenue, 70, 71, 72, 73, 74, 136, 168, 177, 178, 245, 333, 334, 382.
Fourth National Bank, 199.
4th Street, 58.
Fowler, Field, 92.
France, 173, 236, 309, 311.
Frank Leslie's Chimney Corner, 291.
Franklin, Benjamin, 129, 260, 313.
Franklin County, N. Y., 48.
Franklin Institute, 185.
Franklin Square, 211.
Franklin Street, 89.
Frederick Turnpike, 114.
Free Academy, 244, 249, 264.
Free School Society, 37.
Free Soilers, 191.
Fremont, John C., 191, 285, 286.
French Polytechnic, 131, 247.
Frick, Henry Clay, 84.
Front Street, 59.
Fulton, Robert, 36, 41-42.
Fulton Street, 36, 89.

Gaffney (Limestone Springs), S. C., 339-342.
Gallatin, Albert, 45, 127.
Gansevoort Market, 187.
Garden Street, 35.
Gardenier, Jacob Janse, 5.
Gardner Avenue (Brooklyn), 195.
Garfield, James, 299.
Gates, Gen. Horatio, 72, 173.
Gazette (Baltimore), 113.
Geary, James, 59.
Geissenhainer, Frederick W., 201.
General Society of Mechanics and Tradesmen, 13, 247, 264.
George, Henry, 175, 373, 378.
George, P. R., 305.
Germany, 173.
Girard, Stephen, 250.
Girard College, 247, 248.
Gisborne, Frederick N., 219-220.
Gladstone, 284.
Glass Elliott & Company, 233.
Goelet, Peter, 100.
Goodyear, Mr., 296.
Gouge, William M., 126, 128.
Gould, Jay, 180, 216, 348, 353, 375.
Governor's Island, N. Y., 9, 11, 219.
Gowanda, N. Y., 195.
Grace Church, 58.
Graff, Mr., 146.
Gramercy Park, 179, 222, 295.

Gramercy Pond, 73.
Grant, Ulysses S., 288, **301**, 310, 356, 357-358, 363, 365.
Gray, Horace, 203.
Great Britain, 9-10, 45-46, 56, 134, 173, 193, 195, 210, 212, 219, 220, 223, 227-228, 232-233, 236, 298, 309, 360-361, 376.
Great Eastern (ship), 233, 234.
Great Hall (Cooper Union), 245, 260, 267, 269, 272, 332, 333.
Great Kill, 5.
Greeley, Horace, 189, 236, 285, 286, 289.
Green, Andrew H., 352, 354.
Green, Norvin, 240.
Green Engineering Camp, 209, 338.
Greenback Labor Party, 370.
Greenbackism, 293, 357ff.
Greenpoint, N. Y., 322.
Greenwich Lane, 58.
Greenwich Street, 35, 312.
Greenwich Village, 35, 58.
Groom, Wallace, 366, 369.
Gustin, John S., 200, 203.
Gutta Percha Company, 233.
Gwynn, W., 102.

Hackensack, N. J., 57.
Halifax, N. S., 218, 224.
Hall, A. Oakley, 348, 352.
Hall, Charles Henry, 198.
Hall, James, 205.
Halstead, John, 337.
Hamilton, Alexander, 13, 17, 84-85, 124-125.
Hampton, Gov., 34.
Hanover Bank, 199.
Hardenberg, A. A., 373-374, 376.
Harlem, 35, 58, 59, 145, 151, 178.
Harlem Railroad, 141.
Harper, James, 158, 186, 189.
Harper & Brothers, 211, 245.
Harper's, 353-354.
Harte, Bret, 298.
Hartford, Conn., 92.
Hasenclever, Baron, 209.
Havemeyer, William F., 152-153, 186, 189, 190, 354, 356.
Hayes, Rutherford B., 376.
Health, Board of, 347.
Heart's Content, Newfoundland, 234.
Heath, B. S., 371, 372.
Hempstead, N. Y., 43ff., 56-57, 59, 132, 134.
Henery, Mr., 355.
Henry, Joseph, 196.
Herald, 107, 155, 237, 287, 290, 312-313, 329, 335, 362-363, 366, 367, 368, 369, 381.
Herzberg, Constantin, 251.
Hester Street, 195.
Hewitt, Abram S., 72, 95, 117-118, 173-176, 181-182, 192, 194, 195, 197, 199, 205ff., 218-219, 221, 228-229, 236, 240, 241, 242, 247, 251, 261, 263, 264, 265-266, 267, 268, 270, 294, 295, 297, 302, 306, 328, 330-331, 332, 333, 336, 342-343.
Hewitt, Amy, 296.
Hewitt, Charles, 175, 181, 205, 216.
Hewitt, Edward Ringwood, 295, 296, 298-299, 308, 309, 327.
Hewitt, Erskine, 182, 295.
Hewitt, Nellie, 298.
Hewitt, Peter Cooper, 295, 296.
Hewitt, Sarah, 296.
Hewitt, Sarah Amelia Cooper (Mrs. Abram), 76, 165, 172-173, 174, 175, 176, 178, 181, 195, 215-216, 294, 295, 302.
Hewitt, Memorial Building, 338.

Hicks, Elias, 134-135.
Higginson, Lt. Francis, 232.
High Bridge, 145, 148.
Highland, N. Y., 10.
History of the Manufacture of Iron, Swank, 202-203.
Hoboken Trading Station, 4.
Hoffman, John C., 345, 346, 348, 353.
Hoffman House, 292.
Holbrook, Josiah, 130.
Holgate, Jerome Bonaparte, 249.
Home for Old Men and Aged Couples, 299.
Homestead Act, 128.
Hone, Philip, 149.
Honesdale, Pa., 108.
Hopkins, 181.
Hornby, John, 92.
House of Refuge, 133.
Houston Street, 58.
Howard Street, 173.
Howlands, 67.
Hubbard, Gardiner G., 242.
Hudson, N. Y., 46-47.
Hudson River Railroad, 197-198, 199, 315.
Hudson Valley (*see also* specific place), 3ff., 21-23.
Hughes, Thomas, 44, 192, 305.
Hughes, David E., 238-239.
Hughes, Bishop John, 159, 160, 161, 254.
Hughes, Thomas, 286-287, 297.
Hulberd, Calvin L., 352.
Hungerford, Edward, 110, 116.
Hunt, Wilson G., 188, 220, 221-222, 241, 265, 270, 304, 312, 363.
Huntington, Daniel, 221, 375.

Ideas for a Science of Good Government, Cooper, 373.
Illinois, 371.
Illinois Central Railroad, 199.
Independent (Greenback) Party, 370.
India, 361.
Indiana Farmer's Party, 365.
Indianapolis, Ind., 365, 366.
Indians, 299-302.
Indissoluable Nature of the American Union, Capen, 284.
Industrial News, 336.
Ingersoll, Robert, 332.
Interoceanic Canal Commission, 310.
Inventor's Institute, 336-337, 382.
Ireland, 219, 227, 230, 231, 234, 236.
Iron Age, 360.
Irving, Washington, 89.
Irving Place, 246.
Isthmus Canal Company, 310.
Italy, 173.

Jackson, Andrew, 13, 55, 94, 124-129, 278, 369, 374.
Jacksonianism, 87, 124-129, 134, 158, 166, 192, 193, 278ff., 293, 348, 363, 364, 378.
Jacobsen, Mr., 118.
Janse, Jacob (Jacob Janse Gardenier), 5.
Jansen, Claes, 4.
Jay John, 17.
Jefferson, Thomas, 36, 124, 127, 128, 129, 134, 189.
Jeremiah, Thomas, 138.
Jersey City, N. J., 117.
Jervis, John B., 145.
John Street, 89.
Johnson, Andrew, 233, 288.
Johnson, B. M., 311, 318-319.

Johnson, Eleazer, 118.
Johnson, George, 104.
Johnson, Joel, 118.
Journal of Commerce, 78.
Julia, 173.

Kansas-Nebraska Bill, 190-191.
Kellogg, Edward, 358-359, 364, 368, 379.
Kelvin, Lord, 228.
Kendall, Amos, 125, 196, 197, 238-241, 242.
Kensington Museum, 336.
Ketchum, Hiram, 159, 190.
Kinderhook, N. Y., 3, 5.
King, Charles, 264.
King, Clarence, 308.
King, Rufus, 367.
Kings County, N. Y., 80.
Kingsbridge, 186.
Kingsland, 194.
Kipps Bay, 67, 70.
Kirkland's School, Miss., 173.
Knapp, Shepard, 118, 119, 190.
Knight, John Adams, 280.
Knights of Labor, 366, 370-371, 378.

Labor and Other Capital, Kellogg, 358.
Lafayette, 260.
Lafayette Place, 89, 246.
Lake Erie, 316.
Lake Superior, 204.
Lamont, C. A., 336.
Latrobe, John H. B., 111, 112, 113, 115, 116.
Lawrence, Abbott, 129.
Lazeretto Point, Md., 101ff.
L'Ecole Centrale, 264.
Lee, Gideon, 80, 84, 92, 101-102, 118, 122, 138, 184.
Lefferts, John, 44.
Lehigh, Pa., 215.
Lehigh River, 205.
Lenox, Robert, 312.
Leonard Street, 89.
Lester, Charles E., 83.
Lewis, Gov., 47.
Lexington Avenue, 70, 136, 179, 181, 182, 195, 292, 297.
Liberty Street, 89.
Lieber, Francis, 248, 256, 257, 260.
Limestone College, 342.
Limestone Springs (Gaffney), S. C., 339-343.
Limestone Springs Female High School, 341.
Limestone Springs Lime Works, 341.
Lincoln, Abraham, 233, 272-273, 277, 278, 279, 283, 284, 285, 286, 287, 326.
Lispenard Meadows, 35.
Littell, D. F., 321.
Little Dock Street, 18.
Little Raven, Chief, 301.
Liverpool, Eng., 367.
Liverpool & Manchester Railway, 108.
Livingston, 367.
Livingston, Chancellor (canalboat), 88.
Livingstons, 67.
Locofocos, 128, 154-155.
London, 195, 203, 230, 232, 247.
Long Island, N. Y., 3, 43ff.
Long Island Railroad, 199.
Lorillards, 100.
Low, A. A., 233, 277, 304, 363.
Lowber, Robert W., 221, 224.
Lowell Institute, 130, 267.
Lowell lectures, 247.
Lozier, John, 138.
Lyceum of Natural History, 267.
Lyon, Mary, 130.

Mackay, William B., 161.
MacWhorter, Alan, 248, 264.
Madison, James, 55, 373.
Madison Avenue, 70, 177, 195.
Madison Square, 73, 180.
Madison Square Theatre, 292.
Madison Street, 37, 155.
Maiden Lane, 43.
Maine, 44, 372.
Malta, 233.
Malthus, 373.
Mamaroneck, N. Y., 100.
Manhattan Company, 25, 35.
Manhattan Fire Insurance Company, 199.
Manhattan & Gebhard Insurance Company, 199.
Manhattan Water Works, 138.
Manhattanville, 35, 58, 60, 173.
Mann, Horace, 130, 131, 247, 250.
Manual Labor University, 250.
Martin, B. M., 300.
Marxism, 374.
Maryland (railway car), 117.
Maryland (*see also* specific place), 65, 66, 80, 86, 99ff.
Mason, John, (streetcar), 178.
Maspeth Avenue (Brooklyn), 194, 195.
Massachusetts (*see also* specific place), 35, 36, 46, 158, 167, 236.
Master Mechanics' Association, 311.
Matsell, George W., 153.
Matthews, Charles, 248.
Maury, M. F., 220.
McClain, 28.
McClellan, Gen., 286.
McCully, Charles, 102-103.
McCunn, John H., 344.
McGowan's Pass, 38.
McKay, Hugh, 320, 321-322.
McSorley's Saloon, 325.
Meer's Select Classes, Miss., 173.
Mercantile Advertiser, 55.
Mercantile Journal, 366.
Mercantile Library, 246, 267.
Mercer Street, 135.
Mercer Street Church, 135.
Mechanics Society, 244-245.
Merchants' Exchange, 89.
Merchant's State Telegraph Company, 197.
Mercury (locomotive), 116.
Methodism, 6, 21, 23, 29-30, 51.
Metropolitan Health Bill, 347.
Metropolitan Museum, 349.
Mexican War, 185.
Mexico, 298.
Middle Road, 69, 70, 71, 74, 166, 177.
Mill, 373.
Miller, M., 375.
Milwaukee, 195.
Mint (Philadelphia), 211.
Minute Men, 9-10.
Missouri, 191.
Missouri Compromise, 278, 279.
Mohawk & Hudson Railway, 100, 108, 116.
Mollenoux, Jesse, 44.
Monroe, Edmund, 117, 118.
Monroe, James, 300.
Montana (canalboat), 317.
Montgomery County, N. Y., 48.
Mooney, William, 38.
Moore, Ely, 102.
Moravian School (Bethlehem, Pa.), 14.
Morgan, J. P., 333.
Morris Canal, 205, 210.
Morris & Essex Railroad, 199.

Morse, Samuel F. B., 158, 196, 197, 219, 221, 224, 228, 238, 239, 240.
Mott, Dr., 75.
Mott, William W., 138.
Mount Clare, Md., 108.
Mount Clare Railroad Shop, 110-113.
Mulberry Street, 37, 59.
Mullock, Bishop, 219.
Munson, Alfred, 119.
Murray, 128.
Murray Hill, 70-71, 73, 74, 75, 145, 150, 178.
Museum for the Arts of Decoration, 338.
Museum of Natural History, 260.
Mushet-Heath, 216.
Music Hall (New Haven), 366.
Myers, Gustavus, 81-82.

Napoleon III, 298.
Nassau Street, 36.
Nast, Thomas, 353-354.
National Association of Glue Manufacturers, 94.
National Banking Act, 87, 283.
National Emigration Bureau, 299-300.
National (Greenback) Labor Party, 370, 375.
National Labor Congress, 365.
Native-American Party, 158, 186.
Navy Department, 229, 230.
Nebraska, 190-191.
Negroes, 284-285, 288.
Nevins, Prof. Allan, 44, 118, 175, 208, 216.
New Brunswick, Can., 219.
New Church of the Messiah, 135.
New England, 44, 203.
New Hampshire, 175.
New Haven, Conn., 80, 92, 366.
New Jersey, 3, 105, 106, 181, 196, 199, 201, 204ff.
New Jersey Steel & Iron Company, 216-217.
New York & Albany Railroad, 197-198.
New York Central Railroad, 116, 198, 315.
New York Chamber of Commerce, 232, 235, 277, 315, 353, 378.
New York City (see specific person and place)
New York County Agricultural Society, 90.
New York & Erie Railroad, 198.
New York & Flushing Railroad, 199.
New York Gallery of Fine Arts, 184.
New York Gas Company, 89.
New York & Harlem Railroad, 177-178, 197.
New York Historical Society, 266.
New York Indian Peace Commission, 300-301.
New York Juvenile Asylum, 184.
New York Kerosene Oil Company, 199.
New York Life & Trust Company, 199.
New York & New England Telegraph Company, 197.
New York, Newfoundland & London Telegraph Company, 222ff., 227, 234, 235-237.
New York Produce Exchange, 315.
New York Safety Steam Power Company, 320-321.
New York Sanitary Association, 184.
New York Society Library, 246, 269.
New York State (see also specific place), 44, 45, 48, 201.
New York State Canal Convention, 315.
New York State Legislature, 145-146, 148, 152, 153, 160, 161, 162, 184, 188-189, 190, 245, 246, 252, 257, 262, 351-352, 354.
New York State University, 298.
New York Steel Company, 201.
Newburgh, N. Y., 22, 31, 33, 45, 47, 51.
Newfoundland, 218ff., 294.

Newfoundland Electric Telegraph Company, 219.
Newman, William (canalboat), 317, 319.
Newport, R. I., 294.
Newton Creek (Brooklyn), 194, 195.
Niagara (ship), 229, 230.
Niblo's, 197.
Nicaragua Canal, 309, 310-311.
Nichols, Gideon, 44, 53.
Nichols, William, 44, 53.
Nicolls, Gov., 5.
Night Thoughts, Young, 136.
Niles Weekly Register, 114.
Ninth Avenue, 312.
Ninth Avenue Railroad, 199.
Ninth Ward, 69.
North American Telegraph Association, 240-242.
North Carolina, 322.
Northern Pacific Railroad, 380.
Nott, Judge Benjamin, 267.
Nova Scotia, 218, 223, 226, 228, 235, 238.
Novelty Iron Works, 199.

Oberlin College, 130.
O'Brien, James, 354.
Observer, 290-291.
O'Donnell, Columbus, 102.
Ogden, William P., 312.
O'Gorman, Richard, 349-350.
Ohio, 204, 212.
Ohmstead, Frederick, 299.
Old Dominion Steamship Line, 322.
Oliver Viaduct, 114.
O'Malley, Mrs., 306.
108 Street, 38.
113th Street, 100.
114th Street, 100.
125th Street, 60.
126th Street, 59.
155th Street, 38.
Oneida County, N. Y., 46.
Opera House, 246.
Ordnance Bureau, 118.
O'Reilly, Henry, 197.
Ortlieb Constructing Engineers, Frederick, 318.

Pacific Cable, 309.
Palmer, Peter, 244.
Panama Canal, 309-311.
Panic of 1819, 85-87.
Panic of 1857, 230.
Paper Against Gold, Cobbett, 128.
Park Theatre, 35.
Parsons, John E., 247, 265, 270.
Parton, James, 381.
Passaic, N. J., 205.
Patterson, William, 101, 102.
Peabody, George, 230, 250, 251, 339.
Peabody Institute, 251.
Peacock, George, 200.
Pearl Street, 25, 35, 37.
Pease, Francis, 102.
Peekskill, N. Y., 11, 21, 22, 23, 25, 30, 34.
Pekin Legal Tender, 371.
Pender, Sir John, 233.
Pendleton, George H., 364.
Penn, William, 4.
Pennsylvania (see also specific place), 13, 36, 46, 201, 204, 205, 210, 212, 216.
Pennsylvania, University of, 247.
Persian Gulf, 233.
Peru Steel Company, 201.
Peter, John R., 138.

Peter Cooper Glue Factory, 195.
Petersen, F. A., 245.
Petty, Charles, 340.
Philadelphia, Pa., 13, 36, 80, 86, 87, 105, 146, 147, 193, 205, 211, 240, 247, 251, 303, 329, 365.
Phillipsburg, N. J., 205, 210.
Phoenixville, 202.
Pierce, Franklin, 229.
Pine Street, 89.
Pittsburgh, Pa., 215.
Pittsburgh, Ft. Wayne & Chicago Railroad, 199.
Polk, James, 126, 192.
Pomeroy, "Brick," 366, 370, 371, 372.
Pope (canalboat), 319.
Pope, Alexander, 136, 298, 325, 348.
Populism, 364-365.
Port au Basque, Can., 224.
Port Byron (canalboat), 317, 319, 320, 321.
Post, Edwin, 80, 214.
Post Office, 35.
Postal Telegraph Company, 242.
Potomac River, 101, 107.
Poughkeepsie, N. Y., 47, 198.
Powell, Major James, 301.
Pratt, 251.
Presbyterians, 135.
Price, Mr., 102.
Prince Street, 135, 178.
Prince Edward Island, Can., 219.
Princeton University, 298.
Progress and Poverty, George, 373.
Promises of Free Trade, Dixwell, 373.
Protestants, 156-163.
Public Ledger (Philadelphia), 241.
Public School 15, 173.
Public School Society, 133, 155-163, 173, 184, 250.
Public Works, Board of, 351, 352.
Puck, 294.
Pupin, Michael, 327, 329.
Putnam, George, 181.
Putnam County, N. Y. (*see also* specific place), 4.

Quakers, 134-135, 159.

Ramsey, James, 102.
Randall, Capt., 58, 100.
Randall, Mr., 311.
Randolph, John, 104.
Rawlins, Isaac, 249.
Raymond, Rossiter, 206, 332, 342.
Red Cloud, Chief, 301, 302.
Redfield, Herman J., 215.
Reed, Luman, 184.
Reid, John, 361.
Reid, Whitelaw, 181.
Relay House (Baltimore), 114.
Reminiscences, Cooper, 72, 102, 115, 204, 207, 308.
Rensselaer County, N. Y., 48.
Rensselaer Polytechnic School, 129-130, 247.
Republicans, 125ff., 190ff., 272-273, 277ff., 357, 361.
Restelle, Madame, 153.
Resumption Act, 358, 368, 370.
Reuter, Julius, 236.
Revolutionary War, 5, 8, 9-14, 15, 38, 45, 88, 209.
Rhinelanders, 100.
Rich, Josieah, 198.
Richards, T. Addison, 269.
Riker, Richard, 139.

Rimmer, Dr. William, 269.
Ringwood, N. J., 181, 209-210, 212, 214, 216, 294, 305, 338.
Roberts, Marshall O., 218, 221-222, 226-227, 299, 310, 350, 363.
Robbins, Z. C., 336.
Rochester, N. Y., 197, 315.
Rockefeller, John D., 84.
Rocket (locomotive), 108.
Rodgers, Dr. David, 131.
Roebling, John A., 201.
Rogers, Dr., 155.
Rogers, Ann, 71.
Rogers, H. H., 337.
Romaine, William, 38.
Romance of American Railroads, Wright, 110.
Rombonts Precinct, N. Y., 8.
Roosevelt, 370.
Roosevelt, Clinton, 280.
Roosevelt, Franklin D., 380.
Roosevelt, James, 13.
Roosevelt, Theodore, 310.
Rose Hill, 71.
Rosehill mines, 209.
Ruggles, Samuel, 179.
Russell, Robert W., 242.
Russia, 298.
Rutgers, Col., 26.
Ryan, James, 154.
Ryerson, Martin J., 209.

S.P.C.A., 299.
Sage, Russell, 292, 375.
Sailor's Snug Harbor, 100.
St. Gaudens, Augustus, 329.
St. George's Episcopal Church (Hempstead), 51.
St. John's, N. S., 219, 223, 228.
St. John's Park, 89.
St. Lawrence Cable, 226, 227, 238.
St. Lawrence Gulf, 218, 223.
St. Louis, Mo., 367.
St. Mark's Place, 179.
St. Paul's Church, 14, 26, 89.
St. Paul's Island, Can., 219.
St. Pierre Island, 236.
Sands, Nathaniel, 350, 352, 353, 354-355.
Sandy Hill, 100.
Saratoga County, N. Y., 48.
Saratoga & Whitehall Railroad, 199.
Savage's Museum, 40, 259.
Savary, Capt. Benjamin, 167.
Savary, John, 167.
Saw Mill River, 47.
Schenectady, N. Y., 116.
Schermerhorns, 100.
Schieffelin, Henry, 80.
Schiefflin, 69.
Schlesinger, Arthur, Jr., 348.
Schofield, Lewis, 167-168.
School of Design (Cooper Union), 134, 245, 252, 262, 263, 268, 269, 303, 332.
Schultz, Jason S., 361.
Schussele, Christian, 327.
Schuyler, Peter, 3.
Schuylers, 67.
Scribner, Charles, 181.
Scudder's Museum, 17, 40, 89, 259, 260.
Seaman, Lawrence, 53.
Seaman, William, 138.
Second Avenue, 73, 89, 195.
Second Bank of the United States, 85-86, 125-127.
2nd Street, 195.

Second Unitarian Church, 135.
Sedgwick, Theodore, 159.
Serrell, William, 203.
7th Street, 58, 195, 244, 245, 324, 334.
Seventh Ward Bank, 141.
Seventh Ward National Bank, 340.
Seward, William H., 156-157, 272, 278, 288, 309-310.
Seymour, Horatio, 46, 284, 285-286, 288, 346, 364.
Sheridan, Gen., 286.
Shepard, Edward, 297.
Sherman, John, 278, 279, 281, 282, 371.
Sholes, Christopher Latham, 297.
Short History of Paper Money and Banking in the U. S., Gouge, 128.
Shupe, Walter H., 370, 371.
Sibley, Hiram, 239, 240, 242.
Sickels, John S., 59.
Siemens-Martin, 216.
Signet (yacht), 317.
Sigourney & Son, C., 92.
"Six Nations," 239-240.
Sixteenth Ward, 146, 154.
Sixth Avenue, 180, 292, 313.
6th Street, 246.
Sixth Ward, 189.
Slater, Samuel, 85.
Slocum, Lewis B., 57.
Smith, Adam, 127-128, 373.
Smith, F. O. J., 197.
Smith, Junius, 203.
Smith, Melville C., 312.
Smith, Thomas, 119.
Smith, Thomas R., 140.
Smith Island (Brooklyn), 195.
Snell, Thomas, 172.
Sorosis, 298.
South America, 195, 219.
South Carolina, 339-342.
South Carolina Railroad, 116.
Southeast and Southwest Pavilions (Cooper Union), 334.
Southern Relief Association, 288.
Southern Transcontinental Railway, 299.
South Trenton Iron Company, 206.
Southern Pacific Railroad, 380.
Spartanburg, S. C., 339-343.
Spartanburg Baptist Association, 342.
Spaulding, Elbridge Gerry, 283.
Spencer, John C., 160-161.
Sperry's Garden, 58.
Spitzenafski, Baron William, 231.
Spring, Dr. Gardiner, 224.
Stanley, Arthur, 326.
Star, 353.
Staten Island, N. Y., 9, 60.
States Righters, 154.
Stedman, E. C., 298.
Stephenson, George, 108.
Stephenson, John, 178.
Stephenson, Robert, 227.
Sterling Iron Works, 63.
Sterling Steel Company, 201.
Stevens family, 199, 208.
Stevens, Edwin A., 251.
Stevens, Samuel, 138.
Stevens, Thaddeus, 364.
Stewart's, A. T., 25, 173.
Stevens Institute for Engineers, 251.
Stilwell, Silas M., 127, 281-282.
Stockbridge & Pittsfield Railroad, 199.
Stockton & Stokes, 114.
Stourbridge Lion (locomotive), 108, 110.
Stowe, Harriet Beecher, 181.

Stratton, R. M., 148-149.
Stuyvesant, Nicholas W., 244.
Stuyvesant, Peter, 58.
Stuyvesant Hall, 135.
Stuyvesant Institute, 188.
Stuyvesant Square, 89.
Stuyvesant Street, 58, 59, 72, 99.
Stuyvesants, 58, 67.
Suez Canal, 309, 310, 311.
Suffolk County, N. Y., 44.
Sumner, 237.
Sunfish Pond, 70, 73.
Superior Court, 244.
Supreme Court, 222.
Susquehanna (ship), 229, 230.
Susquehanna River, 101.
Sussex Railroad, 199, 210.
Swank, James, 202-203.
Swarthout, Gen., 9.
Sweeny, Peter B., 344, 352, 354.
Syracuse, N. Y., 316, 322, 379, 371.

Taafe, Patrick, 83.
Tabernacle, 189.
Tammany Hall, 17, 38, 138, 139, 140, 141, 154, 186, 187, 190, 191, 278, 294, 344ff., 371.
Taney, Roger B., 126.
Tax Commission, 352, 354.
Taylor, Bayard, 224.
Taylor, Moses, 199, 218, 221-222, 226-227, 335, 350, 353, 363.
Taylor & Sons, William, 317, 318.
10th Street, 58, 173.
Terboss, Henry, 7.
Terboss, Jacobus, 7.
Terboss, Rosekrance, 7.
Texas Central Railroad, 299.
Third Avenue, 22, 58, 59, 73, 99, 100, 169, 173, 177, 195, 200, 244, 245, 312, 333, 334.
Third Avenue Railroad, 187.
30th Street, 312.
31st Street, 70, 195.
32nd Street, 71.
33rd Street, 22, 70, 74, 100, 200.
34th Street, 70, 177.
35th Street, 70, 177.
36th Street, 70, 71.
Thomas, David, 201.
Thomas, Evan, 108.
Thomas, Philip E., 108, 110.
Thompson, George, 202.
Thompson, Henry, 119.
Thompson, John, 70.
Thompson, Jonah, 202.
Thomson, Sir William, 228.
Tibbits, Elisha, 102.
Tiemann, Daniel F., 60, 80, 84, 119, 158, 173, 190, 265, 269.
Tiemann, Martha Clowes, 60.
Tilden, Samuel, 127, 180, 292, 294, 315, 350, 354, 367, 371.
Times, 188, 193, 243, 244, 245, 299, 328, 329, 353-354.
Toledo, Ohio, 370.
Tom Thumb (locomotive), 109-117, 318.
Toncey, Isaac, 229.
Tontine Coffee House, 17, 35.
Townsend, Solamen, 148.
Traveller (locomotive), 116.
Tredwell, John, 44.
Trent Affair, 233.
Trenton, N. J., 105, 174, 181, 204ff.
Trenton & Belvidere-Delaware Railroad, 210.

Trenton Iron Company, 206ff.
Trenton Water Power Company, 204.
Trenton Works, 117-118.
Tribune, 303, 371.
Trinity Bay, Newfoundland, 230, 234.
Trinity Church, 26.
Trowbridge, Henry, 48, 49, 57.
Troy, N. Y., 316, 321.
Trustees, Board of (Cooper Union), 244-245, 265, 266, 267, 269, 329, 336.
Tweed Ring, 180, 187, 190, 315, 344ff., 363.
Twelfth Ward, 122.
20th Street, 136.
21st Street, 89, 100, 180.
22nd Street, 169, 179, 292, 294.
23rd Street, 71, 73, 292.
24th Street, 292.
25th Street, 195.
26th Street, 178.
27th Street, 73, 173, 178, 180.
28th Street, 70, 71, 72, 73-74, 177, 180.
29th Street, 70, 71.
Twilight Club, 382.
Tyndall, John, 331.

Union (New Haven), 366.
Union Emigrant Society, 140.
Union Hotel, 35.
Union League Club, 280.
Union Square, 26, 35, 58, 73, 150, 179, 280.
Unionists, 286.
Unitarians, 134-137, 247, 255-258.
U. S. Arsenal, 69, 133.
United States Court, 244.
United States Sub-Treasury, 125-128, 280.
United States Trust Company, 199.
United Trust, 199.
University Place, 246.
University of Pennsylvania, 247.
University of the State of New York, 298.
Upton, E. W., 92.
Ursuline Convent (Charlestown, Mass.), 158.
Utica, N. Y., 316.

Vail, Alfred, 196, 196.
Vail, George, 228.
Valentia, Ire., 230, 231, 234.
Van Buren, Martin, 94, 125, 126, 127.
Van Cortlandt, Joanna, 23.
Van Cortlandt, Pierre, 23.
Van Cortlandts, 5, 67.
Vanderbilt, Cornelius, 82, 292, 309, 375.
Vanderbilt, William H., 310.
Van Plank, Sen., 128.
Van Rensselaer, Stephen, 129.
Van Rensselaers, 3, 4, 5.
Van Voorst, Cornelius, 4.
Van Wyck, Capt. Richard, 10.
Varian, Isaac L., 161.
Varick, Richard, 17.
Vassar, Matthew, 47, 198, 250.
Vassar College, 47.
Vauxhall, 58.
Vesey Street, 292.
Viggo, Prince, 182.
Vreeland, John, 67-68, 69-70, 80.

Wack, Charles (canalboat), 316.
Wagner, William, 247.

Wagner Institute of Science, 247.
Waldorf-Astoria, 71.
Wales, Prince of, 165, 271-272, 292, 326.
Walker, Robert J., 192, 193.
Wall Street, 17, 18, 37, 89, 194, 383.
Walsh, Mike, 154.
War of 1812, 45-46, 48-49, 56, 57, 88.
War of Commerce, Cooper, 56.
Ward, Thomas, 179.
Ward, W. R. L., 317, 320.
Ward's Island, 187.
Warner, Charles Dudley, 181.
Warren County, N. Y., 48.
Washington, George, 9, 11, 13, 18, 26, 209, 260.
Washington, D. C., 13, 105, 124-129, 192, 196, 211, 240, 277, 294, 299, 300, 356.
Washington County, N. Y., 48.
Washington Market, 26.
Washington Square, 27, 59, 89, 292.
Water Power Company, 166.
Water Street, 17, 18, 59.
Wath-waett, Chief, 5.
Watts, John, 41, 65.
Weaver, James B., 372.
Webster, Prof., 249.
Webster, A. S. (canalboat), 318, 320, 321.
Webster, Daniel, 272, 373.
Weed, Thurlow, 286, 288, 292.
Weekes, 51.
Weeks, Capt. James, 9.
Wells, James N., 138.
West & Company, J. D., 335.
West Indies, 230.
West Point (locomotive), 116.
West Point, N. Y., 10, 13.
West Point Foundry, 116.
Westchester County, N. Y. (*see also* specific place), 10, 145.
Western Union, 197, 237, 239, 241, 242, 328.
Wheeler, William, 346.
Whigs, 166, 198.
White, Chandler, 218, 221, 222, 223.
White, Stanford, 182.
White Mountains, 173, 174.
White Plains, N. Y., 10.
White Street, 89.
Whitefield, George, 6.
Whitehouse, Dr. Edward O., 227, 228.
Whiting, James R., 141, 189, 190.
Whitman, Walt, 134.
Willard, Emma, 130.
William Street, 35.
Wilson, Woodrow, 370.
Winans, Ross, 111, 113, 114.
Winchester, 286.
Winding Creek, 180.
Women's Home, 134.
Wood, Fernando, 153, 186, 187, 188-190, 191, 278, 280.
Wood Point Road (Brooklyn), 194.
Woodhull, Victoria, 332.
Woodward, John, 38, 39.
Working Women's Protective Union, 134.
World, 140, 287.
Worth Street, 37.
Wright, Jonathan, 111.
Wright, Silas, 125-126, **127.**
Wright, W. S., 110.